Digital Ethics
Rhetoric and Re
Online Aggressio..

Digital Ethics delves into the shifting legal and ethical dimensions of digital ecologies and explores productive approaches for theorizing, understanding, and responding to difficult ethical issues online.

Contributions from leading scholars address how changing technologies and media over the last decade have both created new ethical quandaries and reinforced old ones in rhetoric and writing studies. Through discussions of rhetorical theory, case studies and examples, research methods and methodologies, and pedagogical approaches, this collection will further digital rhetoric scholars' inquiry into digital ethics and writing instructors' approaches to teaching ethics in the current technological moment.

A key contribution to the literature on ethical practices in digital spaces, this book will be of interest to researchers and teachers in the fields of digital rhetoric, composition, and writing studies.

Jessica Reyman is an Associate Professor of Digital Rhetoric and Professional Writing in the Department of English at Northern Illinois University, USA. Her research focuses on law and ethics in digital rhetoric, and she is the author of *The Rhetoric of Intellectual Property: Copyright Law and the Regulation of Digital Culture* (Routledge, 2010). Her research has also appeared in journals such as *Rhetoric Review, College English, Computers and Composition, Technical Communication Quarterly,* and *College Composition and Communication.*

Erika M. Sparby is an Assistant Professor of Digital Rhetoric and Technical Communication at Illinois State University, USA. Her research interests include online aggression, memes, identity, and digital ethics, and her work has appeared in *Computers and Composition*. Her dissertation, *Memes and 4chan and Haters, Oh My! Rhetoric, Identity, and Online Aggression,* won the 2017 Hugh Burns Best Dissertation Award.

Routledge Studies in Rhetoric and Communication

The Aboutness of Writing Center Talk
A Corpus-Driven and Discourse Analysis
Jo Mackiewicz

Rhetorical Realism
Rhetoric, Ethics, and the Ontology of Things
Scot Barnett

American Political Discourse on China
Michelle Murray Yang

Professional Communication and Network Interaction
A Rhetorical and Ethical Approach
Heidi A. McKee and James E. Porter

The Rhetoric of Videogames as Embodied Practice
Procedural Habits
Steve Holmes

Orwell's "Politics and the English Language" in the Age of Pseudocracy
Hans Ostrom and William Haltom

The Rhetoric of Oil in the Twenty-First Century
Government, Corporate, and Activist Discourses
Heather Graves and David Beard

Digital Ethics
Rhetoric and Responsibility in Online Aggression
Edited by Jessica Reyman and Erika M. Sparby

For more information about this series, please visit: https://www.routledge.com

Digital Ethics
Rhetoric and Responsibility in Online Aggression

Edited by
Jessica Reyman and Erika M. Sparby

LONDON AND NEW YORK

First published 2020 by Routledge

2 Park Square, Milton Park, Abingdon, Oxon OX14 4RN
605 Third Avenue, New York, NY 10017

Routledge is an imprint of the Taylor & Francis Group, an informa business

First issued in paperback 2021

Copyright © 2020 Taylor & Francis

The right of Jessica Reyman and Erika M. Sparby to be identified as the authors of the editorial material, and of the authors for their individual chapters, has been asserted in accordance with sections 77 and 78 of the Copyright, Designs and Patents Act 1988.

With the exception of Chapter 9, no part of this book may be reprinted or reproduced or utilised in any form or by any electronic, mechanical, or other means, now known or hereafter invented, including photocopying and recording, or in any information storage or retrieval system, without permission in writing from the publishers.

Chapter 9 of this book is available for free in PDF format as Open Access from the individual product page at www.routledge.com. It has been made available under a Creative Commons Attribution-Non Commercial-No Derivatives 4.0 license.

Notice:
Product or corporate names may be trademarks or registered trademarks, and are used only for identification and explanation without intent to infringe.

Publisher's Note
The publisher has gone to great lengths to ensure the quality of this reprint but points out that some imperfections in the original copies may be apparent.

Library of Congress Cataloging-in-Publication Data
A catalog record for this title has been requested

ISBN: 978-0-367-21795-2 (hbk)
ISBN: 978-1-03-217757-1 (pbk)
DOI: 10.4324/9780429266140

Typeset in Sabon
by codeMantra

For anyone who has been a target of digital aggression and harassment.

Contents

List of Figures — xi
Acknowledgments — xiii
*Foreword: Interacting with Friends,
Enemies, and Strangers* — xv
JAMES E. PORTER
List of Contributors — xxiii

1 Introduction: Toward an Ethic of Responsibility in Digital Aggression — 1
JESSICA REYMAN AND ERIKA M. SPARBY

PART I
Ethics of Interfaces and Platforms — 15

2 Hateware and the Outsourcing of Responsibility — 17
JAMES J. BROWN, JR. AND GREGORY HENNIS

3 Values versus Rules in Social Media Communities: How Platforms Generate Amorality on reddit and Facebook — 33
MICHAEL TRICE, LIZA POTTS, AND REBEKAH SMALL

4 Finding Effective Moderation Practices on Twitch — 51
TABITHA M. LONDON, JOEY CRUNDWELL, MARCY BOCK EASTLEY, NATALIE SANTIAGO, AND JENNIFER JENKINS

5 A Pedagogy of Ethical Interface Production Based on Virtue Ethics — 69
JOHN R. GALLAGHER

PART II
Academic Labor in Digital Publics   85

6 Feminist Research on the Toxic Web: The Ethics of Access, Affective Labor, and Harassment   87
LEIGH GRUWELL

7 "Maybe She Can Be a Feminist and Still Claim Her Own Opinions?": The Story of an Accidental Counter-Troll, *A Treatise in 9 Movements*   104
VYSHALI MANIVANNAN

8 Professorial Outrage: Enthymemic Assumptions   123
JEFF RICE

PART III
Cultural Narratives in Hostile Discourses   141

9 Hateful Games: Why White Supremacist Recruiters Target Gamers   143
MEGAN CONDIS

10 Theorycraft and Online Harassment: Mobilizing Status Quo Warriors   160
ALISHA KARABINUS

11 Volatile Visibility: How Online Harassment Makes Women Disappear   179
BRIDGET GELMS

PART IV
Circulation and Amplification of Digital Aggression   195

12 Confronting Digital Aggression with an Ethics of Circulation   197
BRANDY DIETERLE, DUSTIN EDWARDS, AND PAUL "DAN" MARTIN

13 The Banality of Digital Aggression: Algorithmic Data
   Surveillance in Medical Wearables   214
   KRISTA KENNEDY AND NOAH WILSON

14 Fostering *Phronesis* in Digital Rhetorics: Developing a
   Rhetorical and Ethical Approach to Online Engagements   231
   KATHERINE DELUCA

   Index   249

List of Figures

1.1	Digital community moderation and management	7
3.1	GamerGate instructions for creating a Twitter account, by KotakuInAction	41
3.2	Outline of KiA rules from the subreddit, by KotakuInAction	42
3.3	Rules for Ring Shaming Group	45
3.4	"That's it i'm wedding shaming" Facebook search	46
4.1	Hierarchy of moderation on Twitch	57
4.2	Streamer moderation tools/options	57
5.1	Twitter's interface default	78
5.2	Interface redesign that has added friction (Captcha)	78
5.3	Interface redesign that has added friction and alternate greeting	78
5.4	Complete redesign of Twitter's interface	79
6.1	@RealPeerReview tweet	97
10.1	Operational instructions for creating fake online feminist accounts	169
10.2	GamerGate instructions	170
14.1	Front page of the subreddit r/findbostonbombers/	236
14.2	Comments about image posted to reddit by european_douchebag	241

Acknowledgments

We owe many thanks to the many individuals who have provided support as we developed this collection. First and foremost, we thank our contributors for sharing their insights and labor. We appreciate the time and dedication you put into developing your ideas, completing drafts, and revising your chapters. We've enjoyed watching your chapters change and grow individually, as well as come together as a whole as the collection took shape. We are excited to share your work with the world.

Thank you as well to our generous reviewers for providing valuable and supportive feedback that helped shape the knowledge in this collection: Caddie Alford, Timothy Amidon, Brian Ballantine, Estee Beck, Richard Colby, Megan Condis, Melissa Kay Forbes, Bridget Gelms, Kendall Gerdes, Les Hutchinson, Elizabeth Lane, Kyle Larson, Heidi A. McKee, Ersula Ore, Anastasia Salter, Rachel Shapiro, Rebecca Shultz Colby, Kristin Ravel, Donnie Sackey, Ryan P. Shepherd, Wendi Sierra, Kyle Stedman, Annette Vee, and Stephanie Weaver. We are grateful to have been able to tap into your knowledge and expertise, and we appreciate your willingness to share your valuable time.

We must also thank our anonymous reviewers with Routledge who provided early stage feedback on the book proposal and introduction. Your suggestions helped us refine the collection's focus, and strengthen the introduction. Thanks as well to Suzanne Richardson, senior editor, and Eleanor Catchpole Simmons and Richa Kohli, the editorial team, at Routledge who were fantastic about answering our questions and offering support and encouragement along the way.

Erika would like to thank Illinois State University's College of Arts and Sciences for awarding her the New Faculty Initiative Grant in 2017, as well as her colleagues in the English department who endorse and believe in her work. To Adam, thank you for understanding that books (even edited collections) take a lot of time and energy, and for supporting me when I needed to work extra hours or take a nap instead of hanging out. To family and friends (especially my taekwondo families, who help me blow off steam and keep me grounded), thank you for being enthusiastic and supportive about this project—your excitement helped fuel my motivation to complete it.

Jessica would like to thank her academic home, Northern Illinois University, for providing her with the support needed to complete this work. She would also like to express her love and gratitude to her family. To Ryan, Jordan, and Chase, thank you for your patience and understanding during the countless hours devoted to this project, and for providing me with welcome distractions when I needed them the most.

Foreword
Interacting with Friends, Enemies, and Strangers

James E. Porter

I remember a period in the 1990s, in the pre-web and early web days, when Internet groups could organize themselves in semiprivate digital groups (e.g. listserv and Usenet groups). Many of us bought into the utopian ideal of the virtual community based on a more-or-less shared ethos. Of course, yes, there was exclusion, bias, even some aggression in this realm, but less of it, and more easily managed; the ideas of shared ethos, civility in discourse, and open democratic participation all had a chance. Or so it seemed.

We are long past that naïveté now. In 2019, we interact in a Wild West realm of large-scale social media and massive multiplayer online games, where the membership boundaries are not firmly set as with those older digital communities. On Facebook, Twitter, Instagram, and YouTube, we share space with many others who don't agree with us, who don't share the same ethical codes, and who, let's face it, seem to hate us. We can create our own friend networks (on Facebook) or control who follows us (on Twitter), try to manage our spaces, but the platforms are huge, unwieldy, and heavily populated, the boundaries are more porous, and the hate and hostility creep in—or pour in. We have enemies, too. Increasingly, the Internet has become a hostile, angry, and even a dangerous place. We should have guessed there would be trouble.

The researchers in this collection do an excellent job, first, of mapping this new Wild West, cataloguing the range and types of issues we face, focusing mainly on the issue of digital aggression and harassment. The collection focuses on this key question, *What do we do about the problem?* How should we behave, what is right and just, in the way that we express ourselves as writers and communicators in the digital realm? What principles should guide our actions as producers of digital content, whether as professionals or private citizens? These are the fundamental questions linking digital communication with ethics and rhetoric. The distinctive strength of this collection is that its contributors approach these questions combining rhetorical frameworks with writing studies research methodologies to provide practically useful strategies and advice.

A Basic Ethic for Rhetorical Interaction

Let's start with a fundamental ethics question that also happens to be a rhetoric question: *How should we treat others?* In our daily lives, as we walk down the street or as we interact on social media, how should we treat others? As threats to our well-being, as objects to be manipulated for our own gain, as enemies to be defeated and destroyed? Or as fellow beings, comrades, guests, colleagues, brothers and sisters, even friends?

It is helpful to look at what the late 5th-century BCE Greek sophist Isocrates has to say about this. In the Isocratean model, rhetoric and ethics are closely intertwined—their common *telos* being "the best course of action" for the *polis*. According to Isocrates, the purpose of rhetoric is "the good of the state" and "the needs of the commonwealth" (*Panathenaicus*, p. 12). The ultimate goal of the rhetorical enterprise, for Isocrates, is social harmony, concord (*homonoia*) (Benoit, 1991; de Romilly, 1958; Poulakos, 2004). Isocrates's rhetoric focuses on the character of the rhetor, on building and maintaining productive relations, and on promoting justice.

Put bluntly, this ethic of rhetoric says that your purpose as a rhetor does not end with the *audience* but rather with the *polis*. Your communications are not produced only to persuade, instruct, or delight. Your purpose in interacting with the audience serves a larger purpose, a phatic or irenic one (Porter, 2017): to serve the common welfare, to promote justice and equity, to make society better, and to maintain positive relationships with others.

Kinneavy (1982) saw Isocrates's notion of the goal of rhetoric, its *telos*, as arising from "the Athenian notion of a guest's right to protection and compassion" (p. 21), or what was known as *xenia*, the guest–friend relationship: your first obligation, the presumption, about your behavior toward an unknown person was that you were to treat them well, with respect and graciousness, as a friend—because that unknown person might well be a god. Respectful, civil rhetorical interaction is the necessary instrument for *xenia*. It is the means by which we form peaceful, productive relations with strangers, and head off disputes and disagreements. Rhetoric, operating by the principle of *xenia*, provides the alternative to conflict, strife, and war. To violate this principle was to invite the wrath of the gods and bring destruction upon your house—a common theme in Greek tragedies.

In this context, the answer to *What should we do?* becomes very clear: we should greet strangers—or, if not greet, at the very least treat everyone with respect, politeness, civility, and courtesy as human beings—*not just for their sake, and not just for our sake, but for all of our sakes.* The principle of respect for others is, of course, a version of the Golden Rule: *treat others as you would wish to be treated*—a principle found in numerous moral and religious traditions. And this principle is also enshrined as Article 1 of the *Universal Declaration of Human Rights* (United Nations, 1948): "All human beings are born free and equal in dignity and rights. They are endowed with reason and conscience and *should act towards one another in a spirit of brotherhood.*" Or sisterhood. Or personhood.

Respect others ... even when they don't respect you? Ah, there's the rub: Should you always turn the other cheek? The principle of *xenia* says that your first gesture toward others—even, and in fact especially, strangers—should be the rhetoric of the open hand, not the closed fist. That does not mean, however, that harsh, even angry, rhetoric is never a valid option. There are situations and audiences for which a strong, angry, and assertive rhetoric is necessary—times and occasions when you say, *Stop, no more, this is wrong, this must end.* However, the first principle and presumptive stance are clear: treat the stranger as a friend, until you discover that they're not. *Respect others*, but also attach this corollary: *demand respect from others.* It works two ways.

The Integrity of the Game and the Field

For every competitive sport or game I ever played or coached, there was a common guiding set of ethical principles—a sense of fair play that included both respect for the rules of the game and respect for your opponents in the game. The code insisted not only on playing by the rules, but by playing the game with some degree of respect and appreciation for your opponent. *Opponent, not enemy.* After the game is over, you cross the field, shake their hand, and say "good game"—because that is the expected thing to do, the right thing to do.

A listserv, a game world, a social media platform, all are game systems, at least in the respect that they operate by codes, written and unwritten, that govern interaction within the system: everybody is subject to the same rules, and you agree to play by those rules, because without them, there is no game. Sure, you can disagree about application of the rules: Was that pitch a strike or a ball? Was that tennis serve in or out? Heated arguments, sure—and for many games we need referees, even video replay officials, to make the difficult calls for us. But usually we are playing these games on our own, recreationally, and so we settle things among ourselves. We have a momentary heated disagreement, then make a decision and resume playing (usually). Every once in a while, we disagree about the rules themselves, and so we might change the rules to make the game fairer or safer or more interesting.

In any coherent felicitous game system, there is an agreement about the rules: you have written rules, regulations that constitute the strict parameters of the game, and you also have unwritten codes and expectations (e.g. about what does or does not constitute fair play). If somebody cheats at a game, violates the rules consistently or flagrantly, you refuse to play with that person any more. With people who refuse to play by the rules or who fail to respect you, you either have to exclude them, because they don't play well with others, or exclude yourself by leaving the game.

Notice how many times the terms *argue* and *agree* have appeared in this discussion. Because we often disagree, we *argue* in order to come to some kind of agreement or understanding together.[1] The field of rhetoric sits right at this junction, as a coherent guiding system of language interaction developed for the purpose of helping us live more peaceably together. In conjunction with dialectic (which I view as part of rhetoric), this system was developed by the 5th-century BCE Greek rhetoricians to help us arrive at agreement and consensus even when we disagree—because the Greeks understood that (a) there is no avoiding disagreement—it's inevitable among different humans trying to live together; and (b) the alternative to rhetoric is far worse: war, a vicious conflict whose purpose is simply destruction of the other. The Greek rhetoricians were very aware that if rhetoric failed, war ensued.

Should we abandon the playing field, leave the game, and cancel our social media accounts because others are rude, disrespectful, and aggressive? I'm not happy with how Twitter manages our accounts—but they are trying to figure out a way to establish guidelines and rules for interaction while protecting people's right to speak (and yes, of course, protecting their business model). Within this space, I have to decide, as a rhetor, What am I going to do? Should I leave (close my account)—or should I stay?

Well, sometimes, I agree, the only recourse is to leave. However, in the case of Twitter, I see my obligation as to stay, for the time being, and, in my miniscule way, try to make the space better: to be a good tweeter, to model good behavior, and to be a good citizen on a social media platform.

Going back to the principles of Isocratean rhetoric, in addition to respecting our opponents, we also must respect, defend, and uphold *the system* that is in place (e.g. the rhetorical ethical codes that govern interaction) and *the place*, the venue, the platform that is our locus of interaction. We have to respect and protect the rules and the playing field as well because ultimately that is necessary for our overall rhetorical goal—seeking harmony for the *polis*. Ergo, we have a strong ethical obligation not to abandon public space/s to the trolls.

Ethics for Enemies

So what do we do about all those people who don't follow the rules, either the written rules (e.g. terms of service) or the fundamental ethical codes that should govern human relations (e.g. respect for others)? What about those trolls and malicious agents who practice an ethic of hate, intolerance, and exceptionalism? What about the people doing active harm to others: their verbal expressions become harmful, hurtful, and destructive actions that bully and shame others into silence or, even worse, suicide?

First, we have to differentiate—distinguish the merely annoying but relatively harmless trolling, easily ignored, from more serious and systemic forms, such as group bullying, coordinated and sustained attacks, or organized efforts to promulgate fake news. A single mocking statement, where the poster says something rude but then moves on, is different from sustained individual attack over a period of time (bullying), which is different from an organized collective attack by an entire group of racists or misogynists (what happened in GamerGate to feminist media critic Anita Sarkeesian and game developer Zoë Quinn). Our responses, as rhetors, need to account for these differences, as we contemplate how (or if) to respond.

For many of these acts, the verb *troll* is too mild, too benevolent. *Attack* is more accurate. And the hate, antagonism, and attack are often directed at women, at people of color, at the LGBTQ+ community, at the disability community, and at minority populations. The history of attacks on these groups is part of the rhetorical situation. Such attacks need to be historically contextualized: they are not just individual, isolated moments of aggressiveness but are part of a historical pattern that goes well beyond mere disagreement; they are attempts to disenfranchise a person's, or an entire people's, right to speak or, even, exist as members of the *polis*. And verbal aggression is very closely linked with physical violence—let's not forget that. What starts out as hostile speech often shifts to violent acts (Shanes, 2018).

So what do you and I do about these people? How do we respond to the anti-ethic that is poisoning the community well? Should you be civil to a racist? Is it OK to punch a Nazi? These are tough ethical questions for rhetoricians—because fundamentally we trust and believe in symbolic interaction as a way to engage others, to settle our differences, and to find peace and harmony together. And the ethical foundation for that system is respect for others, even when we disagree. What happens, though, in a system when some others don't live by that ethic, who either never learned it or who have rejected it?

There are things that we can do to counter digital aggression. We can leap to the defense of those who are under attack (e.g. Zoë Quinn, Anita Sarkeesian)—so that they are not receiving the attack alone, as individuals. We can denounce the attackers and, to the extent possible, exclude the attackers from participation in the forum, block them, and insist that platform providers like Twitter and Facebook shut down accounts of serial harassers and violators of terms of service. Even when First Amendment law protects certain forms of aggressive expression, as it does, users-in-the-aggregate do have social power and can exercise it to make online spaces more habitable.

With some people, the rhetoric of reasonable, civil conversation just isn't going to work. *Please be respectful* just won't cut it. So you have to resort to a different kind of rhetoric. You ignore them, you denounce them, and you exclude them. Just be careful that in doing so, you don't market their brand and contribute to the ideology: you do not want to become *them*. However we respond, the answer is NOT to ignore such aggression; it has to be named, denounced, and opposed.

We must differentiate, too, between expression and action—because the former is protected, and the latter is not, legally speaking. Speaking purely from the point of view of rhetoric, I would say that all speech is always both expression and action: all speech aims to have an effect, and in that respect it perlocutes. Words are never just words; they also constitute actions (Porter, in press). However, in saying that, I am speaking from the standpoint of rhetoric and ethics, not law—and law, U.S. law anyway, tends not to agree. U.S. First Amendment law draws a fairly hard line between expression and action, and protects a great deal of digital speech/writing as expression—even when it is hateful and aggressive.

The key dividing line is when your speech threatens my own right to speak—silences me. At that point, you have broken the unstated presumption lying at the heart of the rhetorical ethic: that is, the categorical imperative that this code applies to both of us equally; and, ergo, it does not apply to speech that stifles others' right to speech. Your right to free speech does not extend to aggression, harassment, and threats that have the effect of impeding others' right to free speech. Easy enough to say, but when does a discursive action actually stifle my speech? Deciding such questions—determining that dividing line between *allowable strong expression* and *inappropriate/illegal harassing action* in digital spaces—is a matter of vigorous discussion and debate for scholars of law and ethics, for the judicial system, and for the public. Rhetoric scholars have much to contribute.

Conclusion

Digital aggression, harassment, physical threats, mainly directed at women, at LGBTQ+ persons, at members of racial or ethnic minorities—and, let's admit it, mainly coming from white males, often, though not always, affiliated with alt-right and white supremacist groups. This is not the only issue for digital media ethics (Mckee & Porter, 2018)—but it is, I believe, one of the most serious communication issues currently facing us. And it is clearly an issue for rhetoric and writing studies, as our field must be concerned not only with how to write/speak effectively in public spaces but also in how to protect those spaces to make sure that everybody has access to the public dais—which is, in our time, social media.

What does rhetoric teach us? First and foremost, rhetoric teaches us to be aware of audience, particularly the diversity of audiences. It teaches us that people disagree and have different, conflicting views—often strongly held views. People come from different backgrounds, have different senses of humor, and, of course, subscribe to different ethical systems. Rhetoric makes us aware of context and situation, kairotic moments, cultural factors, and power relations. It teaches us to be alert to how symbolic interaction happens in diverse places, in diverse contexts, with diverse audiences. It teaches us that language use has the potential to be harmful and hurtful.

As a system of production and invention, rhetoric is designed to solve precisely what divides us: we talk about it, we come to a shared understanding, and we apologize when we need to. We learn. We adapt our ethics and our language, to suit the new situation, the new audience, the new time and place we're in. If we are reasonable people, we can do this: we can disagree, talk it out, agree to disagree, move on, and be polite with one another. That's what reasonable people do—and this is how rhetoric helps us do it.

There isn't much ethical complexity about the nature of racist and misogynistic attack: it's wrong. But what, what, what should be done about that? And by whom? Owners and managers—listserv and game moderators, game makers, and social media platforms—certainly bear considerable responsibility for policing their own creations. But what do *we* do about it—as responsible public citizens invested in trying to make social media an open, widely available space for public discussion? Or, as teachers and scholars of rhetoric and writing trying to identify, and teach, ethical modes of expression and behavior?

One useful thing we can do is what these contributors are already doing: research online spaces from the point of view of rhetorical ethics, and ask: What are the codes in place governing online interactions? What new codes do we need? How do we address the problems of persistent aggression and harassment, especially of underrepresented or historically victimized groups? What combination of ethical guidelines, platform terms of service, and government regulation will help make social media a more productive place for human interaction?

Obviously, too, we must teach students to navigate the complex world of social media—and to be aware of the rhetorical and ethical complexities of such spaces. We have to teach students to be ethical writers in these spaces, but we also have to teach them how to protect themselves when—not if—they come under attack. We have to teach them to respect others but also to demand respect from others. We must teach them to protect the public spaces themselves. We must teach them to understand why rhetorical ethical principles are vital to the harmony of the *polis*. And, of course, we must model good Internet behavior ourselves. There is a lot we can do.

Note

1 *Argument* in this context should not be confused with *eristic*. Eristic is just shouting at somebody, vilifying them, ridiculing them viciously as a way to defeat them. Eristic, related to the *ad hominem* fallacy, operates mostly as an attack on the rhetor—and that is what we often see as characteristic of online aggression. Argument, on the other hand, does not personalize difference and disagreement: as interlocutors we may disagree, but we respect each other as fellow members of the *polis* even as we disagree.

References

Benoit, W. L. (1991). Isocrates and Plato on rhetoric and rhetorical education. *Rhetoric Society Quarterly, 21*(1), 60–71.

de Romilly, J. (1958). *Eunoia* in Isocrates or the political importance of creating good will. *Journal of Hellenic Studies, 78*, 92–101.

Isocrates. (n.d.). *Panathenaicus*. In G. Norlin (Ed.), Perseus Digital Library. Retrieved from http://www.perseus.tufts.edu/hopper/text?doc=Perseus%3Atext%3A1999.01.0144%3Aspeech%3D12

Kinneavy, J. L. (1982). Restoring the humanities: The return of rhetoric from exile. In J. J. Murphy (Ed.), *The rhetorical tradition and modern writing* (pp. 19–28). New York, NY: MLA.

McKee, H. A., & Porter, J. E. (2018). Digital media ethics and rhetoric. In J. Alexander & J. Rhodes (Eds.), *The Routledge handbook of digital writing and rhetoric* (pp. 401–411). New York, NY: Routledge.

Porter, J. E. (2017). Professional communication as phatic: From classical *eunoia* to personal AI. *Business & Professional Communication Quarterly, 80*(2), 174–193.

Porter, J. E. (in press). Recovering a good rhetoric. In J. Duffy & L. Agnew (Eds.), *Rewriting Plato's legacy: Ethics, rhetoric, and writing studies*.

Poulakos, J. (2004). Rhetoric and civic education: From the Sophists to Isocrates. In T. Poulakos & D. Depew (Eds.), *Isocrates and civic education* (pp. 69–83). Austin: University of Texas Press.

Shanes, J. (2018, November 9). Donald Trump, Pittsburgh, and the lessons of Kristallnacht. *Washington Post*. https://www.washingtonpost.com/outlook/2018/11/09/donald-trump-pittsburgh-lessons-kristallnacht

United Nations. (1948). *Universal declaration of human rights*. http://www.un.org/en/universal-declaration-human-rights/

List of Contributors

Editors:

Jessica Reyman, Northern Illinois University, jreyman@niu.edu

Jessica Reyman is an Associate Professor of Digital Rhetoric and Professional Writing in the Department of English at Northern Illinois University. Her research focuses on law and ethics in digital rhetoric, and she is the author of *The Rhetoric of Intellectual Property: Copyright Law and the Regulation of Digital Culture* (Routledge, 2010). Her research has also appeared in journals such as *Rhetoric Review, College English, Computers and Composition, Technical Communication Quarterly,* and *College Composition and Communication* as well as numerous peer-reviewed articles and book chapters.

Erika M. Sparby, Illinois State University, @Sparbtastic

Erika M. Sparby is an Assistant Professor of Digital Rhetoric and Technical Communication at Illinois State University. Her research interests include online aggression, memes, identity, and digital ethics, and her work has appeared in *Computers and Composition*. Her dissertation, *Memes and 4chan and Haters, Oh My! Rhetoric, Identity, and Online Aggression*, won the 2017 Hugh Burns Best Dissertation Award.

Foreword:

James E. Porter, Miami University

James Porter is a Professor in the Department of English and Armstrong Institute for Interactive Media Studies at Miami University. He co-authored *The Ethics of Internet Research: A Rhetorical, Case-Based Approach* (2009) with Heidi A. McKee and wrote *Rhetorical Ethics and Internetworked Writing* (1998), both of which address digital rhetoric and rhetorical ethics.

Contributing authors:

James Brown, Rutgers University-Camden, jim.brown@rutgers.edu

James Brown is an Associate Professor of English and the Director of the Digital Studies Center at Rutgers University-Camden. He is the author of *Ethical Programs* and the co-author of a chapter in *Precarious Rhetorics* (2018). His research has also appeared in journals such as *Philosophy & Rhetoric*, *Computers and Composition*, and *College Composition and Communication*.

Megan Condis, Texas Tech University, megan.condis@ttu.edu

Megan Condis is an Assistant Professor of Game Studies at Texas Tech University. Her book, *Gaming Masculinity: Trolls, Fake Geeks, and the Gendered Battle for Online Culture*, was published in 2018 by the University of Iowa Press.

Joey Crundwell, Northern Illinois University, jcrundwell1@niu.edu

Joey Crundwell is a Doctoral student at Northern Illinois University. His research interests include video games as literary and rhetorical texts, and as pedagogical tools in college classrooms.

Katherine DeLuca, University of Massachusetts, Dartmouth, kdeluca1@umassd.edu

Katherine DeLuca is an Assistant Professor of English at the University of Massachusetts, Dartmouth. Her work has been published in *Kairos*, the *Journal of Teaching Writing*, *WLN*, and *Computers and Composition*, and she is the coeditor of *The Rhetoric of Participation: Interrogating Commonplaces In and Beyond the Classroom* (forthcoming). Her research focuses on the intersections of digital media studies, composition studies, and rhetoric.

Brandy Dieterle, University of Central Florida

Brandy Dieterle completed her PhD from the Texts & Technology program at the University of Central Florida. Her research interests are in multimodal composition, digital literacies, new media, and gender and identity studies. She works as an Assistant Editor with the journal *Kairos* and serves on the Editorial Review Board of *Xchanges*. Her work has appeared in the *Computers and Composition*, *Composition Forum*, *Kairos*, and the *Journal of Global Literacies, Technologies, and Emerging Pedagogies*.

Marcy Bock Eastley, Northern Illinois University, mbock2@niu.edu

Marcy Bock Eastley is a Doctoral student at Northern Illinois University and holds an MBA in marketing. Building on a successful business career designing digital learning environments, her research interests include rhetoric of digital communities and collaborative practices in the composition classroom.

Dustin W. Edwards, University of Central Florida, Dustin.Edwards@ucf.edu

Dustin W. Edwards is an Assistant Professor of Writing and Rhetoric at the University of Central Florida. He researches digital and material rhetorics, public rhetoric and writing, and the politics of writing infrastructures. His work has been published in *Computers and Composition*, *enculturation*, and *Present Tense*, as well as edited collections such as *Circulation, Writing, and Rhetoric*.

John R. Gallagher, University of Illinois, Urbana-Champaign, johng@illinois.edu

John R. Gallagher is an Assistant Professor of English and Writing Studies at the University of Illinois, Urbana-Champaign. He has published in *Computers and Composition*, *Written Communication*, *enculturation*, and other journals. He researches digital rhetoric and writing, empirical data methods, and online comments. He is working on a manuscript tentatively titled *Update Culture and the Afterlife of Online Writing*.

Bridget Gelms, San Francisco State University, @BridgetGelms

Bridget Gelms is an Assistant Professor of English at San Francisco State University, where she researches writing, digital literacies, and social media cultures. Her work explores the growing issue of online harassment and how it impacts women—their online presences, participations in digital public discourses, and everyday lives. Her research is also concerned with how social media design and governance replicates offline social inequalities in our digital publics. Her work has appeared in *Present Tense*, *enculturation*, and *The Writing Center Journal*.

Leigh Gruwell, Auburn University, lcg0016@auburn.edu

Leigh Gruwell is an Assistant Professor of English at Auburn University, where she teaches undergraduate and graduate courses in writing and rhetoric. Her research centers on digital and feminist rhetorics, composition pedagogy, and research methodologies, and has been published in *Computers and Composition*, *Composition Forum*, and *Present Tense*.

Gregory C. Hennis III, Rutgers University-Camden, gch36@scarletmail.rutgers.edu

Gregory Hennis is an undergraduate student at Rutgers University-Camden, working toward majors in Computer Science and Digital Studies and a minor in English. While at Rutgers, Gregory has participated in the creation of the Rutgers Writing and Design Lab, a peer tutor center that focuses primarily on issues of digital and multimodal rhetoric.

Jennifer Jenkins, Northern Illinois University, jjenkins5@niu.edu

Jennifer Jenkins is a Doctoral student at Northern Illinois University. Her research interests include rhetoric and science fiction, writing studies, and game studies.

Alisha Karabinus, Purdue University

Alisha Karabinus is a student in the Rhetoric and Composition doctoral program at Purdue University. She is interested in the rhetorics of digital communities, games studies, feminist rhetorics, first-year writing pedagogy, and professional and technical writing. She is also a frequent contributor to *Not Your Mama's Gamer*.

Krista Kennedy, Syracuse University, krista01@syr.edu

Krista Kennedy is an Associate Professor of Writing & Rhetoric at Syracuse University. Her research focuses on the ways that humans work with and alongside technologies to produce communication. She is the author of *Textual Curation: Authorship, Agency, and Technology in Wikipedia and the Chambers's Cyclopaedia* (2016), and her scholarship and photographic work has appeared in *College English, Computers & Composition, Communication Design Quarterly,* and *Explorations in Media Ecology* as well as in various American, British, and European venues.

Tabitha London, Northern Illinois University, tlondon@niu.edu

Tabitha London is a Doctoral student at Northern Illinois University. Her research interests include video games in the rhetoric and composition classroom, online gaming communities, and digital literacies.

Vyshali Manivannan, Rutgers University, vyshali.manivannan@rutgers.edu

Vyshali Manivannan is a PhD candidate in Journalism and Media Studies at Rutgers University and holds an MFA in Fiction Writing from Columbia University. Her scholarship has appeared in *Digital Health, Platform,* and *Fibreculture* among others, and her creative work has been featured in literary journals such as *The Fanzine, DIAGRAM,* and *Consequence*. She was nominated for a 2015 Pushcart Prize in Nonfiction and was among those listed in "Notable Essays and Literary Nonfiction of 2014" in *Best American Essays 2015*.

Paul "Dan" Martin, University of Central Florida, paul.martin @ucf.edu

Dan Martin is an Associate Instructor of Writing and Rhetoric and a Coordinator of the Writing Across the Curriculum Program at the University of Central Florida. His research centers on how digital and multimodal writing are shaping knowledge across disciplines. He is also interested in semiotics and the rhetoric of new media, and he tends to investigate digital tools, mediums, and forms through the lens of semiotics.

Liza Potts, Michigan State University, lpotts@msu.edu

Liza Potts is an Associate Professor in the Department of Writing, Rhetoric, and American Cultures at Michigan State University where she is the Director of WIDE Research and the Cofounder of the Experience Architecture program. Her research interests include networked participatory culture, social user experience, and digital rhetoric. She has written *Social Media in Disaster Response* and coedited *Rhetoric and Experience Architecture* with Michael Salvo.

Jeff Rice, University of Kentucky, j.rice@uky.edu

Jeff Rice is the Chair and Martha B. Reynolds Professor of Writing, Rhetoric, and Digital Studies at the University of Kentucky. He is the author of three monographs, four edited collections, and numerous articles and chapters on rhetoric and new media.

Natalie Santiago, Northern Illinois University, nsantiago@niu.edu

Natalie Santiago is a Doctoral student at Northern Illinois University. Her research focuses on digital public spheres, digital rhetoric, and game studies, with a focus in VR/AR/XR.

Rebekah Small, Michigan State University, smallreb@msu.edu

Rebekah Small is a Masters student in the Department of Writing, Rhetoric, and American Cultures and a graduate assistant for WIDE Research. She received a fellowship through the Research Experience for Master's Students (REMS) at the University of Michigan, funded by the Institute of Museum and Library Services. She has also published in places such as *In Media Res and SIGDOC*, and is a 2017–2019 HASTAC Scholar.

Michael Trice, Massachusetts Institute of Technology, mtrice@mit.edu

Michael Trice is a Lecturer in Writing, Rhetoric, and Professional Communication at the Massachusetts Institute of Technology. His research examines how participant experience levels inform user experience in community media platforms, how crowd-sourced instruction rhetorically frames online activism, and how reasoning can be visualized in scientific discourses.

Noah Wilson, Syracuse University, npwilson@syr.edu

Noah Wilson is a Doctoral student in the Composition and Cultural Rhetoric program at Syracuse University. His research interests include digital literacy, rhetorical theory, and surveillance studies.

1 Introduction
Toward an Ethic of Responsibility in Digital Aggression

Jessica Reyman and Erika M. Sparby

Digital aggression in today's digital world is widespread, lacking easily traceable sources and causes and without clear paths for accountability and resolution. In July 2017, the Pew Research Center reported that four in ten U.S. adults (41%) have experienced online harassment and many more have witnessed it. From name calling and public shaming to physical threats and stalking, much of this activity targets women, transpeople, and members of racial or ethnic minority groups. Research shows that one in four Black people has been the target of harassment, and women are twice as likely as men to be harassed online (Duggan, 2017). In addition, religious views and political views and affiliations have also been the basis for aggression. In 2014, GamerGate brought the gendered tensions and gatekeeping practices present in some gaming communities to the attention of the mainstream public. The 2017 white nationalist demonstration in Charlottesville, VA (which was organized largely through Discord, a voice and text chat app), and the online political and public responses following it gave renewed visibility to hate groups. Automation and algorithmic technologies present their own ethical quandaries surrounding digital data. The initial release of Apple Watch was unable to work properly on heavily tattooed or darkly pigmented skin (Profis, 2014), and Fitbit data has been used to catch cheating spouses (Pilon, 2015) and reveal pregnancy (Jackson, 2016). Twitter bots have been credited with influencing the 2016 U.S. presidential election. Facebook's Cambridge Analytica data privacy scandal revealed how the extent of the personal information and data collected through Facebook can be mismanaged and subject to abuse (Granville, 2018).

Within the current context, questions arise about response, responsibility, and accountability that the field of digital rhetoric is uniquely poised to address. The chapters in this collection, as a whole, build on what Porter (1998) has called "rhetorical ethics," which do not constitute a moral code or a set of laws but rather a "set of implicit understandings between writer and audience about their relationship" (p. 68). While Porter's work appeared before the rise of social media, automation, widespread digital data collection, and other contemporary web contexts, we have more recently seen how these implicit agreements extend beyond writer and reader (who often occupy both roles) to also include the individuals, communities, and institutions that build and manage technological spaces for discourse and engagement. Furthermore, as Brown (2015) argues, digital platforms, networks, and technologies themselves carry ethical programs with rhetorical implications.

Following the Association of Internet Researchers' "Ethical Decision-Making and Internet Research" (Markham & Buchanan, 2012), this collection considers digital ethics as deeply embedded within rhetorical contexts. Approaches from our authors take into account Markham and Buchanan's (2012) questions:

- Does the research definition of context match the way owners, users, or members might define it? ...
- Are there distinctions between local contextual norms for how a venue is conceptualized and jurisdictional frameworks (e.g. Terms of Service, other regulations)? ...
- What are the ethical expectations users attach to the venue in which they are interacting? (p. 8)

In doing so, the chapters in this collection seek to understand ethics within dynamic digital ecosystems and ecologies. The authors demonstrate the value of casuistic approaches to studying digital ethics, considering complex ethical issues by analyzing the tensions among regulation-driven and context-driven considerations.

In a time when more people are on Facebook than live in the country of China, when people wear social media in their watches and carry it in their pockets, and when the U.S. president uses Twitter as a political platform, attention to digital ethics is more important than ever. How users participate online and through digital media and how researchers and scholars theorize about ethical participation have the potential to shape the norms, laws, and practices that will determine the future of the social web and digital data. This edited collection provides a discussion of what principles, based on research and theory in rhetoric and composition, *should* guide our thinking about responsibility, accountability, and ethics. Through examinations of unethical practices in digital spaces and through digital technologies, this collection contributes to the field's research and theorizing about ethical participation by providing contextualized, case-based analyses of varying forms of digital aggression and exploring the tensions inherent in minimizing harm in a digital age.

Ethics and Digital Aggression in Rhetoric and Writing Studies

Ethical issues have captured the attention of rhetoric and composition scholars from early iterations of the web to present day. *Foregrounding*

Ethical Awareness in Composition and English Studies (Fontaine & Hunter, 1998) offered a collection of essays on ethical issues relevant to teaching and administrating composition classes and programs at a time when the field was reportedly taking an "ethical turn." In a review essay titled "The Ethical Turn in English Studies" (1999), Harrington asserted a rise in interest in ethics at the time. While she observed that "current discussions vary considerably in approach as well as well as how ethics relates to what we do as teachers and scholars," she located its roots in the connections developing at the time between administrative practices and pedagogical choices to the social, cultural, and political.

At that same time, the web was emerging as a force for communication, civic discourse, public activity, and education, leading rhetoric and composition researchers to define and theorize the concept of "rhetorical ethics" for online rhetoric (Porter, 1998) and later a "digital ethic" (DeVoss & Porter, 2006) for new online environments. New environments for reading and writing presented new ethical issues for consideration by rhetoric and composition scholars. Privacy online was identified early as an ethical issue of rhetorical import by Gurak in *Persuasion and Privacy in Cyberspace* (1999), and has since been examined by Beck et al. (2016). Digital copyright and authorship have been widely examined as contentious legal issues rife with ethical implications (Herrington, 2010; Logie, 2006; Reyman, 2010; Rife, Slattery, & DeVoss, 2011; Westbrook, 2009). Johnson-Eilola (2010) has written about the implications of "spimes" and user data for writers and readers in "Among Texts," where he concludes with "an incomplete list of concerns" that includes issues of privacy and ethics. A 2011 special issue of *Computers and Composition Online* titled "Ethics in Digital Age: Ethics and Digital Media in the Writing Classroom" (Coley, 2011) presents discussion of "ethical literacy" for a digital age, which includes discussions about ethical issues presented by both student composing activities such as photo manipulation and remix and instructor activities such as adopting course management systems. These particular ethical issues—of privacy, of copyright, of remix and attribution—have attracted the interest of scholars interrogating ethics within digital ecosystems and ecologies for composing, communication, participation, and engagement.

As far back as Selfe and Selfe's "Politics of the Interface" (1994), digital rhetoric has been concerned with the ways technologies and interfaces reinscribe dominant ideologies and power structures by their very design, and equally important are explorations of how humans can perpetuate these dynamics through discourse and participation in online spaces. More recently, digital ethics scholarship within rhetoric and composition studies has examined these concerns within the context of human–machine collaborations. Brown's *Ethical Programs* (2015) offers a compelling and extended analysis of the ethics of networked software, showing how software promotes particular arguments and advances an ethical agenda, thus contributing to the complexities of locating responsibility and accountability within and across digital ecologies. Automated systems and algorithms have been addressed as an ethical quandary for rhetoricians studying rhetorical agency (Kennedy, 2016; Miller, 2007; Reyman, 2010).

Other recent work addresses digital aggression through examinations of case studies, analysis of examples, and observations of user activity in online communities. Warnick and Heineman's *Rhetoric Online* (2012) examines cyberterrorism to contribute to an understanding of why and how digital aggression can be so persuasive, revealing the global and political implications for damaging digital discourses (Warnick & Heineman, 2012). Several scholars have observed gendered aggression in online spaces (Cloud, 2009; Jane, 2014; Milner, 2013; Phillips, 2015), including Poland (2016), who provides a first-person exploration of cybersexism and harassment in *Haters: Harassment, Abuse, and Violence Online*. She follows Phillips's (2015) nuanced treatment of the topic, examining different types of trolls and aggressors and acknowledging the intersectionality of harassment and abuse. Clinnin and Manthey (2019), Gruwell (2017), and Sparby (2017) connect what we know (and can learn) about digital aggression to practical applications for teaching writing. They urge writing teachers to engage students in becoming more civically engaged in the digital spaces they occupy.

The field of rhetoric and composition is only just beginning to grapple with and untangle the implications of the widespread abuse and harassment distributed across the social web, the ethical dilemmas presented to us in the writing and rhetoric classroom or through our research, and the complex questions surrounding automation, wearable technologies, and issues of privacy and surveillance. Poland (2016) offers a call to action: "Those of us with the power to do research, educate others, enforce consequences, and build safer spaces have a responsibility to do so" (p. 252). The authors in this collection aim to meet this challenge, offering new frameworks for digital ethics from a uniquely rhetorical perspective.

Toward an Ethic of Responsibility in Digital Aggression: From Not Feeding the Trolls to an Ecology of Response

Typical advice and calls for civility amidst aggression, hate speech, and harassment are frequently too-optimistic, misguided, and ineffectual. Phillips and Milner (2018) critique sentiments such as, "[i]f only people would lower their voices, stop posting rude memes, and quit with the name-calling, we could start having meaningful conversations. We could unite around our shared experiences. We could come together as a nation." Poland (2016) brings attention to the problematic nature of a similar adage for responding to digital harassment: "don't feed the trolls." The idea behind these approaches is that because those who spew hate and harass others online feed on attention, if users simply ignore the comments and behaviors, aggressors will get bored, cease their behavior, and go elsewhere. However well-intentioned, this urging toward civility is inadequate because it flattens contexts, puts an emphasis on intentionality over effect, and can silence the targets of aggression, including already marginalized voices.

Put simply, existing approaches to address digital aggression fail today's digital media users. In contemporary digital contexts, the number of users has risen so dramatically and the boundaries between digital communities are more fluid and diverse than ever before. In *The Internet of Garbage*, Jeong (2018) notes the ways in which such fluidity can contribute to digital aggression:

> When looking through the lens of online harassment, the internet is simply too small. When one platform links to another platform in these cases, it creates a pipeline of hate with very little friction. Even if the targeted platform maintains certain norms, the oncoming invaders ignore them, operating only under the norms of their originating platform. A simple Google search can connect together all the disparate aspects of a person's digital life, allowing bad actors to attack each and every part even without knowing them particularly well to begin with.
>
> (p. 74)

As users move quickly and easily between platforms and spaces, often gaining membership in multiple communities with varying and sometimes conflicting goals, purposes, and values, it's no longer easy to maintain an exclusive online space and drive out those with dissenting opinions or who don't fit within narrow identity categories for participants. Digital spaces are, therefore, rife with conflict, sometimes productive but at other times manifesting as aggression, harassment, and abuse. Such conflict is not necessarily a bad thing, as Milner (2013) points out, because disengagement of marginalized voices can threaten the promise of the Internet as public sphere, and "voice should be evident over exclusion, even if that voice is not monolithic in content and tone."

In these spaces, the advice to "be kind" or "don't feed the trolls" can mean "don't engage" or "don't point out abuse and its effects." In this way, calls for civility problematically place blame for aggression on the target, not the aggressor. Such advice suggests to targets that because speaking within digital spaces leads to harassment, they should no longer speak or even inhabit those spaces at all. Often when someone responds to hostile digital discourse, they are met with "what do you expect when you feed the trolls?" or another such victim-blaming sentiment. In such a way, calls for civility can lead to silencing some of the most marginalized voices online. As Poland (2016) explains:

> Online threats of violence seem to have a very simple purpose: they are intended to act as a reminder to women that men are dominant, that women can be attacked and overpowered if men choose to attack, and that women are to be silent and obedient. Many threats contain ultimatums: if a woman doesn't stop engaging in activities that the men issuing threats find undesirable, she will be punished with physical violence or even death. The intent of threats is to establish offline patterns of violence against women in online spaces.
>
> (p. 53)

Calls for civility can downplay the seriousness of the behaviors that some people experience online. "Troll" sounds playful, harmless even, and belies the serious nature of the range of behaviors that are often grouped under it. But actions like violent rape and/or death threats, stalking, and doxxing—things that invalidate identities and make users feel unsafe beyond digital spaces—are often grouped under this term. "Don't feed the trolls" can suggest that aggressive behaviors shouldn't be taken seriously, and that the effects of abuse aren't real and important to the people who experience them.

Platform providers often approach managing and responding to digital aggression through after-the-fact action and enforcement of punishments rather than through the cultivation of guiding values and preventative measures. Social media platforms, such as Twitter, offer reporting mechanisms for those who experience harassment and technical tools users can employ to block harassers and aggressive content. These mechanisms, however, are limited in their aims and outcomes, and do not do enough to protect the most vulnerable groups (Jhaver et al., 2018). Roberts (2016) has examined the effects that commercial content moderation has on the workers that perform the labor involved in the curation and decision-making processes, what she calls the "dirty work of social media." Immersion in aggressive content—racist, homophobic, misogynistic, and disturbing—can leave workers vulnerable to the potentially devastating effects of daily exposure. Understanding how digital aggression is managed, often through inadequate technical tools or through potentially harmful labor practices that are largely hidden from the general population of Internet users, reveals the limitations of existing approaches. While acknowledging that "content moderation is hard," Gillespie (2018) asserts that social media platforms must embrace their role as "custodians of the Internet":

> This would be a very different understanding of the role of 'custodian'—not where platforms quietly clean up our mess, but where they take up guardianship of the unresolved tensions of public

discourse, hand back with care the agency for addressing those tensions to users, and responsibly support that process with the necessary tools, data, and insights.

(p. 211)

Such an approach requires a new ethic of responsibility to guide the development of platforms, the management of digital communities, moderation practices, and responses to digital aggression. An ethic of responsibility calls for more engagement rather than less, for value in designing for protection against digital harassment rather than after-the-fact cleanup, for accountability and tactical response rather than civility within digital contexts. From platform designers, developers, and managers, to digital community leaders, to everyday users, to content moderators, to policymakers and legal experts, diverse actors must become more aware of their own positionality within particular spaces and moments; the consequences of their decisions, words, and actions; and the embodied experiences of users with which they engage across diverse networks of digital communities. Value systems and ethical principles must be considered from the point of design of platforms, sustained through the careful development and management of communities, and supported through appropriate corrective actions.

We posit that productive digital communities be proactive and act in ways that recognize the multidimensional nature of aggression. Figure 1.1 displays a comprehensive view of such an approach.

1 *Platform designers and developers.* First, we find some responsibility with platform providers, technology developers, and media

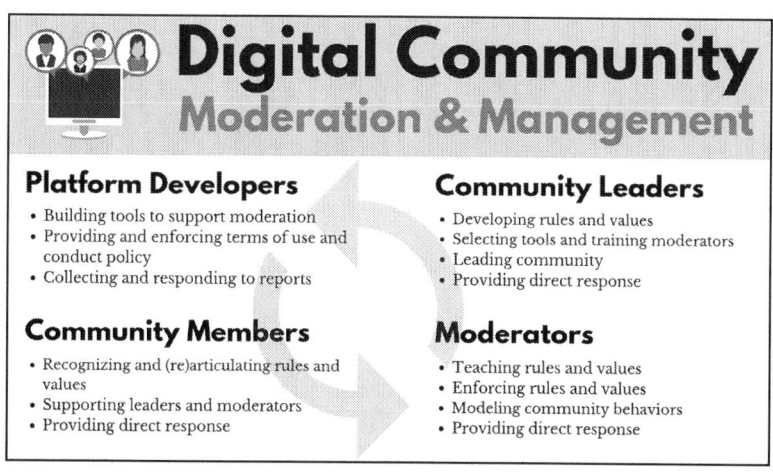

Figure 1.1 Digital community moderation and management (Developed by E. M. Sparby, 2019).

companies to design and offer more powerful tools for moderation and management of aggression, as well as harassment policies and terms of use that can be drawn on to support community members. There must be transparency in actions being taken, tools employed, and terms of use enforced. Some design decisions could benefit from including more diversity in the hiring of developers, managers, and entrepreneurs, as lack of diversity can lead to design decisions with unintended consequences for minority groups and vulnerable populations (Noble, 2018).

2 *Community leaders.* Second, community leaders and content creators themselves must clearly establish and articulate the values and norms of their communities. Leaders can employ technical tools and moderation options made available to them through the platform as well as communicative practices that support values of inclusivity and productive discourse. Community leaders are uniquely positioned to establish these values through the generation of codes of ethics, community mission statements, and through direct responses to transgressions.

3 *Moderators.* Third, human moderators who participate in digital communities can consistently enforce the rules and values of those communities. They can accompany corrections of transgressions and enforcement of rules with reminders to users of the connections between rules and the values established by community leaders. Their actions and comments should aim to support a culture based on a shared value of inclusivity rather than more limited rule-following.

4 *Community members.* Fourth, members and participants who are not official moderators can also help to reinforce values, norms, and rules, and teach others. By distributing the activity of moderation among many participants, community leaders and moderators do not suffer the sole burden. Rather than remaining silent or "not feeding the trolls," participants can respond to aggression with clear articulation of shared values.

This model acknowledges that the multidimensional nature of digital communication requires an ecological response to digital aggression. Much of this work must come from platform designers and developers and social media managers and entrepreneurs, who must build tools that (1) protect vulnerable groups and (2) allow for collective and collaborative management of digital aggression by users and communities. For instance, Citron and Wittes (2017) ask us to consider the impact of features such as shared block lists and Gillespie (2018) proposes *collective* flagging systems where users can identify content as "racist" or "sexual" or "violent," which would then lead to actionable data such as content warnings. Offering design and moderation options would allow users to collectively employ tools and tactics to establish (and reestablish, when needed) values and principles of productive digital discourse and collaboratively cultivate an inclusive community on multiple fronts. In addition, the rhetors within digital spaces—content creators, community leaders, participants, and everyday users—must critically engage to enact positive change.

Chapter Overviews

This collection presents chapters across four sections: ethics of interfaces and platforms; academic labor in digital publics; cultural narratives in hostile discourses; and the circulation and amplification of digital aggression.

Part 1. Ethics of Interfaces and Platforms

In this section, chapters look beyond everyday user interaction to reveal how an interface's design, rules, and community norms impact the potential for digital aggression. James J. Brown and Gregory Hennis open this section with an examination of "hateware" to show how design decisions can enhance or mitigate harassment. Through an analysis of Discord, they advocate for a "design justice" approach, that is, intentionally building interfaces that encourage more inclusive spaces. A large problem with much social media, Brown and Hennis argue, is that platforms outsource responsibility to moderators and users instead of addressing the issue at the design level. Michael Trice, Liza Potts, and Rebekah Small build on this idea in their chapter by examining what they call "communities of harm," such as r/kotakuinaction and LeftBook groups. They argue that rules-based moderation has led to abandoning the values-based moderation often seen in earlier online communities (such as the WELL), allowing the continuation of hate speech and aggression among groups who find workarounds to avoid being shut down by reddit or Facebook. Following Trice, Potts, and Small, Tabitha London, Joey Crundwell, Natalie Santiago, Marcy Bock Eastley, and Jennifer Jenkins point to the shortcomings and potentials of content moderation through a study of four women Twitch streamers. Their findings point to the need for streamers to actively foster inclusive community using the affordances of the Twitch platform, and encourage other users to do the same. This first section concludes by turning to John R. Gallagher for a pedagogical approach to teaching interface design through virtue ethics. Here, Gallagher examines the value of a "virtue approach" and offers a project for students to redesign interfaces to more closely embody their virtues and values.

Part 2. Academic Labor in Digital Publics

In this section, chapters address digital harassment and ethical issues directly related to academic labor. First, Leigh Gruwell provides an autoethnographic exploration of her experiences with past research projects to show how using feminist methodologies to study toxic spaces can endanger researchers, especially women, queer identities, and people of color. She posits a methodology of tactical resistance, which accounts for subverting the Internet's power structures that can silence and exclude marginalized voices. Vyshali Manivannan follows with an autoethnographic treatise (in nine movements) that examines the similarities between academic trolls and the notorious "Reviewer 2," who attempt to undermine nontraditional epistemologies and research methodologies. She offers methods for "counter-trolling" these kinds of attempts at delegitimization. The section closes with a chapter by Jeff Rice, who asks, "When an academic responds publically in anger, does the response constitute academic speech or mere social media outrage? Is public response to professorial outrage the far right oppressing university speech, or is it professorial lack of audience recognition?" To answer these questions, Rice examines rhetorical activity in terms of an "assumed enthymeme" to rethink how the writer and audience in digital networks shape response and rhetorical situation.

Part 3. Cultural Narratives in Hostile Discourses

Part 3 examines the cultural narratives that operate behind and between hostile digital discourses. The section opens with Megan Condis, who explains why video games and video game culture seem particularly suited to recruit members of the alt-right. She examines the rhetorics of race, politics, and play as well as three axioms of online culture to show how the ideologies behind gaming culture coupled with the rise of vocal women and people of color have created a moment ripe for alt-right recruitment. Alisha Karabinus follows with an analysis of the tactics that GamerGaters employed on Twitter. Through the lens of theorycraft, or using mathematical analysis to optimize in-game strategy, she analyzes how aggressors were able to "game" Twitter for use in what she calls "dark activism," or targeted attacks of users to forward their own oppressive ideologies. Bridget Gelms concludes the section, providing stories of two women who have experienced various forms of digital aggression and theorizing a correlation between a woman's visibility online and the amount of harassment she experiences. These stories not only highlight what digital aggression can look like for women, but also exemplify how it works to maintain existing cultural boundaries that exclude women from public discourse.

Part 4. Circulation and Amplification of Digital Aggression

The final section addresses the ways aggression is circulated and amplified in and through digital networks. First, Brandy Dieterle, Dustin Edwards, and Dan Martin draw on case studies of the harassment of Leslie

Jones and the re/circulation of a gif depicting Donald Trump bodyslamming the CNN logo to posit an "ethics of circulation" that promotes inclusivity, social justice, and mindful contemplation. The authors consider how recirculating content is a world-building act that has implications for public discourse: sharing preexisting content assumes and constructs a rhetorical relationship with others and thereby deserves thoughtful contemplation of what such a relationship entails. Next, Krista Kennedy and Noah Wilson examine the Starkey Halo smart hearing aid to investigate surveillance as both necessity and aggression in the use of medical wearables. Kennedy and Wilson conclude with near-future projections for these devices as full health metrics monitors and provide recommendations for best practices in data collection policies for medical wearables. Finally, Katherine DeLuca provides a pedagogical approach that highlights phronesis as an approach that can teach students the effects of their communications in digital environments. Through a case study of communications on two incidents on reddit (the first a subreddit's attempt to locate and reveal the Boston Bomber, the second a thread that started with a surreptitiously taken photo and text mocking its subject), she shows the importance of helping students recognize the humans on the other side of the computer screen and question the ethical implications of the content they post.

Although we chose to divide this collection into sections of overarching themes or objects of study, we could easily have organized them thematically by their takeaways. Rice; Dieterle, Edwards, and Martin; and Gelms each provides guidelines for ethical civic engagements, urging users to be conscious of the impacts of their communications. Condis and Karabinus both examine how hostile discourses—the former related to recruiting, the latter to enacting targeted attacks, both rooted in alt-right and white supremacist ideologies—move through networks and function to perpetuate themselves. Gallagher and DeLuca contemplate pedagogical takeaways, highlighting the ways we can help students understand the impacts of their digital discourses and be good digital citizens. Gruwell and Manivannan provide methodological guidelines for researching in hostile environments, examining how researchers can navigate the sticky issue of publishing about communities that are vocally not only anti-academic and anti-researcher, but also often anti-woman and anti-POC. Brown and Hennis and Kennedy and Wilson discuss ethical technology design, both of the interfaces we use daily and the medical wearables so many users rely on to live their lives. Finally, Trice, Potts, and Small as well as London, Crundwell, Santiago, Eastley, and Jenkins provide suggestions for ethical community moderation, pointing to ways that moderation has become ineffective and how it can regain some effectiveness.

Importantly, although each chapter offers takeaways for how we can address the issues they raise, notice that not all of them are clear-cut.

Gallagher and DeLuca offer us concrete pedagogical strategies, Gruwell provides a new methodology of tactical resistance, and Brown and Hennis offer a design justice approach. But more often, authors call for future research or for more critical awareness. As we hope to show in this collection, digital aggression is messy, and there is no simple solution, no panacea that will solve it in a single instant. Some issues are being highlighted for the first time in this collection (or at least for the first time since the rise of pervasive social media and smartphones) and require further extensive research before anything close to an answer can be found. Our hope is that the chapters that follow begin laying the groundwork for how teachers, scholars, practitioners, and theorists study, think about, and address digital ethics in rhetorical environments from now onward.

References

Beck, E., Crow, A., McKee, H., Reilly, C., Vie, S., deWinter, J., Gonzales, L., & DeVoss, D. N. (2016). Writing in an age of surveillance, privacy, and net neutrality. *Kairos, 20*(2). Retrieved from http://kairos.technorhetoric.net/20.2/topoi/beck-et-al/index.html#

Brown, J. J., Jr. (2015). *Ethical programs: Hospitality and the rhetorics of software*. Ann Arbor: University of Michigan Press.

Citron. D., & Wittes, B. (2017, January 4). Follow buddies and block buddies: A simple proposal to improve civility, control, and privacy on Twitter. *Lawfareblog*. Retrieved from https://www.lawfareblog.com/follow-buddies-and-block-buddies-simple-proposal-improve-civility-control-and-privacy-twitter

Clinnin, K., & Manthey, K. (2019). How not to be a troll: Practicing rhetorical technofeminism in online comments. *Computers and Composition, 51*, 31–42.

Cloud, D. (2009). Foiling the intellectuals: Gender, identity framing, and the rhetoric of the kill in conservative hate mail. *Communication and Cultural Critique, 2*, 457–479.

Coley, T. (Ed.). (2011). *Computers and Composition Online*. Retrieved from http://cconlinejournal.org/fall2011.html

DeVoss, D. N., & Porter, J. E. (2006). Why Napster matters to writing: File-sharing as new ethic of digital delivery. *Computers and Composition, 23*, 178–210.

Duggan, M. (2017). Online harassment 2017. *Pew Research Center*. Retrieved from http://www.pewinternet.org/2017/07/11/online-harassment-2017/

Fontaine, S., & Hunter, S. M. (Eds.). (1998). *Foregrounding ethical awareness in composition and English studies*. Portsmouth, NH: Boynton/Cook.

Gillespie, T. (2018). *Custodians of the internet: Platforms, content moderation, and the hidden decisions that shape social media*. New Haven, CT and London: Yale University Press.

Granville, K. (2018). Facebook and Cambridge analytica: What you need to know as fallout widens. *The New York Times*. Retrieved from https://

www.nytimes.com/2018/03/19/technology/facebook-cambridge-analytica-explained.html

Gruwell, L. (2017). Writing against harassment: Public writing pedagogy and online hate. *Composition Forum, 36*. Retrieved from http://compositionforum.com/issue/36/against-harassment.php

Gurak, L. (1999). *Persuasion and privacy in cyberspace: The online protests over Lotus MarketPlace and the Clipper Chip*. New Haven, CT: Yale University Press.

Harrington, D. (1999). The ethical turn in English studies. *Composition Studies, 27*(1), 85–91.

Herrington, T. K. (2010). *Intellectual property on campus: Students' rights and responsibilities*. Carbondale: Southern Illinois University Press.

Jackson, A. (2016). Husband and wife never expected their Fitbit would tell them this…. *CNN.com*. Retrieved from https://www.cnn.com/2016/02/10/health/fitbit-reddit-pregnancy-irpt/index.html

Jane, E. A. (2014). 'Back to the kitchen, cunt': Speaking the unspeakable about online misogyny. *Continuum, 28*(4), 558–570.

Jeong, S. (2018). *The Internet of garbage*. Washington, DC: Vox Media.

Jhaver, S., Ghoshal, S., Bruckman, A., & Gilbert, E. (2018). Online harassment and content moderation: The case of blocklists. *ACM Transactions on Computer-Human Interaction, 25*(2), 1–33.

Johnson-Eilola, J. (2010). Among texts. In S. Selber (Ed.), *Rhetorics and technologies: New directions in writing and communication* (pp. 33–55). Columbia: University of South Carolina Press.

Kennedy, K. (2016). *Textual curation: Authorship, agency, and technology in Wikipedia and Chambers's Cyclopaedia*. Columbia: University of South Carolina Press.

Logie, J. (2006). *Peers, pirates, and persuasion: Rhetoric in the peer-to-peer debates*. Anderson, SC: Parlor Press.

Markham, A., & Buchanan, E. (2012). Ethical decision-making and internet research: Recommendations from the AoIR Ethics Working Committee (version 2.0). *Association of Internet Researcher*. Retrieved from https://aoir.org/reports/ethics2.pdf

Miller, C. R. (2007). What can automation tell us about agency? *Rhetoric Society Quarterly, 37*(2), 137–157.

Milner, R. M. (2013). Hacking the social: Internet memes, identity antagonism, and the logic of lulz. *Fibreculture, 22*. Retrieved from http://twentytwo.fibreculturejournal.org/fcj-156-hacking-the-social-internet-memes-identity-antagonism-and-the-logic-of-lulz/

Noble, S. U. (2018). *Algorithms of oppression: How search engines reinforce racism*. New York: NYU Press.

Phillips, W. (2015). *This is why we can't have nice things: Mapping the relationship between online trolling and mainstream culture*. Cambridge, MA: MIT Press.

Phillips, W., & Milner, R. M. (2018). The internet doesn't need civility, it needs ethics. *Vice.com*. Retrieved from https://www.vice.com/en_nz/article/pa5gxn/the-internet-doesnt-need-civility-it-needs-ethics

Pilon, M. (2015). Divorced by data. *Wired.com.* Retrieved from https://www.wired.com/2015/06/divorced-by-data/

Poland, B. (2016). *Haters: Harassment, abuse, and violence online.* Lincoln, NE: Potomac Books.

Porter, J. E. (1998). *Rhetorical ethics and internetworked writing.* Greenwich, CT: Ablex.

Profis, S. (2014). Do wristband heart trackers actually work? A checkup. *CNET.com.* Retrieved from https://www.cnet.com/news/how-accurate-are-wristband-heart-rate-monitors/

Reyman, J. (2010). *The rhetoric of intellectual property: Copyright law and the regulation of digital culture.* New York, NY: Routledge.

Rife, M. C., Slattery, S., & DeVoss, D. N. (Eds.). (2011). *Copy(write): Intellectual property in the writing classroom.* Fort Collins, CO: The WAC Clearinghouse.

Roberts, S. (2016). Commercial content moderation: Digital laborers' dirty work. In S. Noble & B. Tynes (Eds.), *The intersectional internet: Race, sex, class, and culture online* (pp. 147–159). New York, NY: Peter Lang.

Selfe, C. L., & Selfe, R. J. (1994). The politics of the interface: Power and its exercise in electronic contact zones. *College Composition and Communication, 45*(4), 480–504.

Sparby, E. M. (2017). Digital social media and aggression: Memetic rhetoric in 4chan's collective identity. *Computers and Composition, 45,* 85–97.

Warnick, B., & Heineman, D. S. (2012). *Rhetoric online: The politics of new media.* New York, NY: Peter Lang.

Westbrook, S. (Ed.). (2009). *Composition and copyright: Perspectives on teaching, text-making, and fair use.* Albany, NY: SUNY Press.

Part I
Ethics of Interfaces and Platforms

2 Hateware and the Outsourcing of Responsibility

James J. Brown, Jr. and Gregory Hennis

In 1999, Herring described a kind of algorithm for "gendered harassment on-line." Though she never specifically calls it an algorithm, she does offer a clear set of steps that she tracks in two different environments: Internet Relay Chat (IRC) and an e-mail list. In both situations, men harassed women by following a clear pattern, and the responses of women were dealt with in predictable ways: initiation of harassment, resistance to harassment, escalation of harassment, targeted participants accommodate to the dominant group norms and/or targeted participants fall silent (Herring, 1999). Herring links this pattern to the libertarian values baked into many online communities:

> Libertarian values of extreme freedom of expression are also present in both discussions, and benefit the most aggressive participants, who happen (not coincidentally) to be male. By maintaining ... that any verbal behavior is authorized, no matter how crude or aggressive, males justify the use of dominating and harassing tactics in the name of free speech.
>
> (p. 163)

Herring's work is as important as it is depressing, since we appear to be living in the exact same world that she described 20 years ago. Contemporary work on online harassment identifies many of the same patterns Herring did, and the end goal remains the same: silencing women and other marginalized groups. Campaigns such as #GamerGate appear to be enacting the same algorithm that Herring saw in IRC and e-mail listservs.

Perhaps it is not fair to say that we are in the *exact* same world, since our current media ecology appears to provide harassers with a more extensive set of tools for coordinated and organized attacks. This has meant that scholars of online harassment have begun to couple the rhetorical analysis of harassment pioneered by Herring and others to the media infrastructures that enable and support such actions (Massanari, 2015; Phillips, 2015; Tarsa & Brown, Jr., 2018). Furthermore, the line between gendered harassment online and off is no longer even clear, and the campaigns we now witness are not confined to our screens or devices. These media ecologies no longer only involve software and screens, since abusers deploy schemes that involve an extensive communications' infrastructure. Targets are swatted by abusers who inform law enforcement that they should send SWAT teams to a target's home, and search algorithms can be gamed to manipulate one's online identity. In short, the harasser has much more than language at his disposal if he wants to exercise his "free speech" to silence others. Following Herring, we see justifications of certain behavior in the name of free speech as misguided in at least two senses. First, the digital platforms we discuss are not operated by U.S. government entities and are thus not constrained by first amendment protections. Second, the use of free speech arguments to support certain abusive behaviors (and also used to justify the hands-off approach of software companies) seems concerned with the free speech of abusers without considering the free speech of abuse targets. Silencing people by way of harassing behavior shows little regard for the free speech rights of targets of abuse.

The assumption that online infrastructures must uphold free speech protections is part of a long and complex history, but our focus in this chapter is on how that assumption has created a useful set of tools for those who want to abuse and harass women, people of color, and LGBTQ groups. In particular, we see Section 230 of the United States Code as being a major contributing factor to our current predicament, a law that we discuss in more detail later in the essay (Protection for screening of offensive material, 1996). Section 230 freed websites of liability for content published by third parties, gave them the ability to make decisions about the publication of content without fear of being labeled a publisher of that content (and thus making them responsible for it), and provided no clear motivation for websites to police third-party content. By pushing this responsibility to users, the rhetoric of libertarianism has simultaneously empowered abusers and asked victims to fix the problem themselves.

This *outsourcing* of responsibility is one of the key features of Discord, the platform we discuss in this chapter. Our goal in this chapter is to describe some of the features of software platforms that enable harassers while disempowering targets and to describe those platforms with a provocative but, we think, useful term: hateware. This concept does not describe a stable category but rather a sliding scale on which we might place a range of platforms when trying to evaluate how or whether their features enable abuse and harassment. Some of these platforms appear at first glance to be general tools or utilities and others are explicitly created to help abusers and harassers. We recognize the problems with placing Twitter and Facebook in the same category as a platform like Hatreon, a short-lived crowdfunding platform for those who wanted to avoid the hate speech policies of sites like Patreon or GoFundMe. While large platforms like Twitter have certainly pushed responsibility to users when it comes to dealing with harassment, it would be counterproductive to collapse the difference between it and sites that openly espouse racist and misogynistic ideologies. Still, by creating a continuum and understanding hateware as part of a broader infrastructural problem, we can begin to track the key features of software that props up and supports abuse and harassment, intentionally or not.

There are platforms that actively attempt to prevent abusive behavior, and these would likely sit outside the hateware spectrum. For instance, an ex-reddit employee named Dan McComas established a social media site called Imzy in 2016. Imzy was an attempt to address, at the level of software design and community norms, some of the problems McComas and others saw at reddit. As Tarsa and Brown, Jr. (2018) argue, Imzy developers recognized that the interface could be complicit in the problem of harassment, and its designers attempt to take a different kind of approach (Tarsa & Brown, Jr., 2018). Unfortunately, the site failed to gain a critical mass of users and shut down in 2017 (Buhr, 2017). The hateware spectrum ranges from "explicitly encourages harassment" to "implicitly encourages harassment," and software that combats harassment is (theoretically) doing neither. Software designed to openly attempt to combat harassment could conceivably find itself on the spectrum because certain design decisions have unintended consequences. However, this does not change the fact that some platforms can avoid being labeled as hateware.

Our hope is that the term "hateware" provides scholars with a theoretical approach to understanding the deep and sometimes invisible infrastructures of harassment. To this end, we start by explaining the term and how we're using it, then move to an extended analysis of the platform Discord. Discord was used to organize the Unite the Right event in Charlottesville, Virginia, which resulted in the death of Heather Heyer as well as two law enforcement officers. Those events put Discord in the spotlight and led to the company banning certain users from the service. However, this attempt to address bad actors and bad behavior after the fact ignores the ways the platform's design actually enables that same behavior. Because Discord uses similar structure and design techniques to other platforms, but also because of these recent events, we found it best to use Discord as our case study. We describe how some of Discord's structure and design decisions make it an example of hateware and how the crowdsourcing of community management (a libertarian infrastructure) creates fertile ground for abusive activity. We close by detailing how the concept of hateware might aid future research on abuse and harassment. In that light, it should also be mentioned that our study is best viewed as a template for analysis of software, rather than a final say on the matter of hateware.

Hateware

Much recent research addressing online harassment has attempted to bring to light how design is contributing to the problem of abuse and harassment, representing a broader interest in design that has long been at the core of digital rhetoric scholarship (Arola, 2010; Jeong, 2015; Kaufer & Butler, 1996; Selfe & Selfe, 1994). Sparby's (2017) work is a key example of this as she examines the "memetic rhetoric" that drives aggression and abuse in spaces like 4chan. The circulation of memes—the cultural units circulated through a community—helps to establish and fortify the identity of a community, and members of that community imitate behaviors in order to participate in identity formation. Sparby offers a detailed account of how this process happens, and she also argues that interface design is an integral part of that story: "users in online collectives often engage in memetic behavior influenced by the interface's technological design, ethos, and collective identity" (Sparby, 2017, p. 86). The design of 4chan and its community norms directly contribute to the community's collective ethos, one that lauds outrageous and shocking behavior. Sparby argues that the platform's anonymity, ephemerality, lack of user registration requirements, short-lived threads, and lack of an archive all contribute to the platform being a haven for hate (Sparby, 2017, p. 88). Interestingly, these design choices are actually put forth as a kind of *lack of design* by the 4chan community itself. This is especially clear when we examine that 4chan articulates its "rules" by saying that there are, for the most part, no rules (Sparby, 2017). As Sparby's research shows, there are indeed many rules, some of which are informed by humans (community norms) and others that are enforced by computation (software design), that establish a platform for a range of uses and abuses.

Massanari has conducted a similar analysis of reddit, a platform that is perhaps second only to 4chan in terms of its fame as a platform for trolling, abuse, and harassment. Massanari uses the term "platform politics" to describe "the assemblage of design, policies, and norms that encourage certain kinds of cultures and behaviors to coalesce on platforms while implicitly discouraging others" (Massanari, 2015, p. 8). She describes how reddit's karma system incentivizes bad behavior, including reposting material across multiple subreddits and making comments that rally behind the community's shared ethos of a "cyber/technolibertarian bent, gender politics, and geek sensibilities" (p. 9). Such activities increase one's karma score, affording more influence in the community. The platform also makes it easy to create multiple accounts, even after a user has been banned. In addition to the karma score and the behaviors it incentivizes, reddit joins many major platforms by providing very little recourse for those who are being harassed (p. 10). Even when moderators are empowered to step in and address abusive behavior, reddit's hands-off ethos often wins the day: "Reddit administrators are loathe to intervene in any meaningful way in content disputes, citing Reddit's role as an impartial or 'neutral' platform for discussion" (p. 11). This idea that a neutral stance somehow stands outside of the fray is prevalent and is a direct result of a regulatory and cultural environment that insists on protecting the free speech rights of users at the expense of the safety of marginalized populations.

4chan and reddit are key examples of sites that are designed to invite certain kinds of behavior, and while they are often held up as a key example of toxic online communities, our analysis in this essay is an attempt to identify how all networked platforms encourage and deter certain kinds of actions. In fact, we aim to provide scholars with a theoretical approach that can be used to examine a broad range of software platforms and not just those that are so obviously filled with what Jane (2016) calls "e-bile." We use the term hateware to describe software that employs policies, algorithms, and designs that enable, encourage, and/ or directly participate in abuse or harassment. This definition certainly accounts for sites like 4chan, but it also helps us examine less obvious examples of software that enables harassment. Software platforms can exist on a sliding scale, ranging from sites and services that openly promote harassment and abuse to those that enable bad actors in more pernicious ways.

Platforms can be positioned along the hateware spectrum and a platform's position on that spectrum can shift depending on changes in functionality, terms of service, or general design. Sites like 4chan and Twitter exist on the extremes, the former being a haven for hate, ignorance, and griefing, and the latter taking an extremely lax, inconsistent, and mostly user-driven approach to policing user behavior and enforcing community standards. Platforms that take any stance on abuse and begin to employ safer techniques can move from a status like 4chan's toward a similar status to Twitter, and some software may even graduate away from the spectrum and join the likes of Imzy. Software that continues to outsource responsibility (like Twitter) can begin tumbling down that slope, and head toward a status similar to 4chan. So, what are the key features of hateware? How do we know where software lies on the hateware spectrum? Given that this chapter is an attempt to open up this question rather than establish a final answer, we offer some provisional ideas about these key features in the hopes that future work will extend and revise our findings here.

In fact, there are many factors that may contribute to a piece of software inching toward hateware status. Our focus in this chapter is on how many platforms allow groups to govern themselves and have few broadly stated community norms. However, there are a number of other features common in hateware. For instance, some platforms selectively allow hypervisibility and simultaneous near invisibility to users, adopting a haphazard approach to anonymity or pseudonymity (an especially complicated issue, given that anonymity can be wielded as a protective tool by targets of harassment). Some have unclear, lax, or vague policies and rules, employ algorithms that are easily gamed and manipulated, and take little initiative to police their user-base. However, hateware's key feature is the outsourcing of responsibility, and this design choice is largely due to the current regulatory environment. Such platforms advertise a hands-off approach, but commonly take steps to at least minimally moderate and filter content. Because they do practice some form of moderation, they appear to recognize their role in managing and addressing online harassment. However, they too often avoid the difficult task of addressing abusive and harassing behavior.

These platforms have begun to dominate the Internet thanks to Section 230 of the United States Code, which was established by the Communications Decency Act of 1996. Section 230 is a landmark portion of the U.S. Code that, among other things, grants immunity to online platforms when one user is harassed by another, whether or not the provider of the platform intervenes. Section 230 states that "no provider or user of an interactive computer service shall be treated as the publisher or speaker of any information provided by another information content provider" (Protection for screening of offensive material, 1996). This language protects websites and social media services (as well as their users) from being treated as publishers. While publishers are at risk of lawsuit due to the publication of libelous or otherwise illegal content, many social media sites, such as Facebook, are not. More than this, the law allows such providers of "interactive computer services" to attempt moderation without opening themselves up to legal action:

> No provider or user of an interactive computer service shall be held liable on account of—
>
> A any action voluntarily taken in good faith to restrict access to or availability of material that the provider or user considers to be obscene, lewd, lascivious, filthy, excessively violent, harassing, or otherwise objectionable, whether or not such material is constitutionally protected; or
> B any action taken to enable or make available to information content providers or others the technical means to restrict access to material described in paragraph (1).
> (Protection for screening of offensive material, 1996)

Providers are allowed to moderate content, but they are not required to. Prior to the establishment of Section 230, websites *could* be held liable if they attempted to moderate anything at all, and this was thanks to the fact that traditional defamation law was applied to such cases prior to the introduction of Section 230 in 1996. Section 230 was meant to provide an incentive for platform providers to moderate their content, by allowing them to retain immunity even when they moderate. In reality, this law has created fertile ground for abuse and harassment. Platform providers continued to neglect moderation, because what Section 230 failed to do was to provide a *disincentive for not moderating*.

This brings us to today, a moment when providers continue to do minimal work when it comes to moderation, allowing hate and abuse to thrive. Hateware, then, exists as a consequence of this new kind of software platform emerging in the 21st century. Unwilling to claim full responsibility but also unwilling to completely step away from moderation, platforms like Facebook and Twitter straddle the (admittedly blurred) line between a media organization and an information tool. In order to understand the role these sites play in the current problems with online harassment, it is crucial that we see their decisions regarding moderation as not just a matter of policy but also a matter of design. Through their design decisions, these platforms have (knowingly or not) built a set of tools that bad actors have seized upon in order to troll, harass, and abuse others.

This portion of the U.S. Code is arguably the most important piece of our current digital infrastructure and has been described by Eric Goldman, a leading legal scholar on Section 230, as "the law that gave us the modern Internet," the "most important law in tech," and "the law that makes the Internet go" (Goldman, 2017). Section 230 has been at the center of a number of court cases since its passage, most recently in *Fields v. Twitter* (2017), a lawsuit attempting to make Twitter liable for the actions of terrorists using their platform. In January 2018, the Ninth Circuit Court of Appeals ruled in Twitter's favor, though it largely "sidestepped Section 230, leaving it [sic] applicability for another day and another court" (Goldman, 2018). Section 230 continues to be at the center of many legal and legislative battles, but its impact on our contemporary digital infrastructure is undeniable. Provided with legal coverage by Congress and the courts, not only have companies taken a hands-off approach to managing communities and policing harassment, they have actually shifted that responsibility to their users by crowdsourcing such activities.

Sowing Discord

Discord is a platform that has emerged as an important part of the conversation surrounding software and online harassment. At first blush, it seems to be little more than a chat application. However, our analysis demonstrates that Discord is much more than this and that its design provides those aiming to abuse and harass others with key tools for doing so. Designed to provide gamers with the ability to chat while gaming, it is akin to IRC chat rooms, and it allows users to create their own servers to host like-minded conversations. Each server is divided into different channels, which are similar to chat rooms. So, each server has one or more channels, and each user can be a part of multiple servers. There is also a permissions system in place: the creator of a server can assign different roles to users with different permissions. Permissions dictate what users with particular roles can and cannot do, from what channels they can post in all the way down to *what* they can post in those channels. The permissions' system is most often used in hierarchy style: the server owner can have the most power and highest permissions, and they can create other roles, such as administrators and moderators.

Discord also gives users the option of remaining anonymous. There is not necessarily a real name attached to any Discord account: just a username, password, and an e-mail that realistically a user only ever needs access to once, to confirm the account. Users can also create a temporary free account that is automatically deleted if it is not confirmed via an e-mail address. Discord doesn't *require* anonymity, and users can link social media and gaming accounts to Discord accounts (such as Facebook, Twitter, YouTube, reddit, Battle.net, Twitch, and Steam). Even if users decide to connect these accounts, they have the option of not showing them on their profile. Much of what takes place on Discord takes place behind the scenes in a sense: user servers can be (and most often are) configured to be private and only accessible by desired parties (though, we will demonstrate below that infiltration of servers is indeed possible). This is a departure from the way platforms like Twitter and reddit work, because the latter platforms focus on providing the possibility of users to interact with those outside of their immediate social networks. In addition to attempting to silo conversations with its server model, Discord also allows a range of other features, including video calling and screen sharing, as well as an API that allows for the integration of Discord directly within specific games.

Discord is an interesting case study in hateware given that, at first glance, it is little more than a platform that makes communication among gamers easier. Players of online games such as *Overwatch* can establish a server and easily use Discord to chat while playing. Thus, one might initially balk at the idea that Discord enables abuse and harassment, and we would not fault such a response. If Discord is hateware, then what about e-mail platforms? What about text messaging? We have two responses to such questions. The first is that any platform or application could indeed be placed on the hateware spectrum, depending on design choices and features offered to users, and this is why we insist on understanding hateware as a sliding scale rather than a category. Our second response is that, upon closer analysis, Discord is much more than a mere chat application. Discord's design offers features that many have exploited to abuse, harass, and troll. We want to focus on Discord's general approach to content moderation as well as techniques used by those abusing others on the platform. Discord outsources the labor of community management to users, a design decision that is core to nearly any social networking application or platform in use today. This establishes an environment that is rife with bad behavior. Those wanting to harass others have used a number of techniques, including the use of invitation links that allow users to invite others to join their server.

Discord could not exist without the extensive labor carried out by its users. The platform offers very little in the way of community management, and it relies on users to report bad behavior. As we have noted, this is the norm with contemporary websites and services, and it is largely due to Section 230 establishing an environment that disincentivizes any attempt to actively filter content or police behavior. It also allows companies like Discord to avoid paying a labor force of content moderators and community managers. Even after raising massive amounts of venture capital in 2017, Discord had hired only five customer experience personnel and zero moderators (Menegus, 2017). Discord provides tools to those administering servers; however, they do not necessarily make life very easy for server administrators. For instance, the default setting for any Discord server is "no verification," meaning that if an administrator makes no changes to the settings, they are inviting anyone to join the conversation without having to verify their identity (Ravenscraft, 2016). This is, of course, an open invitation to those who want to disrupt a server.

A number of journalistic accounts have pointed out that Discord has shown little concern for harassment. Menegus of *Gizmodo* has offered a frank evaluation of Discord's approach to this problem: "From what I've seen, users who wish to engage in harassment, raid servers, or bombard chats and users with child pornography suffer no lasting repercussions for doing so" (Menegus, 2017). While this approach changed after the Unite the Right controversy (which we address later), the overall approach from Discord appears to be one of unconcern. One Discord user quoted by Menegus even describes a number of de facto moderation techniques that administrators have had to develop on their own. For instance, many administrators have had to create entire channels for new users, a kind of holding pen for the abusers that arrive to disrupt the conversation. This strategy results in a kind of "manual verification process, where new users can only talk in two rooms which the majority of the server have muted" (Menegus, 2017). Creating these containment rooms (one can imagine a chatroom in which harassers scream at one another without an audience) has now become a normal operating procedure for administrators attempting to deal with harassment.

Those using Discord to harass others have developed a range of techniques, and we will focus on the most common: server raiding. Discord uses invitation links to allow users to send invitations to particular servers, and these invitations can be set to expire after a period of time determined by the user. This is an easy way to invite people to a server, but it is also an easy way to infiltrate a discussion and cause chaos. This kind of action is known as a raid on a Discord server, and it happens fairly regularly. Invitation links can be generated by those posing as members of the community. These users essentially embed themselves in order to later invite other trolls and abusers. One can sit in the weeds, participate in the discussion, and after a certain amount of time gain the permission to generate invitation links. They can then invite others to raid the server, meaning that a swarm of users arrives to post offensive material and to overrun the conversation with thousands of simultaneous posts. However, these invitation links are not only generated by harassers—they are often used by members of a server to draw in new members. They are a convenient way to gain community members, and therefore many server administrators continue to use them even if they do invite raids. One server administrator described the problem to Menegus:

> Some time ago, the owner of the server put out a few invite links on Reddit, and as such, the search term "furry discord" brings up the Reddit post containing said link as one of the top results.... The simplest way to stop these raids is to revoke said link, however doing so cuts off the main source of legitimate people wishing to join.
> (Menegus, 2017)

Thus, server administrators are caught between creating the possibility of growing their community and inviting raids on their server.

Discord claims to be updating the software to address raids, which the company says is a violation of their terms of service and is against their values. However, certain updates seem to have actually exacerbated the problem. For instance, one 2017 change log explains that the default expiration time for links was changed from 30 minutes to 24 hours, "so less people run into dead ends and more people get to hang with their fun friends" (Nelly, 2017). Furthermore, the same change log provides a claim that Discord has upgraded systems to address raiding, but we are given no details. Instead, we get cute Internet lingo: "A ton of internal systems have been added to combat spam and raiding. THEY ATTAC. WE PROTEC" (Nelly, 2017). Discord has also attempted to address this problem with verification levels, which establish "a basic level of security a user must meet before they're allowed to send text messages in a channel" ("What are verification levels?," n.d.). Implementing such changes does attempt to address raids and the creation of invitation links by nefarious actors. However, it still places the onus on users (those administering servers) to address the problem. This design decision is framed as the one that gives users freedom, but the result is that administrators are tasked with dealing with raids and attacks on a regular basis. Apparently, with freedom comes overwhelming responsibility.

To fully understand how Discord has responded to problematic users, it's best to turn to the event that put Discord in the spotlight—the Unite the Right rally and subsequent protest in Charlottesville, Virginia. Originally designed for gaming communities, Discord does play host to other conversations, including a collection of alt-right organizations. These organizations communicated (privately and out of sight) with each other on Discord to organize the rally, plan raids on other servers, and target individuals for abuse. The ultimate impact of their digital actions (a real-life hate rally) was immense and demonstrated that online harassment does not necessarily remain online. The actions of these Discord users exploded into the real world, and that seemed to be where Discord began to draw the line. The Unite the Right rally was not organized overnight and the hatred exhibited was not spontaneous: Discord servers that helped organize the event (such as National Socialist Army, Führer's Gas Chamber, Blood and Soil, /pol/, and Centipede Central) had been hosting forms of abuse since before the creation of this messaging client. But in addition to raiding other servers, groups were also organizing internally. Their outwardly facing harassment doesn't always reveal what is happening within the walls of the servers, where "they posted swastikas and praised Hitler" (Roose, 2018). Hatred was the norm even inside those walls, with defamation of certain groups of people and blatant hate speech running rampant. According to *New York Times* reporter Kevin Roose, even infighting between these various servers was common, meaning no one was safe.

The biggest offense of the alt-right on Discord, however, *was* outwardly facing (and extremely so): the Unite the Right rally in Charlottesville, Virginia, which led to the death of Heather Heyer. This form of harassment was not innovative. In fact, it was depressingly banal. Simply by exploiting the platform and its features, users of the alt-right servers were able to organize themselves and coordinate a massive meet-up. There was no special tactic used here, like the ones we discussed earlier on in this chapter, no server raids, no invitation link sharing. They merely took advantage of Discord's hands-off approach to community management in order to hide in plain sight.

After years of being aware that their platform had been utilized by the alt-right, white supremacists, and neo-Nazis, Discord finally began taking action by eliminating servers and issuing warnings to others (Newton, 2017). After the Unite the Right rally, Discord said that it was taking a proactive, long-term stance to deal with those violating terms of service. Interestingly, they policed this behavior by, once again, relying on users to report bad actors: "Though we do not read people's private messages, we do investigate and take immediate appropriate action against any reported ToS violation by a server or user" (Alexander, 2018). However, Discord also claims to track certain patterns that are associated with raids, such as the use of bots to swarm a server, meaning that their trust and safety team is not only relying on user reports. The details of these measures are closely guarded by the company: "We do not disclose the exact measures we take as we don't want to give people clues for how to work around those measures" (Alexander, 2018). Still, Discord insists that they never listen in and that they are not policing the content of a server.

This insistence of remaining at a remove from content and staying out of the nitty gritty of actual language is in keeping with the hands-off nature of the libertarian bias of many digital spaces, a bias that we can see at least as early as the harassment studied by Herring. Language is not policed, because this would violate the free speech ethos that still dominates many digital platforms. Discord will go to great lengths to not police actual speech (or to convince users that they are not doing so) for fear of alienating users who would see such policing as off-putting. But Discord can also just as easily claim that it is following current U.S. law, which does not require them to engage in this way. Furthermore, the very draw of Discord for alt-righters (and perhaps others) is the anonymity and privacy of Discord servers. This is key to their platform, and a violation of it would actually transform their service. Discord remains adamant that the company will only track conversation on a metalevel, and that they don't and will not track content. They have removed people for abuses of terms of service in their messages, but only after receiving tips via other users. All of these ways of dealing with abuse deal in technicalities. One way to understand this is that Discord avoids the question of ethics altogether. Another way to understand it—the way we choose to read the situation—is that the company's ethics are embedded in the platform, its policies, and its community. However you understand it, it should be clear that Discord's approach leaves a lot of wiggle room for offenders. Alt-right servers such as The Right Goys and Centipede Central are still active even after Discord banned a number of servers in the wake of Charlottesville (Liao, 2018).

Design Justice and Insourcing Responsibility

In a 2017 *BuzzFeed* story, Discord CEO Jason Citron laid out the company's design philosophy in clear terms: "We're very focused on making an amazing communication product for gamers.... I had a hunch that it would be used outside of gaming, but it wasn't anything we thought specifically about" (as quoted in Bernstein, 2017). When asked about the popularity of his platform among the alt-right, Citron essentially shrugged his shoulders: "It's inevitable that there will be actors using the product for things that are not completely wholesome"

(Bernstein, 2017). Seven months later, it became clear just how unwholesome some of Discord's users were. Those organizing the Unite the Right rally in Charlottesville had exploited many of the platform's features to gather together white supremacists at an event that resulted in the death of Heather Heyer and two law enforcement officers. The most prominent of these organizers was Jason Kessler, who proclaimed on Twitter that Heyer was a "a fat, disgusting Communist" and said her death was "payback" for deaths caused by Communists (Pearce, 2017). Discord had been a key tool for Kessler and others, something that Citron knew about in January. However, he seems to have seen such uses of his platform as collateral damage, something that would inevitably happen in a space that took a hands-off approach to moderation. Even after Charlottesville, Citron has said that the company has no plans to change its model of relying on users to report bad actors (Crecente, 2017).

But what would Discord look like if Citron and the rest of the design team "thought specifically about" the other potential uses of Discord? What if software designers began to think more deeply about how their platforms might be enabling bad behavior and designed these platforms with such potentialities in mind? How might the designers of these platforms *insource*, rather than outsource, responsibility? This is the kind of approach many scholars are beginning to advocate for. For instance, Costanza-Chock has argued for a "design justice" framework that sees design as directly tied to questions of racism, sexism, and domination:

> For example, at the personal level, we might explore how interface design affirms or denies aspects of a person's identity through features such as, say, a binary gender dropdown during account profile creation. More broadly, we might consider how design decisions play out in the impacts they have on different individual's biographies or life-chances. At the the community level, we might explore how platform design fosters certain kinds of communities while suppressing others, through setting and implementing community guidelines, rules, and speech norms, instantiated through different kinds of content moderation systems. At the institutional level, design justice asks us to consider the ways that various design institutions reproduce and/or challenge the matrix of domination in their practices.
>
> (Costanza-Chock, 2018, p. 5)

We believe that the term "hateware" can be a key part of a design justice approach since it presents critics and designers with a way of analyzing and evaluating platforms that are enabling the abuse of marginalized people. Understanding the rhetoric and ethics of harassment will require that we do more than just analyze the language and actions of those carrying out this abuse. As many scholars have already noted, the analysis of bad behavior will have to be coupled with an understanding of how our digital infrastructure is a crucial part of this story.

Discord's name suggests from the very start that disharmony and disagreement are core to what users might expect. As Milner (2014) has argued, disagreement and agonism are important for healthy, thriving communities. Drawing on the work of Chantal Mouffe, Milner argues that we should notice the difference between agonism and antagonism in online communities. Antagonism describes argument between "enemies," while agonism describes disagreement between "adversaries." Discord's problem with raiding demonstrates that its siloed model provides for agonism on particular servers but also too easily allows for *antagonism*:

> Antagonism… [pushes] voices out of the public sphere. For the logic of lulz [to] afford vibrant, agonistic public discourse, multiple perspectives and counter perspectives should be evident. Voice should be evident over exclusion, even if that voice is not monolithic in content or tone.
>
> (Milner, 2014)

Antagonism is built on exclusion and silencing others, and certain design decisions can encourage that kind of behavior. Discord is but one example of a site that has made such design decisions without fully recognizing the far-reaching implications of those decisions. Section 230 and a broader notion of free speech drive a great deal of design on the Internet, meaning that nearly every site and service on the Internet outsources responsibility.

The concept of hateware is our attempt to understand how design can help address problems of abuse, harassment, and antagonism by thinking more carefully about the design of software and community standards. Rather than addressing these problems after the fact, design justice can attempt to address them when building platforms and communities. Rather than outsourcing responsibility, design justice can insource it. To prevent the problems of hateware, we will need to identify and diagnose the portions of software that are easily gamed toward nefarious ends and then learn from those lessons as we attempt to build software that avoids landing on the hateware spectrum.

References

Alexander, J. (2018, February 28). Discord is purging alt-right, white nationalist and hateful servers. *Polygon*. Retrieved from https://www.polygon.com/2018/2/28/17061774/discord-alt-right-atomwaffen-ban-centipede-central-nordic-resistance-movement

Arola, K. L. (2010). The design of web 2.0: The rise of the template, the fall of design. *Computers and Composition, 27*(1), 4–14.

Bernstein, J. (2017, January 23). A thriving chat startup braces for the alt-right. *BuzzFeed News*. Retrieved from https://www.buzzfeed.com/josephbernstein/discord-chat-startup-braces-for-the-alt-right

Buhr, S. (2017, May 24). R.I.P. Imzy. *TechCrunch*. Retrieved from http://social.techcrunch.com/2017/05/24/r-i-p-imzy/

Costanza-Chock, S. (2018). Design justice: Towards an intersectional feminist framework for design theory and practice. *Social Science Research Network*. Retrieved from https://papers.ssrn.com/abstract=3189696

Crecente, B. (2017). Discord: 87M users, nintendo switch wishes and dealing with alt-right. *Rolling Stone*. Retrieved from https://www.rollingstone.com/glixel/news/discord-87m-users-switch-dreams-dealing-with-alt-right-w513598

Goldman, E. (2017). The ten most important Section 230 rulings. *Social Science Research Network*. Retrieved from https://papers.ssrn.com/abstract=3025943

Goldman, E. (2018, January 31). Twitter didn't cause ISIS-inspired terrorism. Fields v. Twitter. *Technology & Marketing Law Blog*. Retrieved from https://blog.ericgoldman.org/archives/2018/01/twitter-didnt-cause-isis-inspired-terrorism-fields-v-twitter.htm

Herring, S. (1999). The rhetorical dynamics of gender harassment on-line. *The Information Society, 15*, 151–167.

Jane, E. A. (2016). Online misogyny and feminist digilantism. *Continuum, 30*(3), 284–297.

Jeong, S. (2015). *The internet of garbage*. Jersey City, NJ: Forbes Media.

Kaufer, D. S., & Butler, B. S. (1996). *Rhetoric and the arts of design*. Mahwah, NJ: Lawrence Erlbaum.

Liao, S. (2018, February 28). Discord shuts down more neo-Nazi, alt-right servers. *The Verge*. Retrieved from https://www.theverge.com/2018/2/28/17062554/discord-alt-right-neo-nazi-white-supremacy-atomwaffen

Massanari, A. (2015). #Gamergate and The Fappening: How reddit's algorithm, governance, and culture support toxic technocultures. *New Media & Society, 19*(3), 329–346.

Menegus, B. (2017). How a video game chat client became the web's new cesspool of abuse. Retrieved from https://gizmodo.com/how-a-video-game-chat-client-became-the-web-s-new-cessp-1792039566

Milner, R. (2014). FCJ-156 Hacking the social: Internet memes, identity antagonism, and the logic of lulz. *The Fibreculture Journal, 22*. Retrieved from http://twentytwo.fibreculturejournal.org/fcj-156-hacking-the-social-internet-memes-identity-antagonism-and-the-logic-of-lulz/

Nelly. (2017, July 21). 7.21.17—Change Log. Retrieved from https://blog.discordapp.com/7-21-17-change-log-c9acad667d67

Newton, C. (2017, August 14). Discord bans servers that promote Nazi ideology. Retrieved from https://www.theverge.com/2017/8/14/16145432/discord-nazi-ban-white-supremacist-altright

Pearce, M. (2017). Tweet from the account of Charlottesville rally organizer insults slain protester Heather Heyer. Retrieved from http://www.latimes.com/nation/la-na-charlottesville-organizer-20170818-story.html

Phillips, W. (2015). *This is why we can't have nice things: Mapping the relationship between online trolling and mainstream culture* (Reprint edition). Cambridge, MA: The MIT Press.

Protection for screening of offensive material, 47 U.S. Code § 230 (1996). Retrieved from https://www.law.cornell.edu/uscode/text/47/230

Ravenscraft, E. (2016, August 17). Discord is the voice Chat App I've Always Wanted. *Lifehacker.* Retrieved from https://lifehacker.com/discord-is-the-voice-chat-app-i-ve-always-wanted-1785403197

Roose, K. (2018, January 20). This was the alt-right's favorite chat app. Then came Charlottesville. *The New York Times.* Retrieved from https://www.nytimes.com/2017/08/15/technology/discord-chat-app-alt-right.html

Selfe, C. L., & Selfe, R. J. (1994). The politics of the interface: Power and its exercise in electronic contact zones. *College Composition and Communication, 45*(4), 480–504.

Sparby, E. M. (2017). Digital social media and aggression: Memetic rhetoric in 4chan's collective identity. *Computers and Composition, 45,* 85–97.

Tarsa, B., & Brown Jr, J. J. (2018). Complicit interfaces. In W. S. Hesford, A. C. Licona, & C. Teston (Eds.), *Precarious rhetorics* (pp. 255–275). Columbus: Ohio State University Press.

What are verification levels? (n.d.). *Discord Server Setup.* Retrieved from http://support.discordapp.com/hc/en-us/articles/216679607-What-are-Verification-Levels-

3 Values versus Rules in Social Media Communities
How Platforms Generate Amorality on reddit and Facebook

Michael Trice, Liza Potts, and Rebekah Small

In this chapter, we examine issues of ethics in online communities, presenting a historical account of an online community ethos juxtaposed against modern rules-based communities of harm. By communities of harm, we mean communities that place the individual's freedom to act aggressively above any common community value or long-term goal. Of particular interest in these communities of harm are the rules used to maintain their presence on platforms, like Facebook, Twitter, and reddit, by either subverting platform rules or following the rules while disengaging with the values behind those rules. This rule subversion might manifest as a reddit thread banning doxxing[1] and dogpiling[2] while still serving to aggregate targets for a campaign or harassment. It might also manifest itself as a closed Facebook group that tightly regulates how posts are reported so that concerns about content never reach Facebook itself.

For this critique, we examine historical online communities such as the WELL, an early online community, and the writings about these spaces by Rheingold (2000) among others. The ethos and practices of these foundational communities are then juxtaposed with the GamerGate controversy as it played out on reddit's/KotakuInAction (KiA) subreddit, a news aggregator and forum for the GamerGate community, and the transformation of LeftBook, the network of left leaning Facebook groups that began as places for community discourse and slowly devolved into spaces for shaming and personal attacks. The KiA subreddit is widely recognized as the primary reddit home for GamerGate with over 30,000 subscribers, and its persistence as one of the last centralized hubs of GamerGate rests in its ability to follow the rules of reddit while promoting the hostile ethos of GamerGate. LeftBook is not as well known, but the activity of some of their "Shaming" groups—where members post images with the intent of the community shaming individuals for rings, weddings, nails, etc.—has recently garnered the attention of news media for their dogpiling and criticism of those not involved in the community. LeftBook intentionally circumvents Facebook moderation to protect its own shaming ethos. These two spaces represent dynamic opposites with regard to the ways in which community ethos is built and content is moderated—GamerGate is quite public about following the rules of reddit, while shaming groups hide from Facebook as closed communities with tight internal moderation. Our findings suggest that, even in the absence of the aggressive ideology found in the KiA subreddit, groups that are predicated on rules rather than values fall to the same demise. When values are not communicated through positive messaging but rather through rules which steer the community in the direction of certain behaviors, those communities find ways to skirt positive values while still following the rules. Ultimately, regardless of the intentions behind the creation of groups like KiA and LeftBook, their rules-based moderation has led them into similar patterns of messaging and behavior.

To explore this issue of rules versus values in full, we first examine the intersections between community governances, rules, and ethics. Here, we take a look at both the history of ethical moderation within online communities and how the field of technical communication has wrestled with the issue of ethical governance historically: from codes of ethics to social justice to community *phronesis* as the palpable outcome of UX design. We then apply this understanding to KiA and LeftBook to demonstrate the ethical limitations of rules-based moderation and how the practice of rules-based moderation bridges ideological classifications in its ethical shortsightedness.

Governance versus Ethos in Online Communities

In comparing ethos and rules, it is worth discussing a bit of the history of online governance. Ideological radicalization online has been a concern since the turn of the century. In fact, following the U.S. presidential elections in 2000, Jenkins and Thorburn (2004) felt it necessary to rebuff these concerns by explaining that while radicalism on the left and right were rampant online, the current audience of Internet media paled by comparison to cable and network television. For them, broadcast media would never allow such radicalization to expand due to the enormous audience advantage of broadcast media. Of course, much has since changed in the size of online audiences.

Less than ten years later, Zittrain (2008) proposed the rise of a new kind of civil libertarian ideal online: a *netizenship* informed by the communal practice, success, and ethics of Wikipedia. Roughly concurrently, Coleman and Blumler (2009) questioned ceding public deliberation to Twitter and Facebook by suggesting that only a BBC-like government-funded (yet politically independent) platform could properly capture the values of civic deliberation. By 2013, Tufekci documented the rise of the activist celebrity as a newly christened master node in networked deliberation. Tufekci's work, in particular, has proven prescient as it anticipated the importance of individual broadcast nodes as tastemakers on Twitter and Facebook. Quickly, the debate moved from why we need governance online to what form of online governance would best serve the public good.

Haas and Eble (2018) recently drew technical communication directly into this debate by calling attention to how the tensions between globalization and local communities create opportunities for oppression that we must be attuned to. In many ways, the communities of harm we examine are responding to global platforms by resisting the stated values of these platforms in order to indulge more freely in antisocial and amoral behavior. It is worth examining how they do that and why it matters when rules arise from values and not individualistic rebellion.

Code of Ethics and Accountability

At the close of World War II, Bush (1945) asked a pivotal question in the history of science and engineering: What next? In "As We May Think," Bush's proposal of the memex offers a less compelling moment than the ethical pivot the article personifies as a description for how disciplines should adapt to the postwar era. In hindsight, we can note that the decades that followed gave rise to technical achievements from ARPANET to the moon landing. That same period also led to a growing codification of the ethics within engineering. In 1946, the National Society of Professional Engineers released their initial Canon of Ethics for Engineers expanding upon the rules of ethics that had preceded it. The first canon (National Society of Professional Engineers, 2018) expressed a particular commitment to public welfare as ethos: "Hold paramount the safety, health and welfare of the public in the performance of their professional duties."

While codes of ethics existed prior to the end of the war, many of those that came after the war had changed. In the late 19th and early 20th centuries, professional codes of ethics often focused upon issues of individual honor and honesty. For example, the 1912 code of ethics for the American Institute of Electrical Engineers opened with: "While the following principles express, generally, the engineer's relations to client, employer, the public, and the engineering fraternity, it is not presumed that they define all of the engineer's duties and obligations." Yet by 1950, the American Institute of Electrical Engineers code opened:

> Honesty. justice, and courtesy form a moral philosophy which, associated with mutual interest among men, constitutes the foundation of ethics. The engineer should recognize such a standard, not in passive observance, but as a set of dynamic principles guiding his conduct and way of life. It is his duty to practice his profession according to these Canons of Ethics.
>
> (American Institute of Electrical Engineers, 1950)

Additionally, by the second half of the 20th century, the codes of organizations like the National Society of Professional Engineers (NSPE) (1961) and American Society of Mechanical Engineers (ASME) (1976) shifted to prioritize canons that placed a commitment to the "welfare of the public" or "human welfare" as a key principle. Many trends within the engineering organizations likely fed such shifts. The Work Progress Administration led to numerous nationalized public works; World War II generated both a sense of national professional unity and opposition to the horrors of science and engineering run amok in Germany, and communication technologies began to challenge the local versus the national versus the global. Perhaps few codes epitomized all three movements quite so well as the World Medical Association, which was formed explicitly to address the concerns about global ethical issues in medicine after the atrocities of World War II (World Medical Association, 2018). This ethics-centered shift in professional community behavior from personal integrity to the ethics of public welfare is an important historical note to revisit when considering how governance has evolved online, especially given the technical communications' historic relationship with these codes.

Katz (1992) addressed part of what inspired this shift in codified engineering ethos in "The Ethic of Expediency: Classical Rhetoric, Technology, and the Holocaust." In his analysis of Nazi communication regarding the improvement of trucks for more efficient slaughter of human life, Katz identified an ethos that prioritized scientific and engineering efficiency over human life. This efficiency ran deeper than the communication itself. Historians have noted that Germany adapted Soviet technology in its gas vans as it eased the minds of the executioners. Where soldiers often suffered ill effects from the shooting of unarmed women and children, the vans removed this emotional and personal connection. Importantly, the process as well as the communication of the process was designed to empower unethical, inhumane, monstrous behavior by distancing the actor from the action and the victim. The entire Nazi platform was predicated on creating an environment where the unconscionable became psychologically palatable. The resistance to such an atmosphere became the centering of humanistic values as central to governance across national, professional, and organizational communities. Canons centered on a commitment to the public welfare became the norm.

The move from individual accountability as ethos to an ethos of service to humanity offers a compelling comparison for those of us looking at social media platforms. As we discuss later with the WELL, personal accountability can be derived from a community ethos. In fact, Zittrain's (2008) evaluation of Wikipedia's ethos and the *netizenship* that rose from it suggests that it is this shared collaborative vision that promotes the governance necessary to maintain the community. These two examples of the WELL and Wikipedia contrast sharply with our later modern examples of community online, KiA and LeftBook's shaming groups.

Importantly, these communities maintain strict community rulesets, but they do so around an ethos less shaped on positive, ethical contributions than amoral recreation and harassment. Essentially, they propose rules of accountability to the community, but not to a greater ethical consideration, either the platform, society, or humanity at large. In this way, it is not simply a rejection of social justice and ethics, but a redefining of what it means to be social and a rejection of justice outside of the community's standards.

In many ways, the response of communities like KiA and Ring Shamers can be viewed as part of the populist response to growing globalization that Haas and Eble (2018) ask us to consider as technical communicators. Populist anger and a desire to lash out with that anger is a known nemesis of the social justice Haas and Eble promote. It is not unlike the one Bush (1945) responded to as part of his postwar call to something greater—the Internet has channeled anger into destructive communities that lack accountability beyond the community as well as lacking a community ethic that seeks positive change. The flexibility, anonymity, and generative power of online networks make them excellent realms for fighting oppression, but those features make these networks efficient at enacting oppression at the individual, organizational, national, and global levels (Tufekci, 2017).

The connection between ethics and governance matters as it relates to both organizations and platforms. Part of the reason for exploring amoral groups on platforms arises from our wish to focus upon how platforms might offer a means to create ethos rather than simply codes of conduct. For us, that means a similar transition as occurred after World War II, a move from personal accountability as rules to an affirmation of a community's positive contribution to the world around them and the sense of personal accountability that might arise from such a mission. In this way, we also hope to express how a commitment to positive applications of social justice might alleviate the oppressive populism that had arisen in the face of tensions between globalization and the individual.

Early Online Communities

Social networks, forums, content management systems, wikis, mobile apps, and dedicated messaging services all offer a range of rhetorical purposes, possible audiences, and functional capabilities that make a universal online community difficult to reliably define. Before we referred to these digital spaces as social media platforms, researchers and practitioners were examining what were primarily text-based technologies such as e-mail, chat, and online bulletin board systems. Researchers noted that "cyberspace is essentially a reconceived public sphere for social, political, economic, and cultural interaction" (Fernback, 1997, p. 37), and as such studied it as a phenomenon. Many of the early, celebrated work about online communities focused on the positive potential of the Internet, often framed around ideas connecting counterculture with technoculture (Johnson, 1997; Raymond, 1999; Rheingold, 2000). This work served to inspire a growing community of leaders and participants in these digital spaces. While academic scholarship questioned ethical issues of identity and representation in these communities (Baym, 2000; Ess, 1996; Herring, 1993), it was often drowned out in industry by cyberlibertarian voices in early incarnations of publications such as *Wired* magazine and others (Warnick, 2002).

The ethos of these early digital spaces was buoyed by the influential, often utopianistic writings of the major influencers of this time. These spaces were heralded as places where "the common man and the information worker—cowboy or infocraft—can search, manipulate, create or control information directly; he can be entertained or trained, seek solitude or company, win or lose power" (Benedikt, 1991, p. 123). Virtual communities thought leaders such as Howard Rheingold (2000), open-source leaders such as Richard Stallman, and popular culture shaped a lot of these ideas. In these spaces, there was a strong spirit of positivity with regard to creating community, volunteerism, and shared governance. While trolling and worse certainly existed (Turkle, 1995), there was a sense that the "virtual" Internet would be better than "real life." There were expectations for civil discussion. The kind of anonymity that existed was still tied to a name, or user "handle" of some sort, that would often voluntarily follow you from online board to online board.

While many of these spaces saw the early Internet as a space of utopian vision, others noted that "cyberspace is an arena of power" (Fernback, 1997, p. 37). These individualistic beliefs held in many early spaces can be summed up in the hacker ethic by Levy (1984):

1 Access to computers—and anything which might teach you something about the way the world works—should be unlimited and total.
2 All information should be free.
3 Mistrust authority—promote decentralization.
4 Hackers should be judged by their hacking, not bogus criteria such as degrees, age, race, or position.
5 You can create art and beauty on a computer.
6 Computers can change your life for the better.

(pp. 27–33)

Not too surprisingly, even though this utopian vision carried a promise of something better, the examples explored later in this chapter took that spirit of individualism and connected it to power without any ethical safeguard. In fact, they frequently placed the right of the individual to misbehave as the core value of the community. Rather than individualism feeding art and beauty, it would feed hate, envy, and self-indulgence.

WELL

The WELL (Whole Earth 'Lectronic Link) is an online community that began in 1985 and is still running today. On the website's "About" section, the writers describe the site as "a cherished destination for conversation and discussion... widely known as the primordial ooze where the online community movement was born—where Howard Rheingold first coined the term "virtual community" (2019). Built in Sausalito, a city near San Francisco and north of Silicon Valley, it was a place for writers, artists, thinkers, and tinkerers populated by people with community-building skills (Evans, 2018, p. 132). Its cofounder, Stewart Brand, an early counterculture entrepreneur, had built the Whole Earth Review from which the WELL's name sprung.

Today, the WELL describes itself as a space for "artisanal conversations" where members create a space "distinguished by the quality of our non-anonymous participants, and by uncommon policies." These policies include the axiom "real people, real names" (2019). It is this "real names" policy that immediately distinguishes it from platforms like reddit where anonymity is a core value. And the WELL's policies on creating a space where "mutual respect and cooperation" are paramount make for a very different kind of community than the combative nature of many subreddits.

To examine this ethos further, consider this statement on the WELL's website (2019):

> The WELL was launched in 1985 with minimal rules and a freewheeling spirit. The aphorism crafted to greet users at the time was "You Own Your Own Words." This now classic and carefully tended policy has been expanded into The WELL Member Agreement with detailed explanations of the implications of "YOYOW," as members refer to it.

This focus on YOYOW is symbolic of the ethos of responsibility devoid of government oversight. This catchphrase seems jovial, but it demands that participants be responsible for their actions and work together to create a better digital society.

Participants on the WELL refer to themselves as "WELL-beings" who are engaged with their community for positive growth. Describing his entry into this online community, Rheingold (2000) states,

> Finding the WELL was like discovering a cozy little world that had been flourishing without me, hidden with the walls of my house; an entire cast of characters welcomed me to the troupe with great merriment as soon as I found the secret door.
>
> (p. xv)

This secret door created a space that flourished in its community.[3]

Reddit's KiA

While the WELL offers a view of a community focused upon non-anonymous communities of high-quality conversations, reddit's KiA serves as something of a direct counterexample for how chan culture has shifted away from the WELL's vision. Much like the wider chan culture, KiA strongly encourages anonymity over real names. It also aims for a populist and raw discourse more interested in cutting insults than quality of conversations. As discussed later, this attitude bleeds over to a rejection of most publishers and sources considered valid outside the community and an ethos closely tied to the harassing nature of the GamerGate movement that founded KiA.

GamerGate began in mid-2014 from an angry rumor-filled breakup rant posted online. The details of that story have been recounted by other articles (Chess & Shaw, 2015; Mortensen, 2016) and by the initial target of GamerGate, Zoë Quinn (2017), but a quick primer will assist in contextualizing the key issues around GamerGate as it relates to current ethical issues in community governance. First, from Zoë Quinn to Seth Rich, online conspiracies often move from blog rumors to 4chan fodder to social media activism as anarchy, even as they remain the tragedy and drama of actual human beings. Second, they are first and foremost rumor mills. They start as personal accusations that are made to appear as vetted claims via focused discussion on chan boards and YouTube. They develop into deep networks of actors and technical platforms to support and defend the rumors, they often build a culture and counterculture around the rumors, and they apply this sense of community to target both ideological opponents and long-standing institutions they see as threats (Chess & Shaw, 2015). As a matter of ethics, the method and purpose of these networks matter. Rather than guided by a principle of bettering the public welfare, they are attack engines. In addition, they are attack engines driven by rumor and drama over knowledge and information. With all of that in mind, a brief recap of GamerGate follows.

The originating post, full of sordid, personal, largely unsubstantiated claims about infidelity and betrayal quickly found its way to 4chan. As the target of the blog post was an independent game developer—and the accusations revolved around unsupported claims of sex with journalists for positive coverage of her games—channers used the blog post as a rallying cry against games journalists and feminists in game design and critique. From 4chan, conversations about the rumors spilled over into a network of YouTube channels dedicated to criticizing feminism and cultural criticism. Eventually, the rumor mill moved to Twitter.

On Twitter, 4chan users attempted to trend several hashtags, including #quinnspiracy, #fiveguys, and #FiveGuysBurgersAndLies. The hashtags make clear that Quinn was the target and that the ridicule was focused upon the rumors of supposed infidelities in the original blog post.

Values versus Rules in Social Media Communities   41

The hashtags failed to capture much attention until actor Adam Baldwin coined the tag #GamerGate while retweeting a YouTube video about the incident. Organizers quickly took advantage of Baldwin's interest and latched onto his hashtag in a behavior pattern that would become central to GamerGate success: involve conservative celebrities and pundits to amplify the message. From there, a number of articles covered Baldwin's involvement and the backlash to it. Pushback against these articles critical of GamerGate soon spiraled into a massive Twitter fray pitting culture critics against GamerGate and conservative pundits like Milo Yiannopoulos, Christina Hoff Sommers, Cathy Young, and Mike Cernovich. The inclusion of these pundits would do little to abate the original harassment and rumormongering even as a veneer of media criticism focused on challenging feminist culture critics was added to the discussion. GamerGate as a machine for rumor and accusation relished in flat structure and largely rejected anything resembling governance or accountability.

When GamerGate did generate rules, those rules tended to be technical, not ethical. There are no canons of GamerGate. For example, as shown in Figure 3.1, GamerGate frames its Twitter instructions as a how-to for new users. Yet buried in these instructions are a number of implicit values: anonymity, connected networks, in-group/out-group definitions, and prioritization of certain accounts. What GamerGate saw as an ethos was largely volume and power.

As GamerGate transitioned to reddit, this rule structure was modified (see Figure 3.2). The site's rules explicitly banned many of the tactics

RULES

1	Don't be a dickwolf.
2	No Personal Information
3	Posting Guidelines
4	Please tag posts for flair
5	We are not your personal army
6	Archive as much as you can
7	Don't post bullshit
8	No Reposts
9	No Metareddit posts

If you have any questions or concerns, please message the moderators before private messaging an individual moderator.

You can find our rules and much more in our Wiki.

Figure 3.1 GamerGate instructions for creating a Twitter account, by KotakuInAction. Screencapture by M. Trice, 2015.

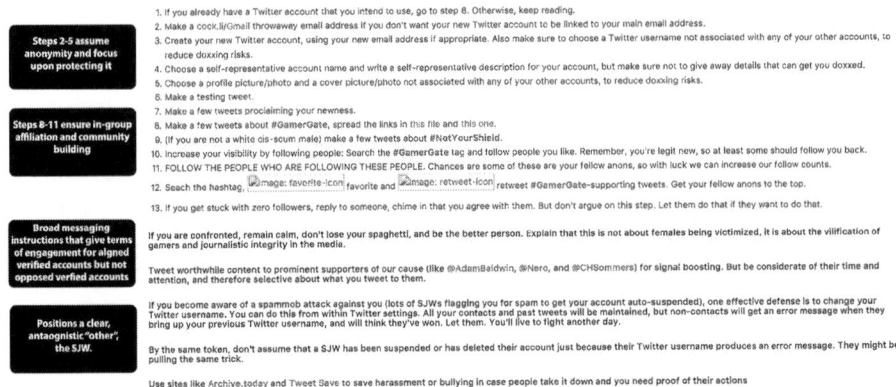

Figure 3.2 Outline of KiA rules from the subreddit, by KotakuInAction. Screencapture by M. Trice, 2018.

popular in the community. Actions such as linking to a target's tweet or article could result in the subreddit being banned. In fact, as numerous aggressive and harmful subreddits were removed, KiA survived due to an aggressive enforcement of its rules. As a result, KiA's effort to survive on reddit resulted in mitigating the acceptable behavior of the subreddit's users. What did not happen was a shift in values. The rules do not state an affirmative community purpose or a set of guiding principles. What they outline are the behaviors that are unacceptable, thus leaving anything else open to the community. Thus, the community remained heavily focused upon its animosity toward targets. While this prevented direct organization and harassment of targets from the subreddit, it also maintained the ethos of hostility and dehumanizing behavior that fed the culture of the harassment.

The discourse of the KiA rules remained resolutely that of Gamer-Gate's, starting with the language of Rule 1, a reference to a rape joke from a popular online comic. The commitment to anonymity (Rule 2) also remained present. This anonymity is an interesting feature when compared to YOTOW of the WELL, which regulated a freewheeling community via accountability for the type of speech a person used. This accountability is largely lacking on KiA. While certain behaviors were banned, KiA aggressively disavows any responsibility beyond these rules for what a user says. Another rule worth mentioning is Rule 5: "We are not your personal army." In the expanded clarifications for these rules, KiA moderators state:

> Don't post a call to action to downvote some submission on reddit you disagree with. In fact, all links to other subreddits' comment sections will be automatically removed by AutoModerator.

> Don't make posts like "let's give that idiot a piece of our mind!"
> if you come across something stupid someone said on the internet.
> (KotakuInAction, 2019)

These rules highlight a significant move away from the 4chan operation side of GamerGate that focused heavily upon directing mass movement to and away from certain publications and individuals. It is one clear case where the rules completely altered the standard behavior of GamerGate on reddit. The discourse of the rules became a means to express the aggrieved purpose of the community even as the rules restrict the old behavior patterns.

While KiA became a muted form of GamerGate due to the need to meet the rules of the reddit platform, KiA's discourse and rules help demonstrate that the core values of aggrievement within the community remained largely unchanged even as the activities allowed by the community were limited. Since KiA strictly enforced rules against targeting and mob action, those elements exceptionally common to the Twitter and 4chan versions of GamerGate disappeared from the site (though not necessarily disappearing from incarnations on other platforms). KiA also maintained a focus on multiple targets (social justice, feminists, and journalists), though the method of linking shifted to images rather than live links. Thus, the foes remained the same even as the engagement with those foes shifted.

The ability to rein in the GamerGate community so that it could survive on reddit demonstrates some intriguing possibilities about the role of community rules in other online spaces. First, it suggests that community values can be entwined into the functional representations of platform, similar to hashtags on Twitter and Facebook. Word choice and personalization matter in these rule systems. Yet, a tension remains in that the values of reddit are not reflected in the KiA community. By following the reddit rules as a technical obstacle, KiA users managed to maintain values of aggrievement and harassment even as they took the actual behaviors offsite.

Facebook's LeftBook as a Space for Shaming Groups

In *The Presentation of Self in Everyday Life*, Goffman (1959) posits a scenario in which a woman observes a man at a party in order to perceive the man's impression of a third partygoer. This woman carefully notes the man's facial expressions, proximity, and body language, and in doing so becomes the "unobserved observer," who watches but is not watched. As we examine our next group of users attempting to build community, in an age where platforms preach stoicism and neutrality instead of affirmative values, we witness the consequences of an unobserved observer becoming the observed. The network of individuals we examine next has created a system of their own to vet users and content. LeftBook is not official, unified, or transparent, but it includes a vast web of Facebook users who have joined groups of like-minded users to discuss almost everything, from tacky weddings to late stage capitalism. While part of the downfall of this network was the far-right groups opposed to their activity (upset at their inability to troll from outside of the closed groups), the real undoing came down to Facebook's inability to moderate its own users.

Named for the many groups with a far-left political affiliation, Left-Book refers to the unknown number of Facebook groups that utilize rules-based moderation and are quick to ban users who abuse said rules. While like-minded users see this as a valuable effort to promote a specific environment within a group, others (whose ideals are not valued or welcome) perceive the insular nature of this as toxic and threatening. Regardless of personal politics, this network subverted Facebook's functionality, utilizing it for their own purposes and evading the Facebook moderators' attention as much as possible. And as a result, the groups that began as facets of a value-based community morphed over time into a strict rules-based system focused on subverting Facebook's platform and approaches to moderation (see Figure 3.3).

Three factors contribute to governance issues on LeftBook:

- The practice of official Facebook moderators' completely shutting down groups which generate too many blocks/reports.
- The authority placed in the hands of a select few users/moderators, who control the atmosphere of the group.
- Clashes with the public (on Facebook and other media) over the content, rules, or values of the groups.

Facebook's lack of nuanced moderation led to the authority being placed in the hands of a few individuals who seem to be as ill-suited to moderate as the 7,500 moderators employed by Facebook (Koebler & Cox, 2018). Because of this failure to effectively govern their platforms, Facebook moderation has become a feature of the website that is avoided at all costs in these groups. The rhetoric behind the antifascist statement "we don't call the police" as response to police brutality is echoed in LeftBook groups' adoption of the practice "we don't report users," the insinuation being that to flag a group or user would cause more problems than it would solve. One change led to another, and the vast majority of LeftBook addressed their lack of moderation by instituting their own rules. Facebook's failure to moderate their users directly led to the rules-based moderation we see throughout LeftBook today.

Because users do not trust Facebook to properly moderate their groups and pages, LeftBook groups are run by individual moderators or administrators, called "modmins" by some. These administrators are charged

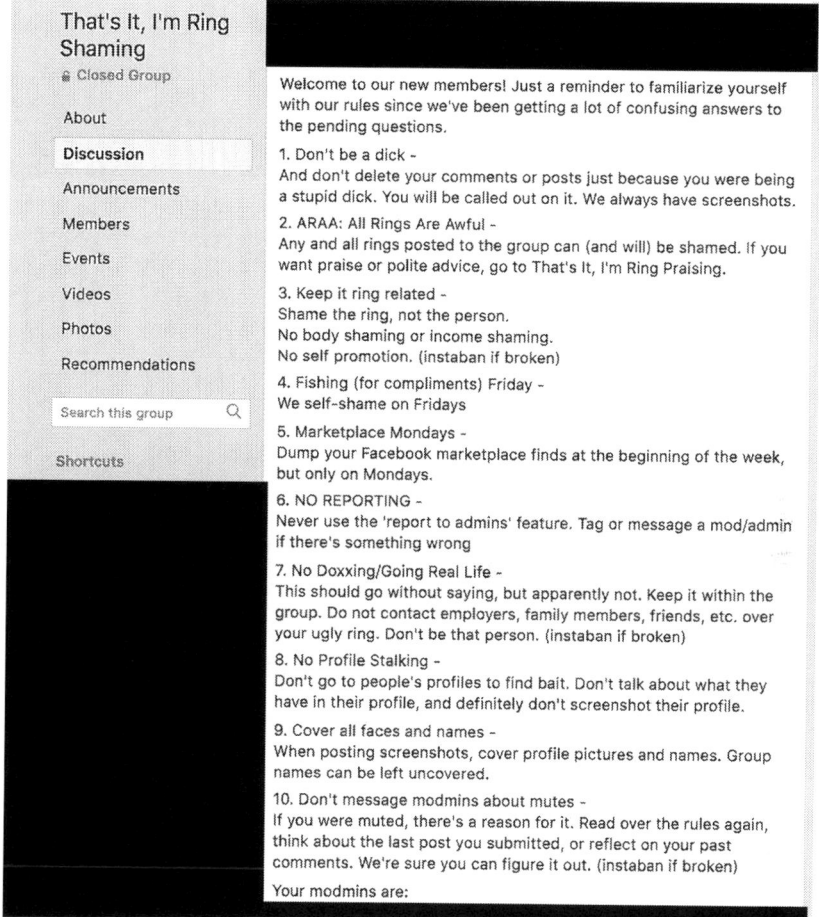

Figure 3.3 Rules for Ring Shaming Group. Screencapture by R. Small, 2018.

with making sure that the rules of their group are followed, admitting new members on a case-by-case basis, and dealing with interpersonal conflicts within the group swiftly. Instead of alerting the officials, users are told to tag a modmin, who will quickly review the situation and do what needs to be done so that the group can continue to function. This rule is paramount especially considering that a vast majority of these groups are intended for humorous but anonymous criticism of any expression of personal taste, meaning that personal attacks are common, and they span across themes including cultural appropriation, cosmetics, or even humorous examples of technology-illiterate generations using the platform "incorrectly." Because of the fine line holding the ethos of these groups together, they simply cannot tolerate those who would ignore their rules. As such, these groups are known for being "ban-happy," sometimes so much so that splinter groups form, who self-proclaim to not ban as many users (see Figure 3.4).

It is hard to consider the amount of time these modmins invest in this endeavor without drawing comparisons to the early AOL days and the labor-intensive volunteer program used to moderate chats and update community bulletins (Postigo, 2009). But while AOL recognized (albeit with miniscule reimbursement) the labor it took to run their community, Facebook does not. In fact, that lack of consistency from Facebook when it comes to moderation is expressly what led to the authority now given to modmins. Facebook users, like many others on social media, have

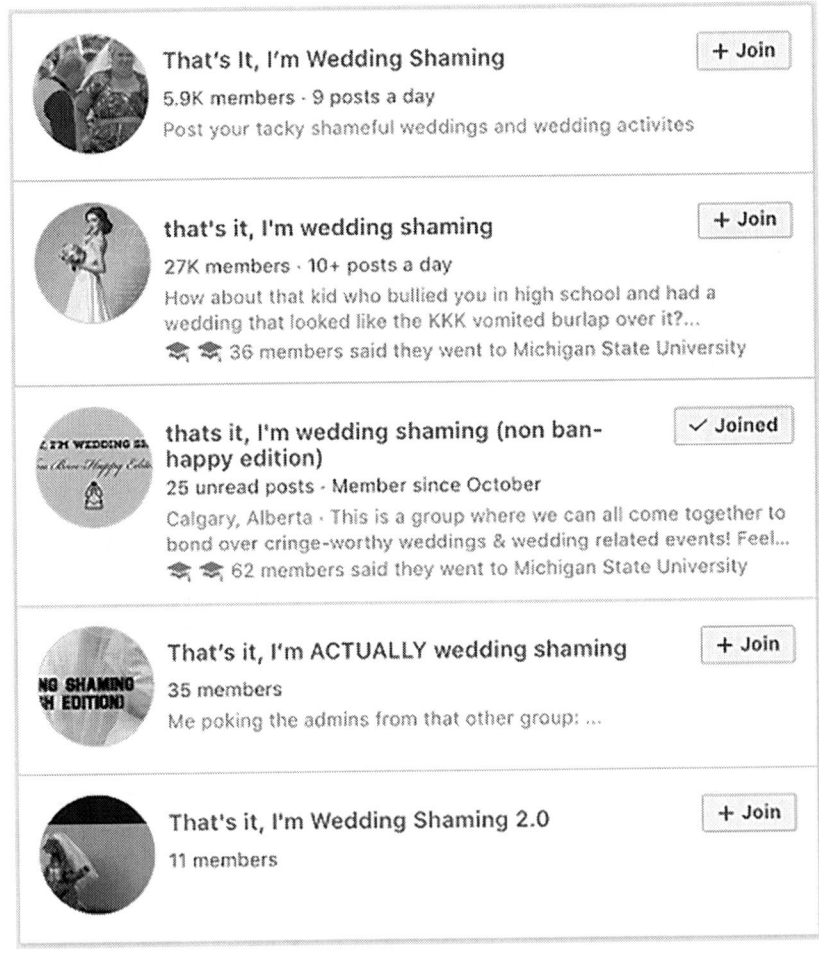

Figure 3.4 "That's it i'm wedding shaming" Facebook search. Screencapture by R. Small, 2018.

found disappointment when looking to large social media platforms for help handling abuse and harassment. Twitter and Facebook have both famously failed to suspend or ban bad actors. Due to their ad hoc "Community Standards," which rely on hard lines and "objective" workflows, Facebook claims that they have not had the time to think ethically about their policy as they are already overwhelmed with time-sensitive cases (Koebler & Cox, 2018). The problems that users, especially those in groups, have found with Facebook led the modmins of these groups to, like KiA, take measures to avoid appearing on the radar of official moderators and the public.

The effect of viral posts reported through media outlets like *Slate* and *The Today Show* had a profound effect on these groups as they found themselves in the public eye (Withers, 2018). While the content and tone of these viral posts were very different, the result was the same: splintering groups, anger expressed at those in the groups who shared the content outside of it, and even more dramatic efforts to hide from the platform and the public.

One attempt to hide from Facebook moderators, and the general public, was employed by the group titled "That's It, I'm Ring Shaming," which received viral attention several times regarding content that was cross posted to other social and news media sites. In order to hide from the media attention, as well as the deluge of new member applications that the attention attracted, they changed the name of the group to "gnimahS gniR m'I ,tI s'tahT" which is the name of the group written backward so that it would not show up in Facebook's or Google's search engine.

In the end, as these groups garner attention and then lose it again, one thing is clear: the rules holding them together are not enough to shape their actions and attitudes. And while this case may seem like the confluence of several missteps, the consistent differences between groups who follow rules (or do not with disastrous consequences as seen here and above in the case of KiA) and those who base their community around affirmative, positive values suggests otherwise. It is also worth mentioning that within the network of LeftBook, there are several groups that do focus on affirmative values. The flip sides to all of the shaming groups are "That's it, I'm ___ Praising" groups, which have not garnered media attention due to the harmless, positive nature of their behavior. These groups employ the same set of rules, but do not have the same problems as the shaming groups. The center *can* hold if online communities mold themselves around productive, positive, fruitful goals and values.

Conclusions

The goal of this chapter is to update Rheingold's (2000) call: "more than ever before, we need to ask the right questions today about what kind of people, what kind of societies might emerge from social cyberspaces tomorrow" (p. 323). Now that tomorrow has become today, the types of communities have diversified with disturbing trends. Rules that focused on personal accountability have gradually lost sight of ethical value. YOYOW now means skirting Facebook moderators or behaving just well enough on reddit to avoid subreddit shutdown. Accountability only goes so far as survival. Minus some greater call to public welfare, social justice, or even positive contribution, many digital communities have descended into an ethos of aggrievement and harm. As platforms enact universal rules of conduct to promote sitewide values and behaviors, KiA and LeftBook demonstrate how these values are often resisted. As a result, groups only avoid offenses that might invite outside human intervention within the community. Platforms must ask themselves whether these rules have ethical meaning, and if they do not, what purpose do the rules serve?

Notes

1 Doxxing is the revealing of personal identification in an online community. This might include the name of pseudonymous accounts or contact information, like addresses, employment, and phone numbers.
2 Dogpiling is signaling for a mass of users to respond to a thread or specific account, often to create a flood of overwhelming responses.
3 Much of the early design and discussion around online communities focused on the counterculture of the times. Noting that the demographic of the WELL was "thirty-year old white guys," Evans (2018) quotes an early WELL employee, Nancy Rhine, as saying "The WELL stood for Whole Earth 'Lectronic Link, but it did not represent the whole Earth" (p. 133). While men were the majority of participants in these online spaces, this did not mean that women were also not engaging. In a similar vein, examining the following modern examples suggests that while a gender divide persists ideologically online, that divide has still led to similar failures in ethical governance, leading us to conclude that neither gender is absolved when ethics are developed with an ethos of chaotic neutrality and applied inconsistently across a platform.

References

American Institute of Electrical Engineers. (1912). Code of principles of professional conduct (1912). Retrieved from http://ethics.iit.edu/ecodes/node/5068.
American Institute of Electrical Engineers. (1950). Code of principles of professional conduct (1950). Retrieved from http://ethics.iit.edu/ecodes/node/3232.
American Society of Mechanical Engineers. (1976). Codes of ethics of engineers (1976). Retrieved from http://ethics.iit.edu/ecodes/node/6297.
Baym, N. (2000). *Tune in, log on: Soaps, fandom, and online community*. Thousand Oaks, CA: Sage Publications.
Benedikt, M. (1991). Cyberspace: Some proposals. In M. Benedikt (Ed.), *Cyberspace: First steps* (pp. 119–224). Cambridge, MA: MIT Press.

Bush, V. (1945). As we may think. *The Atlantic Monthly, 176*(1), 101–108.
Chess, S., & Shaw, A. (2015). A conspiracy of fishes, or, how we learned to stop worrying about #GamerGate and embrace hegemonic masculinity. *Journal of Broadcasting & Electronic Media, 59*(1), 208–220.
Coleman, S., & Blumler, J. G. (2009). *The Internet and democratic citizenship: Theory, practice and policy*. Cambridge: Cambridge University Press.
Ess, C. (1996). *Philosophical perspectives on computer-mediated communication*. Albany, NY: SUNY Press.
Evans, C. (2018). *Broad band: The untold story of the women who made the internet*. New York, NY. Penguin Random House.
Fernback, J. (1997). "The individual within the collective: Virtual ideology and the realization of collective principles." In S. G. Jones (Ed.), *Virtual culture: Identity and communication in cybersociety* (pp. 36–54). Thousand Oaks, CA: Sage.
Goffman, E. (1959). *The presentation of self in everyday life*. New York, NY: Random House.
Haas, A. M., & Eble, M. F. (Eds.). (2018). *Key theoretical frameworks: Teaching technical communication in the twenty-first century*. Logan: Utah State University Press.
Herring, S. C. (1993). Gender and democracy in computer-mediated communication. *Electronic Journal of Communication, 3*(2). http://www.cios.org/EJCPUBLIC/003/2/00328.HTML
Jenkins, H., & Thorburn, D. (2004). *Democracy and new media*. Cambridge, MA: MIT Press.
Johnson, S. (1997). *Interface culture: How new technology transforms the way we create and communicate*. New York, NY: Basic Books.
Katz, S. B. (1992). The ethic of expediency: Classical rhetoric, technology, and the Holocaust. *College English, 54*(3), 255–275.
Koebler, J., & Cox, J. (2008, August 23). "Here's how Facebook is trying to moderate its two billion users." *Motherboard*. Retrieved from motherboard.vice.com/en_us/article/xwk9zd/how-facebook-content-moderation-works
KotakuInAction. (2019). Rules. *Code of conduct for KotakuInAction*. Retrieved from https://www.reddit.com/r/KotakuInAction/wiki/rules#wiki_5._we_are_not_your_personal_army
Levy, S. (1984). *Hackers: Heroes of the computer revolution*. Garden City, NY: Anchor Press/Doubleday.
Mortensen, T. E. (2016). Anger, fear, and games: The long event of# GamerGate. *Games and Culture, 13*(8), 787–806.
National Society of Professional Engineers. (1961). Code of ethics for engineers. Retrieved from http://ethics.iit.edu/ecodes/node/3262
National Society of Professional Engineers. (2018). NSPE code of ethics for engineers. *History of the Code of Ethics for Engineers*. Retrieved from https://www.nspe.org/resources/ethics/code-ethics/history-code-ethics-engineers
Postigo, H. (2009). America online volunteers: Lessons from an early co-production community. *International Journal of Cultural Studies, 12*(5), 451–469.
Quinn, Z. (2017). *Crash override: How GamerGate (nearly) destroyed my life, and how we can win the fight against online hate*. New York, NY: Hachette.

Raymond, E. (1999). The cathedral and the bazaar. *Knowledge, Technology, and Policy, 12*(3), 23–49.

Rheingold, H. (2000). *The virtual community: Homesteading on the electronic frontier* (Revised edition). Cambridge, MA: MIT Press (Original work published in 1993).

The WELL. (2019). *The WELL.* Retrieved from https://www.well.com/about-2/

Tufekci, Z. (2013). "Not this one": Social movements, the attention economy, and microcelebrity networked activism. *American Behavioral Scientist, 57*(7), 848–870.

Tufekci, Z. (2017). *Twitter and tear gas: The power and fragility of networked protest.* New Haven, CT: Yale University Press.

Turkle, S. (1995). *Life on the screen: Identity in the age of the internet.* New York, NY: Simon & Schuster.

Warnick, B. (2002). *Critical literacy in a digital age: Technology, rhetoric, and the public interest.* Mahwah, NJ: Lawrence Erlbaum Associates.

Withers, R. (2018, August). Inside the semiprivate Facebook Groups where people shame others' weddings. *Slate.* Retrieved from https://slate.com/technology/2018/08/wedding-shaming-facebook-groups-are-a-little-harmless-judgmental-fun.html

World Medical Association. (2018). History. Retrieved from https://www.wma.net/who-we-are/history/

Zittrain, J. (2008). *The future of the Internet—And how to stop it.* New Haven, CT: Yale University Press.

4 Finding Effective Moderation Practices on Twitch

Tabitha M. London, Joey Crundwell, Marcy Bock Eastley, Natalie Santiago, and Jennifer Jenkins

Introduction

Researchers have documented online harassment across the Internet, with gendered harassment against women being of particular note for our study. Such discussions often explore elements of anonymity, platforms, and rhetorical dynamics including asynchronous and synchronous communication (Herring, 1999; Poland, 2016). Addressing harassment against women is complicated by many factors as incidents like GamerGate and other misogynistic and targeted movements have shown. One popular conception of the Internet is that it promises anonymity and space to reinvent identity. However, Poland (2016) offers evidence to show that societal roles and cultural norms, whether tied to gender, race, sexuality, or any other facet of identity, are very much still in place in online environments. This concept of offline sociocultural influence in online spaces is, of course, not new. Herring (1999) established in her analysis of interaction in an IRC (Internet Relay Chat) and listserv that "gender stereotyping and gender-based discrimination carrying over from the 'real world' are free to operate" (p. 152).

Alongside discussions of harassment targeting women, scholars have begun to argue that the role of the collective in online social spaces is important to consider with regard to collaborative moderation of toxic behavior. Milner (2013) argues for engagement, saying that countering trolling and antagonistic behavior on 4chan and reddit results in richer interaction than simply suppressing such discourse (p. 62); "publics need counterpublics; trolls need countertrolls" (p. 88). Similarly, Gillespie (2018) acknowledges the need for balance when moderating disruptive behavior and content along with the complexities that come with determining what to moderate and when. Gillespie identifies moderation as a social responsibility and calls on all stakeholders to recognize their role as custodians of the Internet. These ideas of engagement and social responsibility are, of course, at odds with the phrase "don't feed the trolls," which is still accepted by many users of online spaces as a guiding principle for online interactions. Scholars such as Poland (2016) argue that such statements disempower users and encourage the status quo (p. 62).

Our research of the online streaming platform Twitch builds on the work of Poland and others. Based on our observations of four Twitch livestreamers who use the platform for livestreamed video game play, we assert that ignoring harassment, vitriolic language, and sexism online has serious consequences for user participation. Much of the Internet is no longer defined by clear lines of division the way popular online spaces of the past were. Where forums, chat rooms, and other participatory sites were once a final destination for users, where a person's activities were exclusive to that site, the pervasiveness of social media and sites like Twitch means that users might hop from one space to another in the space of a minute. A person might see a retweet of a viral video clip from Twitch on their Twitter timeline, which may lead them to the Twitch stream that the clip came from, where they might then click on the Twitch streamer's social media links to learn more about them. Twitch-specific users also find new streamers by Twitch's own recommendations, browsing categories related to their interests, searching for specific games or types of games, or when a streamer hosts another streamer's channel, which is a form of recommending content. With this frequent and fluid movement, users often shift among roles and explore a variety of spaces (Phillips & Milner, 2017); harassment can bleed across communities, channels, and platforms, creating continuous cycles of toxicity in these spaces.

As a platform, Twitch further complicates our understanding of moderating harassment due to several factors: cross-pollination, platform-provided moderation tools, and the burden of moderation placed on content creators (streamers). We define cross-pollination as the movement between channels, with users bringing the norms and expectations (both positive and negative) of previous channels and "seeding" the new channel with behavior shaped by the culture of the previous channel or channels. Platform-provided tools for moderation include bots, administrative powers to time-out and ban users, and mediation from global moderators and administrators when necessary. Even with these tools, the burden of moderation is on the streamer, who has to produce their own chat rules, designate their own moderators, manage bans, and cultivate a community culture that reinforces the rules and guidelines they set forth. With this chapter, we set out to examine the moderation of gendered harassment on Twitch, specifically asking what multilayered moderation practices look like on the platform and what strategies seem most effective in the channels of women streamers. We build on previous scholarship that has addressed politeness (Graham, 2017) and general moderation strategies (Seering, Kraut, & Dabbish, 2017) on the platform. By further examining the moderation practices of Twitch streamers and the tools available to them, it is our desire to begin the work of understanding how moderation practices inform and shape these varied and thriving communities and what the implications might be for other online communities across the Internet.

Twitch, a subsidiary of Amazon, hosts an average of one million viewers daily, capturing higher peak Internet traffic than sites like Facebook and Amazon's own site ("Twitch Jobs," 2018). Content ranges from video game play (the most popular content on the site) to creative and IRL (in real life) streams ("Twitch Statistics and Charts" 2018). The site consists of individual channels managed by streamers, some of whom make their living off revenue earned from subscriptions, donations, and sponsored content. Twitch users form communities around these channels due to the participatory nature of the site. Alongside the stream is a chat window, which allows users to interact by posting text messages and emotes (Twitch-specific emojis). Through the chat feature and donations, users can interact with the streamer. User engagement on this site is unique, in part, due to the synchronous nature of livestreaming and the adjacent chat feature.

One of the greatest challenges facing Twitch streamers is the management of harassment due to the responsibility the platform places on them in regards to moderating their channel while producing live content. In particular, women and minorities face habitual harassment (Campbell, 2016; Fagone, 2015). Webcams are used in most channels, and the streamer is the literal face of the channel and community and can therefore be exposed to vitriolic and aggressive messages. These streamers are regularly engaged in a balancing act between fostering their communities and managing disruptive behaviors, which can undermine the very content of their channels. Through a careful analysis of four Twitch streamers, our research demonstrates the effectiveness of several different moderation strategies. Most notably, we posit that direct streamer engagement with disruptive users coupled with the fostering of a community that will do the same offers a model for effectively managing gendered harassment and aggression online.

Methodology

Through livestreamed recordings and Twitch and channel-specific policies, we examined practices occurring within four distinct communities. We received approval from our institution's Institutional Review Board to capture livestreamed and publicly available content on Twitch. Our research questions asked whether women streamers received gendered harassment in this space, how that harassment manifested itself, and how these streamers addressed such harassment. By studying the streamed activities of these four women streamers, we observed, recorded, and analyzed instances of harassment and the moderation practices used to address them.

Written Policies

Practices aimed at mitigating harassment are typically informed by platform policies and channel-specific rules. Prior to observing participants, we gathered a baseline of moderation tools and support documentation. Twitch's "Terms of Service" (2018) and "Community Guidelines" (2018) provide expectations for user conduct. Both detail unacceptable behavior on the platform including illegal activity, violence, hateful conduct, the sharing of private information, and the regulation of sexual content. Consequences for violating these policies include temporary or permanent removal from the site and its services. Twitch also provides a "How to Manage Harassment in Chat" article in the Help Center (2018). Additionally, most streamers provide a set of chat rules either posted below their streams or as a pop-up message that appears upon entering their chat. Similar to the platform-provided information, streamers indicate prohibited behaviors. Comparing this information enabled us to gauge moderation provided by Twitch relative to the moderation practices of individual streamers.

Streamer Selection

This study assumed that harassment occurs frequently enough in online spaces that it would be easy to capture on Twitch, and our objective was to look at how such instances are moderated and managed. Given the prevalence of gendered harassment, we chose to focus our efforts specifically on female-identifying streamers. We observed activities of four streamers (20 hours each) assumed to experience some level of harassment in the Twitch environment.

We wanted popular and professional streamers—we define professional streamers as those who maintain a consistent schedule, stream a significant amount, and whose primary income comes from their streaming activities—offering some level of predictably scheduled streaming activities to facilitate data collection. We chose four women from three countries who play a variety of games, with a range of 350,000–800,000 followers, channel views in excess of ten million, and at least four years of experience streaming on Twitch. We determined that games in the online shooter genre such as *PUBG*, *Overwatch*, and *Fortnite* provided likely opportunities to observe harassment due to their emphasis on competition. Therefore, all four streamers played at least one of these games. We have assigned the pseudonyms Freya, Alruna, Sigrun, and Kara to our four streamers to protect their anonymity.

Each streamer has a slightly different streaming strategy, level of interaction, and differing moderation strategies. Perhaps the single greatest distinction among the streamers is their approach to balancing gameplay with community interaction. Freya and Alruna are similar in that they emphasize gameplay over constant interaction with viewers, while Kara and Sigrun seem to value community engagement over gameplay. Examining moderation practices, we recognized Freya as having a well-moderated channel, while the others were not particularly noted in this regard. Through observing these four streamers, we were able to catalogue and analyze moderation behaviors for individuals with similar demographics (including age and language spoken) and histories on the site but varied personalities and differing approaches to streaming.

Recorded Livestreams

As we were examining community norms, we chose to remain observers in this space, so as not to potentially disrupt the ecology of the channels. We recorded the selected streamers for 20 hours each at various times throughout January and February 2018. In order to capture our desired gameplay genre, we occasionally had to rely on archived streams accessible via individual channels rather than recording the livestreams.

While watching the recorded streams, we specifically focused on identifying instances of harassment and moderation. While the language captured was jarring, we chose to report explicit content without censor to accurately represent the harassment and resulting experience for all involved. Within chat, harassment included disruptive comments or images unrelated to gameplay or the stream.

Limitations

Our research was intentionally limited to observation of the selected streamers. We chose to study depth rather than breadth of experience and did not want to influence behavior by acting as participants ourselves. While we invited personal interviews with the streamers, we received no replies, possibly due to the streamers' popularity and the time limitation of this study. We also chose to limit our results to trends and examples of prevalent behaviors. As patterns emerged, we began collecting and coding only obviously moderated activities or unique occurrences. Due to automated deletion via Twitch moderation tools, some harassment activities were immediately deleted and unavailable for observation. In these cases, we analyzed the moderation based on context and moderator or streamer commentary.

Findings: Harassment and Moderation

The language of Twitch's "About" page establishes the site as a "community where millions of people and thousands of interests collide in a beautiful explosion of video games, pop culture, and conversation" (2017). However, we found toxicity present on the site. From individuals posting harassing messages in chat to organized attempts targeting streamers, harassment exists on the platform. Video game websites and sources like *The New York Times* have published multiple articles discussing the impact of swatting, racism, and harassment of marginalized groups on the platform (Campbell, 2016; Fagone, 2015). As a note to readers, the following section includes examples that contain explicit, hateful, and sexual language.

Gendered Harassment

Harassment of women on Twitch manifests itself in both familiar and sometimes unique ways, occurring most frequently in the IRC channel. Our study documented various forms of harassment including comments directly about gender ("Chat, is [Freya] a boy or a girl?"), unsolicited comments on appearance ("U always look so creepy when ur eyes move like that"), and sexually explicit remarks ("you are sexy," "show boobs," "you have nice boobs," and "my Brazillian friend rafael wants to smell you"). Our observation of moderation across the four channels showed users openly commenting about the respective streamer's gender, often with implicit surprise or intrigue ("Is that a girl gamer," "it's a girl!" "Fun to see a girl play"). These comments did not occur as frequently as unsolicited remarks on appearance or messages with sexually charged content, which were sometimes more pervasive and aggressive ("Are u a prnstar cause i just cummed 4 times and still beating my meat," "ARE THOU A T h o t ... ANSWER ME YOU WHORE"). All users (streamers, moderators, and viewers) on Twitch are exposed to vitriol, hate, and sexism when these comments are posted in chat and allowed to persist. Due to the seamless nature of Twitch (viewers may easily move between channels), such behavior and discourse sometimes pervade the space, crossing from one community to the next. Users often reference coming from other channels when entering chat and use emotes from other channels, marking their membership in other communities. In fluid environments like this where boundaries/lines are not as readily drawn as other spaces and platforms, the potential for harassment to expand and impact users seems even greater. For example, a user banned for harassing a streamer in their channel can enter any other channel and continue the same behavior there, or even direct users in the new channel back to the channel where they were originally banned. Many popular streamers, all four of our subjects included, also include links to their social media accounts on their channel, meaning a banned user can continue their harassment on multiple other platforms with one simple click. We observed gendered harassment targeting women to varying degrees in each of the four selected channels, and it was prevalent enough to suppose a sense of frequency not only in the channels but across the platform.

Moderation Tools

Part of what makes Twitch unique as a platform is the potential for users to interact with streamers synchronously via chat. Twitch grants its users this interaction as it encourages participation and community growth. However, this affordance presents many complications for streamers wishing to regulate activity on their channels. In fact, streamers who do not regulate the discourse from their communities may find themselves with a toxic following and could even be in violation of Twitch's guidelines. Further complicating moderation on Twitch is the nature of chat rooms. Depending on the number of concurrent viewers, any channel's chats can see high-volume traffic, with multiple messages from hundreds of participants posted in chat per second.

While Twitch provides its users with conduct guidelines, they have historically left much of the enforcement up to streamers, providing various tools for moderation and the opportunity for multitiered moderation strategies. See Figures 4.1 and 4.2 for a description of moderation roles and tools available on Twitch. In addition to Twitch's guidelines and moderation tools, streamers often provide rules for their channels. Channel rules tend to reflect Twitch's policies, but streamers may shape them to serve the needs of the particular channel and its community. These rules provide a framework of acceptable and unacceptable behavior and discourse in the channel, often prohibiting the posting of links, political and religious discussion, and the bad-mouthing of streamers and moderators. We commonly found requests to "please be respectful"

Hierarchy of Moderation on Twitch
Administrators - Twitch staff who enforce policies and *Terms of Service* across the platform.
Global Moderators - Experienced users with the same privileges of a channel moderator but platform-wide.
Streamers - Channel owners with access to various moderation tools *see following table.
Channel Moderators or "mods" - Users (generally unpaid) selected by streamer whose primary function is to help moderate the chat. Moderators have the ability to timeout or ban viewers and have access to various commands affecting participation in the channel chat.

Figure 4.1 Hierarchy of moderation on Twitch, by T. London, 2018.

Streamer Moderation Tools/Options
Bots - Programmable tools which automatically perform tasks in chat such as reminding viewers of channel rules and purging content.
Chat Modes - Streamers and moderators may place the channel chat in follower-only mode, subscriber only mode, and emote only mode, affecting user participation. They may also use the "Slow" command, which affects how often viewers can post messages.
Timeouts - Streamers and moderators may temporarily ban viewers from chat.
Bans - Streamers and moderators may permanently ban viewers from chat.

Figure 4.2 Streamer moderation tools/options, by T. London, 2018.

in channels across Twitch. However, channel rules are often written with language lacking explicit direction and fail to mention repercussions for violation. Despite the multiple avenues of moderation the platform provides, much of the burden for regulation and enforcement rests on streamers, their communities, and general viewers who also have the ability to block and report fellow users. While Twitch's approach to moderation allows streamers flexibility in addressing disruptive behavior, it also opens the door to inconsistent moderation strategies, which may make mitigating harassment more difficult.

Moderation Practices

In the 80 hours of livestreaming that we viewed, we observed the implications of subtle changes and approaches to moderation on the levels and kinds of harassment received on a platform where the chat feature opens the door to hateful exchanges, hyperlinks to inappropriate content, and harassment campaigns. AutoMod (a Twitch-provided tool that automatically blocks inappropriate content), bots, and moderators serve to limit these messages, but neither algorithm nor human can filter and address every inappropriate utterance. Preventing harassment before it enters a channel can be difficult—as many channels do not regularly employ subscriber-only chat, nor would this prevent harassment entirely. The only true filter preventing disruptive viewers from posting messages is the requirement of a Twitch account, which is free and set up with ease.

Regardless of the platform's policies, streamers are left with much of the burden of enforcement, which complicates their role even further. The primary purpose of Twitch is to provide entertainment for its users. Streamers play the role of entertainer and content creator on a platform designed with viewer participation in mind. This places pressure on streamers to balance entertainment and encourage participation in chat while also enforcing the rules of the platform and their own channel.

Our observation of Freya, Alruna, Sigrun, and Kara revealed a range of moderation strategies/moderative responses. For example, Freya's channel has explicit rules for the chat (including a statement prohibiting hate speech), which are regularly enforced. In comparison, Kara's chat rules emphasize participation and positivity and fail to mention consequences for disruptive behavior; as a result, we rarely observed corrective behavior in her channel. Only a handful of messages were deleted in the observed hours and countless messages were posted by users (nonsubscribers and subscribers) commenting on Kara's appearance in both nonsexual and sexual ways. More than 100 of the logged messages were sexually explicit, such as "you are so hot," "that ass," and "Get the tittys out." Despite these messages, Kara chose not to regulate chat. While Alruna does not provide many channel rules, she and her moderators timed out disruptive users as much as, if not more than, Freya. Both Alruna and Sigrun fall somewhere in between Freya and Kara. Both have rules for their channels, but acts of moderation appear at times sporadic and inconsistent; however, harassment does not go entirely unchecked. To account for differences in moderation, it seems possible that some streamers believe strict regulation of chat—and participation—will limit the success and growth of their channels, which they may rely on for regular income. Another possibility is that streamers do not know how to moderate their chats in a way that would mitigate harassment or that they believe ignoring harassment is the best option. It may also be that streamers do not have the appropriate resources to consistently address harassment, such as not having enough moderators online to assist.

If Alruna and Sigrun represent a middle ground in moderation, Freya and Kara represent opposite ends of the moderation range we observed. For example, users frequently bombarded Kara's channel chat with comments on her appearance that were often sexual in nature. These comments did not generally elicit response from either Kara, moderators, or other viewers. At times, viewers would goad each other on or build off each other's inappropriate comments such as when one viewer said, "Do your buttons not work on your shirt?" and another replied, "You might as well get them out" or when a viewer called attention to Kara's appearance saying, "I see your............like a porn star" and a second viewer said, "hahaha @viewer." On multiple occasions, we observed viewers responding to sexually explicit messages with humor and escalation—a behavior that appears normalized in the channel.

We did note a few occasions where viewers called for moderation. In Example 1, Sc00terXX posted messages in chat for some time, trying to attract Kara's attention. The initial comments went unaddressed by the community, Kara, and her moderators for some time (ellipses indicate intervening messages in chat):

Example 1:
Sc00terXX: @Kara I Love youooo
...
illpandas: BAN HIM PLS
9watched: (emote) that guy is scary

Sc00terXX comments up to this point included "I love you," "Why are u so pretty," and "I'm just going to say it but.....your so fucken hot." Sc00terXX's comments were persistent and spammed the chat. It wasn't until nearly 30 minutes of messages in chat that a user called for someone to ban the disruptive user. Part of what makes this instance interesting is that after illpandas called for moderation, another user, 9watched, commented on the exchange, reiterating that Sc00terXX's comments were unwelcome. This suggests that while many inappropriate messages go unchallenged in Kara's chat, not all users are comfortable with such content; however, they do not seem to be emboldened until someone else, moderator or fellow user, takes that first moderative step.

While observing Kara's channel, only a handful of messages in chat—from separate users—were removed/deleted. Several of the messages were deleted during the same livestream, which may suggest that a certain threshold of harassment had been reached from the perspective of the active moderators. The comments deleted were especially sexually explicit in nature and represent content even beyond the norm of more general sexual remarks normally observed in the channel. The deleted comments include "Are u a prnstar cause i just cummed 4 times and still beating my meat" and "id fuck ur brains out mmm." On occasion, Kara would verbally react to especially determined users in chat. One such user, mo_the_turtle, persisted with asking who was in the house with Kara, posting over 25 messages in the exchange and finally saying "do u have a roommate? @Kara." No moderators stepped in to address these remarks though; instead, Kara verbally addressed mo_the_turtle saying, "When I'm ready to tell you about that kind of stuff mo_the_turtle I will 100% I'm just not yet..." At that point, mo_the_turtle reluctantly wrote "ok" and stopped participating in chat. However, moderative acts from Kara and her moderators were infrequent, and much of the harassment observed in her channel went unchecked. Neither Kara nor her moderators made full use of the tools available to them to address harassment. Due to this lack of moderation and clear channel rules, harassment persisted in the channel, often resulting in the chat being so overrun by sexually explicit content (and other disruptive commentary) that more appropriate discourse was lost in chat and, we speculate, was even actively discouraged by the kinds of messages being posted and allowed in Kara's channel.

In comparison, Freya's channel demonstrated consistent and dynamic moderation in response to gendered harassment. We observed multiple examples where Freya or her moderators directly addressed disruptive behavior in chat. Moderation occurred frequently in chat and followed similar patterns of behavior on the part of the moderators and Freya—a norm of moderation seems present in this channel. Moderators consistently removed overtly aggressive, violent, persistent, and sexual comments from chat including spam and remarks or questions about Freya's appearance, with users generally receiving a time-out. Deleted messages include "will you be my waifu" (Japanese nerd culture slang for "wife"), "I'm slapping u," "yes, she has a charismatic face," "Hey Freya – I think I saw you on OKCupid...Very Cute ^_^," "u suk," "BEGONE T H O T" (derogatory slang for "that ho over there"), and "ugly dyke."

Generally, otherwise questionable or confrontational discourse did not immediately result in a time-out. Instead, moderators would engage with the viewer, redirecting or correcting. For example, one viewer asked Freya, "do you have a tic disorder," and one of the moderators responded by saying, "question is kinda rude." While the viewer's comment may not reach the level of harassment, the moderator identified it as inappropriate and chose to respond in a way—calling the comment out—that would not cut off the viewer's participation in the space in the same way that a time-out or ban would. We observed this kind of moderative check in chat many times in Freya's channel from several moderators, which suggests an underlying strategy specific to the channel probably guided by Freya who behaved similarly on several occasions. Example 2 demonstrates the dynamics at play when streamers choose to directly address problematic content in chat.

Example 2:

silversmoke: How come every time I stop by this stream , she seems like she's in pain? Reminds me of that girl on Twilight. I never see a smile or hear a laugh. Maybe I just come at the wrong times?

...

blitz5: silversmoke maybe because life sucks?

Freya (verbal): "How come every time I stop by the stream she seems like she's in pain? Maybe because you cause me such great pain every time you show up. Maybe it's you. I'm allergic to you."

BookerLIVE [sub]: rekt

...

DaBestCanadian [sub]: oof
Zeus789 [sub]: damn
Sorrowfulravens
[Twitch Prime]: Hahaha

...

silversmoke: Freya aww sorry to hear that then. Caught you in a few stream with talkingdonut, guess its just me. Well, hope ya feel better.

...

Freya (verbal): "Yeah, I don't know. We already had like this whole discussion today about people expecting streamers to be smiling constantly while playing video games. And how it's an unrealistic expectation to have. Cause I'm sure if you like set up a camera and recorded your own face while you played video games...I don't know, I wonder how much—I wonder if you'd be surprised by how little you actually smile when you're playing a competitive shooter that requires intense focus and listening skills like..."

In this example, Freya takes the time to speak to silversmoke, which essentially places the stream on hold for a moment. By doing this and saying things like "Maybe it's you," she draws viewer attention to silversmoke's messages and sets a standard for what is allowed in chat. Her initial response is reacted upon by other viewers in the chat favorably, with humor and the sense that silversmoke has been corrected or put in their place. Fellow viewer responses such as "rekt" and "oof" further place silversmoke's message on display. When silversmoke posts again, somewhat apologetically ("Freya aww sorry to hear that then"), Freya continues to engage with dialogue, pointing out the unrealistic cultural expectation that streamers should always appear happy. She is able to address silversmoke's comment live, shaping expectations in her community in real time. The goal is not to silence viewers, but to realistically allow them to participate within the norms established by the streamer. From examples like this, we believe that Freya, and by extension her moderators, believe in striking a balance between allowing viewers a space to express themselves and moderation. Her strategy draws a line of what is acceptable in the channel but does not shy away from stronger acts of moderation like time-outs when necessary. We noted that Freya spoke directly to disruptive viewers several times during our observations, and found it to be a somewhat frequent act of moderation in her channel, supported by members of the community.

Due to the moderation that occurs in Freya's channel, viewers can quickly gain an understanding of what is acceptable chat behavior. Channel rules are provided in chat and moderators regularly enforce those rules by intercepting harassment and inappropriate content in chat, following the example that Freya has set for them. Freya's previously detailed moderation strategy—of calling out inappropriate behavior and explaining why it is unwelcome or disruptive—does not necessarily alienate offending viewers and allows them to continue participating in the channel as long as they operate within the established rules. We believe that Freya's moderation strategy represents an effective approach for mitigating harassment on Twitch while balancing entertainment and participation. Her strategy requires planning and a commitment to consistency, but it demonstrates that harassment can be addressed and mitigated in online communities. Freya's approach is more successful than Kara's, which lets harassment generally go unchecked. The fact that several Twitch users commented on Freya's community and the consistency of moderation in her channel also speaks to the need for moderation in this space. In one exchange, a viewer wrote, "this is one of the nicest chats ive ever ben to, to be honest lol," and another agreed, saying, "its because its actually a modded chat @viewer lol." Some viewers on Twitch do recognize the need for moderation and express appreciation for the community Freya has fostered. This offers an interesting contrast to the viewer who entered Kara's channel and posted a message testing the freedom of the chat saying, "Kara plays...with herself" and then followed with "I was expecting a timeout" seconds later. This viewer expected to be timed out because they had, presumably, enough experience on the platform to know the conventions of the space. This example also demonstrates the fluidity of viewer movement across Twitch—channel rules do carry weight in that they build expectations viewers then bring to other channels. It's channels like Freya's that help to set standards of moderation and show that harassment can and should be managed. The example set in Freya's channel is, unfortunately, the exception as many channels on Twitch reflect uneven moderation strategies such as those found in Sigrun's and Alruna's channels or the extreme found in Kara's channel. However, Freya's channel does show that more civil spaces can be fostered on the platform through active moderation.

Community Moderation

While Twitch provides policies, guidelines, and tools to enforce appropriate use and to address disruptive users, the power of human interaction cannot be ignored. During our study, we observed many forms of harassment and noted the limitations of the platform's tools and algorithms as well as shortcomings in streamers' moderation strategies. Analyses of two of the selected channels demonstrate another form of moderation, what we are calling "community moderation." We observed community members, both subscribers and nonsubscribers, actively addressing harassment, engaging with trolls, and calling for formal moderation, particularly in Freya's channel. Example 3 illustrates how community members sometimes work together to mitigate problematic messages.

Example 3:
GoldieBoi: is that a grill? <message deleted>
...
GoldieBoi: a gamer gril? <message deleted>
...
GoldieBoi: your thicc <message deleted>
...
NotJohnny (sub): (KaraFail emote)
Freeze81: (FailFish emote)
4reel: ban this idiot jesus
...
BurritoGainz (sub): @GoldieBoi youre a creep

In this example, GoldieBoi's offensive messages are clearly meant to draw attention from both viewers and Freya. The user asks if Freya is a "grill" (slang for "girl"), calling into question her gender based on her appearance, then asks if she is a "gamer gril," which is generally a derogatory phrase in gaming culture implying that the subject is not a "true" or "serious" gamer. When GoldieBoi has established Freya's gender as female, they then comment on her appearance, calling her "thicc," which in this space is typically used as slang to sexualize the recipient. GoldieBoi was successful in garnering attention as the messages were eventually deleted when GoldieBoi was temporarily timed out or banned by the moderators. 4reel called out GoldieBoi while also asking for response from moderators.

Similarly, BurritoGainz, a subscriber to the channel, says to GoldieBoi, "youre a creep." 4reel's and BurritoGainz's contributions to the exchange establish acceptable corrective discourse in the community—publicly calling out the inappropriate behavior. Resorting to name calling, often considered juvenile or immature in other contexts, is in this community an effective method of mitigating harassment. While purely speculative, we believe this may be due to the fact that this kind of language draws attention from other users and may result in an aggregation of name calling from several users, ultimately drawing the attention of mods or the streamer. This example is important in that it demonstrates how community members apart from streamers and moderators have agency to directly respond to offensive utterances and that they expect streamers and moderators to use the available tools in response. Multiple viewers responded to GoldieBoi's messages through typed responses and emote use, admonishing GoldieBoi's messages, reacting with "Lul," and even correcting GoldieBoi's grammar. Because this discourse occurs in the public space of the channel chat, both viewers participating in chat and lurkers (viewers who watch the stream but rarely, if ever, contribute to chat) are witness to (1) what the community deems inappropriate behavior and (2) response to disruptive messages which may be modeled when confronting future instances of harassment.

Freya's community has normalized the corrective behavior seen in Example 3, which appears to be the result of modeling users of authority (streamers and moderators). Freya will call out disruptive viewers, but mostly relies on her moderators to maintain a civil chat. Moderators in her channel were quite active, with two or more observed in chat at any given time. Viewers praised moderators and expressed surprise and appreciation at how welcoming and helpful the community was. This reflects the community Freya has fostered where both moderators and subscribers frequently welcome new viewers and seek to engage in conversations regardless of status within the channel. With the number of moderators in chat and their level of participation in both addressing disruptive behavior and general chat discourse, they set a daily precedent for acceptable behavior in the channel. This is also a reminder that moderation consists of more than the tools available and that the human component should not be ignored.

In general, moderators across channels correct behavior through simple statements ("stop," "don't go there") and discourse that establishes consequences ("stop being creepy or you won't be able to chat here anymore"). Viewers then model statements like these, particularly in channels where the community plays a significant role in moderation. Example 4 demonstrates how viewers in Freya's channel address offensive content in a manner that closely resembles moderator behavior.

Example 4:

xGamingbrox: I cream myself and I'm 5 inches

...

Extremebean (sub): @xGamingbrox tmi dude

...

xGamingbrox: @Extremebean sorry I'll stop trolling I appreciate the appropriate response

...

Extremebean: @xGamingbrox yeah just pelase abide to the rules of this chat

...

xGamingbrox: Ok np

...

xGamingbrox: Ngl if you have [guest_streamer] on your team it's a guaranteed L she so bad that even a sloth could beat [guest_streamer] but Freya a great Moira even tho Moira the easiest hero <message deleted>

Teh_Truth (mod): don't be rude

This exchange demonstrates how willing Freya's community is to correct and redirect disruptive behavior rather than have moderators immediately ban viewers like xGamingbrox. After being confronted, xGamingbrox posts a message giving the impression that his behavior may change. In response, Extremebean, a frequent participant in the channel, calls for xGamingbrox to "abide to the rules of this chat." Directing a user to the chat rules is a rhetorical move moderators regularly employ in many channels. Extremebean's response is both appropriate given the context and demonstrates Extremebean's sense of responsibility in maintaining appropriate discourse in the chat. However, xGamingbrox goes on to dismiss the streamer Freya was playing with at the time as well as minimize Freya's skill in the game *Overwatch*. A moderator then stepped in, deleting the disruptive messages and added "don't be rude."

Examples 3 and 4 show that viewers, regardless of status, have the rhetorical ability to challenge and admonish problematic messages and viewers seeking to harass streamers and disrupt their communities. This kind of community moderation is not a strategy that streamers or moderators can practice, necessarily. It is the result of an apparently unspoken, collaborative effort in which moderators, subscribers, and general viewers enforce the explicitly stated chat rules and the implied community norms by way of social correction. While it is conceivable that a streamer might engineer a community with built-in community moderation, in the communities that we observed it seemed to be naturally occurring among participants, due to the streamer's own personality and approach to moderation. On Twitch, many channels have 1,000+ concurrent viewers (some boast upward of 20,000+) with the potential for hundreds of viewers actively participating in chat. Depending on the flow of a channel's chat, it is impossible for moderators to delete every message or time out every disruptive viewer. Inevitably, some offensive messages will slip by in chat. In the case of Freya's channel, the community has stepped up to address this gap in moderation. The frequency with which these community members address offensive content sets this channel apart from the other three. Due to its impact, we believe community moderation is a significant rhetorical model for study and an interesting part of multilayered moderation strategies in online spaces.

Conclusion

Ignoring harassment results in the spreading of misogyny, hate, and sexual content online. And enough scholarship has shown that ignoring harassment is neither an acceptable nor an ethical response (Gillespie, 2018; Milner, 2013; Poland, 2016). When it comes to Twitch, both the platform and streamers have an obligation to address harassment in this space. Channels like the ones we observed demonstrate that harassment, particularly gendered harassment, is very much alive on the Internet. And while the task of grappling with this reality may seem difficult, Freya, her team of moderators, and her community prove that moderating harassment with consistent and transparent measures has an impact.

A significant factor in what makes Twitch unique as a platform is the position of the streamer as a central speaker—as rhetor—with access to a variety of moderation tools. Because Twitch leaves so much of the responsibility for moderation on streamers, they must acknowledge the role they play and the significance of the available tools; otherwise, ignoring harassment continues a cycle of disruption and vitriol present on so much of the Internet. If streamers ignore harassment in their own channels, they increase the likelihood that their viewers will cross over to other channels and repeat the same behavior. As our observations show, creating rules for the community and enforcing those rules with a unified team of moderators can work to curtail harassment and set expectations for acceptable discourse in this space.

While Freya's channel represents a small space on a much larger platform, impactful moderation is possible on Twitch. In some ways, Freya is fortunate to operate on a platform that offers multiple tools for moderation, enabling her to strategize ways to address harassment, tailoring moderation to her channel and community. Freya's approach to moderation shows that channels with explicit rules and consistent enforcement address harassment with greater immediacy and effect. What streamers and moderators failed to address with consistency across the four channels continued to occur, often without comment from other viewers. And while explicit rules make public the kind of behavior and discourse allowed in a channel, enforcement of those rules by moderators appears to have the greatest impact on harassment received by streamers. This study of harassment on Twitch has implications for other platforms and social media. The tools Twitch provides are extensive and go beyond what other platforms offer, involving content creators and general viewers in the process of determining inappropriate content and responding to harassment. Is this an ideal model of moderation? Does such an approach encourage social responsibility in users? We think so, but these are only a few of the questions that require further study on this platform. Perhaps harassment cannot be eradicated entirely on the Internet, but consistent moderation can be successful in addressing inappropriate conduct and toxicity.

References

About Twitch. (2017). *Twitch.tv*. Retrieved from https://www.twitch.tv/p/about
Campbell, C. (2016, May 12). Racism, Hearthstone and Twitch. *Polygon*. Retrieved from https://www.polygon.com/features/2016/5/12/11658440/twitch-abuse-hearthstone
Fagone, J. (2015, November 24). The serial swatter. *The New York Times*. Retrieved from https://www.nytimes.com/2015/11/29/magazine/the-serial-swatter.html
Gillespie, T. (2018). *Custodians of the internet: Platforms, content moderation, and the hidden decisions that shape social media*. New Haven, CT: Yale University Press.
Graham, S. L. (2017). Politeness and impoliteness. In W. Bublitz & C. R. Hoffman (Eds.), *Pragmatics of social media*, (pp. 459–491). Berlin: De Gruyter Mouton.
Herring, S. C. (1999). The rhetorical dynamics of gender harassment on-line. *The Information Society, 15*, 151–167.
How to Manage Harassment in Chat. (2018). *Twitch.tv*. Retrieved from https://help.twitch.tv/customer/en/portal/articles/2329145-how-to-manage-harassment
Milner, R. M. (2013). FCJ-156 hacking the social: Internet memes, identity antagonism, and the logic of lulz. *The Fibreculture Journal, 22*. Retrieved from http://twentytwo.fibreculturejournal.org/fcj-156-hacking-the-social-internet-memes-identity-antagonism-and-the-logic-of-lulz
Phillips, W., & Milner, R. M. (2017). *The ambivalent internet: Mischief, oddity, and antagonism online*. Cambridge: Polity.
Poland, B. (2016). *Haters: Harassment, abuse, and violence online*. Lincoln, NE: Potomac Books.

Seering, J., Kraut, R., & Dabbish, L. (2017). Shaping pro and anti-social behavior on Twitch through moderation and example-setting. Proceedings from *2017 ACM Conference on Computer Supported Cooperative Work and Social Computing.* Portland, OR.

Twitch Community Guidelines. (2018). *Twitch.tv.* Retrieved from https://www.twitch.tv/p/legal/community-guidelines/

Twitch Jobs. (2018). *Twitch.tv.* Retrieved from https://www.twitch.tv/p/jobs/

Twitch Statistics and Charts. (2018). *Twitchtracker.com.* Retrieved from https://twitchtracker.com/statistics

Twitch Terms of Service. (2018). *Twitch.tv.* Retrieved from https://www.twitch.tv/p/legal/terms-of-service/

5 A Pedagogy of Ethical Interface Production Based on Virtue Ethics

John R. Gallagher

Introduction

Interfaces govern user actions on the Internet and, specifically, social media platforms. They are, according to media theorist Alexander Galloway (2012), "the point of transition between different mediatic layers within any nested system" (p. 31). On Instagram, the image-sharing platform, life is beautiful because the platform's interface enables and habituates image beautification. Twitter is snarky and deleterious to such a degree that the microblogging platform issued a call-for-proposals to address "healthy metrics" in the spring of 2018. The site asked for ways to "encourage more healthy debate, conversations, and critical thinking" while reducing abuse, spam, and manipulation (Twitter, 2018). The snark that Twitter wants to eliminate is in many ways tied to its interface: the strict character limit that sets Twitter apart from other platforms produces habits of snark, abuse, and harassment.

The habits that arise from these interfaces come from designers, who engage in complex ethical choices. As Selfe and Selfe's "The Politics of the Interface" (1994) argued, computer interface design has "complex political landscapes" (p. 481) that can reproduce "colonial mentalities" (p. 482). Interfaces are not value-neutral technologies. They inscribe thoughts and actions into users, as all technologies do (Johnson-Eilola, 1997). Those who create interfaces and other user design architectures therefore need to consider the complex consequences on users who deploy their interfaces. "The Politics of the Interface" inaugurated a critical turn in writing studies: writing technologies, so crucial to composition teachers and writing theorists, need to have their interfaces and designs interrogated ideologically, politically, and culturally.

The publication of "The Politics of the Interface" (1994) led writing studies scholarship to critique interfaces, templates, and other features of user design (Arola, 2010, 2017; Boyle & Rivers, 2016; Brooke, 2009; Brown & Tarsa, 2018; Carnegie, 2009; Gallagher, 2015; Oswal, 2013; Potts & Salvo, 2017; Rivers & Söderlund, 2016; Selber, 2004; Warnick, 2005). While these scholars either critique interfaces or advocate for speculative design (imagining different types of design), I advocate for not only critical attention but also actual production. As instructors of digital rhetoric, we need to teach students to critique interfaces *and* produce interfaces in responsible ways. Consequently, I reorient this conversation to the *ethical production of interfaces*.

My exigence for this approach is the prevalence of online harassment and trolling (Eckert, 2017; Herring et al., 2002; Jane, 2015; Massanari, 2017, 2018; Phillips, 2015; Rowe, 2015; Sparby, 2017). Addressing this milieu of misogyny, racism, and homophobia requires more than trite calls for civility, which often have resonances of white privilege. Rather than retheorizing digital public spheres, an effort blunted by the U.S. election campaigns of 2016 and 2018, we can alternatively teach students to ethically (re)design interfaces on their screens. To do this, we need, of course, to teach students technical skills of interface design, including HTML, CSS, JavaScript, basic computer coding (e.g. Python, C++, etc.), image manipulation, and wireframing, as well as communicative practices, including creating user personas, work flow techniques, user testing, and content management. But we also need to teach them *ethical approaches* to better inform and complement these technical and social skills. A pedagogy of ethical interface production, I believe, will help students to hone design practices that can reduce the possibility of online harassment and vitriolic exchanges that target women, minorities, the LGBTQIA+ community, and the disability community. An immediate philosophical challenge confronts this pedagogy: if we are teaching students to be ethical producers of interfaces, then what are the ethical paradigms, systems, and foundations we would draw upon? Responding to this question assists digital writing and rhetoric instructors with developing a starting point for classroom discussions of ethics and crafting assignments about ethics.

The rest of this chapter focuses on a pedagogy of ethical interface production. After discussing interfaces as being habit-related, I introduce virtue ethics, an ethical paradigm, that urges habits and character traits over rules or outcomes. Virtue ethics provides the ethical framework for a pedagogy of ethical interface production. Next, I provide a brief case study of Whitney Wolfe Herd, the creator of the mobile software application Bumble. I frame Herd as an exemplar of respect. The Bumble application, I contend, is an example of the way virtues are transposed from an exemplar to an interface. Following this discussion of Herd and Bumble, I describe a pedagogy of ethical interface production, with an emphasis on user testing and continuous redesign. Before concluding, I address the concern of manipulation when designing interfaces.

Interfaces and Habit Formation

Interfaces mediate digital communication. To attend interface design and production in holistic terms, we must accordingly develop a robust definition of interface including but *exceeding* electronic screens. To echo

Boyle, Brown, and Ceraso's (2018) recent argument, "As we cannot locate *the* digital only on a screen or solely in distributed networks, no one encounter with the digital adequately disposes our rhetorical sensibilities towards productive engagements" (p. 257; emphasis in original). Following Boyle, Brown, and Ceraso's lead, I turn to a definition that encompasses design thinking and theory based in and around screens while including objects, people, and habits. Carnegie (2009) takes such a view of interfaces, writing the following of the term:

> Basically, the interface is a place of interaction whether the interactions are between user and computer, user and software, computer and software, user and content, software and content, user and culture, and the user and other users. In fact, it would be impossible to separate out the various interactions as they layer over each other: a user communicating with another user requires interaction with the computer, the software, the graphics, and a set of cultural norms. The interface is the common meeting point and place of interaction for the technological, human, social, and cultural aspects which make up computer-mediated communication and, more specifically, new media.
>
> (p. 165)

Carnegie's approach to interface focuses on screens while having a broader connotation. We can conceive of interfaces as being technical, cultural, political, economic, material, and ethical in nature. Such a perspective is promising for digital ethics because interface, from Carnegie's expansive view, can include the behaviors between users, i.e. people, objects, machines, and algorithms. Screen-based interfaces, such as those on Twitter, become behavioral meeting places between users having discursive exchanges.

If Carnegie's perspective on interfaces locates a relationship that exceeds screens, then, by extension, it accounts for power relations and the ethics of those power relations, including habits. While interfaces do not dictate user behavior, they clearly influence those habits and dispositions. As instructors of design thinking and multimodality (Arola, 2010; Eyman & Ball, 2014; Marback, 2009; Palmeri, 2012; Purdy, 2014), we need not only to have students produce interface affordances and functionalities but also consider the desired habits of possible users as an ethical endeavor. In more pedagogical terms, we ought to blend a focus on interface design, layout, and affordances with conversations surrounding the kinds of habits students want to inculcate in potential users. We need, of course, to advocate for denaturalizing or "defamiliarize[ing] commonsensical impressions of technology in educational settings" (Selber, 2004, p. 88) so that users do not simply accept the interfaces of devices and software as the only way of communicating. But we also need to design pedagogical materials, encourage classroom conversations, and plan active-learning activities that support analysis and production of user habits. The broader issue facing pedagogies of interface design, then, is to consider habit formation when producing interfaces.

When we focus on the broad question of habit and habit formation, we rapidly encounter ethical questions. What kinds of habits should we have students consider? What kinds of habits are appropriate for interface production? What ethical frameworks should we engage to answer these questions? If students are designing and producing interfaces, to what extent are they manipulating users? While I'll address this last question in my conclusion, this set of questions motivates a consideration of effective ethical paradigms when teaching interface design.

Virtue Ethics: An Ethical Paradigm for Interface Production

These questions present a task for instructors: if we aim to develop ethical examinations of interfaces, then we need to buttress our pedagogies with ethical frameworks. Doing so will avoid *ad hoc* approaches that result in students equating the term "ethical" with "personal preference," a concept known as emotivism. Ethical frameworks such as deontology (rule-based ethics) and consequentialism (outcome-based ethics) cannot account for the rapid transformations and mutations of digital media discourse because they are not contingent enough. Deontology is concerned less with the outcomes, in this case the actual habits of users, than an adherence to rules. The equivalent here would result in students strictly considering an interface's affordances rather than the habits developed by users of that interface. For consequentialism, students would consider the outcomes of users' behaviors rather than the affordances themselves—and outcomes cannot be guaranteed. In both cases, the issue of *contingency* arises: the kinds of habits we would need to advocate and teach depend on various contextual factors, including time, location, platform, and exigency.

A lesser known ethical paradigm, called virtue ethics, is contingent enough to provide guidance about what sorts of habits we should teach for interface design and production while still providing normative claims, e.g. *should* or *ought* claims (Colton & Holmes, 2018; Duffy, Gallagher, & Holmes, 2018; Gallagher, 2018). While an entire review of virtue ethics is outside the scope of this chapter, I will provide some brief background for context. Virtue ethics has a long history in Greek philosophy (Aristotle, *Nicomachean Ethics*, 1984), experiencing a revival in the latter part of the 20th and early 21st centuries (see the following for selected pivotal pieces: Annas, 1993; Anscombe, 1958; Foot, 2003; Hursthouse, 1999; MacIntyre, 1984; Slote, 1983, 1992; Vallor, 2016; Zagzebski, 2010). Virtue ethics in composition and rhetoric is somewhat sporadic but nevertheless still attended (Bizzell, 1992; Colton & Holmes, 2016, 2018; Colton, Holmes, & Walwema, 2017; Duffy, 2014, 2017; Duffy, Gallagher, & Holmes, 2018; Friend, 1999; Spigelman, 2001). Feminist theory (Jaggar, 1991), ethics of care (McLaren, 2001), and Buddhist ethics (Goodman, 2015) have picked up—among many others—virtue ethics as a useful framework because it is flexible enough to account for diverse contexts while still providing sources of normativity, i.e. exemplars or people who are worthy of emulation due to their demonstration of a particular virtue or character trait. A crucial thread throughout virtue ethics is the emphasis on virtues as a guide to action and how one ought to behave ethically. This ethical framework can be summarized as drawing on exemplars' virtues or character traits for guidance in ethical decision-making processes.

In a virtue ethics' paradigm, communities try to find exemplars with character traits *worthy of emulation*. In pedagogical terms, instructors would ask students to find character traits the classroom community deems worth of emulation; students would need to come to an agreement about what virtues are worthy of emulation. These character traits provide the foundations for ethical discussions and conversation as well as a shared understanding of what constitutes "ethical" and not simply personal preference. The people who demonstrate virtues, as agreed upon by the classroom community, are considered exemplars, and hence why the framework is contingent yet normative.

Exemplars provide instructors with a normative and contingent way of conceptualizing habits when producing ethical interfaces. People such as Whitney Wolfe Herd, who designed the dating application Bumble that enables women to make first contact for heterosexual matches, can be considered an exemplar of respect. In a less successful example, Dan McComas, founder of the defunct social news aggregator Imzy, might be an exemplar of friendliness. Imzy, branded as a friendly alternative to social news aggregator reddit, was designed by McComas, the former product chief of reddit, to combat the vitriol present in and around reddit. Wolfe Herd and McComas provide us, as instructors, with habits that can, in turn, help inform interface production across the rhetorical canons, including invention, style, arrangement, memory, and delivery.

Pedagogically, using virtues and exemplars as an ethical framework in the classroom usefully avoids formulaic imperatives or outcomes, thereby providing students with the opportunity to address complex ethical issues. Drawing upon virtues and exemplars means that a pedagogy of ethical interface production is not static. Students would design and produce interfaces in multiple, iterative ways with different character traits during the revision process. Students might ask themselves: What does a patient exemplar look like? How does a courageous exemplar act? To respond to these questions, we need to look for actual people who embody these virtues. I'll offer one example in the next section: Wolfe Herd and her feminist application Bumble.

Wolfe Herd as an Exemplar of Respect

Wolfe Herd was formerly a cofounder of the dating application Tinder, which sought to speed up the social mores of dating. Tinder is a known as a "hook up app" dominated by men. Leaving Tinder after suing the company for sexual harassment, Wolfe Herd went on to create Bumble. Bumble is in many ways the "anti-Tinder" dating application. As journalist Leora Yashari (2015) writes, Bumble is "a self-proclaimed feminist dating app where women have to make the first move." In an interview with Yashari (2015), Wolfe Herd says of Bumble:

> If you look at where we are in the current heteronormative rules surrounding dating, the unwritten rule puts the woman a peg under the man—the man feels the pressure to go first in a conversation, and the woman feels pressure to sit on her hands. I don't think there is any denying it. If we can take some of the pressure off the man and put some of that encouragement in the woman's lap, I think we are taking a step in the right direction, especially in terms of really being true to feminism. I think we are the first feminist, or first attempt at a feminist dating app.

Strikingly, Wolfe Herd didn't set out to build a dating application. Instead, she set out to build "a female-only social network 'rooted in compliments and kindness and good behavior'" (Tepper, 2018). Wolfe Herd's Bumble took the opposite approach of Tinder and many other dating applications: to change the habits of users by allowing women to make first contact when dating. She aimed to inculcate the habit of patience in men who used the application. And the application allows for being friends with other people, which Tinder does not (to be fair, Tinder is partnered with a separate application that focuses on friendship). In the end, Wolfe Herd achieved her original purpose anyway.

The Bumble application is an example of an exemplar's virtues, in this case respect and possibly patience, being transposed into the desired habits of an interface. Interface designers consistently draw upon their own experiences, with the Wolfe Herd–Bumble example being no different. Wolfe Herd experienced inappropriate workplace behavior at Tinder. Using her experiences, she produced an interface with desired habits: the interaction between men and women needed to be more respectful. The habit of respect, then, is baked into Bumble's architecture, overtly and covertly shaping users' habits as they navigate Bumble.

While there are many other people that we might hold up as exemplars affecting interfaces, Bumble is a high-profile example that started with the habit *first*. In other words, Wolfe Herd is on the record as wanting to establish a "female-only social network" and not a dating application. The habits informed the interface design, rather than coming after or in tandem with the production of a sleek interface. If we use exemplars that follow Wolfe Herd, then our pedagogies should ask students to consider user habits *before* design concepts and technological affordances. The discussion of ethics comes first, foregrounded as equally if not more important than interface functionalities.

Into the Classroom

I now turn to a concrete discussion of a pedagogy of ethical interface production. Like many other pedagogies, this sort of interface production involves brainstorming ways to wireframe and mock-up user interfaces, which necessarily draws on textual, visual, aural, and haptic modalities. Students can be encouraged to build mock-up interfaces with paper, whiteboards, clay, and other mediums. However, emphasizing virtues and exemplars in pedagogical materials and classroom discussions shifts students' focus from interfaces (things and objects) to designers (people and habits). They need to study how *people* conceive of user behavior and how habits are formed before they mock up any designs. Like Wolfe Herd, students come up with the habits first and try to use affordances to achieve that purpose.

Practically, this project takes about a month of a semester and can be taught in a variety of technical writing courses, first-year writing courses, and any courses with a design or multimodal component. In terms of more formal readings, I assign Duffy (2014, 2017) as well as Arola (2010), thereby introducing students to virtue ethics and interface design in tandem. I typically assign short selections from various virtue ethicists (cited earlier) and design thinking, including Potts and Salvo (2017). This provides students with a theoretical basis for a pedagogical approach to ethical interface production.

Simultaneously, I ask students to identify examples of online harassment or bullying. We search for examples of platforms that experience these problems as well as platforms that seem to have fewer of these examples. We search for habits worthy of emulation, as well as designers of the successful platforms; I playfully label this activity the search for digital dispositions. I task students with finding people who seem, to them, to have a designed a platform with particular habits in mind. I emphasize to students that they are looking for normative behavior not based on static rules or ideal outcomes but on the character traits they see worthy of emulation. A productive route for emphasizing exemplars is to ask students to contact designers. My students often send e-mails in order to schedule phone interviews or video chats. Interviewing is crucial because it allows students to hear the personal experiences of designers, thereby further contextualizing students' chosen virtues.

A critical component of this approach—one that virtue ethicists would advocate—is that the exemplar is worthy of emulation not only from a personal viewpoint but also from a community's. Consequently, in such a pedagogy, students would need to acclimate themselves to a community, seeking out the community's norms. In my courses, students present these preliminary reflections to the rest of the class, wherein our classroom community attempts to identify habits worthy of emulation as a group.

Students then produce multiple models of interfaces they believe will lead users to emulate respective exemplars. Students have the freedom to select a community, as well as platform, of their choice. I subsequently ask students to generate various physical models, while stressing that the interface is less important than the habits they wish to inculcate. Rather than one specific interface, then, they iterate on several designs, which echoes Arola's (2010) canonical argument about interface design.

> Teachers can ask students to redesign an interface—either in an image-editing software program or with crayons and paper—for a different purpose or a different audience. For example, ask students to "design a MySpace interface for your Grandmother," or "design a MySpace interface that encourages you to meet people with whom you share similar musical tastes." Such prompts get students producing their own designs and help them enact visual rhetorical choices.
> (Arola, 2010, p. 12)

I provide students with various supplies to produce model interfaces but with a key distinction: visual rhetorical choices are backgrounded, while exemplars and habits are foregrounded. Furthermore, while this approach has shared resonances with recent work on speculative design (Rivers & Soderlund, 2016) and speculative redesign (Brown & Tarsa, 2018), it provides a normative ethical framework for such interface design. That is, in previous approaches to interface design, scholars have provided no ethical source of normativity. With the approach I advocate here, our sources of normativity are habits or virtues. More specifically, the sources of normativity are exemplars of virtues.

Because students build interfaces with habits and exemplars in mind, they have the scaffolding to recognize that design procedures are naturalized rather than immutable truths handed down from platforms, websites, and corporations. Ethical interface production thus seeks to identify user behavior, via dispositions, across a wide spectrum rather than on one website or platform. Like Brown and Tarsa's speculative redesign (2018), this approach "…draw[s] attention to how design enables and constrains activity—it suggests that no set of functions or features is 'natural' and that each engagement with an interface is a new human-technology assemblage" (Brown & Tarsa, 2018, pp. 259–260).

Because students have the scaffolding for denaturalizing interfaces, we subsequently generate ideas, approaches, and strategies for habit inculcation during in-class activities. Students thus move from exemplars to concrete habits as they might be constituted in an interface for a habit-forming purpose. Using exemplars as a guide, we design interfaces with affordances that reflect the selected virtues. Students find numerous users that they want to emulate but they also need a vocabulary for moving from the language of virtues (e.g. respect, patience, etc.) to the language of user experience.

Take, for instance, the virtue or disposition of patience, which is a common habit that students want to inculcate in their designs. When this virtue comes up, I ask them to consider the design concept of friction, or deliberate interactions that slow user engagement. Examples of friction include needing to check a box before proceeding or users needing to confirm their identities in some way. Yet, friction is also a user habit shaped by designers' choices. In terms of friction, then, I ask students to consider why designers try to create friction and interview designers about why patience is crucial to user habits. The habit of patience and its design counterpart friction are important when considering the role that speed plays in terms of online harassment. As Brown and Tarsa (2018) eloquently write,

> Abusive behavior thrives on speed—firing off message after message, jumping from thread to thread, or even just a cycle of copy-paste-submit. This kind of behavior doesn't require speedy thinking, just speedy fingers and a broadband connection—and those fast-paced repetitive motions are part of the pleasure. Designing an actionary mechanic that targets that pleasure is simple: delay the rate of input allowed, record only every other keystroke, or activate a script that deletes any words that exceed an average (or reduced) typing speed every thirty seconds.
>
> (p. 271)

Bullies, trolls, and harassers flourish in our hyper-discursive digital world. But how are we to deal with this kind of harassment, other than to eliminate it? What would we replace it with? My response is to postulate virtues as a way to combat harassment and prevent certain kinds of behaviors, as in Brown and Tarsa's compelling argument, while providing a positive path to follow, one that is flexible to account for the diversity of activity in online environments. Ethical interface production, through a virtue ethics framework, engenders a constructive and positive course of action for students.

Actual production separates my approach from more speculative approaches like Brown and Tarsa's. I ask students to use a variety of open-source software, including image-editing and manipulation software, wireframing programs, and JavaScript kits for interface interactivity. The open-source community is especially useful to draw upon here so that students are not constrained by proprietary corporate software, thereby reducing their means of expression.

78 *John R. Gallagher*

In my assignments, I include images (I designed them in image-editing software) that demonstrate interface production with an emphasis on the virtue of kindness (Figures 5.1–5.4).[1] Figure 5.1 shows Twitter's standard update field. Figures 5.2–5.4 update the template field to enact the virtue of digital kindness. Figures 5.2 and 5.3 attempt to create habits of kindness in user behavior. Figure 5.4 attempts to influence user behavior overtly by disrupting any user naturalization with a heart as the shape of Twitter's update field. The goal of the latter three figures (Figures 5.2–5.4) is not to settle on one particular interface design but rather multiple designs. In this sense, ethical interface production destabilizes interface design and, more broadly, design thinking as having an endpoint. Continuous redesign—and moving into production with those redesigns—enacts an ethical stance toward design theory.

Figure 5.1 Twitter's interface default. Screencapture by J. R. Gallagher, 2018.

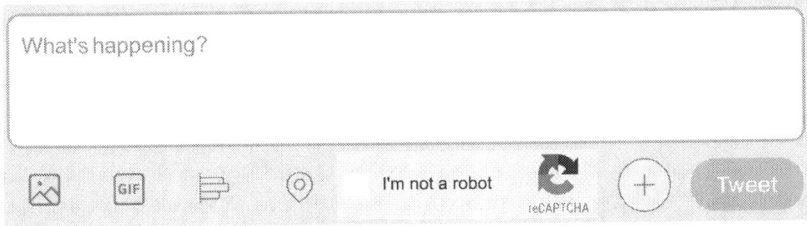

Figure 5.2 Interface redesign that has added friction (Captcha), by J. R. Gallagher, 2018.

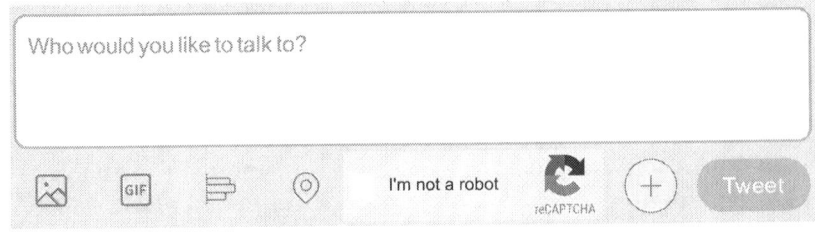

Figure 5.3 Interface redesign that has added friction and alternate greeting, by J. R. Gallagher, 2018.

Figure 5.4 Complete redesign of Twitter's interface, by J. R. Gallagher, 2018.

Past student examples have included redesigns of Goodreads, Tumblr, Pinterest, Vox, Craigslist, YouTube, and many others. I have found that providing students with time in class to workshop their interfaces is especially helpful. Digital poster sessions, with an example of the proposed interface, leads to productive peer feedback. Peer review sessions are crucial to brainstorming and mocking up different models. Ultimately, interface aesthetics and affordances are less important than the discussion and investigations of habits, along with the ethical queries that arise from those discussions and investigations.

User Testing as an Ethical Activity

After the production of these models, students user-test their models to determine how users react to their redesigns. In ethical terms, asking students to determine how their designs succeeded or failed assists them in seeing how design choices become ethical choices that users naturalize into habits. Students have the direct experience of seeing their design(s) taken up and utilized while building pragmatic ethical skills of user testing.

Conceptually, this user testing means that such interfaces are not endpoints but permutations of a process. A pedagogy of ethical interface production emphasizes not a final product but a process of *looking at* an interface as well as *through* an interface.[2] Boyle (2015) usefully crystallizes such an approach in his discussion of glitch art, one I would extend to interfaces: "Looking at and through becomes less productive a heuristic when that which we look at or through is a dynamic and shifting process and not a stable object" (p. 18). Interfaces, in the scope of my argument, become processes aimed at encouraging and inculcating ethical habits and behaviors rather than static screen-based affordances or multimodal texts.

Practically, students can use a variety of means to achieve these ends. They use survey software, such as Qualtrics or Google forms, to user-test their designs, thereby "involving the audience" (Breuch, 2015; Breuch et al., 2016; Johnson, 1997). They can also observe how potential users take up an interface, either through in-person observations or screen-recordings. Students mock up interfaces using more wireframing and other available software to observe and record how users will take up their designs. They can thus determine to what extent their designs have produced the habits they aim to encourage. Implicit in this pedagogy is that repetition, practice, and iteration are all valuable, productive activities that seek a type of embodied knowledge transcending criticism and discursive production. Boyle (2015) offers a version of this approach that distinguishes such knowledge from mere knowing.

> We might more productively consider rhetoric and glitch through metastable orientations as resistance training. To put this another way, much like when we exercise in a gym, straining regions of the body we rarely use (much less know), so too might practices like those involved with glitch art attune us to the embodied medial conditions that inform us. These practices... help inform, transduce, and exercise a rhetorical manner of being in ways that are not reducible to what we see or know, but aim to increase and intensify what we can do.
>
> (p. 27)

User testing moves students away from a predictive type of knowledge confined to classroom practices and toward an unpredictable approach to interface design. Because students are not seeking out designs but rather habits, they need to have the freedom (and I argue agency) to produce interfaces that may fail in the inculcation of desired habits and virtues.

User testing, in the context of ethical interface production, seeks out user habits and ways to create those habits by way of exemplars. It does not seek to make monolithic determinations about interface affordances. Mistakes and iterations, as well as audience engagement, are all valuable activities in this process because it means that we do not have easy answers to tasks such as reducing online harassment or productive civic exchange. Indeed, without exemplars, we cannot know what civic exchange is or how to productively inculcate it in a way that accounts for the diversity and variety of digital discourse.

Ethical Concerns of Manipulation

With its focus on habits, ethical interface production raises concerns about manipulation. The concern may be articulated as follows: students designing interfaces as described previously may not be providing users with agency if they are prescribing habits through interface affordances. This concern is not limited to the ethical approach I have presented because all-interface design is likely a type of coercive manipulation. In the scope of the project I have described, however, manipulation might be described as a type of *emulation*. Students ask potential users to emulate the exemplars the class community has chosen. From a virtue ethics perspective, we might redescribe manipulation as emulation.

Emulation, in my view, is crucial due to the vitriol prevalent online. The task of stopping online hatred, sexism, racism, and homophobia may not be possible by banning users or dictating a series of unacceptable behavior. This approach does not provide a framework for what kinds of behaviors or habits are positive and worthy of emulation. It also puts the onus on victims to report or "warn" automated writing systems (Laquintano & Vee, 2017) rather than on perpetrators. As such, emulation through design is an alternative for prescribing positive behaviors. Nevertheless, if scholars and instructors are to engage deeply with a pedagogy of ethical interface production, then the conversation about potential manipulation should be addressed by future scholarship.

Conclusion

Interfaces need to be continuously rethought and redesigned as communities grow and adapt. Virtue ethics, with its emphasis on virtues and exemplars, can assist theorists, practitioners, and teachers with producing ethical interfaces, thereby informing design practices, interface theories, and classroom pedagogies. This chapter has linked virtue ethics, interface design, and classroom teaching through the common thread of habits, habit formations, and exemplars. While much of what I have written here involves technology and is in fact predicated upon the Internet and social media, the framework is based on virtues of those who demonstrate those character traits, specifically exemplars.

I have endeavored to provide a normative way of seeking out desired behaviors and habits rather than a negative framework that seeks to reduce online harassment. Affirmative examples, I believe, are useful for nurturing ethical frameworks that students may bring with them in their careers. Students exposed to an ethical interface production could, hopefully, bring this ethical framework with them to their professional endeavors, perhaps sparking more systemic change. Students exposed to this approach thus have the power to traverse specific technological tools, cultivating deliberate virtues based on exemplars. Virtue ethics thus may help to lessen the responsibility of the victim to report violations of social media harassment because, as a contingent yet normative ethical framework, virtue ethics provides positive interactions, through exemplars, rather than defining behavior that is not allowed.

Notes

1 Please contact me if you would like to use Figures 5.1–5.4. These are available as SVG (scalable vector graphics) files. I can readily supply them in a high-resolution format.
2 See Lanham's *The Electronic Word* (1993) and Brooke's *Lingua Fracta* (2009) for more on this at/through distinction.

References

Annas, J. (1993). *The morality of happiness*. Oxford: Oxford University Press.
Anscombe, G. E. M. (1958). Modern moral philosophy. *Philosophy, 33*(124), 1–16.
Aristotle. (1984). *Nicomachean ethics*. (H. G. Apostle, Ed.). Des Moines, IA: The Peripatetic Press.
Arola, K. L. (2010). The design of web 2.0: The rise of the template, the fall of design. *Computers and Composition, 27*(1), 4–14.
Arola, K. (2017). Indigenous interfaces. In D. Walls & S. Vie (Eds.), *Social writing/social media: Pedagogy, presentation, and publics*. Parlor Press, WAC Clearinghouse Perspectives on Writing Series.
Bizzell, P. (1992). The politics of teaching virtue. *ADE Bulletin, 103*, 4–7.
Boyle, C. (2015). The rhetorical question concerning glitch. *Computers and Composition, 35*, 12–29.
Boyle, C., Brown, J. J., & Ceraso, S. (2018). The digital: Rhetoric behind and beyond the screen. *Rhetoric Society Quarterly, 48*(3), 251–259.
Boyle, C., & Rivers, N. A. (2016). A version of access. *Technical Communication Quarterly, 25*(1), 29–47.
Breuch, L. K. (2015). Glocalization in website writing: The case of MNsure and imagined/actual audiences. *Computers and Composition, 38*(Part B), 113–125.
Breuch, L.-A. K., Bakke, A., Thomas-Pollei, K., Mackey, L. E., & Weinert, C. (2016). Toward audience involvement: Extending audiences of written physician notes in a hospital setting. *Written Communication, 33*(4), 418–451.
Brooke, C. G. (2009). *Lingua fracta: Towards a rhetoric of new media*. Cresskill, NJ: Hampton Press, Inc.
Brown, J., & Tarsa, R. (2018). Complicit interfaces. In W. Hesford, A. Licona, & C. Teston (Eds.), *Precarious rhetorics* (pp. 255–75). Columbus: Ohio State University Press.
Carnegie, T. M. (2009). Interface as exordium: The rhetoric of interactivity. *Computers and Composition, 26*(3), 164–173.
Colton, J. S., & Holmes, S. (2016). A social justice theory of active equality for technical communication. *Journal of Technical Writing and Communication, 48*(1), 4–10.
Colton, J. S., & Holmes, S. (2018). *Rhetoric, technology, and the virtues*. Logan: Utah State University Press.

Colton, J. S., Holmes, S., & Walwema, J. (2017). From NoobGuides to #Op-KKK: Ethics of Anonymous' tactical technical communication. *Technical Communication Quarterly, 26*(1), 59–75.

Duffy, J. (2014). Ethical dispositions: A discourse for rhetoric and composition. *JAC, 34*(1–2), 209–37.

Duffy, J. (2017). The good writer: Virtue ethics and the teaching of writing. *College English, 79*(3), 229–250.

Duffy, J., Gallagher, J. R., & Holmes, S. (2018). Virtue ethics. *Rhetoric Review, 37*(4), 321–392.

Eckert, S. (2017). Fighting for recognition: Online abuse of women bloggers in Germany, Switzerland, the United Kingdom, and the United States. *New Media & Society, 20*(4), 1282–1302.

Eyman, D., & Ball, C. E. (2014). Composing for digital publication: Rhetoric, design, code. *Composition Studies, 42*(1), 114–7.

Foot, P. (2003). *Virtues and vices and other essays in moral philosophy*. Gloucestershire: Clarendon Press. Original work published 1978.

Friend, C. (1999). Resisting virtue: Rhetoric, writing pedagogy, and popular moral discourse. *Composition Forum, 10*(1), 16–29.

Gallagher, J. R. (2015). The rhetorical template. *Computers and Composition, 35*(1), 1–11.

Gallagher, J. R. (2018). Enacting virtue ethics. *Rhetoric Review, 37*(4), 379–384.

Galloway, A. R. (2012). *The interface effect*. Cambridge, UK: Polity Press.

Goodman, C. (2015). Virtue in Buddhist ethical traditions. In L. Besser-Jones & M. Slote (Eds.), *The routledge companion to virtue ethics* (pp. 89–98). New York, NY: Routledge.

Herring, S., Job-Sluder, K., Scheckler, R., & Barab, S. (2002). Searching for safety online: Managing "trolling" in a feminist forum. *The Information Society, 18*(5), 371–384.

Hursthouse, R. (1999). *On virtue ethics*. Oxford: Oxford University Press.

Jaggar, A. M. (1991). Feminist ethics: Projects, problems, prospects. In C. Card (Ed.), *Feminist ethics* (pp. 78–104). Lawrence: University of Kansas Press.

Jane, E. A. (2015). Flaming? What flaming? The pitfalls and potentials of researching online hostility. *Ethics and Information Technology, 17*(1), 65–87.

Johnson-Eilola, J. (1997). *Nostalgic angels: Rearticulating hypertext writing*. Santa Barbara, CA: Praeger.

Johnson, R. R. (1997). Audience involved: Toward a participatory model of writing. *Computers and Composition, 14*(3), 361–376.

Lanham, R. (1993). *The electronic word*. Chicago, IL: The University of Chicago Press.

Laquintano, T., & Vee, A. (2017). How automated writing systems affect the circulation of political information online. *Literacy in Composition Studies, 5*(2), 43–62.

MacIntyre, A. (1984). *After virtue* (2nd ed.). Notre Dame: University of Notre Dame Press.

Marback, R. (2009). Embracing wicked problems: The turn to design in composition studies. *College Composition and Communication, 61*(2), 397–419.

Massanari, A. (2017). #Gamergate and The Fappening: How Reddit's algorithm, governance, and culture support toxic technocultures. *New Media and Society, 19*(3), 329–346.

Massanari, A. L. (2018). Rethinking research ethics, power, and the risk of visibility in the era of the "alt-right" gaze. *Social Media + Society, 4*(2), 1–9.

McLaren, M. A. (2001). Feminist ethics: Care as a virtue. In P. DesAutels & J. Waugh (Eds.), *Feminists doing ethics* (pp. 101–117). Lanham, MD: Rowman & Littlefield Publishers.

Oswal, S. K. (2013). Accessible eportfolios for visually-impaired users: Interface, designs, and infrastructures. In K. V. Wills & R. Rice (Eds.), *ePortfolio performance support systems: Constructing, presenting, and assessing portfolios* (pp. 135–153). Anderson: Parlor Press.

Palmeri, J. (2012). *Remixing composition: A history of multimodal writing pedagogy.* Carbondale: Southern Illinois University Press.

Phillips, W. (2015). *This is why we can't have nice things: Mapping the relationship between online trolling and mainstream culture.* Cambridge, MA: MIT Press.

Potts, L., & Salvo, M. J. (2017). Introduction. In *Rhetoric and experience architecture* (pp. 3–16). Anderson, SC: Parlor Press.

Purdy, J. P. (2014). What can design thinking offer writing studies? *College Composition and Communication, 65*(4), 612–641.

Rivers, N. A., & Soderlund, L. (2016). Speculative usability. *Journal of Technical Writing and Communication, 46*(1), 125–146.

Rowe, I. (2015). Civility 2.0: A comparative analysis of incivility in online political discussion. *Information, Communication & Society, 18*(2), 121–138. doi: 10.1080/1369118X.2014.940365.

Selber, S. (2004). *Multiliteracies for a digital age.* Carbondale: Southern Illinois University Press.

Selfe, C. L., & Selfe, R. J. (1994). The politics of the interface: Power and its exercise in electronic contact zones. *College Composition and Communication, 45*(4), 480–504.

Slote, M. (1983). *Goods and virtues.* Oxford: Clarendon Press.

Slote, M. (1992). *From morality to virtue.* Oxford: Oxford University Press.

Sparby, E. M. (2017). Digital social media and aggression: Memetic rhetoric in 4chan's collective identity. *Computers and Composition, 45*, 85–97.

Spigelman, C. (2001). What role virtue? *JAC, 21*(2), 321–348.

Tepper, F. (2018, May 13). Whitney Wolfe Herd doesn't care what she's supposed to do: How Bumble's founder turned a dating app into a movement. Retrieved from https://techcrunch.com/2018/05/13/whitney-wolfe-herd-bumbles-founder-doesnt-care-what-shes-supposed-to-do/

Twitter. (2018). Twitter health metrics proposal submission. Retrieved from https://blog.twitter.com/official/en_us/topics/company/2018/twitter-health-metrics-proposal-submission.html

Vallor, S. (2016). *Technology and the virtues: A philosophical guide to a future worth wanting.* Oxford: Oxford University Press.

Warnick, B. (2005). Looking to the future: Electronic texts and the deepening interface. *Technical Communication Quarterly, 15*(3), 327–333.

Yashari, L. (2015, August 7). Meet the Tinder co-founder trying to change online dating forever. *Vanity Fair.* Retrieved from https://www.vanityfair.com/culture/2015/08/bumble-app-whitney-wolfe

Zagzebski, L. (2010). Exemplarist virtue theory. *Metaphilosophy, 41*(1–2), 41–57.

Part II
Academic Labor in Digital Publics

6 Feminist Research on the Toxic Web
The Ethics of Access, Affective Labor, and Harassment

Leigh Gruwell

The Internet presents significant opportunities for feminist researchers, both in terms of identifying new locations for research as well as developing new research methods and methodologies. But, as writing studies scholars very well know, the Internet can be a hostile place for women, people of color, and other marginalized groups. Black and Hispanic Americans, for example, experience online harassment at disproportionately high rates, while women tend to face more severe forms of online harassment than men (Duggan, 2017). Feminist researchers have thus worked to understand how and why gendered and raced oppression persists online (Cole, 2015; Jane, 2014; Mantilla, 2013; Megarry, 2014; Noble, 2018). This well-documented toxicity, however, doesn't only affect Internet *users*—it can also shape the work of Internet *researchers*, particularly those who are committed to enacting feminist methodologies.

Writing studies has recognized how the Internet may complicate research practices, and scholars have eagerly explored questions of researcher positionality and identity (Almjeld & Blair, 2012; Sapienza, 2007), relationships with participants (Blair, 2012; Dadas, 2016), and the distinction between public and private (McKee & Porter, 2010). Feminist research methodologies have been particularly influential in these conversations, as researchers have asked how best to enact ethical research practices in digital spaces. However, the field has largely overlooked the very real challenges that a toxic Internet presents to feminist researchers. Internet technologies are enmeshed in structures of power that can devalue feminist rhetorical practices, including feminist methodologies that foreground social justice and attempt to undo gendered and/or raced power imbalances. How then can feminist researchers gain access to such spaces while still honoring their commitment to conduct socially responsible research? How should we conceptualize the affective labor that often accompanies researching toxic online spaces? How ought feminist researchers manage their own privacy and safety online while also performing transparent, effectual research?

In this chapter, I draw on my own research experiences—as well as the experiences of other feminist Internet researchers—to explore how this toxic environment can undermine the feminist methodological principles of reciprocity, reflexivity, and transparency. I suggest that the specific dynamics of online spaces, interactions, and relationships may heighten these difficulties and present new risks for Internet-based feminist research, specifically in terms of affective labor, access, and harassment. After reviewing how feminist methodologies have imagined ethical research practices, I explore how specific case studies challenge these existing feminist methodologies. I then conclude by outlining a heuristic for what I call a methodology of tactical resistance, which exploits the same networks that sustain the toxic web to create space for feminist research and researchers online. Based on the acknowledgment that all research is rhetorical, tactical resistance's particular attunement to power makes it an especially productive methodology not only for feminists doing research online, but for any Internet researchers who hope to perform meaningful and ethical research in and on the toxic Internet.

Feminist Methodologies: The Methodological Is Political

Feminist methodologies—in writing studies and beyond—are as diverse as feminism itself. On the most general level, though, feminist research methodologies emerge from feminism's interest in identifying and rectifying gendered power inequities, although other embodied differences such as race, sexuality, and ability are often foregrounded as well. Feminist methodologies generally reject positivist characterizations of knowledge as objective and transcendent and instead insist that knowledge emerges from specific, culturally situated bodies (Deutsch, 2004; Harding, 1993; Hartsock, 1988). It is this understanding of knowledge as partial, situated, and relational that results in feminist researchers' general commitment to "become answerable for what we learn how to see" (Haraway, 1991, p. 190). Feminist methodologies therefore stress that researchers should acknowledge the material and discursive structures that shape their own epistemological commitments.

Feminist methodologies, however, are not solely concerned with complicating the production of knowledge: they are also sharply attentive to social justice outcomes, most typically centered on women, people of color, and other historically oppressed groups (Kirsch, 1999; Lather, 1991; McKee & Porter, 2010). If research is to do political work and improve the lives of participants—as feminist researchers say it should— then methodologies that neglect to consider how their theoretical assumptions line up with the everyday practices of participants undermine the emancipatory potential of research. This means reimagining how we relate to participants, seeing them not as distant objects to be studied but as cocreators of knowledge. Research *on* women (or other marginalized groups) should work *for* women to improve their circumstances. Importantly, these political goals also demand research that is accessible, transparent, and consequential (Blair, 2012; Kirsch, 1999; McKee &

Porter, 2010). For feminist methodologies, then, ethical research results from a reflective researcher (who has carefully interrogated and accounted for her own positionality) co-constructing (ideally with participants) knowledge that will potentially better the lives of women and other oppressed groups. In short, feminist research methodologies might be best characterized by the three interconnected principles of *reflexivity*, *reciprocity*, and *transparency*.

Because feminist researchers accept that knowledge-making is not a detached, neutral process but is inevitably tied to one's embodied, socially specific location, *reflexivity* is integral to any research project. Such "self reflexivity and critical consciousness about one's own position, gender, and status are key features of feminist thinking," argue McKee and Porter (2010, p. 155). Feminist researchers understand reflexivity as a process, not as an isolated event. A recursive movement between the researcher and the research, reflexivity acknowledges the difficulty of separating the two and asks scholars to critically reflect on "how the researchers' identity, experience, training, and theoretical framework shape the research agenda, data analysis, and findings" (Kirsch, 1999, p. 5). Reflexivity, in short, demands that researchers interrogate their own positionality to consider how it may shape their research outcomes.

Feminist methodologies emphasize the importance of self-reflexivity as a means of accounting for the partiality and specificity of knowledge production, but they also understand research as an explicitly political stance that values and amplifies the experiences and knowledges of oppressed groups. It is this political motivation that has led many feminist researchers to approach participants as collaborators. Feminist researchers like Cushman (1996), Kirsch (1999), Powell and Takayoshi (2003), and Royster (2000) (among many others) have shown us how seeking "mutually enriching relationships between researchers and their subjects" can produce ethically sound research (Powell & Takayoshi, 2003, p. 394). While it may be difficult—or even impossible—to fully eliminate any power disparities between researcher and participants, feminist methodologies value *reciprocity* between researcher and participants as a means of dissembling traditional power dynamics and centering the voices of marginalized groups.

While reciprocity helps produce research that does political work and improves the lives of participants, it is certainly not the only means of doing so. *Transparency* is an equally important principle for feminist researchers, because it not only aids in the creation of more equitable relationships with participants, but it also makes their voices accessible and effectual. Transparency, for feminist researchers, is largely concerned with creating positive outcomes for researchers and participants alike, and, as Kirsch (1999) argues, involves a thoughtful examination of "the possible consequences—material, social, political—of our research, particularly if it involves others over whom we have power" (p. 83). As a result, feminist researchers are preoccupied with the "so what?" question, rethinking how to create research that transforms the oppressive structures it studies (Lather, 1991; McKee & Porter, 2010). Transparency thus guides relationships with participants and helps researchers make choices about how and where to publish their research, with the goal of amplifying marginalized voices and ultimately bettering the lives of participants.

The feminist research methodological principles outlined earlier—reflexivity, reciprocity, and transparency—inform feminist researchers who study digital spaces and communities. In their study of digital feminist researchers, McKee and Porter (2010) found that most researchers consistently enact and value these principles, even as new media technologies introduce a host of new ethical considerations. Feminist researchers have written about the difficulties of articulating and creating identities within online communities (Almjeld & Blair, 2012; Dadas, 2016), the challenges of creating dialogic relationships with participants in digitally mediated spaces (McKee & Porter, 2010; Sapienza, 2007), and the imperative to conduct digital research grounded in women's experiences and focused on participant empowerment (Blair, 2012; Hawisher & Sullivan, 1998). But this work tends to overlook the sometimes-precarious landscape in which digital feminist research occurs. The Internet is still in many ways a toxic place for women and other oppressed groups and this research, while valuable, is yet to fully grapple with the question of how this toxicity might affect our research practices.

The Internet comprises incredibly diverse spaces and users, but it is dangerous to view it—or any digital technology—as a neutral tool. Technologies are products of their culture, designed by people with their own biases, assumptions, and motivations, and therefore any researcher studying Internet technologies must account for the ways in which online spaces are not only embedded in but can perpetuate exclusionary power relationships. Feminist researchers, in particular, should pay close attention to how gendered power relations manifest online and how those power relations might influence their own ability to research. Feminist research methodologies have yet to thoroughly interrogate the difficulties a toxic Internet presents, despite an abundance of scholarship that suggests that the Internet has been, and continues to be, unwelcoming or even dangerous to women, people of color, and other marginalized groups (Banks, 2006; Hawisher & Sullivan, 1998; Jane, 2014; Nakamura, 2008; Noble, 2018). For this reason, I suggest it is imperative that we recognize how the structure of the Internet itself, as well as the communities that inhabit it, may disempower feminist researchers and methodologies.

One of the most visible manifestations of this dynamic is harassment. While online harassment is almost certainly as old as the Internet itself, Jane (2014) argues that it "is getting more prevalent, it is getting uglier, and it has a number of distinctly gendered characteristics" (p. 534). Women—particularly young women—experience sexual harassment and abuse online at much higher rates than men, and are much more likely to find the experience troubling (Duggan, 2017; Lenhart et al., 2016). Black Internet users also experience disproportionately high rates of harassment online (Duggan, 2017), as do LGBTQ users (Lenhart et al., 2016). These users are more often the targets of the most severe forms of harassment, including exposure of private data, stalking, and physical threats. Accordingly, women, people of color, and LGBTQ users tend to censor themselves more online, and many have left certain platforms or communities altogether (Lenhart et al., 2016). This research—along with the work of others (Cole, 2015; Mantilla, 2013; Megarry, 2014)—demonstrates how online harassment can create a research setting marked by sexism, racism, and homophobia.

Although harassment may be one of the most visible manifestations of the Internet's toxicity, there are also deeper inequalities built into the structures of Internet technologies themselves. In her book *Algorithms of Oppression*, Noble describes how "algorithmically driven data failures that are specific to women and people of color" can disempower certain users (p. 4). To illustrate this "algorithmic oppression" at work, Noble (2018) shares the example of how a Google search for "black girls" produced a long list of pornographic, demeaning websites that figured Black girls and women as sexual objects. Noble's work suggests that online hostility is not just the product of a few bad actors within a community; rather, it is the very design of the technology itself that can result in a sexist, racist environment that may be antagonistic to feminist researchers and methodologies.

This toxicity is in many ways inextricable from the most basic functions of the Internet, and correspondingly, it manifests in some of the most popular online platforms. Researchers have identified sexist, racist, and/or homophobic practices in communities like YouTube (Döring & Mohseni, 2018), Wikipedia (Gruwell, 2015; MacAulay & Visser, 2016), Twitter (Cole, 2015), and Facebook (Dadas, 2016). Of course, it's important to note that a good deal of feminist, anti-racist, and other forms of equality-focused activism have found success online—the Internet is certainly not wholly hostile to feminist rhetorics or research, and it is well worth our time to complicate simplistic technological narratives. However, given the frequency and magnitude of online toxicity, it is likely that Internet researchers will encounter hostility, especially if they claim a specifically feminist identity. Researchers, then, must be prepared to ethically navigate the difficulties these potentially hazardous environments can present to feminist methodologies, particularly in terms of reflexivity, reciprocity, and transparency.

Reflexivity

Internet feminist researchers value reflexivity, even as they recognize how it can change in online spaces that complicate researcherly identities in sometimes-unexpected ways. Almjeld and Blair (2012), for example, note that "the shift toward new media creates further challenges regarding ways researcher identity is created and how that identity impacts both how we approach questions in the field and what we are willing to question" (p. 99). Enacting reflexivity means that researchers must not only interrogate their own epistemological positioning but also consider their relationships to the individuals and communities that they study, especially as online spaces blur the lines between the "multiple roles of researcher, participant, and observer" scholars may inhabit (McKee & Porter, 2010, p. 166). While this research raises important questions about how researcherly identities are created through Internet technologies, it has largely not considered how the toxic Internet further complicates how researchers understand and articulate those identities.

Because feminist Internet researchers can easily find themselves working in toxic environments, it is important to consider the role affect, or emotion, plays in embodied identity formation. Feminist researchers have long argued that emotions are an important component of feminist reflexivity, as they can have immediate and profound effects on research (Bizzell, 2000; Deutsch, 2004; Jaggar, 1989). Blakely (2007), for example, argues that "Researchers' emotions... are an untapped resource of information, lending insight into the research process [and] the findings of the study" (p. 61). But given the sometimes-precarious nature of Internet-based research, feminist scholars can experience complex emotional reactions that feminist reflexivity is yet to fully interrogate.

It wasn't until I began a project on online harassment (Gruwell, 2017) that I was forced to confront the limits of reflexivity and the affective demands on feminist researchers online. As I was researching the relationship between online harassment and public writing pedagogies, I collected examples of harassment on Twitter and YouTube. Drawing from the work of Jane (2014), I felt that it was important to represent the full, often vulgar and violent, range of harassing language online in order to illustrate the extent of the problem. However, I was surprised by—and thus unprepared for—the intense emotional reactions I experienced after spending hours at a time sorting through hateful, violent, misogynistic language. The process of researching online harassment not only angered me, but made me feel tired and defeated. At its worst, the harassment I was researching got to my core, making me question the value of my worth as a woman and researcher. Most research is draining in one respect or another, but there was something especially taxing about intentionally reading content meant to silence women like me—feminists committed to identifying and resisting sexism, racism, and homophobia online.

Other feminists who study online harassment report similar emotional reactions. In her dissertation on online harassment, Gelms (2018) writes honestly about the emotional toll such work can take, noting that in the course of her research, she experienced "stress and anxiety" (p. 42). She concludes that

> in conducting inquiry into online harassment, a researcher is likely to expose herself to shocking, depressing, and triggering stories or language [which can] ensure that the researcher will have to take on a significant amount of emotional labor or strain.
> (Gelms, 2018, p. 43)

Likewise, Vera-Gray (2017) argues that the emotional toll of researching online harassment can create "hidden added labour forming an invisible backdrop to the methodological decisions of feminist researchers" (p. 62). These experiences echo Duggan's (2017) finding that witnessing online harassment can produce significant emotional stress.

A hostile environment can significantly alter how we understand ourselves and our research, and it's important to be honest about all the factors that shape our researcherly identities, including the affective labor that can often undergird Internet research. Given the extent of toxicity online, it is likely that even feminist researchers who are not directly researching harassment or hate speech will encounter graphic, abusive content, which can create anxiety and potentially even discourage feminist researchers from studying Internet spaces. Without a more capacious understanding of reflexivity—one that accounts for the widespread hostility found online—feminist researchers may find themselves unable to fully account for their embodied identities, thus falling short of the feminist methodological goal of being accountable for our knowledge claims. Online spaces can shape our researcherly identities in ways we may not expect—and thus it is critical that we develop reflexive practices that accommodate the complexities of Internet research.

Reciprocity

Internet technologies can also call into question traditional understandings of feminist reciprocity, which foregrounds the importance of creating ethical relationships between researchers and participants. Recognizing that researchers occupy a specific (often privileged) position, feminist reciprocity insists that researchers be explicit as possible in order to create collaborative, mutually beneficial interactions with participants and their communities (Cushman, 1996; Kirsch & Ritchie, 1995; Powell & Takayoshi, 2003). This imperative likely accounts for McKee and Porter's (2010) finding that most researchers using feminist methodologies in online spaces "strongly favored respecting the wishes of the individuals and the community being studied" (p. 158). Such an approach to reciprocity online not only creates more equitable relationships with participants, but it can also offer more complex—and therefore more accurate—technological narratives.

Feminist reciprocity is thus often figured as a way to correct power inequities that often disadvantage participants. But the Internet's toxicity can sometimes complicate or cloud power relationships. Massanari (2018), for example, points out that a researcher studying alt-right hate groups online can become vulnerable due to extreme power imbalances. Reciprocity on the toxic Internet, then, can be difficult to navigate, and often presents sticky ethical challenges when it comes to dealing with participants, especially when those participants have more power than researchers.

I encountered this dynamic myself when I conducted a person-based study of women Wikipedia writers (Gruwell, 2015). I sought to interview some of these women in order to learn more about the causes of and potential solutions to Wikipedia's gender gap. Early in my research, I discovered that Wikipedia ran a research committee, the Wikimedia Foundation Research Committee (RCom), which allows researchers to negotiate the terms of their relationship with the community. First, a researcher creates a project page describing her research. Committee members then review the page and either ask for revision or offer support. The committee notes that they value "community engagement," and that they insist on "(Re)Contribution," so that "Wikimedia and/or the community [benefits] in some way from participating in your work" ("Notes on good practices," 2011). RCom thus seemed to perfectly facilitate the feminist reciprocity I sought.

As I wrote my project page, I explained my desire to work with Wikipedians to help make the community more inclusive, and clarified that I would happily share any conclusions or recommendations that resulted from my research with the community. Weeks, then months, passed before I received feedback from committee members. While some comments were helpful, it was evident that most users were not familiar with feminist research practices. For example, one user urged me to study something more precise than "women's experience." I did my best to revise my proposal in response to these concerns, but the fact was that I received very little feedback at all—only four users responded to my request over a year and a half. I certainly didn't want to force anyone to help me design my study or recruit participants, and I knew that, as a nonprofit organization that partially relies on volunteers, Wikimedia's RCom is likely understaffed. But I was concerned about the apparent misunderstandings about what constituted feminist research. Ultimately, I decided to rethink my approach: I discovered a Wikipedia Gender Gap listserv and decided to introduce my project there. Although I had still not received any official endorsement from RCom, several women agreed to participate in my study right away, and others graciously introduced me to other feminists working with Wikipedia. I eventually gathered enough participants to complete my study, which concluded that neither Wikipedia's editorial policies nor its community interactions support feminist epistemologies. Little wonder, then, that I found it so difficult to enact feminist methodologies.

In my case with Wikipedia, I chose to work *around* the community rather than to work *with* it, collaborating with Wikipedia-adjacent groups to recruit participants. Yet, I questioned my decision to reach out directly to female Wikipedia editors rather than completing the review process through RCom. I worried that going around the official community channels was somehow unethical. Was I unfairly representing the community I had intended to help? How might my results have differed had I been able to recruit participants through RCom? I couldn't deny these concerns, but I also recognized that this was, at base, a question of power: Wikipedia is a well-organized community that can decide which research projects to support (or not).

During my Wikipedia research, I came across another feminist researcher who had similar difficulties negotiating a relationship with Wikipedia. Kate, a scholar in a field dominated by quantitative methods, planned a qualitative study of female Wikipedia editors that claimed a specifically feminist methodology.[1] Kate also found the process of requesting support difficult, as RCom seemed to be unfamiliar with feminist methods. She recalled: "When I said that I was going to be using feminist interview techniques, one of the members of the Research Committee came back and said, 'what does that mean?'" Kate reported feeling uncertain about the motivations of the research committee, noting, "I felt like it was more about power than protecting the community." In short, Kate worried that the methodologies valued by the Wikipedia community did not support the methodology she valued as a feminist researcher. Happily, however, Kate was able to work with research committee and revise her project page to receive their support in participant recruitment.

While Kate and I were both able to make the best of a challenging research situation, it's clear that researchers using methodologies that are unfamiliar or unacceptable to the community are at a disadvantage in terms of negotiating community support. Researchers should always be cautious about exerting their power ethically, and certainly should avoid coercing participants. But these experiences suggest that digital feminist researchers might have difficulty gaining access to participants that don't share their methodological or political commitments, especially when dealing with larger, well-organized communities. Feminist reciprocity insists that researchers should announce their scholarly identity and intentions, but this can result in ethical dilemmas. In many ways, then, feminist reciprocity's goals of collaborating with participants and advocating for women and other marginalized groups can be at odds on the toxic Internet.

Transparency

The feminist methodological principle of transparency is a culmination of reflexivity and reciprocity, as researchers aim for openness and accountability at every stage of a research project, often well past publication. In particular, researchers have celebrated the potential of the Internet "to diminish the stark division between personal self and public scholar" (Almjeld & Blair, 2012, p. 107). This blurring of lines has resulted in feminist scholars reimagining what transparency might look like online. Not only can researchers use digital tools like social media to cultivate a feminist research identity, they can also use online networks to circulate research widely, making it more accessible to participants and other stakeholders in order to create the transformative structural changes feminist research desires (Morrison, 2018; Nagy-Zekmi & Hollis, 2010).

Like reflexivity and reciprocity, though, Internet technologies can challenge what feminist transparency looks like in practice. With the increased pressure to use Internet technologies to make research accessible to participants and public audiences alike, feminist researchers can find themselves in a dangerous bind as simply maintaining a public presence online as a feminist researcher can invite harassment. Writing in *Inside Higher Ed* about their study on the harassment of female scholars, Veletsianos and Hodson (2018) argue that "online harassment continues to impact the ways in which women in higher education can and do participate in online spaces." The toxic Internet, that is, may make simply existing as both a feminist and a researcher in online spaces dangerous.

Historian Mary Beard, for example, experienced harassment after posting online about the ethnic diversity of Roman British society (Boseley, 2017), and classicist Sarah E. Bond was likewise targeted after making similar claims disputing the assumed whiteness of ancient Greek and Roman statuary (Quintana, 2017). Vera-Gray (2017) received a flood of harassment and threats as a result of her decision to publicly recruit (women) participants online. Such gendered harassment can be further compounded for academics of color. Sociologist Tressie McMillan Cottom (2015) has written about how entreaties to make research public can ignore the real risks publicity presents to her as a Black woman: "As a public writer, academic and black woman, my location at the bottom of a racist, sexist social hierarchy mitigates the presumed returns on academic public engagement," she writes. Researchers who have been harassed online report feelings of fear, shame, and paranoia (Campbell, 2017; Gelms, 2018)—feelings that can ultimately silence feminist researchers online.

Feminist scholars need not even actively publicize their research to become targets. While the mass organizing power of social media platforms makes it easier than ever for public audiences to circulate feminist research, those audiences are not always friendly. I learned this firsthand when the Wikipedia study I described earlier was featured on a Twitter account called @RealPeerReview on October 28, 2016. This account, which has more than 50,000 followers, is meant to "provide a lighthearted, satirical view of most questionable specimens of modern academic peer review process," according to its (anonymous) moderator ("Twitter account," 2017). When my article's abstract was featured along with the (misleading) summary "Wikipedia is anti-feminist because its editorial policy doesn't allow you to just make things up" (Figure 6.1), I didn't find out until a few days later when a commenter tagged my Twitter account, which I primarily use to cultivate a public identity as a feminist researcher.

While most young scholars might be pleased to find their research featured in such a visible platform, it was more than a bit shocking to see my work spotlighted in what was clearly meant to be a derogatory way. Comments were uniformly critical and dismissive, as users called me and my work "lunatic academic fringe," "idiotic and misogynistic," and argued "that without feminist morons, the world would be a

New Real Peer Review
@RealPeerReview

Follow

Wikipedia is anti-feminist because its editorial policy doesn't allow you to just make things up

sciencedirect.com/science/articl ...

Abstract

Compositionists have celebrated Wikipedia as a space that privileges collaborative, public writing and complicates traditional notions of authorship and revision. Yet, this scholarship has not considered the implications of Wikipedia's "gender gap"—the highly disproportionate number of male editors over female editors. In this article, I explore how Wikipedia functions as a rhetorical discourse community whose conventions exclude and silence feminist ways of knowing and writing. Drawing on textual analysis of Wikipedia's editorial policies, as well as interviews with female users, I argue that Wikipedia's insistence on separating embodied subjectivity from the production of knowledge limits the site's ability to facilitate any substantial, subversive feminist rhetorical action. These limitations, I suggest, should inform a critical pedagogical approach to Wikipedia.

7:32 AM - 28 Oct 2016

735 Retweets **880** Likes

♡ 65   ⟲ 735   ♡ 880

Figure 6.1 @RealPeerReview tweet. Screencapture by L. Gruwell, 2016.

less stupid place." One commenter even wrote, "Red scum need to be summarily SHOT!!," referring to me, presumably, as the red scum in question. Many comments also specifically took issue with my use of feminist methodology and framed it as antithetical to "real," objective knowledge and scientific practice. Comments like "Its [sic] OK to subvert the patriarchy at the expense of knowledge and scientific progress" and "Academic feminists are out to destroy science in its name" seemed to suggest that because my work was explicitly feminist, it was automatically specious.

With 735 retweets and 880 likes as of June 2018, this is likely the largest public audience that will ever engage with my research. Scholars expect their published work to be subject to scrutiny and criticism, but since the account only posted the abstract (along with a link to my paywalled article), it was hard to imagine that most who responded were engaging with my actual argument rather than the reductive framing offered by @RealPeerReview. Even today, reading these comments is upsetting, especially since several named me and my university directly. I was relatively lucky, however: in at least one case, @RealPeerReview tweeted the C.V. of a recent PhD, ostensibly to make fun of her dissertation title, complete with the scholar's home address.[2]

@RealPeerReview co-opts the process of peer review—which is typically blind, and undertaken by subject area specialists—and makes it public, framing scholars who engage in feminist research as subject to additional, external public surveillance (and, of course, ridicule). Indeed, this account largely targets qualitative research in perceived "soft" fields such as women's/gender/sexuality studies, postcolonial studies, and critical race studies that all tend to reject the positivist epistemology @RealPeerReview seems to endorse. Targeting feminist researchers in this way makes the prospect of even traditional academic publication daunting and suggests that feminist researchers need to be prepared for the possibility of their work going public, even if they do not actively seek to do so. Coupled with the increasing demand to maintain some kind of public presence online, the transparency offered by Internet technologies can undermine the emancipatory goals of feminist research and can even put scholars' privacy and safety at risk.

Tactical Resistance: Researching the Toxic Internet

It is clear that a toxic Internet presents serious challenges for feminist methodologies. How, then, can feminist researchers continue to explore these spaces critically, ethically, and safely? I suggest that feminist researchers navigating potentially precarious online environments adopt what I term a methodology of tactical resistance. This methodology takes seriously the feminist methodological imperatives of reflexivity, reciprocity, and transparency, but does so with the recognition that the

Internet often silences or excludes feminist rhetorics and methodologies. Situational and potentially subversive, a methodology of tactical resistance offers feminist researchers tools to recognize and work around structures of power, continuing to redefine what counts as research.

This methodology is rooted in de Certeau's well-known distinction between strategies and tactics. Strategies, according to de Certeau, are practiced by the powerful, and depend upon "a specific type of knowledge, one sustained and determined by the power to provide oneself with one's own place" (1984, p. 36). A strategy, in other words, is a practice of those who already possess the authority to speak or act. A tactic, by contrast, is the "art of the weak," a practice determined "by the *absence of power*" (1984, p. 38; emphasis original). While feminist methodologies are already well-suited to identify power differentials, a methodology of tactical resistance offers feminist researchers who have determined that they occupy "the space of the other" (deCerteau, 1984, p. 37), a means to intervene in the structures of power that may exclude or otherwise silence them.

Practicing a methodology of tactical resistance thus involves first recognizing the power relations that may preclude feminist research practices and then identifying the multiple networks that surround a research site. Based on an acknowledgment that power is intersectional, polymorphic, and rarely fixed (particularly in potentially hostile online spaces), a methodology of tactical resistance helps researchers navigate the varied relations that structure research, highlighting resistant networks as well as locating ruptures and gaps in power that feminist researchers can then exploit. Because it understands research as always rhetorical and therefore political, a methodology of tactical resistance is an unapologetically activist approach to research that recognizes the responsibility of the feminist researcher to resist the systemic disempowerment of women and other marginalized groups.

Choosing a methodology is a thorny—and often risky—process that demands thoughtful reflection. Every research situation is unique: a methodology of tactical resistance may simply not be appropriate for all research projects. However, because tactics are inherently kairotic, relying "on a clever *utilization of time*, of the opportunities it presents and also of the play that it introduces into the foundations of power" (de Certeau, 1984, pp. 38–39; emphasis original), a methodology of tactical resistance offers a flexibility that is well-suited to the varied spaces Internet researchers may inhabit. The following heuristic questions, then, are starting points meant to help feminist researchers identify tactical opportunities within the specific research environments they may inhabit:

- Who or what are you studying? What are their goals and how do they align with (or differ from) a feminist perspective? Who or what stands to benefit (or lose) from your research?

- What networks surround the participants/community you are studying? How might those networks support and/or undermine your research?
- What power dynamics exist between/around participants and yourself? How might the Internet technologies you use complicate these already-complex relationships?
- How are you constructing your identity as a researcher, as a public figure, and/or as a private citizen of the Internet? Are there any overlaps or contradictions within these positions? How might your participants want to resist the identity you've created?
- Which parts of your identity will you share, and which will you obscure? Have you taken appropriate steps to ensure your privacy and safety?
- How will you share your results? Which audiences (intended or otherwise) might potentially engage with your research?
- Have you created opportunities for self-care throughout your research? What networks—on and offline—exist to support you, including, potentially, other feminist researchers?

While the methodology of tactical resistance I outline here is primarily meant to help feminist researchers navigate the sometimes-hostile spaces of the Internet, it can also inform digital research more broadly. Most notably, it highlights the ways in which any online community is surrounded and sustained by other (digital and/or offline) networks, and suggests that researchers ought to begin acknowledging and connecting with these networks in order to fully account for the complexities of Internet-based rhetoric. While it is tempting to understand digital communities as stable, isolated entities, it is more productive to recognize how they bleed into and overlap with other online spaces and material structures. As a result, a methodology of tactical resistance can illuminate the degree to which power structures inform and are perpetuated in digital spaces. A methodology of tactical resistance, then, offers just one means to the ultimate end: equalizing the web's hierarchical structures to make it easier for feminist rhetorics—and for feminist methodologies—to have a place online.

Notes

1 "Kate" is a pseudonym. To further safeguard her identity (and her continuing relationship with Wikipedia), I am being purposely vague regarding Kate's field of study.
2 For the sake of further protecting this scholar's privacy, I won't include her name or the title of her dissertation.

References

Almjeld, J., & Blair, K. (2012). Multimodal methods for multimodal literacies: Establishing a technofeminist research identity. In K. L. Arola & A. F.

Wysocki (Eds.), *Composing (media)=composing (embodiment)* (pp. 97–109). Logan: Utah State University Press.

Banks, A. J. (2006). *Race, rhetoric, and technology: Searching for higher ground.* Mahwah, NJ: Lawrence Erlbaum.

Bizzell, P. (2000). Feminist methods of research in the history of rhetoric: What difference do they make? *Rhetoric Society Quarterly, 30*(4), 5–17.

Blair, K. (2012). A complicated geometry: Triangulating feminism, activism, and technological literacy. In L. Nickoson & M. P. Sheridan (Eds.), *Writing studies research in practice* (pp. 63–72). Carbondale: Southern Illinois University Press.

Blakely, K. (2007). Reflections on the role of emotion in feminist research. *International Journal of Qualitative Methods, 6*(2), 59–68.

Boseley, S. (2017, August 6). Mary Beard abused on Twitter over Roman Britain's ethnic diversity. *The Guardian.* Retrieved from https://www.theguardian.com/uk-news/2017/aug/06/mary-beard-twitter-abuse-roman-britain-ethnic-diversity

Campbell, E. (2017). 'Apparently being a self-obsessed c**t is now academically lauded': Experiencing Twitter trolling of autoethnographers. *Forum: Qualitative Social Research, 18*(3). doi:10.17169/fqs-18.3.2819

Cole, K. K. (2015). 'It's like she's eager to be verbally abused': Twitter, trolls, and (en)gendering disciplinary rhetoric. *Feminist Media Studies, 15*(2), 356–358.

Cushman, E. (1996). The rhetorician as an agent of social change. *College Composition and Communication, 47*(1), 7–28.

Dadas, C. (2016). Messy methods: Queer methodological approaches to researching social media. *Computers and Composition, 40*, 60–72. doi:10.1016/j.compcom.2016.03.007

de Certeau, M. (1984). *The practice of everyday life.* (S. F. Rendall, Trans.). Berkeley: University of California Press.

Deutsch, N. L. (2004). Positionally and the pen: Reflections on the process of becoming a feminist researcher and writer. *Qualitative Inquiry, 10*(6), 885–902.

Duggan, M. (2017, July 11). *Online harassment 2017.* Retrieved from http://www.pewInternet.org/2017/07/11/online-harassment-2017/

Döring, N., & Mohseni, M. R. (2018). Male dominance and sexism on YouTube: Results of three content analyses. *Feminist Media Studies*, 1–13. doi:10.1080/14680777.2018.1467945

Gelms, B. (2018). Volatile visibility: The effects of online harassment on feminist circulation and public discourse (Doctoral dissertation, Miami University).

Gruwell, L. (2015). Wikipedia's politics of exclusion: Gender, epistemology, and feminist rhetorical (in)action. *Computers and Composition, 37*, 117–131. doi:10.1016/j.compcom.2015.06.009

Gruwell, L. (2017). Writing against harassment: Public writing pedagogy and online hate. *Composition Forum, 36.* Retrieved from http://compositionforum.com/issue/36/against-harassment.php

Haraway, D. J. (1991). *Simians, cyborgs, and women: The reinvention of nature.* New York, NY: Routledge.

Harding, S. (1993). Rethinking standpoint epistemology: What is "strong objectivity"? In L. Alcoff & E. Potter (Eds.), *Feminist epistemologies* (pp. 49–82). New York, NY: Routledge.

Hartsock, N. C. M. (1988). The feminist standpoint: Developing the ground for a specifically feminist historical materialism. In S. Harding (Ed.), *Feminism and methodology* (pp. 157–180). Bloomington: Indiana University Press.

Hawisher, G. E., & Sullivan, P. (1998). Women on the networks: Searching for e-spaces of their own. In S. C. Jarratt & L. Worsham (Eds.), *Feminism and composition studies: In other words* (pp. 172–197). New York, NY: MLA.

Jaggar, A. M. (1989). Love and knowledge: Emotion in feminist epistemology. *Inquiry, 32*(2), 151–176.

Jane, E. A. (2014). 'Your a ugly, Whorish, slut': Understanding e-bile. *Feminist Media Studies, 14*(4), 531–546. doi:10.1080/14680777.2012.741073

Kirsch, G. E. (1999). *Ethical dilemmas in feminist research: The politics of location, interpretation, and publication*. Albany, NY: SUNY Press.

Kirsch, G E., & Ritchie, J. S. (1995). Beyond the personal: Theorizing a politics of location in composition research. *College Composition and Communication, 46*(1), 7–29.

Lather, P. (1991). *Getting smart: Feminist research and pedagogy within/in the postmodern*. New York, NY: Routledge.

Lenhart, A., Ybarra, M., Zickuhr, K., & Price-Feeney, M. (2016, November 21). *Online harassment, digital abuse, and cyberstalking in America*. Retrieved from https://www.datasociety.net/pubs/oh/Online_Harassment_2016.pdf

MacAulay, M., & Visser, R. (2016). Editing diversity in: Reading diversity discourses on Wikipedia. *Ada: A Journal of Gender, New Media, and Technology, 9*. doi:10.7264/N36M3541

Mantilla, K. (2013). Gendertrolling: Misogyny adapts to new media. *Feminist Studies, 39*(2), 563–570.

Massanari, A. L. (2018). Rethinking research ethics, power, and the risk of visibility in the era of the 'alt-right' gaze. *Social Media+ Society, 4*(2), 1–9.

McKee, H. A., & Porter, J. E. (2010). Rhetorica online: Feminist research practices in cyberspace. In E. K. Schell & KL Rawson (Eds.), *Rhetorica in motion: Feminist methods and methodologies* (pp. 152–171). Pittsburgh, PA: University of Pittsburgh Press.

McMillan Cottom, T. (2015). 'Who do you think you are?': When marginality meets academic microcelebrity. *Ada: A Journal of Gender, New Media, and Technology, 7*. doi:10.7264/N3319T5T

Megarry, J. (2014). Online incivility or sexual harassment? Conceptualising women's experiences in the digital age. *Women's Studies International Forum, 47*, 46–55.

Morrison, A. (2018). Of, by, and for the Internet: New media studies and public scholarship. In Sayers, J. (Ed.), *The Routledge companion to media studies and digital humanities* (pp. 76–86). New York, NY: Routledge.

Nagy-Zekmi, S., & Hollis, K. (2010). Questions of response/ability: Public intellectuals in the information age. In S. Nagy-Zekmi & K. Hollis (Eds.), *Truth to power: Public intellectuals in and out of academe* (pp. xv–xxi). Newcastle upon Tyne, England: Cambridge Scholars Publishing.

Nakamura, L. (2008). *Digitizing race: Visual cultures of the Internet*. Minneapolis: University of Minnesota Press.

Noble, S. U. (2018). *Algorithms of oppression: How search engines reinforce racism*. New York, NY: NYU Press.

Notes on good practices on Wikipedia research (2011, September 5). Retrieved June 24, 2018 from Wikipedia: https://meta.wikimedia.org/wiki/Notes_on_good_practices_on_Wikipedia_research

Powell, K. M., & Takayoshi, P. (2003). Accepting roles created for us: The ethics of reciprocity. *College Composition and Communication,* 54(3), 394–422.

Quintana, C. (2017, June 17). For one scholar, an online stoning tests the limits of public scholarship. *The Chronicle of Higher Education.* Retrieved from https://www.chronicle.com/article/For-One-Scholar-an-Online/240384

Royster, J. J. (2000). *Traces of a stream: Literacy and social change among African American women.* Pittsburgh, PA: University of Pittsburgh Press.

Sapienza, F. (2007). Ethos and research positionality in studies of virtual communities. In H. A. McKee & D. N. DeVoss (Eds.), *Digital writing research* (pp: 89–106). Cresskill, NJ: Hampton Press.

Twitter account mocking 'questionable' left-wing papers is shrouded in secrecy amid threats of hacking. (2017, February 14). *Fox News.* Retrieved from http://www.foxnews.com/us/2017/02/14/twitter-account-mocking-questionable-left-wing-papers-is-shrouded-in-secrecy-amid-threats-hacking.html

Veletsianos, G., & Hodson, J. (2018, May 29). *Inside Higher Ed.* Retrieved from https://www.insidehighered.com/views/2018/05/29/dealing-social-media-harassment-opinion

Vera-Gray, F. (2017). 'Talk about a cunt with too much idle time': Trolling feminist research. Feminist Review, 115(1), 61–78.

7 "Maybe She Can Be a Feminist and Still Claim Her Own Opinions?"

The Story of an Accidental Counter-Troll, *A Treatise in 9 Movements*

Vyshali Manivannan

Movement 1[1]

In 2017, troll scholars Whitney Phillips, Jessica Beyer, and Gabriella Coleman published a piece challenging the mass media's narrative about the role of trolls, 4chan, and the alt-right in Trump's election. They contended that "trolling," already overused shorthand for "disruption," doesn't apply to white nationalism; that anonymous and pseudo-anonymous communities like 4chan and reddit fluctuate in terms of ideology and demographics; and that the alt-right's visibility depended on journalistic amplification and far-right media outlets' sudden ability to set the narrative agenda for mainstream news (Phillips, Beyer, & Coleman, 2017). They legitimized these challenges by asserting, "We've been studying online communities and subcultures for years," with a "combined total of over thirty years of research experience" (Phillips, Beyer, & Coleman, 2017). As evidence, they're not alone in their research; they link to pieces by other scholars and to *Fibreculture*'s issue on troll theory, which includes my work on 4chan.

Their argument is worth making, but the article instigated a thread on 4chan's Politics (/pol/) subforum to document and evaluate the potential value or threat these troll scholars posed to the subculture. The authors' photos were posted, with talk of punitive action. Most of the rhetoric was misogynistic and intellectually belittling, such as "women/scholars: choose," "if anyone is a scholar on memetics, they are on 4chan and 100% not a woman," and a post quoting the authors' credentials and commenting, "MY SIDES," judging the list laughable (Anonymous, 2017a, b). Measuring status and expertise by duration of research isn't uncommon. But a combined total of years of study is a nonsensical metric for substantive merit, and basing prestige on genre and quantity instead of quality of publication is anathema to a subculture that prides itself on its anti-celebrity, meritocratic ethic. This backlash also speaks to 4chan's long-standing resentment of scholars, journalists, and other epistemological gatekeepers who became careless historians for a community without a centralized archive. Maybe it's an accusation that as academics, especially when we extol accuracy, we're supposed to care about getting it right.

If we call it misogyny, then I'm a strange opportunity to pass up: a nonwhite, queer, disabled female scholar and novelist who browsed 4chan daily and published work on its purposely repellent subcultural logics (Manivannan, 2013). I used to think that readers were skipping the prefatory material including my name, which codes as Tamil female, but I want to suggest that these trolls examine our scholarship and recalibrate their strategies to fit our culture more than their ideology. As Overstreet (2018) argues, they're strategic rhetoricians who "define, and are defined by, each other and the world from which they emerge" (p. 158). That is, misogyny is reserved for trolling women, homophobic slurs and taunts about virility for men. When they target academics, they become an intersubjective effect of a given academic field, its particular disciplinary allegiances, its hostility to novel approaches, minorities, women, and its oppositional criticism (Berkenkotter, 1995, pp. 245–247; Olson & LaPoe, 2018, p. 273).

This is the stereotype of Reviewer #2, the academic boogeyman of the peer review system, which promises professional quality control over scholarly publication. Less a number than a discursive mode, Reviewer #2 is popularly seen as the one most inflexible, harsh, adversarial, and married to their discipline's preferred paradigm. Peer review grants epistemic credibility. It's the currency of competence for graduate students seeking a way in, non-tenure-track faculty seeking to hold on, faculty seeking promotion or tenure. Caught somewhere between scholar and troll myself, I see Reviewer #2 as a gift for trolls from communities like 4chan or reddit who target academics in order to infiltrate and dismantle scholarly gatekeeping, particularly when it comes to representations of trolling cultures. Coordinating in anonymous or pseudo-anonymous spaces and acting in identity-based social networks like Twitter, these "academic trolls" borrow the language of agonistic peer review to walk among us as one of us, to critique the scholarly community for leveraging the link between higher education and morality to condemn what older trolling cultures still do. Reviewer #2 offers them a way to exaggerate, amplify, and publicize the ways in which peer review—the linchpin of the research enterprise—is riddled with sexism, racism, elitism, incivility, and confirmation bias.

Academic trolls adopt as their primary rhetorical strategy the ad hominem, adversarial, and intellectualist discourse of a stereotypical Reviewer #2, so normalized that it has achieved meme and hashtag status, but which, by virtue of belonging to higher education, signals civility, morality, and good taste, regardless of what's being said. Practically a readymade defense.

Embracing our priorities, academic trolls harass scholars with the rhetoric normalized in peer review, a rhetorical performance that prevents, dismantles, or otherwise limits alternate epistemic forms. They flay the hypocrisy of progressive academic tolerance to the bone, and use it as a proof of our duplicity in labeling trolling practices "hate speech" when the same speech acts in peer review are normalized as "constructive criticism."

Movement 2

Tannen (2002) argues that much of our academic exchange is founded on an accepted ideology of agonism that, especially in its extreme forms—like Reviewer #2—is destructive for knowledge-making. Conventional frameworks ask scholars to find fault and oppose,

> engendering a lack of respect for colleagues and for the cultural diversity of our disciplines. Unfair criticism often grows out of a failure to understand or appreciate the disciplinary context in which other researchers are working, and the methodologies they employ.
> (Tannen, 2002, p. 1665)

This unfair criticism applies especially to interdisciplinary work, which betrays a given discipline's paradigm. Autoethnography occupies a similarly contested space: its site of inquiry and use of aesthetic, poetic, and performative techniques undermine the mind/body schism carefully maintained by scholarly communities invested in preserving their discipline's "objective" paradigm. This belief in objectivity is steeped in the myth that the pursuit of knowledge and those who pursue it can be separated, and that authors aren't hurt or silenced by sneering blind reviews, equating Reviewer #2 with 4chan trolls and their project of training others, through trolling, to suppress their emotional response (McCosker, 2014; Tannen, 2002).

Let's call it "academic trolling," a triple entendre that enfolds trolls trolling scholars, scholars trolling scholars, and scholars trolling trolls. Moses (2018) finds the same core belief in the alt-right and higher education: that sabotage, hoax, and provocation—the tools of 4chan trolls—are appropriable strategies that can gut or empower scholars or politicians.

Trolls "argue by reflecting the mannerisms, arguments, and personality traits of their interlocutors back at them, *ad absurdum*" (Moses, 2018, p. 13). With trolls targeting scholars, their aggressive meta-discourse becomes about the problematic rhetorical performances of quality control in academic publishing, especially where it reifies older, more rigid methods and styles (Moses, 2018, p. 20).

Failing to acknowledge the overlap between scholars and academic trolls permits us to condemn. This condemnation, too, is easily weaponized against the scholarly community as hypocrisy.

Movement 3

Since academic trolls accuse us of poorly defining our terms, we should differentiate between trolling on 4chan and trolling on social media sites like Twitter, where many scholars, many of them female and/or nonwhite qualitative researchers, report being digitally harassed. Generally speaking, trolling exists on a continuum, and as it's not a fixed or pregiven aspect of a discursive environment, how we define it depends on its context. Coleman (2012) describes trolling as ambivalent, with disparate agendas executed through morally questionable, spectacular actions. It tends to embrace meritocratic norms and information transparency and hinges on lulz, or the active disruption of another's emotional equilibrium. On boards like 4chan, this manifests as a rhetorical, mimetic device intended to destabilize the basis for normatively rational conversation (Coleman, 2012, pp. 114–115). 4chan and its clones, like 7chan and 8chan, are fast-paced, interest-based, anonymous imageboards, housing 50+ topical subforums, each offering a robust alternative to social media and the logics of self-promotion. Between 2006 and 2016, content suppression and ideological rifts caused factions of 4chan users to defect to IRC, 7chan, and the "free-speech-friendly" 8chan. /pol/, short for "Politically Incorrect," was first created as a "containment board" for unironic expressions of white supremacy on 4chan, and operates on both 4chan and 8chan today (Marwick & Lewis, 2017, pp. 11–12). Knuttila (2011) finds that the central experience of 4chan is contingency, the absolute lack of certainty, where users emerge in relation to an environment in constant flux and other anonymous users negotiating that environment. Content on *chan boards refreshes automatically, and expired content is permanently removed unless users save it in personal folders or community-run archives like Chanarchive, or if automated 4chan web crawlers like Holla Forums archive snapshots. As the *chans lack an automatic, centralized repository, preserved threads and paratexts identify material deemed important to collective memory (Knuttila, 2011). So does the practice of self-documentation, in temporary and persistent forms, from memes to near-mythologizing entries on Encyclopedia Dramatica. Although the nature of 4chan's discourse is such that anything can be archived, most of it isn't, generating a resistance to archival memory—fixed, unchanging documents—in favor of Herwig's (2011) conception of repertoire, an embodied knowledge that requires continual presence and connection to yield a history that is ever-changing (p. 46).

It seems natural, then, that scholarship making assertions about 4chan's culture and history in finalized, permanent formats would always be suspect to the community.

The same features of the interface also cultivate a culture of automatic dissent, less mobilized by ideological difference than by a performative contrarian stance (Auerbach, 2012). The *chan troll offers counterdiscourses to any discourse offered as hegemonic, regardless of its content, particularly when lulzy responses are anticipated. In keeping with what Auerbach (2012) calls anonymous forums' economy of unreality, participation constitutes a kind of insincere masquerade. This is diametrically opposed to the secrecy of peer review and lack of accountability for Reviewer #2's evaluations, which are more sincere than lulzy since they aren't intended to generate response. For lulz-oriented trolls, the desired outcome is emotional outburst, and the attendant suggestion that the inability to quell your emotions means you're intellectually inferior, incapable of rational discourse (McCosker, 2014, p. 201). Scholarly communities, particularly where disciplinary clashes arise over methodological differences, insist on erasing emotions too, rejecting personal presence in scholarship and enthroning disembodied intellect. After all, if the text is separable from the scholar, it's acceptable to sneer (Tannen, 2002, p. 1665).

In contrast to 4chan trolls, social media trolls on sites like Twitter that value identity and social prestige acquire the rhetorical dynamics particular to those values. Ott (2017) observes that "Twitter ultimately trains us to devalue others, thereby cultivating mean and malicious discourse" (p. 60). Tweets are simple and impulsive, and the ones that reach peak popularity possess intense, often negative charge, creating a space conducive to heartfelt incivility. Identity-based flame wars, or abusive exchanges that degrade or hijack the subject of debate, thrive on Twitter, particularly what Mantilla (2013) calls gendertrolling: the expression of sincere misogyny; the coordinated participation of numerous participants; longevity and intensity across online and offline sites; and the reliance on vicious, credible gender-based insults and threats to suppress women's response to sexism (p. 564). Unlike the academic trolls collaborating on 4chan, whose onsite ethos resists fanaticism and treats nothing as sacred, gendertrolls are true believers in the issues of the manosphere. In many ways, this limits their rhetorical actions to flame war, and makes them as vulnerable to outrage as those they target. Academic trolls originate on a site where users pride themselves on maintaining emotional equilibrium and adapt that culture to social media sites like Twitter, slowly hyper-exaggerating Reviewer #2's extreme rhetoric to the point of absurdity, laughing until anyone catches on, and earning the bonus of wresting the narrative agenda away from academic experts (Moses, 2018).

In many ways, Twitter seems like an ideal space for academic trolls to make conspicuous the fact that academics, as agents of epistemological power, are biased in their gatekeeping. It's an ideal site to target and undercut academic prestige, especially since many scholars use it to discuss their workflow, share and promote their publications, and otherwise reveal their personality, process, and research agenda. Marginalized scholars are easily transformed into objects of hate for a community already prepared to cohere around flaming. Motivation doesn't excuse or forgive the actions a troll may undertake, as victim perception is crucial to the trolling act (Marwick & Lewis, 2017). But when we conflate variants of *chan-style trolling, in this case academic trolling, with hate, we misrepresent it and do ourselves a disservice. Hate-attribution is a rhetorical endgame, its performative force stemming from its ability to drain any position, gesture, or speech act of any political or representational agency, reducing it to thoughtless reprehensibility. It's often a tool deployed by liberal political theory to define itself against an enemy Other opposed to its ideals of "love," "compassion," "empathy," and "tolerance" (Duncan, 2017). Higher education aligns itself with these ideals, so hate-attribution doesn't stick to Reviewer #2 the same way it does to trolls. Thus, Reviewer #2 is the dream role in an online masquerade designed to simultaneously expose academic hypocrisy and commandeer a significant node in the information economy.

Threads from reddit and from /pol/ archived by the automated indexer Holla Forums indicate that academic trolls understand peer review and trolling as twin discursive modes of social control: marked by misogyny, status-based prejudice, intolerance of newness or change, derision or snark, and ambiguity about the writer's real beliefs. This allows academic trolls to cloak themselves in our decorum to perform within what Auerbach (2012) calls anonymous culture's pervasive sense of unreality and economies of offense and suspicion: a steady equilibrium of offense designed to exclude those sympathetic to mainstream norms like personal fame; and a persistent skepticism that cultivates a disposition toward accepting nothing at face value and engaging in frequent detective work (pp. 12–18).

These economies have no place on Twitter, which privileges reputation and popularity. But scholars—often white, male, working in quantitative disciplines—perform and accept all three economies on social media, taking to Twitter to allege a loss of empiricism and theoretical rigor due to methods like autoethnography or interdisciplinarity. Some of these approaches emerge in troll scholarship, especially around 4chan, because continual presence is required for understanding, pointing to a possible personal stake that academic trolls have in controlling representations of trolling (Herwig, 2011; Knuttila, 2011). I'm assuming for the moment that the Twitter scholars I've mentioned earlier are who they say they are and not academic trolls, the variant using Reviewer #2's language for the lulz. It's sometimes impossible to tell.

Movement 4

The academic world is the one in which a scholar's research endeavors are shaped by metrics like number of peer-reviewed publications, journal rankings, and citation count per publication. Peer review includes internal and external reviews of tenure dossiers, grant applications, classroom performance, publication, and departmental decision-making procedures. Reviewer #2 arises out of blind peer review processes that determine publication, wherein experts in the discipline appraise the quality of work produced by a scholar in the same field. However, even at its most equitable and merit-based, a junior scholar's peers aren't equals but higher-ranked gatekeepers like full professors, editors, or scholars with different disciplinary orientations. Anonymity is used to prevent social bias, but disciplinary differences can cause referees to read in different ways. Diverse disciplinary allegiances can be advantageous, potentially introducing the author to multiple perspectives and research methods, but only if the referees aren't suspicious of approaches that diverge from theirs (Berkenkotter, 1995, pp. 246–247).

Peer review can and does work when it couples quality control with the encouragement of innovation and, to accommodate reading in different ways, an openness to interdisciplinarity, a careful attendance to authors' contributions instead of their failings. The discursive mode we call Reviewer #2—agonistic, oppositional debate aimed at "exposing weaknesses and faults in another's scholarship, [resulting in] odd assumptions about what belongs in a paper and what does not" (Tannen, 2002, p. 1657)—and the trepidation this inspires in junior scholars renders the peer review process unsound. Peer review remains "a social mechanism through which a discipline's 'experts' maintain quality control over new knowledge entering the field" (Berkenkotter, 1995, p. 245), and a space where Reviewer #2 seems freed by anonymity to rhetorically perform the same antagonistic, irreverent, hateful humor that scholars ascribe to the *chans, while rejecting the premise that we have normalized this as well.

So this isn't to say we should abolish peer review. We need to recognize how its usefulness is imperiled by the destructive consequences of combative referees, and how our tolerance of this makes us vulnerable to sophisticated disinformation disseminated online by academic trolls pretending to be us. To academic trolls, Reviewer #2's rhetorical performance is steeped in their culture of automatic dissent—an inflexible contrarian commitment to a concept, method, or discipline at odds with the author's operational goals—but also in celebrity discourse of the self, which is antithetical to onsite *chan culture. It's rare that a figure is both target and method of targeting, utilitarian and lulzy. Coupled with the reductive characterization of 4chan by many academics—many of whom are derided by the community for misunderstanding insider slang or relying on personal prestige to legitimize their arguments—it's reason enough to target us for "redpilling[2]," or turning us, our work, and Reviewer #2's rhetoric to their advantage.

Autoethnography, for instance, often derided as unverifiable, easily falsified "mesearch," is a primary target for academic trolling from *chan users because Reviewer #2 treats it similarly. Audiences who witness academic trolling performed by seemingly established scholars are likely to reject autoethnography and the interdisciplinarity it entails. There's even a chance that the autoethnographer will turn on systems of academic gatekeeping. After all, "Shit My Reviewers Say," with over 47,000 followers, and the Facebook group "Reviewer 2 Must Be Stopped," with nearly 16,000, indicate a willingness to broadcast abusive feedback. Threatening the impartiality of peer review is tantamount to threatening its social, psychological, and epistemic legitimacy, discrediting the knowledge vetted by this process. Silencing interdisciplinary, innovative approaches like online ethnography and autoethnography—especially given that journalists and feminist scholars like Adams (2017), Campbell (2017), Jane (2017), Vera-Gray (2017), and others disclose the autoethnographic origins of their research—means exploiting knowledge-making processes that directly impact troll cultures. So for academic trolls, either result is a victory. Either way, they expose how the language of peer review is inclined toward suspicion, offensiveness, and a sense of unreality in its project of defending what legitimate knowledge production is.

However well- or ill-intentioned, reviews of autoethnography tend to legitimize research siloes, mainstream sites of study, and conventionally rigorous approaches. Wall (2008) reflects on evaluations of an autoethnographic article, where critiques called it without theoretical grounding and "legitimate" method. Holt (2003) observes that feedback on an autoethnographic article consisted mainly of universal critiques of autoethnography, not specific comments, and that some of his referees questioned its rigor, while others didn't think it constituted research at all, stating, "The author does not convince me of the significance of the methodology for reflective purposes" and "Time does not equate to quality. There is no evidence of rigor in this narrative" (pp. 21–24). This last comment is interesting, given that Phillips, Beyer, and Coleman (2017) use time spent in the field as a proof of expertise, and 4chan trolls, like this reviewer, similarly complained.

In coordination threads on /pol/, *chan users create literature review matrices to contrast these rebuttals to feminist, autoethnographic, and interdisciplinary areas with the research itself. Coleman (2012) mentions that trolls may act as informal, armchair ethnographers and archivists, recording their own history (p. 111). *chan users preserve what is culturally significant, so it says something that they save these literature reviews and practice the official discourse of Reviewer #2, whose adversativeness transforms a potentially illuminating, warranted review into scholar-enacted academic trolling. That is, it isn't impossible for them to grasp conventions across disciplinary traditions for the purpose of lulz and *a posteriori* construction of arguments about picking your battles, lurking, learning. By contrast, despite ties to the moral enterprise of civil, progressive academic culture, Reviewer #2 prefers oppositional debate, which online might as well be known as lulzily, ceaselessly feeding the trolls.

Movement 5

Can you tell which quote comes from Reviewer #2's gatekeeping, which from academic trolls?

a "Self-obsessed cunt" ≡ "The navel-gazing characteristic of a woman's diary"?[3]
b "Massive wall of text saying nothing of substance" ≡ "Entire premise of the work [is] utterly theoretically bankrupt"?[4]
c "High was my expectation, and so much deeper was my disappointment" ≡ "For trolling scholars they don't seem to know what trolling even is. Also I love their bias and double standards"?[5]

d "It is essentially an opinion piece that editorializes shamelessly about the superior methods of a recent paper in the first person" ≡ "We've got to come up with new ways of interacting with and analyzing movements, because methods used to interpret older, more rigid models of organization don't necessarily apply"?[6]

Best demonstrated in (a), Reviewer #2's feedback is a more polite form of trollish misogyny. (b) and (c) evince similar levels of snark. And in (d), oddly enough, it's the academic troll who recognizes what Reviewer #2 can't, that you can't study new phenomena using unsuitable methods.

What does this say about us?

Movement 6

In a crowdsourcing thread on /pol/ where my name is mentioned, a user observes, "The real win for us is to redpill the authors, generating a cascade event until they are shut down" (Holla Forums, 2017). Another user replies:

> You assume that a redpilled author will be free to publish redpilled material or withdraw from the publication of bluepilled[7] material. In truth, any hint of redpilling within the academy is ruthlessly isolated and prevented from spreading. Grants aren't given to researchers who don't produce the conclusions the funders want to hear. Bluepilled peer reviewers will demand changes. Bluepilled journals will deny publication. Bluepilled faculties will take disciplinary action. All academics know this. They know the game and they know their career track.
>
> (Holla Forums, 2017)

Maybe we instinctively bristle at this, but trade "bluepilled" for "contrarian," "inflexibly committed to a pet discipline," "unwilling to believe as well as doubt," or "adhering to hierarchical power structures wherein authorship is taken as mastery and the author is always lesser, never an author/ity," or other characteristics of Reviewer #2, and the charges start to stick.

All methodologies warrant a critical eye, but the rhetoric of Reviewer #2, which finds its double in academic trolls, positions female scholars, creative methodologies, and style as toxic threats to the idyllic safe space of academic culture: intellectual rigor (i.e. established, appropriate methods and sites of inquiry), bourgeois norms of taste and decency (i.e.

concealing emotional labor), the veneration of overwork and expertise (i.e. not understanding comes with high stakes).

Harassed over her supposed "narcissism, lack of scientific prowess, and dullness" (Campbell, 2017), autoethnographer Elaine Campbell observes that this abuse mirrors that of autoethnography's scholarly detractors, who contend such research "reads like a woman's diary, not like a scientific piece of work" (Shit My Reviewers Say, 2017, August 30). Vera-Gray (2017), gendertrolled for the feminist positioning of her research, was additionally criticized by academic trolls using the language of Reviewer #2, as in "Male scientists don't get involved in these kinds of things because they are busy researching real things that may have an impact on the world" (p. 73). To a wider audience, civility makes gender-based critique more acceptable than "self-obsessed cunt"; for the narrower audience of academics being targeted, academic trolls use the professional rhetoric that produces the disciplinary identities that scholars come to occupy to remind academics that their own field—crystallized in Reviewer #2—wants to see them fail.

Olson and LaPoe (2018) find that women are hindered from fully participating in academic discourse, as men are framed as more articulate, argumentative, rational, and diligent. This leaves women scholars both accustomed and vulnerable to digital silencing on social media by gendertrolls, who aim to create a "digital Spiral of Silence," mediated intimidation by a vocal minority to compel female academics to disengage from social media to protect themselves and their careers (Olson & LaPoe, 2018, pp. 273–274, 278). But 4chan trolls generally don't want their targets to disengage. Silence contravenes the project of lulz, which requires a steady stream of impassioned response. So, while academic trolling mimics gendertrolling in its preference for scholars who resist the cultural violence and erasure of academic discourse, those most vocal about the hypocrisy of liberal, progressive academic culture, most disenchanted with the failures of peer review and the limits of academic meritocracy, it's in service of "the real win." These scholars seem most open to conversion.

If 4chan trolls are a barometer for sociocultural significance, given their extensive ethnographic fieldwork on potential targets, then perhaps they view these scholars as having underrecognized importance in knowledge communities, and therefore as being most important to redpill. Interdisciplinary, autoethnographic approaches, for instance, are as alienated and stigmatized as a 4chan troll. We're maybe seen as most likely to study repugnant sites. We're maybe presumed savvy enough to know where to publish, how to write in ways that evade an outright "no" from "bluepilled" peer reviewers or journals, straddling a line between unpacking a problematic academic phenomenon and rehabilitating academic trolling in progressive outlets.

If we're silenced, the only loss is lulz. If we resist academic culture by publishing redpilled material, "generating a cascade event," that's the "real win."

I find myself on this trajectory, an accidental counter-troll, a scholar like the targets listed earlier whose work and merits were summarized and debated by academic trolls on /pol/, more generously than Reviewer #2, perhaps because I strived to account for the ethic of the community I was writing about in my style of writing. I drew from my experience, but didn't supplement with credentials. I adopted phrasing that accepted what academic culture often resists: the language of lurking and continual learning, not of absolute expertise.

And maybe because I have been a troll, I accidentally wrote like one, unintentionally attempting to troll the trolls.

Movement 7

"I got curious and found something interesting," a user writes, "This Vyshali Manivannan is either one of us or has a very sharp eye. Almost all of his scholarly articles are on imageboard culture" (Holla Forums, 2017). Another disagrees, "The faggot who wrote these articles is probably a 4channer who thought they could turn their autistic waste of a life into an academic career" (Holla Forums, 2017). What does that make me, if they're not entirely wrong? A harmless, possibly advantageous voice, whose "trendy" hybrid methods and autoethnographic work and "one of them" experience with digital autoethnography could help them rewrite the narrative agenda? Or a liberal academic drunk on the Kool-Aid, "a possible ping for high-knowledge threat in the future" (Holla Forums, 2017)?

If I had to distill it down, maybe lurking, thoroughness, and "writing like a troll"—that is, flexibly accommodating both a serious academic tone and an ironic one—in this article about 4chan shielded me, but I doubt my situation is common. I happened to have been an insider, familiar with the subcultural argot and practices I was analyzing. In these threads, at least, users evaluated the substance of my work before noticing my gender, ethnicity, or sexual orientation by checking the rest of my online presence. They singled out the bio on my blog, which included an author photo and descriptions of my research agenda, writing projects, and institutional affiliations, and a post reflecting on my experiences as a graduate student. The post was an obvious choice. I had tagged it "autoethnography." I'd taken inspiration from feminine *mêtis*. I'd included a dream log from my bullet journal, popularly cast as feminine pursuits (Manivannan, 2016). But then, paradoxically for those hoping to pigeonhole me as a "pozzed feminist shill," I criticized doctoral programs for academic hazing in written and oral feedback, hostility toward competing agendas and "reprehensible" sites of inquiry (like 4chan), and bias against women, minorities, the disabled. I argued that biomedicine and social science needed to value artistic integrity. I acknowledged that, as a doctoral student and professor, I was part of the machine, and therefore, potentially, part of the problem. I was trying to say, despite my precarious status, that academic departments and the scholarly journals we covet for employment or promotion are built on rigid hierarchical processes that need to change.

This same post was received by academic trolls very differently. One poster, focusing on a section where I put "research" in quotes—interpreted as self-deprecatory awareness that narrative and autoethnography aren't "real" research but should be—insisted I'd "been absorbed completely into the academy" (Holla Forums, 2017). Some dismissed me as a "woman justifying her inability to reason" (Holla Forums, 2017), despite the *Fibreculture* article that seemed to resonate with them, but others momentarily floundered at this, that I sounded like a /pol/ user, that, somehow, this was also how a real feminist would sound. One poster noted: "Difficult, isn't it? She demonstrates the kind of understanding of our ways that can only be gained by steady long-term acclimation, to the point I begin to see any of the academy-vomit she spews as a kind of mockery" (Holla Forums, 2017). What was there to do, since they had already praised the article for its accuracy, but rationalize my position by deciding I was "a high-caste Indian woman. I would assume she isn't 'one of us,' but just sharp and has an inherited affinity for the Aryan mindset" (Holla Forums, 2017). But to some of them, I was engaging in their kind of doublespeak, where my assertions could be read seriously or sarcastically—as when I asked, "What counts as evidence?," and where my jargon-laden sentences could be derisive ingratiation to academic culture's intellectual elitism, or as tongue-in-cheek as *chan-coordinated prank phone calls. Perhaps most significantly, a poster questioned,

> Maybe she can be a feminist and still claim her own opinions? You might feel similarly if you were a woman in academia. Ironically, many of the comments you all have made about her prove some tenets of feminism to be true. (outgrouping her based on sex and left leaning politics, then proceeding to discredit her and assign an enemy status).
>
> (Holla Forums, 2017)

In other words, an academic troll of the second variety, a scholar trolling scholars, who maybe also slipped into the third variety, the scholar trolling trolls, by writing in doublespeak in parsing the relationship between person, jargon, and argument, especially with regard to a decentralized, anonymous forum where identity is always fluid, emergent, and relational.

Movement 8

Academic trolling is a discursive mode with three prongs: trolls trolling scholars, or those who coordinate on 4chan and confront their targets on social media; scholars trolling scholars, as in Reviewer #2 whose rhetorical strategies resemble a civil, bourgeois version of onsite 4chan discourse; and scholars trolling trolls—a kind of counter-troll, or vaccine, perhaps, for the other two types of academic troll. Maybe, my near miss suggests that counter-trolling can be a valid academic practice, necessitating a reevaluation of the place of academic trolling—particularly scholars trolling trolls—in scholarly publishing, and that we need to dismantle Reviewer #2, restoring personhood to scholarship and refining our modes of disagreement.

Academic trolls may ignore identity factors if the content is "fair" and the paper well-written (which isn't the same as being kind). A redditor praised that *Fibreculture* article because "the emphasis on context and understanding the rules of the community from the inside was great" (u/Entelluss-Gloves, 2015). The same thread indicates that, while many academic trolls use search terms to arrive at preconceived notions before they read—combining "ctrl-F" + "autoethnography," "misogyny," "feminist," or "hate"—actually reading and comprehending articles crowdsourced for a literature review is imperative. Two users in this reddit thread separately remarked, "10 reasons evil misogynist [sic] thing I don't like is just like every other evil transmisogynoirist thing I don't like" and "CTRL + F 'misog' = 32 results, W T F," and were gently chastised by the original poster, "At least read the article first? This is academic anthropological analysis, not the Huffington Post" ("Understanding gg," 2015).

The words they search for are telling, as is what they choose to target or learn from, and if we want to inoculate ourselves by becoming academic trolls, rhetorical context is important. Counter-trolling means that our phrasing, citation, and hate-attribution matter, and that our rhetorical strategies should emerge relationally, without sacrificing substance.

Reframing Reviewer #2 doesn't mean eliminating oppositional debate. It asks referees to prioritize respect and conciliation, to look for strengths before attacking weaknesses, to remember that people exist behind the page, to consider language in context and the effects of our agonistic discourse (Tannen, 2002, p. 1667), since this agonistic discourse provides motive (oppositional debate = never-ending lulz) and strategy (Reviewer #2 = familiar discursive mode and post hoc defense) to the academic trolls who target us. To them, Reviewer #2 recasts any academic department that tallies peer-reviewed publications for promotion or tenure as legitimizing destructive agonism, which undermines the ability of those academics to criticize linguistic strategies used to demonize and discredit a community. To extend Tannen's suggestions, I think we should consider how dichotomizing how knowledge should be created and organized makes us vulnerable to not only editors, referees, and other members of the scholarly community but also trolls who see us as lolcows, highly exploitable for humor, or redpillable, highly exploitable for derailing a narrative about academic gatekeeping, epistemological production, and progressive tolerance, to paint journalists and academic scholars—the major offenders in misrepresenting troll cultures—as corrupt, self-interested, and hypocritical, motivated by reputational mechanisms more than meritocracy or collaboration. Maybe one of the reasons these academic trolls let my blog post slide was that I too appeared to be calling out the hypocrisy of maintaining an idyllic safe space by using hate-attribution to protect your ranks. Or, if their goal is to identify both "high-knowledge threats" and disenchanted scholars, maybe it was better to see if my work could be rehabilitated.

Movement 9

I think we should acknowledge that we sometimes fail to do the work we insist others to do: observe even reprehensible cultural phenomena on their own terms, and learn the languages of those we study from a distance in horror. I think because of what Duncan (2017) identifies as "liberalism's struggle to yoke itself to 'love' [having] as its eerie double a struggle to locate among its ideological and political enemies an increasingly reified 'hate,'" we worry that if we do this work, we'll become the targets of hate-attribution ourselves, stripping us of effective political agency. But comprehension and instruction don't necessarily mean becoming an advocate or apologist. Rather, candid reflexivity would create opportunities for polemical counteraction, planned and rhetorically performed with a (potentially) equally strategic eye.

As Overstreet (2018) says, this means we have to accept that words don't, or differently, matter (p. 161), as with the nomadic, paralogic writing characteristic of Vitanza's (1987) "antibody rhetoric," which itself enacts a self-commentary and orthographic play akin to 4chan's onsite trolling and makes a similar bid for epistemic uncertainty, echoing its culture of contingency. This is a "sub/versive" rhetoric, a non-disciplinary rhetoric unconcerned with adjudicating knowledge claims, aimed instead at locating and exploiting rhetorical differences. This is rhetoric weaponized against narrow definitions of composition theory, enacted in Vitanza's article as provocation that resists the traditional rules of argumentation and fosters a nondisciplinary, nonlogical poetic growth of knowledge (p. 44). This "antibody rhetoric," meant to "struggle against author/ity," has "the ability to suspend, counterbalance readings interminably. In this view, The Antibody Rhetoric is a mobile army of counter-sub/versions composed *not* of, but constituted by, the differences that shuttle between metaphor and irony" (Vitanza, 1987, p. 49). It's intended to "cure" rhetoric of its tendencies to exploit, repress, and exclude. It evades the academic, disciplinary, and grammatical system of rhetoric that has disenfranchised creative, nonlinear, playful, and open-ended ways of inquiring and knowing, in favor of the illusion of mastery, legitimacy, and finality.

This is a restoration of the creative principle to language, as in rhetorical guerilla warfare, which academic trolls have been innovating much longer than us, perhaps summed up by the user who suggests that the real interest in our scholarship is: "whether we can a) use it to further our own reinforcement of our culture and protect it from future subversion and b) develop countermeasures to future subversion that might arise from (((someone))) using the knowledge within" (Holla Forums, 2017). Rhetoric as a tool for social exploitation, language as a war game presumed invisible to scholars who have forgotten the "anti-tradition tradition of being such a provocateur" (Vitanza, 1987, p. 57). That is, academic trolls know that most knowledge communities still reject the antibody.

If there's a conclusion to be had, maybe it's this. By modulating Reviewer #2's rhetoric, by writing like antibody-wielding counter-trolls in anticipation of academic trolling, we can sidestep vitriolic reactions and threatening coordination threads, as occurred around Coleman, Phillips, and Beyer (2017). This means understanding the rhetoric of academic trolls, opening ourselves to unwelcome affects, experimenting with a less didactic paralogy, and accepting that we share common ground. They're dissatisfied with our current version of knowledge-making and author/ity. Lacking a permanent, centralized repository for their history, they're concerned with preserving an accurate representation. Challenging their tactics on their own terms may best guard against them while allowing us to research and write about subjects that may imperil us online.

Notes

1 To better simulate and communicate the experiences presented and analyzed in this project, I have adopted the formats and stylistic conventions of online discussion forums, which are single-spaced, rarely indent, indicate paragraph breaks and cognitive and emotional processing with white space, and encourage creative experimentation with orthography.
2 Being redpilled means diverging from mainstream interpretations and interrogating the narratives crafted by mass media.
3 (Campbell, 2017) ≥ (Shit My Reviewers Say, 2017, August 30).
4 (Anonymous, 2017b) ≤ (Shit My Reviewers Say, 2017, September 22).
5 (Shit My Reviewers Say, 2016, November 26) ≤ (Anonymous, 2017b).
6 (Shit My Reviewers Say, 2017, October 27) ≤ (u/Entelluss-Gloves, 2015).
7 Being bluepilled means consuming, believing, and creating mainstream narratives.

References

Adams, C. (2017)."They go for gender first." The nature and effect of sexist abuse of female technology journalists. *Journalism Practice, 12*(7), 850–869.
Anonymous. (2017a). Can /pol/ recover? [Thread 117816868]. Messages posted to https://archive.4plebs.org/pol/thread/117816868
Anonymous. (2017b). When were you when /pol/ was btfo? [Thread 117905983]. Messages posted to https://archive.4plebs.org/pol/thread/117905983
Auerbach, D. (2012). Anonymity as culture: Treatise. *Triple Canopy*. Retrieved from https://www.canopycanopycanopy.com/contents/anonymity_as_culture__treatise
Berkenkotter, C. (1995). The power and the perils of peer review. *Rhetoric Review, 13*(2), 245–248.
Campbell, E. (2017). "Apparently being a self-obsessed c**t is now academically lauded": Experiencing Twitter trolling of autoethnographers. *Forum: Qualitative Social Research, 18*(3). http://www.qualitative-research.net/index.php/fqs/article/view/2819
Coleman, G. (2012). Phreaks, hackers, and trolls: The politics of transgression and spectacle. In M. Mandiberg (Ed.), *The social media reader* (pp. 99–119). New York, NY: New York University Press.
Duncan, P. (2017). The uses of hate: On hate as a political category. *M/C Journal, 20*(1). Retrieved from http://journal.media-culture.org.au/index.php/mcjournal/article/view/1194
Herwig, J. (2011). The archive as the repertoire: Mediated and embodied practice on imageboard 4chan.org. In G. Friesinger, J. Grenzfurthner, & T. Ballhausen (Eds.), *Mind and matter: Comparative approaches to complexity* (pp. 39–56). Piscataway, NJ: Rutgers University Press.
Holla Forums. (2017). Research journal article on Holla Forums? [Thread]. Messages posted to https://hollaforums.com/thread/7833773/politics/research-journal-article-on-holla-forums.html
Holt, N. (2003). Representation, legitimation, and autoethnography: An autoethnographic writing story. *International Journal of Qualitative Methods, 2*(1), 18–28.
Jane, E. (2017). Feminist digilante responses to a slut-shaming on Facebook. *Social Media + Society, 3*(2), 1–10.

Knuttila, L. (2011). User unknown: 4chan, anonymity, and contingency. *First Monday, 16*(10). Retrieved from https://firstmonday.org/article/view/3665/3055

Manivannan, V. (2013). Tits or GTFO: The logics of misogyny on 4chan's Random - /b/. *Fibreculture, 22.* Retrieved from http://twentytwo.fibreculturejournal.org/fcj-158-tits-or-gtfo-the-logics-of-misogyny-on-4chans-random-b/

Manivannan, V. (2016, August 21). "Artistic integrity is a problem for you" [Blog post]. Retrieved from https://vyshalimanivannan.com/artistic-integrity-is-a-problem-for-you/

Mantilla, K. (2013). Gendertrolling: Misogyny adapts to new media. *Feminist Studies, 39*(2), 563–570.

Marwick, A., & Lewis, R. (2017). Media manipulation and disinformation online. *Data & Society.* Retrieved from https://datasociety.net/output/media-manipulation-and-disinfo-online/

McCosker, A. (2014). Trolling as provocation. *Convergence, 20*(2), 201–217.

Moses, G. (2018). In defence of the academic troll: A word on the new heroes of infotainment. *Droste Effect Magazine, 7.* Retrieved from http://www.drosteeffectmag.com/bulletin-7-defence-academic-troll-new-heroes-infotainment/

Olson, C., & LaPoe, V. (2018). Combating the digital spiral of silence: Academic activists versus social media trolls. In J. Vickery & T. Everbach (Eds.), *Mediating misogyny* (pp. 271–291). London, UK: Palgrave Macmillan.

Ott, B. (2017). The age of Twitter: Donald J. Trump and the politics of debasement. *Critical Studies in Media Communication, 34*(1), 59–68.

Overstreet, M. (2018). Feeding the troll: Online hate speech as communal act. In C. Ball, C. Chen, K. Purzycki, & L. Wilkes (Eds.), *The proceedings of the annual computers and writing conference: 2016–2017.* Fort Collins, CO: The WAC Clearinghouse. Retrieved from https://wac.colostate.edu/resources/wac/proceedings/cw2016-2017/

Phillips, W., Beyer, J., & Coleman, G. (2017, March 22). Trolling scholars debunk the idea that the alt-right's shitposters have magic powers. *VICE Motherboard.* Retrieved from https://motherboard.vice.com/en_us/article/z4k549/trolling-scholars-debunk-the-idea-that-the-alt-rights-trolls-have-magic-powers

Shit My Reviewers Say. (2016, November 26). "I was originally very excited to review this paper" [Tumblr]. Retrieved from https://shitmyreviewerssay.tumblr.com/post/146158730729/i-was-originally-very-excited-to-review-this

Shit My Reviewers Say [YourPaperSucks]. (2017, August 30). "This paper reads like a woman's diary" [Tweet]. Retrieved from https://t.co/6e372VVfUw

Shit My Reviewers Say [YourPaperSucks]. (2017, September 22). "I found the entire premise of the work to be utterly theoretically bankrupt" [Tweet]. Retrieved from https://t.co/5VtO2ItziC

Shit My Reviewers Say [YourPaperSucks]. (2017, October 27). "It is essentially an opinion piece that editorializes shamelessly about the superior methods of a recent paper in the first person" [Tumblr]. Retrieved from https://shitmyreviewerssay.tumblr.com/post/166849280910/it-is-essentially-an-opinion-piece-that

Tannen, D. (2002). Agonism in academic discourse. *Journal of Pragmatics, 34,* 1651–1669.

u/Entelluss-Gloves. (2015, August 5). Understanding gg as a cultural phenomenon [Thread]. Retrieved from https://www.reddit.com/r/AgainstGamerGate/comments/3fybnj/understanding_gg_as_a_cultural_phenomenon/

Vitanza, V. (1987). Critical sub/versions of the history of philosophical rhetoric. *Rhetoric Review, 6*(1), 41–66.

Vera-Gray, F. (2017). "Talk about a cunt with too much idle time": Trolling feminist research. *Feminist Review, 115*(1), 61–78.

Wall, S. (2008). Easier said than done: Writing an autoethnography. *International Journal of Qualitative Methods, 7*(1), 38–53.

8 Professorial Outrage
Enthymemic Assumptions
Jeff Rice

On December 24, 2016, Drexel University professor of politics and global studies George Ciccariello-Maher tweeted, "All I want for Christmas is white genocide." Shortly after, condemnations of Ciccariello-Maher surfaced in a variety of media outlets and led Drexel's president to denounce the tweet as well. After the Las Vegas mass shooting on October 1, 2017, at the Route 91 Harvest music festival, Ciccariello-Maher received further negative attention for a tweet he wrote connecting Donald Trump to the killings. "White people and men are told that they are entitled to everything. This is what happens when they don't get what they want," Ciccariello-Maher (2017a, October 2) wrote. He additionally commented in a related tweet that connected the event to "white genocide":

> It is the spinal column of Trumpism, and most extreme form is the white genocide myth. The narrative of white victimization has been gradually built over the past 40 years.
> (Ciccariello-Maher, 2017b, October 2)

After another round of public condemnation for his association of the massacre with Trump, Drexel responded by placing Ciccariello-Maher on administrative leave. Ciccariello-Maher eventually resigned from Drexel, blaming white supremacists for the negative attention to his tweets. Ciccariello-Maher is not the only academic whose tweets either prompt public backlash or lead to employment scrutiny. When posted by academics, tweets or Facebook status updates about politics, racial tension and discrimination, global events, sexual harassment, and other topics demanding public debate often lead to attacks on the professor posting online.

Much of the vitriol directed against professors for expressing these kinds of opinions online has been attributed to either a conservative body hostile to university discourse, as Ciccariello-Maher suggested, or even worse, a right-wing conspiracy to shut down academic speech in general. Within academic writings, public discourse surrounding this issue argues that a crisis regarding free speech has emerged. Ciccariello-Maher, thus, represents for many not a singular instance of public indignation at a professor's outrage, but a movement directed against academic speech. Ciccariello-Maher, this rhetorical framing posits, is one of many academic victims of right-wing abuse. As Quintana and Read (2017) write in *The Chronicle of Higher Education*,

> Review enough such cases of faculty polemic gone viral, and an archetype starts to emerge—an assembly line of outrage that collects professors' Facebook posts, opinion essays, and classroom comments and amplifies them until they have become national news.

Ray (2017), writing for *Inside Higher Ed*, argues that "the political right has developed a coordinated network to systematically target the free speech of presumably left-wing professors." In the same publication, Daniels and Stein (2017) view right-wing attacks on leftist professors as evidence "that colleges and universities need to do a much better job of protecting academic freedom in a digitally networked age." Regarding these charged social media incidents and the reactions they generate, Newfield (2017) proclaims, "The right clearly feels threatened again today." Writing an op-ed in *The Washington Post* after being placed on leave, Ciccariello-Maher (2017c, October 10) agreed with these kinds of positions, arguing

> More and more, professors like me are being targeted by a coordinated right-wing campaign to undermine our academic freedom—one that relies on misrepresentation and sometimes outright lying, and often puts us and our students in danger.

As these critics note, there was no shortage of conservative response to Ciccariello-Maher's tweets, including expected criticism from notable conservative outlets such as *Breitbart*, *The Blaze*, and *Infowars*. In his op-ed, Ciccariello-Maher lists fellow academics whose social media posts also have attracted the wrath of conservative websites and news: Saida Grundy, Zandria Robinson, Tommy Curry, and Johnny Eric Williams. With so many incidents, the pattern suggests much of what Ciccariello-Maher proposes, or it at least insinuates focused attention on leftist-oriented professors who use social media to express outrage at a variety of events or political figures.

Rather than follow that line of thinking, however, I want to examine professorial outbursts differently and from a rhetorical, rather than political or conspiratorial, angle. I want to examine professorial anger on social media and the responses that follow as a question of audience recognition and response, and not as one of organized conservative conspiracy. I choose to focus on professorial posts because academics, one might assume, command a specific understanding of rhetoric (or at least, professional discourse), and because professors represent professionals who teach and, in theory, perform critical thinking when engaging with either contemporary or controversial issues. Critical thinking suggests an overall knowledge of rhetorical situations and the audiences one attempts to reach. Critical thinking, as well, assumes that there exists an audience for a given speech or writing act. By offering this specific focus, I hope to bring attention to problems regarding professorial assumptions about audience, assumptions which misdirect academic attention away from the discourse itself in favor of other types of assumptions driven by enthymemes. The power of the enthymeme, particularly in online discourse, challenges academic responses to not just events, but academic response in general.

In a given social media rhetorical situation, what does professorial anger assume regarding audience and audience reception? When a professor makes an argument regarding white genocide or draws a connection between a mass shooting and the president, what assumptions does the professor make about his or her audience's contextual knowledge or even political sympathies? Does the professor assume the existence of an audience, does the professor assume audience agreement, or does the professor assume that the tweet in question serves as entryway or participation into a larger debate? Or does the professor simply assume agreement with the logic behind the tweet? Does the professor assume that the tweet or Facebook post will generate a rhetorical situation that can be academically debated or eventually agreed upon? How, in other words, is response imagined by the rhetor? Bitzer (1959) canonically posed the rhetorical situation as one of response.

> To say that rhetoric is situational means: (1) rhetorical discourse comes into existence as a response to situation, in the same sense that an answer comes into existence in response to a question or a solution in response to a problem; (2) a speech is given rhetorical significance by the situation, just as a unit of discourse is given significance as answer or as solution by the question or problem.
>
> (pp. 5–6)

For Bitzer, rhetoric is situational because of how it functions in response to a given exigence. Response, in turn, participates in creating a reality. "Rhetoric is a mode of altering reality," Bitzer (1959) argues, "by the creation of discourse which changes reality through the mediation of thought and action" (p. 4). Bitzer's example of Kennedy's assassination focuses not on the killing of Kennedy but on the different types of responses the president's death evoked, and thus, whether in eulogy or reporting, the ways these responses created realities for different audiences, including more contemporary realities such as conspiracies regarding the president's killing.

In social media outbursts of anger, the exigence for professorial outbursts stems from a given problem, and the tweet or post intends to form a new situation, but the response to these outbursts, as well, affects another rhetorical situation separate from the specific problem (such as Ciccariello-Maher's understanding of the Las Vegas shootings or what he calls "white supremacy"). The question for rhetoric and social media is to distinguish between these two distinct rhetorical moments—a professorial moment of anger as response to a given event or moment and a public response to that response. In this chapter, I approach this question via a discussion of the enthymeme in order to better understand these moments as more complex than a right-wing conspiracy or as coordinated political attacks. The enthymeme, I argue, offers rhetoric a way to better comprehend both the outburst and the response within digital contexts. The digital platforms where these outbursts occur are important because digital audiences are not always obvious and digital discourse spreads differently from print or oral exchange. By focusing on enthymemes and the assumptions they must contain within their utterances, I am not endorsing nor denying the existence of troubling responses that often follow outbursts such as Ciccariello-Maher's: death threats, calls for rape, hate mail, or any other act of violence. Nor am I commenting on the legality of response, as in the University of Illinois's decision to withdraw an offer of employment to Steven Salaita, a case I will later discuss. Instead, I am focusing on the assumptions implicit in many of the professorial moments of social media outrage that eventually earn public attention. I am focusing on the enthymeme as a rhetorical practice of digital assumption and how that practice makes assumptions about audience and rhetorical delivery.

The Enthymeme

Enthymemes have long been a focus of rhetorical studies. Ong (2004) explains Peter Ramus's definition of the enthymeme as the origin of contemporary usage, "a syllogism which is 'imperfect' in the crude, *simpliste* sense that one of its premises is suppressed" (p. 187). This definition, though championed by Ramus, stems from Aristotle's brief note in *The Rhetoric* that the enthymeme is an "imperfect syllogism." That question of imperfection has led to a great deal of commentary and analysis on what an enthymeme actually is or how it should be defined or differentiated from the syllogism. Poster (1992) traces the vast influence of Aristotle's statement, noting the many contradictory definitions of enthymemes among rhetoricians and teachers of rhetoric. Out of the many citations Poster offers, she cites Bitzer's 1959 *Quarterly Journal of Speech* essay "Aristotle's Enthymeme Revisited" and Bitzer's focus that "the premises of the enthymeme be supplied by the audience" (as cited in Poster, 1992, p. 5). Following a discussion of the traditional breakdown of major and minor premises, Bitzer (1959) also states, "The missing materials of rhetorical arguments are the premises which the audience brings with it, and supplied at the proper moment provided the orator is skillful" (p. 407). Following Bitzer, I concentrate on the audience-directed aspect of enthymemic discourse.

For many scholars, enthymemes depend on assumptions regarding audience knowledge. "The structure of the enthymeme," Gage (1983) writes, "derives function from the relationship between a writer's intended conclusions and an audience's pre-existing assumptions" (p. 39). In his pedagogical analysis of effective enthymemes, Gage draws attention to the assumptions "shared by or derived by the writer's audience" (40). "Essentially," Raymond (1984) argues similarly, "enthymemes may be defined as assumptions used in public discourse" (p. 144). Walker (1994) reintroduces the basic aspect of enthymemic thinking as the "tendency to emphasize the dialogic relation between writer and audience by requiring the writer to include the audience's thinking in the invention process" (pp. 46–47). Walker draws upon Anaximenes and not Aristotle, stating that in an enthymemic moment, "The audience is to feel not simply that the speaker's claims are true or probable, but that both speaker and claims are good and admirable, and the very opposite of what is false, bad, and detestable" (p. 50). Enthymemes, therefore, carry an element of ethos with them, assuming that the audience will recognize that the speaker/writer and the content of the statement are valid and good. When a speaker/writer makes a public announcement about the president or a racially charged issue, the speaker will assume his or her ethos is being read positively. A tweet indicates credibility ("professors must know what they are talking about; therefore, you will believe what I write").

In his discussion of enthymemes, Walker (1994) deviates from the traditional emphasis on the syllogism and instead focuses on inference, "from probable assumptions granted by one's audience" (p. 47). This non-Aristotelian enthymeme, Walker describes

> is a strategic, kairotic, argumentational turn that exploits a cluster of emotively charged—value-laden oppositions made available (usually) by an exetastic buildup in order to generate in its audience a passional identification with or adherence to a particular stance, and that (ideally) will strike the audience as an "abrupt" and decisive flash of insight.
>
> (p. 53)

In such a stance, an audience, the speaker/writer assumes, will treat the rhetorical moment as insightful (i.e. "the reason the Las Vegas massacre occurred was because of Trump or white privilege"). A tweet or post, as a particularly compressed form of digital rhetorical expression, is posed as one such flash of insight in which limited characters focused on a passionate issue (race, the president, politics, global conflict) can produce audience identification. To reach that audience, however, one assumes that the audience in question exists and shares the tweet or post's passion. This point is key to how digital professorial outrage is responded to by an assumed audience. These outbursts, such as wishing for white genocide (whether as literal act or critique of white response to genocide or critique of white supremacists' imaginary fear of their own genocide), eventually are not read as insightful nor identified with by a specific and vocal audience. The eventual controversies, such as the one that led to Ciccariello-Maher's administrative leave and resignation, work counter to the speaker/writer's assumption regarding ethos, insight, and audience.

While Walker dismisses the term "enthymeme" as not relevant to rhetorical work and as too tied to Aristotle, I keep the term as an essential feature of digital interactions across social media platforms. I add the word "assumed" to the overall definition of enthymeme that associates the term with audience. Assumed, a term present in many definitions of audience-based enthymemes is not tied to the rhetorical gesture in a concrete way, but it should be, particularly when we discuss digital or social media interactions. Emotionally charged statements, identification, the differentiation between what is good and what is bad, ethos, preexisting belief—these are rhetorical assumptions made when addressing an ambiguous and not always identifiable social-media-based audience whose connections and networks make it both fluid and present during an interaction. A social media declaration offers its audience an assumed enthymeme. One public response to such declarations, and also an assumption based on enthymemic construction, is the invocation of academic speech.

Academic Speech

Academic freedom or academic speech, an important point of Ciccariello-Maher's defense of his tweets and the focus of much of the professorial rhetoric I will examine, is an enthymemic phrase. The utterance of this phrase makes several audience assumptions. For instance, the claim for academic freedom is an argument that academic writing or speech should be protected as free speech in order to allow for the transmittal and circulation of controversial ideas or ideas that seem controversial for challenging the status quo (but which, in fact, may become the status quo at some point). Thus, any speech act or writing (digital or print) delivered by an individual who holds an academic position should be protected as academic freedom in order to ensure academics the ability to pursue knowledge without fear of retribution from those who disagree. In turn, the argument often proceeds, tweets by a professor about white genocide constitute academic freedom and should be protected regardless of their reception. To arrive at that final point, however, is to believe in either the preceding premises or that the final point follows those premises. An audience who is persuaded that a call for white genocide is simultaneously protected as academic freedom is persuaded that the call is academic speech. The audience who thinks differently is not persuaded by the assumed premises and therefore calls for a professor's dismissal in response. Both positions, however, arrive at their assumptions via a variety of previous interactions and beliefs. Based on these interactions, an assumption emerges regarding whether to accept the tweet as legitimate academic speech or to express anger at the tweet, or to regard the backlash at the tweet as uninformed or malicious. Academic speech depends greatly on an assumption of clarity regarding its previous premises.

Academic speech is a highly persuasive term for professorial discourse. Enthymemes are often used for purposes of persuasion. For instance, in the history of social protest, the enthymemic "I Am a Man" sandwich boards worn by garbage workers striking in Memphis in 1968 were meant to persuade local government and a largely white television audience that (1) if all men are created equal, as the second paragraph of *The Declaration of Independence* states, and if (2) African American garbage workers in Tennessee are men, then (3) African American garbage workers deserve to be treated as equally as their white counterparts. For "I Am a Man" to be effective and to persuade white Americans that the garbage worker's demands be met, a 1968 audience must recognize a variety of previous interactions and beliefs. These include *The Declaration of Independence* reference, the role of discriminatory Jim Crow laws, the legacy of slavery, and the overall inequality experienced by an African American worker in the 1960s. Similarly, "I Am a Man" assumes that audiences are familiar with and possibly sympathetic to issues relevant to Civil Rights, voting rights, labor rights and related issues dominant during or leading up to 1968. An audience must compute, as Flusser (2011) argued in his concept of the technical image, a variety of positions, images, experiences, and knowledge into a singular image (such as the image of a protester wearing a sandwich board) in order to draw a conclusion. The "I Am a Man" image, Flusser would likely argue, is a technical image, a series of layered images that are presented as singular and whose enthymemic effect depends on assumptions audiences make based on what they layer or computate into that image.

Flusser (2011) called this layered image the technical image because of viewers' ability to layer within a single representation a number of other representations (whether they know they are doing so or not). Flusser attributed the technical image to computer or digital culture, noting how technology facilitates the process of aggregating into one space a variety of assumed beliefs and positions. While Flusser does not describe the technical image as enthymemic, he does indicate how audiences make assumptions based on how a given image is layered. "All technical images have the same basic character," Flusser (2011) wrote, "on close inspection, they all prove to be envisioned surfaces computed from particles" (p. 33). These "particles" consist of the various previously encountered images and ideas we bring to a reading of a present image. All present images, for Flusser, are programmed images. The images are not natural but are composites of other images whose overlap programs an ideology, a bias, a position, a posture, a representation, and so on. "I Am a Man" is a programmed image. It is not neutral because it depends on a layering of preceding imagery, such as what I previously outlined. Ciccariello-Maher's "white genocide," as well, is a programmed image dependent on previous understandings of genocide, critiques of "whiteness," and white complacency or involvement in discriminatory or oppressive practices.

> Although they appear to do so, technical images don't depict anything; they project something. The signified of a technical image, whether it be a photograph of a house or a computer image of a virtual airplane, is something drawn from the inside toward the outside. ...To decode a technical image is not to decode what it shows but to read how it is programmed.
> (Flusser, 2011, p. 48)

Flusser's technical image is not too far removed from Barthes's (1977) rhetoric of the image. The image, Barthes (1977) writes, is "a message without code" because of the connotations and associations viewers bring to its reception (p. 154). Barthes's canonical example of an Italian advertisement that aggregates images associated with Italian food—tomatoes, garlic, red and green colors, pasta, onions—produces what he calls "Italianicity" because audiences assume—based on their exposure to previous tropes of Italian food—that the ad represents an authentic Italian gastronomy. The "icity" addition to Italian is meant to signify that the advertisement is not, in fact, Italian, but an aggregation or layered image of being Italian based on viewers' assumptions regarding inferred premises of Italian food. "All images are polysemous," Barthes (1977) declares: "they imply, underlying their signifiers, a 'floating chain' of signifieds" (p. 156). But where do such signifieds come from? From our previous interactions. What anchors the viewer in the image is the given signified the viewer fixates on, such as what one imagines Italian food to be or what an audience might assume about the terms "white" or "genocide."

A social media outburst is an image in the Barthesian sense of imagery. "The myth of photographic 'naturalness,'" as Barthes (1977) calls it, is also the myth of social media naturalness (p. 158). There is no natural expression online (or, of course, offline), nor should there be an assumption that one's digital outburst "just is." As Barthes (1977) argues, "in the total image [connotations] constitute discontinuous or better still scattered traits" (p. 162). The question for rhetorical studies is whether the reader of an image can recognize these traits or not. Ciccariello-Maher may believe that yes, a reader can understand his implicit scattered traits and particles; the public outcry, on the other hand, did not.

The Social Media Audience

Social media audiences are often described in a fairly basic manner: within our social networks, we have strong ties (who we know well such as our family, our friends, and our coworkers) and weak ties (who we barely know or not at all). The average person, Facebook's former head of global brand design Paul Adams (2011) writes, has "fewer than ten strong ties, and many have fewer than five" (p. 60). While we might assume that strong ties are an individual's most powerful connections in a given social media network and our most readily available audience, weak ties, in fact, are more powerful and more prevalent. Communication may take place more often among strong ties (paying attention to each other's updates or tweets on a regular basis), but for every 150 weak ties (Adams's number for the average member of a network), each one of those 150 has another 150 weak ties, and so on. Each set of weak ties can connect to what we say or share online. One will always have far more weak ties than strong ties. With every public like or share, this vast network is connected to us, as well; each sees our social media interactions or has our interactions shared with them. Strong ties are more likely to pass over controversial remarks or not share them with unsympathetic audiences. Weak ties—those 150 and then 150 beyond—may be more likely to share because their viewpoints will diversify. "Weak ties," Adams (2011) argues,

> are at the periphery of our social network, which means they are connected to more diverse sets of people than our strong ties, which are more central in our network. These diverse ties pass on more novel information, and so they can often know more than our strong ties do.
>
> (p. 64)

In an audience driven rhetoric motivated by enthymemic exchange, how can one account for so many weak ties and their assumptions? One cannot.

My interests, therefore, are in extending the enthymeme (and its technical image counterpart) to an examination of what I call the assumed enthymeme, particularly for how it functions in social media spaces' vast networks of differing and unknown assumptions, and even more specifically, among academics in social media spaces. As with the Ciccariello-Maher case, in the last few years, there have been a plethora of controversial moments in which an academic tweets or posts a Facebook update that generates a considerable response. The initial post is typically angry, and the consequential responses, which typically spread out over weak ties as opposed to only right-wing conspiracists, are angry as well. In addition to assumptions regarding scattered traits and layered meanings, the immediate posting may be written with the assumption that only like-minded readers (strong ties) will encounter it, or that, at the least, an audience is limited to those who follow or who are friends, not the weak ties extending outward and who may differ in political viewpoint and technical image. Along with the technical image aspect of assumed enthymemes—the layered meanings within the image—is the question of connectivity and assumption.

Twitter often functions as a platform for projected anger as an enthymemic expression. Twitter's basic unit of connectivity is following, which provides exposure to other Twitter users' tweets. One may heart a tweet (signifying agreement) or retweet (sharing the tweet with one's own social network of close and weak ties and, as well, signifying agreement). "On Twitter," Marwick and boyd (2010) write, "there is a disconnect between followers and followed" (p. 117). Marwick and boyd summarize their research via the observation that this disconnect stems from Twitter users neglecting audience.

> They are uncomfortable labeling interlocutors and witnesses as an "audience." In bristling over the notion of audience, they are likely rejecting a popularly discussed act of "personal branding" as running counter to what they value: authenticity. In other words, consciously speaking to an audience is perceived as inauthentic.
>
> (p. 119)

Twitter offers a "mode of expression," Murthy (2011) writes, "in that the unintended audience has an incongruous understanding of what the speaker may have actually intended" (p. 780). Naaman, Boase, and Lai (2010) call tweets "social awareness streams," the networking of personal–public communication, brevity of content, and highly connected spaces. Part of their quantitative study revealed that the "majority of [Twitter] users focus on the 'self'" (Naaman, Boase, & Lai, 2010). Self-focus, in some situations, can lead writers to assume that audience belief is the same or like-minded because the self tweets (or simply communicates) via its own technical images. Twitter users might assume that the tweets they project outward to their followers, and consequently, their followers' followers, are, without any question, persuasive on their own terms and not programmed computations, as Flusser

(2011) might argue. Following Marwick and boyd's (2010) analysis, the projected technical image may not believe that there exists an audience for a rhetorical situation, or at the least, there isn't an audience who disagrees. Thus, on Twitter, I express my beliefs, and whether there is an audience or not, my expression is self-understood as persuasive. Audiences, of course, do exist, but the assumption of audience agreement often confuses public proclamations on social media and causes one to forget that point. The call for murder, as one very public case of Twitter self-expression demonstrates, reveals that confusion.

When then Virginia Tech professor Steven Salaita tweeted on June 19, 2014, "You may be too refined to say it, but I'm not: I wish all the fucking West Bank settlers would go missing" (Salaita, 2014a, June 19), he was referencing the Hamas kidnapping and murder of three Israeli teenagers: Naftali Frankel, Gilad Shaar, and Eyal Yifrach. Salaita's tweet, which would eventually be listed among other tweets as reason to not hire him at the University of Illinois, prompted considerable outcry both against Salaita's online commentary and in support of academic speech. Salaita's tweet assumes a few things about his readership who follow his self-expression: (1) readers believe that Israel unjustly occupies the West Bank; (2) Israelis living in the West Bank do so illegally; (3) the murder of Israelis who are in the West Bank is, therefore, justified because they are illegally present. On the same day, Salaita tweeted, "Zionists: transforming 'antisemitism' from something horrible into something honorable since 1948" (Salaita, 2014b, June 19). In this case, the enthymemic tweet depends on two premises for an audience to agree: (1) anti-Semitism was previously bad; (2) Zionism, the Jewish nationalism formed in the 19th century and which led to the creation of Israel in 1948, is so egregious that it has created a current situation in which it is acceptable to be anti-Semitic; (3) it is now acceptable to be anti-Semitic.

At this point, one can read Salaita's tweets as directed toward perceived sympathetic political or anti-Israel audience assumptions. However, another layer in this communicative stream occurs as one particular audience, mostly academic but sometimes journalistic, conveys its own enthymemic assumptions whose focus is not the anti-Israel sentiment but the nature of the speech itself. The final enthymemic points of Salaita's two tweets build off of the two previous premises I draw attention to, though public reaction in support of Salaita did not acknowledge this progression of thought. Instead, those academics who supported Salaita built into the tweets not these premises (or some variation) but instead a completely different enthymemic conclusion based on the question of academic speech and its assumed enthymemic stance. (1) A professor tweets about Israel (or any other subject). (2) Because the tweet was written by a professor, the tweet is academic speech. (3) The tweet is therefore protected from retaliation of any sort (critical or professional employment). There are two levels of enthymemic assumption occurring: one regarding Israel and anti-Semitism and one regarding what an academic is allowed to say on social media without fear of retribution or critique. How these two assumptions are read and then circulated as response determines how the speaker is interpreted (his or her ethos) as well how the speaker interprets public reaction (response to the rhetorical situation).

The Salaita case allows for a return to the question of academic freedom as an enthymemic assumption. The fact that academics would concentrate on the technical image of academic freedom and not the racism within Salaita's tweets is fairly predictable since academic freedom is central to professorial concerns and discourse. As a technical image, academic freedom projects any number of images and beliefs among its professorial audience, which eventually translate into assumptions about professorial discourse in general. Many of these images and beliefs are based on previous actions by disparate universities to limit what professors can write about or say within the university, as well as the accompanying professorial fear that follows these actions.

Part of this image may be based on post-World War II McCarthy-influenced requirements that teachers sign pledges or loyalty oaths that they did not belong to the Communist Party or other "subversive" groups. Or this image may be partly based on the University of Chicago's 1967 Kalven report, often cited in academic freedom discussions. The report argued "By design and by effect, it is the institution which creates discontent with the existing social arrangements and proposes new ones. In brief, a good university, like Socrates, will be upsetting" (Kalven Committee, 1967). The university, the report continues, "arises out of respect for free inquiry and the obligation to cherish a diversity of viewpoints" (Kalven Committee, 1967). Within this image may also be the 1967 Supreme Court ruling in *Keyishian v. Board of Regents* that the University of Buffalo could not force faculty to sign pledges that they had never been a member of the Communist party nor could the university prohibit faculty from distributing materials or speech deemed "subversive." The American Association of University Professor's *1940 Statement on Principles of Academic Freedom and Tenure* outlined a number of points to protect teacher rights including its important first provision:

> Teachers are entitled to full freedom in research and in the publication of the results, subject to the adequate performance of their other academic duties; but research for pecuniary return should be based upon an understanding with the authorities of the institution.
>
> (Committee on Academic Freedom and Academic Tenure of the AAUP, 1940)

But the document also contains the broader statement, likely folded into contemporary technical images professorial discourse identifies as authentic:

> College and university teachers are citizens, members of a learned profession, and officers of an educational institution. When they speak or write as citizens, they should be free from institutional censorship or discipline, but their special position in the community imposes special obligations. As scholars and educational officers, they should remember that the public may judge their profession and their institution by their utterances. Hence they should at all times be accurate, should exercise appropriate restraint, should show respect for the opinions of others, and should make every effort to indicate that they are not speaking for the institution.
> (Committee on Academic Freedom and Academic Tenure of the AAUP, 1940)

In addition to his professorial status, Steven Salaita was a citizen as he tweeted anti-Semitic language to both his followers (strong ties) and his followers' followers (weak ties). If one has layered into a technical image of academic speech the image of the professor as citizen, then that part of the technical image may override other possible image inclusions such as being "accurate" or exercising "appropriate restraint," particularly as an audience (of self or others who agree) is assumed among one's social media followers.

Among the many cases of professors losing or failing to gain tenure due to internal disagreement, institutional debate, publication controversy, contested classroom practice, or other issues, there emerge new layers that constitute the technical image called academic freedom or academic speech. All of these items aggregate into one image called academic freedom. Assumptions about the technical image are based on which items are drawn upon as premises. The University of Illinois's decision to withdraw an offer of employment to Salaita was read by supporters of Salaita as a challenge to academic freedom (Salaita is read as citizen and as professor) and not as a response to racist discourse or the call for murder. The two premises leading to each of the tweets, as I outline them, do not seem to influence the various critiques of academic speech violations or play a role in declaring an academic speech violation. Indeed, none of the supporters of Salaita address the implied premises of his tweets.

Instead of reading the content of the tweets and forming a response based on the tweets, Salaita's supporters read the technical image of academic speech and based its response on the already circulated fears of its erosion. This difference is important as it directs attention toward the kinds of assumptions audiences made and then circulated throughout various media—blog posts, newspaper interviews, or other social media responses. These assumptions are based on exposure to previously articulated issues regarding academic speech. "The summary dismissal of Professor Steven Salaita from a tenured faculty position at the University of Illinois is the single most brazen attack on freedom of speech in American universities in my lifetime," University of Chicago law professor Brian Leiter (2014) argued in his opening remarks to a sponsored Salaita talk. Writing for the American Association of University Professors, Kirstein (2016) summarizes much of the Salaita coverage and concludes with a claim about academic freedom, not the actual tweets Salaita wrote or the assumptions that they make.

> In reporting the news, the media serve the common good. When revelations surface that students are being denied professors who are free to teach so that they are free to learn, education is protected.
> (Kirstein, 2016)

The New York Times (Dunn, 2014) covered the Salaita incident by reporting on academics who cancelled talks at the University of Illinois in protest. Each cancellation was based on a concern over academic freedom. As University of Minnesota History professor Allen Isaacman is quoted,

> The University of Illinois's recent decision to disregard its prior commitment to appoint Professor Salaita confirms my fear of the administration's blatant disregard for academic freedom.
> (Dunn, 2014)

"Don't Speak Out," Perry's (2014) essay in *The Chronicle of Higher Education* was titled. Perry's conclusion regarding Salaita's case is not based on the enthymemic postings or what their assumptions might be, but the generic issue of academic speech which, for him, is layered with public response as improper (his calling out of "bloggers and local papers").

> We need to open pathways for more academics to speak out in public, not punish Salaita for doing so in ways that have provoked such strong feelings. But we can't ask scholars to embrace the risks of engagement in a system in which partisan bloggers and local papers can push timid administrators to fire, or in this case unhire, academics who leap into public debates.

In *The Nation*, Palumbo-Li (2014) called the Salaita affair McCarthyite and a "shock wave" sent throughout the university community. "A Six Figure Settlement on Campus Free Speech," an *Atlantic* headline read after the University of Illinois settled with Salaita, transforming the issue into one of paying off denied speech, and not the tweets themselves (Chandler, 2015).

What we witness in these responses is an enthymemic response (academic speech) outside of the enthymemic assumptions the tweet initially made. Academic speech is a powerful and well-circulated enthymemic assumption within academic discourse. The shock at Salaita's predicament emerges from the vast social networked audience cognizant of the premises of an enthymemic academic speech declaration. The racist declarations of murder or anti-Semitism implicit in the tweet's premises, however, are not strong enough for this particular audience to override the academic speech technical image in favor of other types of technical images that might have been drawn from for meaning. These layered images might include those associated with anti-Semitism such as murdering Jews because of where they live (a history of pogroms in many countries, including the Middle East), associating Zionism with racism (the U.N. declaration in 1975) or the legacy of the 1967 Six Day War (and consequent de-legitimatization of Israel conquering the West Bank after Jordan's assault). This disconnect demonstrates how assumed speech is not "just is" when projected, among other places, online and in social media platforms where audiences can be imagined but not seen directly. Assumed speech is layered; it depends on previous interactions and engagements, whether the image is a protest against 1968 labor discrimination or a call to murder Israelis. But assumed speech also depends on the assumption of an audiences' existence, as well as that particular audience's like-minded technical images.

Conclusion

In this chapter, I have focused briefly on two cases of professorial outrage and the role of the assumed enthymeme within that outrage. Anger at a political moment, global conflict, territorial debate, or similar issues lead to social-media-based rhetorical situations in which audiences are assumed to exist, but the premises of the tweets or updates, as well, are based on assumptions. "Few of us are called upon to address an audience," Hauser (1999) begins *Vernacular Voices*.

> Most of our communication directed at persons or groups has some immediacy, and we know them in some way. We experience our transactions with them in concrete terms as addressed discourse: our own thoughts, our intended message, a specific audience to which we have adapted and that audience's perceived response.
>
> (p. 5)

The broader issue questions audience transactions as being based on assumptions, not concrete, addressed discourse. Assumptions regarding audience comprehension, agreement, or immediacy complicate how a rhetorical situation and the response it evokes are read across professional and personal communication. A tweet associating the U.S. president with a mass murder in Las Vegas may feel to its poster like a stance whose "flash of insight" (as Walker, 1994 notes) will convince an assumed audience of truth or validity. But when that tweet is read as a different set of enthymemic premises than the poster appears to intend, any assumptions of immediacy prove irrelevant. Weak ties override strong ties and bring to their reading of the tweet their own technical images—whether regarding mass shootings, presidential ethos, Las Vegas itself, professors as anti-government leftists, or something else. Ciccariello-Maher, Salaita, and those who support each professor may believe that the negative response to their tweets was based on either right-wing or Zionist conspiracies, but a rhetorical answer to their falling out in academia demonstrates the complexity of audience response overall, the role technical images play in public response to public social media displays, and how enthymemic assumptions depend on which set of assumed premises might support the tweet or Facebook post's projection of meaning. Viewed this way, we are forced to consider our digital expression and our reading of digital expression far more closely than we currently do.

References

Adams, P. (2011). *Grouped: How small groups of friends are the key to influence on the social web*. Berkeley, CA: New Riders.

Barthes, R. (1977). The rhetoric of the image. *Image music text* (S. Heath, Trans.). New York, NY: Hill and Wang.

Bitzer, L. (1959). Aristotle's enthymeme revisited. *Quarterly Journal of Speech*, 45(4), pp. 399–409.

Chandler, A. (2015, November 12). A six figure settlement on campus free speech. *The Atlantic*. Retrieved from https://www.theatlantic.com/national/archive/2015/11/a-six-figure-settlement-on-campus-free-speech/415680/

Ciccariello-Maher, G. [@ciccmaher]. (2017a, October 2). White people and men are told that they are entitled to everything. This is what happens when they don't get what they want [Tweet]. Retrieved from https://twitter.com/ciccmaher/status/914861355835981824

Ciccariello-Maher, G. [@ciccmaher]. (2017b, October 2). It is the spinal column of Trumpism, and most extreme form is the white genocide myth [Tweet]. Retrieved from https://twitter.com/ciccmaher/status/914862098311770112

Ciccariello-Maher, G. (2017c, October 10). Conservatives are the real campus thought police squashing academic freedom. *The Washington Post*. Retrieved from https://www.washingtonpost.com/news/posteverything/wp/2017/10/10/conservatives-are-the-real-campus-thought-police-squashing-academic-freedom/?noredirect=on&utm_term=.10b3b805bbd5

Committee on Academic Freedom and Academic Tenure of the AAUP. (1940). Statement of principles on academic freedom and tenure. AAUP. Retrieved from https://www.aaup.org/report/1940-statement-principles-academic-freedom-and-tenure

Daniels, J., & Stein, A. (2017, June 26). Protect scholars against attacks from the right. *Inside Higher Ed.* Retrieved from https://www.insidehighered.com/views/2017/06/26/why-institutions-should-shield-academics-who-are-being-attacked-conservative-groups

Dunn, S. (2014, August 31). University's rescinding of job offer prompts an outcry. *The New York Times.* Retrieved from https://www.nytimes.com/2014/09/01/education/illinois-university-prompts-outcry-for-revoking-job-offer-to-professor-in-wake-of-twitter-posts-on-israel.html

Flusser, V. (2011). *Into the universe of technical images* (N.A. Roth, Trans.). Minneapolis: University of Minnesota Press.

Gage, J. (1983). Teaching the enthymeme: Invention and arrangement. *Rhetoric Review,* 2(1), pp. 38–50.

Hauser, G. (1999). *Vernacular voices: The rhetoric of publics and public spheres.* Columbia: University of South Carolina Press.

Kalven Committee. (1967). Report on university's role in political and social action. *University of Chicago.* Retrieved from http://www-news.uchicago.edu/releases/07/pdf/kalverpt.pdf

Keyishian v. Board of Regents, 385 U.S. 589 (1967). Retrieved from https://www.law.cornell.edu/supremecourt/text/385/589

Kirstein, P. N. (2016, January–February). Steven Salaita, the media, and the struggle for academic freedom. *AAUP.* Retrieved from https://www.aaup.org/article/steven-salaita-media-and-struggle-academic-freedom

Leiter, B. (2014, October 7). Salaita appearance at U of Chicago tonight. *Leiter Reports.* Retrieved from https://leiterreports.typepad.com/blog/2014/10/salaita-appearance-at-u-of-chicago-tonight.html

Marwick, A., & boyd, d. (2010). I tweet honestly, I tweet passionately: Twitter users, context collapse, and the imagined audience. *New Media and Society,* 13(1), pp. 112–133.

Murthy, D. (2011). Twitter. Microphone for the masses? *Media, Culture & Society,* 33(5), pp. 779–789.

Naaman, M., Boase, J., & Lai, C.-H. (2010). Is it really about me? Message content in social awareness streams. *ACM Digital Library.* Retrieved from https://dl.acm.org/citation.cfm?id=1718953

Newfield, C. (2017, October 19). Feeding a dangerous fiction. *Inside Higher Ed.* Retrieved from https://www.insidehighered.com/views/2017/10/19/why-universities-should-not-crack-down-free-speech-essay

Ong, W. (2004). *Ramus, method, and the decay of dialogue: From the art of discourse to the art of reason.* Chicago, IL: University of Chicago Press.

Palumbo-Li, D. (2014, August 27). Why the "unhiring" of Steve Salaita is a threat to academic freedom. *The Nation.* Retrieved from https://www.thenation.com/article/why-unhiring-steven-salaita-threat-academic-freedom/

Perry, D. (2014, August 20). Don't speak out: The message of the Salaita affair. *The Chronicle of Higher Education.* Retrieved from https://www.chronicle.com/article/Dont-Speak-Out-The-Message/148393

Poster, C. (1992). A historicist recontextualization of the enthymeme. *Rhetoric Society Quarterly,* 22(2), pp. 1–24.

Quintana, C., & Read, B. (2017, June 22). Signal boost: How conservative media outlets turn faculty viewpoints into national news. *The Chronicle of Higher Education.* Retrieved from https://www.chronicle.com/article/Signal-Boost-How-Conservative/240423

Ray, V. (2017, June 30). Weaponizing free speech. *Inside Higher Ed*. Retrieved from https://www.insidehighered.com/advice/2017/06/30/right-using-comments-left-wing-professors-delegitimize-higher-ed-essay

Raymond, J. C. (1984). Enthymemes, examples, and rhetorical method. In R. J. Connors, L. S. Ede, & A. A. Lunsford (Eds.), *Essays on classical rhetoric and modern discourse* (pp. 140–151). Carbondale: Southern Illinois University Press.

Salaita, S. [@stevesalaita]. (2014a, June 19). You may be too refined to say it, but I'm not: I wish all the fucking West Bank settlers would go missing [Tweet]. Retrieved from https://twitter.com/stevesalaita/status/479805591401922561?lang=en

Salaita, S. [@stevesalaita]. (2014b, June 19). Zionists: Transforming "antisemitism" from something horrible into something honorable since 1948 [Tweet]. Retrieved from https://twitter.com/stevesalaita/status/490651053101441025?lang=en

Walker, J. (1994). The body of persuasion: A theory of the enthymeme. *College English, 56*(1), pp. 46–65.

Part III
Cultural Narratives in Hostile Discourses

9 Hateful Games
Why White Supremacist Recruiters Target Gamers

Megan Condis

In 2014, a subset of gamers, encouraged by alt-right wunderkind Milo Yiannopoulos, converged around the hashtag #GamerGate and harassed and threatened progressive game developers and critics.[1] A few years later, YouTube gaming celebrities PewDiePie and JonTron got into hot water for making anti-Semitic jokes (Mulkerin, 2017), using racial slurs and repeating white nationalist[2] talking points, respectively (Sarkar, 2017) on their wildly popular channels. More recently, professional gamers and commentators like Matthew Trivett (Alexander, 2018), Félix Lengyel (Gallagher, 2018), Tyler Blevins (Tamburro, 2018), and Matt Vaughn (Hansen, 2017) also faced discipline for broadcasting racial slurs on the popular streaming service Twitch. And in 2017, Bethesda, the publisher of the newest entry in the *Wolfenstein* franchise (a series of first-person shooter video games in which the player fights against Nazis in an alternate reality where the Axis powers won World War II), angered some fans with their game's marketing campaign, which centered around the slogan "Make America Nazi-Free Again" (Axford, 2017). The slogan was deemed by these fans to be too overtly political and too critical of President Donald Trump and the alt-right. It might seem strange that online video game culture has become a serious recruiting ground for white supremacists. However, a closer look at the historical intersections of race, politics, and play in these spaces reveals why Internet gaming culture is particularly susceptible to white supremacist rhetorics. Such an investigation is important not only because it provides a vital framework for understanding what is going on in this particular subculture but also because it functions as a useful case study of Riche's (2017) concept of "rhetorical vulnerability" or the differential effects that rhetorical appeals have on different populations and the conditions that may prime certain audiences to be vulnerable to certain appeals.

I identify three axioms of online culture that explain why gamers (as a subculture) are especially vulnerable to white supremacist recruiters. First, on the Internet (following the famous Internet adage called "Godwin's Law"), *every*one is a Nazi according to *some*one. The term "Nazi" is thrown around so often as to essentially have lost all meaning, a fact that offers ample cover for those who actually espouse white nationalist beliefs. Second, gamers reason, if everybody is calling everybody else Nazis all the time, then it is most likely the case that nobody is *really* a Nazi. After all, the people they see online getting called neo-Nazis and fascists by those on the left don't look or sound like the Nazis they see commonly depicted in video games. Finally, given the distrust gamers feel for politicians (and progressive politicians, in particular) over the failed attempts at video game censorship that took place in the 1990s, any group who claims to be against social justice and political correctness (such as the neo-Nazis and white supremacists on the alt-right) starts to look like a friend to gamer culture.

Many on the left believe (or at least hope) that the rise of white supremacy online can be attributed either to a bunch of silly, childish trolls acting edgy to get attention (and who should therefore be ignored by serious-minded adults) or a bunch of ignorant, know-nothing, hate-filled rubes who will be easy to defeat in the culture war currently being waged for the hearts and minds of the next generation of voters. This kind of dismissive, disdainful thinking on the part of the left is dangerous in that it makes it difficult to recognize the sophisticated tactics neo-Nazis actually use to recruit. Nazis put a lot of thought into how to make their ideology appealing to young people, and anyone who wants to argue effectively against those appeals will first need to thoroughly understand white supremacist "pitches" as well as why it is that they are choosing the targets that they are. This essay looks at the specific appeals aimed at the subculture of online video game players as a case study in how neo-Nazis break down the beliefs, desires, and fears of a particular target group to make them seem to fit neatly into that group's worldview. My hope is that this exercise will serve as a template to help anti-racist activists and academics combat fascism and white supremacy more effectively by helping them to understand the rhetorical strategies that they will face and to shape their rebuttals accordingly.

Neo-Nazi Recruitment: The Basics

Hate groups have been using the Internet as a recruitment tool since the earliest days of the web (Duffy, 2003, p. 292). According to Keipi et al.,

> White supremacists in the US were among the very early users of the electronic communication network during the 1980s. Hate is said to have gone online as early as March 1984 when neo-Nazi publisher George Dietz used the bulletin board system (BBS) as a method of online communication. The White Aryan Resistance BBS followed, adopting this form of communication in 1984 and 1985.
>
> (2017, p. 56)

Their ideal target demographic are "isolated, lonely, insecure, unfulfilled, bitter young men who feel that society at large has abandoned them and denies them the opportunities they feel entitled to" (Deo, 2017). Historically, this demographic consisted mostly of working-class white men who felt that they had lost their place of prominence within the broader culture (their status as providers and patriarchs) due to the pernicious influences of feminism and multiculturalism (Beck & Tolnay, 1995, pp. 122–123). The formation of hate groups therefore functions as "a mechanism of power and oppression, intended to reaffirm the precarious hierarchies that characterize a given social order" (Perry, 2001, p. 10).

With this in mind, it becomes easy to see why gaming culture provides an ideal environment for the recruitment and radicalization of young white men. After all, during the 1980s and the 1990s, video games were marketed almost exclusively to these same young white men as a way to escape the constraints of the real world. Games were billed as utopian spaces where geeky guys could indulge in masculinist power fantasies without reprisal (Kimmel, 2009, p. 150; Salter, 2017).[3] However, as the audience for video games began to grow more and more diverse and critics began calling for more diversity both within games and in the gaming industry, a subset of gamers started to feel as though their escapist fantasies were being "invaded" by outsiders and that straight white men were being replaced as the dominant demographic in gaming culture (Condis, 2018, p. 44).

#GamerGate was a perfect distillation of these frustrations, and white supremacists quickly noticed that the hashtag was easily exploitable as a recruitment opportunity. According to Cross,

> GamerGate has successfully radicalized a disaffected group of mostly – not exclusively, but mostly – young white men who feel put-upon by structural changes in society, but for whom videogames are one of the most important and personal manifestations of that. And so it follows a very familiar pattern that we see in reactionary movements of late capitalism where that latent sense of resentment – of birthrights not being fulfilled, privilege no longer counting for as much as it used to, at least in the eye of the privilege beholder – is being exploited now as a source of movement energy.... There's a very strong isomorphism between the idea of "they're going to take our videogames away" and "they're going to take our country away."
>
> (as cited in Van Veen, 2015)

As a result, white supremacists rallied around the #GamerGate hashtag, using it as a vehicle to spread their ideology under the cover of a discussion of popular culture.[4] One poster on the neo-Nazi message board *Stormfront* chatted about how "GamerGate is widely supported by young White men who might otherwise be oblivious to political matters" and would therefore be "a perfect opportunity to slowly wake them up to the Jewish question" (WakeUpWhiteMan, 2014). Another wrote:

> The best thing GamerGate can do is create a perpetual assault to slow down feminists and the Judeo-Left until some sort of political opposition arises. They also need to expand their interests beyond video games, queers and "womyn" in your video games are simply a symptom of a Jewish media, academia, government, and economic hegemony, if they want to push their anti-social virtues they will do it whether you like it or not.
>
> (GreekRebel, 2014)

More "serious" white supremacist publications like *Radix* (a journal founded by Richard Spencer) also entered the fray, publishing articles warning that "gamers protesting that they should be 'left alone' will fail unless they can actually ground their beliefs in something deeper and systematic" and that "ultimately, #Gamergate matters because it is one front in a war that encompasses our entire culture. Indeed, it is a war that determines whether something called 'culture' can even continue to exist" ("Gamergate and the End of Culture," 2014). First they came for the video games and I said nothing…

The notion of piggybacking onto some event in the popular zeitgeist and using it as a vehicle to introduce white supremacist ideology to the masses has long been a key part of the neo-Nazi playbook. In fact, journalists recently discovered the actual playbook, a "style guide" designed to teach writers for *The Daily Stormer* how to best present their views for the consumption of the unindoctrinated. The style guide recommends that their writers should

> Always hijack existing cultural memes in any way possible…. Cultural references and attachment of entertainment culture to Nazi concepts have the psychological purpose of removing it from the void of weirdness that it would naturally exist in, due to the way it has been dealt with in the culture thus far, and making it a part of the reader's world. Through this method we are also able to use the existing culture to transmit our own ideas and agenda…. Packing our message inside of existing cultural memes and humor can be viewed as a delivery method. Something like adding cherry flavor to children's medicine.
>
> (Feinberg, 2017)

Gamson (1995) describes neo-Nazi recruiters as "media junkies" who monitor popular culture looking for useful carriers for their message of white supremacy (p. 85). When it comes to recruiting in online gaming culture, this means utilizing popular memes and image macros, the lingua franca of the Internet, to showcase their beliefs while also utilizing a thin veil of plausible deniability, making it intentionally unclear whether a particular racist message comes from a place of sincere hatred or if it is just some troll shitposting "for the lulz." According to white supremacist-turned-peace-activist Christian Picciolini (2018), it also means establishing a presence in virtual spaces where their targets congregate, including popular multiplayer online games like *Fortnite* (Epic Games, 2018) or *Minecraft* (Mojang, 2011), to search for potential converts.

They have also taken to modifying popular video games like *Doom* (id Software, 2016) and *Counter-Strike* (Valve Corporation, 2000) to turn them into explicit celebrations of the Holocaust (Khosravi, 2017) and even developing their own independent titles like *Angry Goy* and *Angry Goy 2*, which give players the chance to shove Jewish characters into ovens and to shoot up an LGBTQ nightclub and a news station called the "Fake News Network" (Dillon, 2018). The intent of these overtures is to demonstrate to the target that white supremacist beliefs "fit in" with the rest of gaming culture by referencing the same cultural touchstones they hold dear.[5] And, at least according to the Nazis themselves, their strategy seems to be working; famed neo-Nazi hacker Andrew "Weev" Auernheimer bragged that #GamerGate was "by far the single biggest siren bringing people into the folds of white nationalism" (Futrelle, 2015).

However, it is not enough for neo-Nazi recruiters to simply repeat popular memes back at their targets with minor tweaks. A shared love of *Skyrim* or *Pokémon*[6] alone is not going to magically make someone convert to a radical right-wing viewpoint. In order to be effective, these recruitment tactics need to connect with something that already exists within the worldview of the target, something that neo-Nazis can use to make their own beliefs seem more palatable and compatible with the target's existing beliefs. Within gaming culture, the first of these potential "hooks" stems from the tendency of people to default to hyperbole when communicating online; on the Internet, just about *everybody* is a Nazi in *somebody's* eyes.

On the Internet, Everybody Is a Nazi (According to Somebody)

In 1990, Mike Godwin was tired of seeing the word "Nazi" being thrown around willy-nilly online. Just about any time that a debate broke out on the Internet, he thought, somebody would end up labeling their opponent a Nazi sympathizer, even when discussing the most innocuous of topics. "Invariably," he later wrote,

> the comparisons trivialized the horror of the Holocaust and the social pathology of the Nazis. It was a trivialization I found both

> illogical (Michael Dukakis as a Nazi? Please!) and offensive (the millions of concentration-camp victims did not die to give some net blowhard a handy trope).
>
> (Godwin, 1994)

So, he decided to try and counteract this trend by creating "a counter-meme designed to make discussion participants see how they are acting as vectors to a particularly silly and offensive meme ... and perhaps to curtail the glib Nazi comparisons" (Godwin, 1994). What he created came to be known as Godwin's Law of Nazi Analogies, which states that "as an online discussion grows longer, the probability of a comparison involving Nazis or Hitler approaches one" (Godwin, 1994).

Godwin's Law was intended to be descriptive. It was supposed to be a "law" in the same sense as, say, the Law of Thermodynamics, not a legalistic restriction of acceptable speech. However, perhaps due to confusion about its name, it was "quickly adopted as a social rule, with general agreement that the guy who fell back on a Hitler analogy had lost the argument" by default (Weigel, 2005). Ugilt calls this use of Godwin's Law the evoking of the "Nazi-card-card":

> At some point most of us have witnessed, or even been part of, a discussion that got just a little out of hand. In such situations it is not uncommon for one party to begin to draw up parallels between Germany in 1933 and his counterpart. Once this happens the counterpart will immediately play the Nazi-card-card and say something like, "Playing the Nazi-card are we? I never thought you would stoop that low. That is guaranteed to bring a quick end to any serious debate." And just like that, the debate will in effect be over. It should be plain to anyone that it is just not *right* to make a Nazi of one's opponent. The Nazi-card-card always wins.
>
> (Ugilt, 2012, p. 1)

In other words, according to this misinterpretation of Godwin's Law, calling someone a Nazi online must always already be an exaggeration and a falsification of the beliefs of one's opponents, a rhetorical strategy that only the ignorant, the shrill, or the unscrupulous would deploy. As such, the Nazi-card-card provides excellent cover for actual white nationalists, white supremacists, and neo-Nazis,[7] who can feel free to espouse all manner of racist, fascist, even genocidal beliefs with the knowledge that, whenever someone calls them out for sounding like a Nazi, *they* will be the ones who seem like calm, logical, rational thinkers to an outside observer, while their accusers will seem unhinged and overly emotional.

Further muddying the waters is the fact that the neo-Nazis that gamers encounter online don't really look anything like the Nazis that they are used to seeing. In fact, the depictions of Nazis that gamers have become accustomed to seeing are drawn using such extremely broad brush strokes that *no one* particularly resembles them.

These "Very Fine People" Don't Look Like Nazis

Nazis have a long tradition of serving as the "baddies" in American video games, the enemies that the player can slaughter with abandon without having to feel guilty about it. They typically come in one of two different flavors: the cartoonish caricature or the blank slate. The cartoonish caricature is an over-the-top character resembling a comic book super villain who is purely and unrelentingly evil simply for the sake of it (Ugilt, 2012, p. 3) and who poses a threat that goes beyond mere military might and tips into the science fictional or the occult. The most well-known example of this version of the video game Nazi is Mecha-Hitler, the robot-suited final boss of *Wolfenstein 3D* (id Software, 1992).

The Führer also appeared in *Bionic Commando* (Capcom, 1988) for the Nintendo Entertainment System, albeit in a loosely disguised form. The American version of the game was censored, and transformed the Nazi bad guys into a generic group of enemies called the "Badds." But the title of the Japanese version of the game translates to *The Resurrection of Hitler: Top Secret* and features a plot to bring the great dictator back to life so that he can help them build a super weapon. And although the names have been changed in the American version, it is obvious who the player is supposed to be fighting, considering that the final boss, now called "Master D," has a character portrait that looks exactly like the leader of the Third Reich. In both games, the deaths of these characters are rendered in excruciatingly gory detail, considering the graphics engines of the time, a fact that emphasizes the moral permission developers and players gave themselves to enjoy a bit of ultraviolence so long as it was aimed at a murderous fascist equipped with advanced technology (Kalata, 2017).

If these games inflate the Nazis into monstrous, superhuman threats, other games tend to reduce them to empty shells with no ideology or personality to speak of whatsoever. Games like *Call of Duty* (Infinity Ward, 2003), *Medal of Honor* (DreamWorks Interactive, 1999), and *Battlefield 1942* (Digital Illusions CE, 2002) provide endless waves of functionally identical Nazi soldiers as "fodder for [the player] to shoot at without needing to feel bad about it" (McKeand, 2018). They are "soulless machines" (Reuben, 2017), empty shells presented without any political context. In many ways, they resemble another video game enemy staple: the mindless zombie (McKeand, 2018). In fact, several games and game expansions have combined the two ideas, making shooting Nazi Zombies into the ultimate guilt-free form of target practice.

So, why is this a problem? Well, first, it means that video games rarely depict what it is about the Nazis that make them despicable in the first place. We never see their genocidal policies. We never hear their racist rhetoric.[8] We just see Nazi paraphernalia like SS uniforms and swastikas slapped onto interchangeable enemies. To use video gamer parlance, Nazism becomes a "skin," a cosmetic choice that serves as an easy shorthand for "scary bad guys" with no substance and no explanation of what it is exactly that makes them bad besides the fact that they are wearing the "bad guy costume."

Second, when these comic book villains are the only images of Nazis that gamers see depicted in their favorite medium, it becomes difficult for them to recognize neo-Nazis in the real world. This is because real-world Nazis don't necessarily look anything like the ones that gamers are familiar with. White supremacist recruiters online often go out of their way to distance themselves from well-known Nazi imagery and vocabulary, "rely[ing] heavily on dogwhistles and crypto-fascist terminology" (Deo, 2017) and using labels like "identitarian" or "ethnonationalist." They also work hard to create an atmosphere of camaraderie in their online communities, often targeting unpopular, disillusioned young men who feel rejected by their peers and telling them that they have a home in their movement (Deo, 2017). Finally, as described earlier, they mask some of their most vile beliefs behind a veneer of irony. Again, according to the official *Daily Stormer* style guide, "Most people are not comfortable with material that comes across as vitriolic, raging, non-ironic hatred. The unindoctrinated should not be able to tell if we are joking or not" (Sparrow, 2017). This purposefully cultivated layer of plausible deniability allows actual neo-Nazis to simultaneously disavow Nazism ("Of course I was just kidding when I said on my livestream that Hitler did nothing wrong! Only a monster would say something like that and really mean it.") even as they go about spreading white nationalist talking points.

Thus, neo-Nazis disguise their ideology when talking to new recruits, a process that is much easier when the image that those recruits have in their head of what actual Nazis look like is so cartoonish and silly. But even that is not enough to win many people over to their way of thinking. To seal the deal, they must demonstrate not only that white supremacists can seem friendly when they want to but also that they and their target convert share a common enemy.

The Enemy of My Enemy Is My Friend

When one looks at the rhetoric used by gamers to describe their community, it would seem that they shouldn't have many political enemies. Many, in fact, declare that they abhor politics in games of all sorts and that they just want to be left alone to play their games in peace without real-world issues showing up in their virtual playgrounds and ruining the fun (Condis, 2018). One source of this hostility to politics is an echo of the threat of censorship that politicians posed to video games back in the 1990s, the memory of which is still fresh in many gamers' minds. During this period, games like *Mortal Kombat* (Midway Games, 1992) and *Doom* (id Software, 1993) were causing parents to worry about the prevalence of violence in products that were thought of as being for children. In 1993, Democratic Senator Joe Lieberman held a U.S. Congressional hearing on the possibility of forming a federal commission to oversee the games industry, prompting the creation of the Entertainment Software Rating Board (Hsu, 2018). In the meantime, a lawyer named Jack Thompson began a crusade against video games, filing lawsuits on behalf the family members of school shooting victims blaming game designers for the deaths of their loved ones (Benson, 2015). Later, when it was discovered that the Columbine shooters played the computer game *Doom* (id Software, 1993), both Republican House Speaker Newt Gingrich and President Bill Clinton called for an investigation into the effects of violent video games on children (Hsu, 2018). And, as recently as 2005, Senator Hilary Clinton partnered with Senator Joe Lieberman to push for legislation that would punish retailers for selling games with adult themes to kids (Peterson, 2015).

The last of these provided a convenient talking point for white supremacists who wanted to recruit gamers to their cause in the run-up to the 2016 U.S. presidential election. By repeatedly identifying Hillary Clinton (and, by extension, the left as a whole) as "anti-video game" and by decrying feminist and anti-racist video game criticism as an attempt to censor or silence game designers, they were able to convince many gamers that they had common cause with the alt-right (Sherr & Carson, 2017). In fact, some journalists have noted that "a proportion of Trump's most vocal supporters are gamers" (Tait, 2018) and that #GamerGate brought many gamers into the Trump camp (Condis, 2018; Tait, 2018).[9]

Creating a Cheat Code to Defeat Hate

Because of the history outlined earlier, gamers are rhetorically vulnerable to certain recruitment tactics employed by white nationalists, white supremacists, and neo-Nazis. Rhetorical vulnerability is an idea developed by Riche (2017) that seeks to acknowledge the uncomfortable openness and exposedness that communication entails and that some bad faith actors such as trolls or peddlers of propaganda seek to exploit. So, what can we do about it? How can we push back against the ever-evolving narratives being put forth by neo-Nazis, not only within gaming culture but across mainstream culture? I don't claim to have all the answers, but I do want to make a couple of suggestions here that I think will help.

First, we need to demand that the gaming industry "pick a side" in the fight against white supremacy in the games they create and on the platforms they build. We also must acknowledge that when companies refuse to acknowledge the presence of Nazis in gaming culture or try to dodge the responsibility of dealing with them for fear of seeming "too political," they are already choosing a side. They are choosing to allow white supremacists to feel at home in the spaces they create. Take, for example, Steam, the humongous digital gaming distribution platform with a "near monopoly" on PC game sales (Colwill, 2017), which hosts thousands of user-created groups featuring white nationalist themes, Nazi imagery, and copious racial slurs (Campbell, 2018). In October of 2017, Emanuel Maiberg, a reporter for *Motherboard*, discovered that

> searching Steam Groups for the term "Nazi" brings up 7,893 results. Searching for the n-word brings up 4,520 results. When I searched Steam Groups for the term "white power" I found a group called "Power to Whites" that has 85 members. In its "About" section it says that "We are a group deticated [sic] to killing Jews, Crips, Gays and Blacks.

And while Valve, the company that owns Steam, does "have a habit of quietly removing specific hate groups any time they're mentioned in the press" (Grayson, 2018), their official moderation policy remains extremely hands-off (EJ, 2018).

This desire on the part of technology companies to wash their hands of their responsibility to moderate their platforms is a key feature for white supremacists and other hate groups to exploit. And it *is* a feature in the eyes of developers, not a bug. According to Salter (2017),

> Since social media and crowdfunding sites also receive a share of income from user activity, they profit directly from the major spikes in traffic associated with controversies.... This implicates platforms financially in online abuse in disconcerting ways, raising unanswered questions about their business model and their duty of care to others.
> (p. 16)

In other words, technology companies have a strong financial incentive to ignore hate speech and Nazi activity on their platforms, both because they want to avoid the expense of hiring human beings to make the judgment calls involved with deciding what constitutes "hate" and because they profit from the increase in user engagement associated with flame wars and harassment campaigns. This means that, as consumers, we need to hold technology companies to account and invest our money in those that are willing to invest the time and money necessary to moderate their platforms.

Furthermore, as scholars and teachers, we need to learn to listen to the language that white supremacists are speaking to their targets before we can ever hope to speak persuasively against it. Neo-Nazis are using the mediums that gamers are familiar with and deeply care about to communicate their message, including memes, game mods, and social media platforms. They are going to where the gamers are (Steam, reddit, 4chan, Discord) to speak directly to them in their own spaces. We need to enter those spaces as well, both to observe what is being said and to make our own arguments against fascism and hate wherever we can. Academic discussions taking place within the ivory tower about the horrific perniciousness of white nationalism are not an effective way to study how to fight back. We need to get out into the world, listen to, and directly engage with people if we want to make our own messages heard. To that end, I also suggest that academics practice writing in modes other than those we are used to. We need to create our own memes and make our own games to teach others about how Nazis recruit and to push back against white supremacist rhetoric.

These modest proposals will not bring about the end of white supremacy online, but my hope is that they will enable a conversation to take place. Right now, most of the conversations being had on this topic within the academy are taking place at a far remove from where neo-Nazi recruitment is actually taking place. As a result, the presence of hate online is becoming normalized. It is our responsibility, then, to look at the ways that our communications' technologies are constructed, to find effective ways to moderate our online communities, and to create digital content of our own. To do otherwise is to cede gamer culture, or perhaps even the Internet writ large, to the Nazis. And, as we should all know by now, Nazis are never satisfied with conquering just one small region of public life.

Notes

1 Very briefly, #GamerGate was a harassment campaign aimed at feminist and anti-racist video game critics and developers that masqueraded as a consumer revolt. For more information, see Dewey (2014) and Condis (2018).
2 In this piece, I am going to be using the terms "white supremacist," "white nationalist," and "Nazi" pretty much interchangeably, although technically they all represent different political philosophies. For example, white supremacists believe that the white race is inherently better (healthier, more intelligent, more civilized, etc.) than all other races. White nationalists, on the other hand, are proponents of the creation of a nation-state that is reserved only for white people. While it is theoretically possible for someone to be a white nationalist but not a white supremacist (they believe that all races are inherently equal; they just want to make sure that race mixing doesn't happen within their own nation) or for someone to be a white supremacist but not a white nationalist (they believe that whites are inherently superior to others but don't advocate for the creation of a white ethnostate); in practice, these groups overlap quite a bit (Perlman, 2017). Nazis and neo-Nazis, on the other hand, are a specific subgroup of white nationalists who model themselves on Hitler's Germany and the Third Reich (Gao, 2018). The reasoning behind my collapsing of these terms is as follows: first, in the wake

of recent events like the Unite the Right rally in Charlottesville, Virginia, which included white supremacists, white nationalists, representatives from various neo-Nazi groups, neo-Confederates, and the KKK, it makes sense to me to discuss these groups as interconnected with one another. Although one group or another might prefer to refer to themselves using one particular term over another, they are seemingly happy to work together with other groups to push a shared political agenda. Second, I don't want to get bogged down in a maze of labels that has been intentionally designed to derail the larger conversation about what these hate groups are actually advocating. I argue that pedantry is a luxury that we cannot afford in the fight against literal fascists and that the benefits of taking the time and energy to parse out the minute differences between these groups are vastly outweighed by the drawbacks associated with further muddying the waters for those who are observing this debate and who are not up to date on the latest fashionable euphemisms for hate.

3 This is not to say that only men play games. Rather, since the mid-1980s, the games industry has been pitching their products as "toys for boys," turning games into an activity that is thought of as a "masculine" pursuit. See Condis (2018) and Lien (2013).

4 This is not the first time that white supremacists have attempted to hitch their wagon to a subcultural community rooted in some aspect of popular culture. They have also buried their messages of hate in punk and folk music, heavy metal, and, just recently, a new genre of electronic dance music called "fashwave" (Love, 2017, pp. 265–268).

5 In fact, as van Veen (2015) discussed in a roundtable for *First Person Scholar*,

> GamerGate's 'campaigns' are produced through online strategies that are similar to hacktivism, and its culture of enjoyment produces a reward system for active participation that is not unlike gaming itself except that its targets are very real people, suffering from very real forms of harassment and violence.

In other words, one of the ways that white supremacists prove to gamers that they are ideologically compatible is by transforming the kinds of activism they encourage people to engage in online *into a kind of game*. See also Cross (2016).

6 In 2016, Andrew Anglin of *The Daily Stormer* made a post about the idea of posting neo-Nazi fliers featuring, among other things, an image of Pikachu dressed as Hitler, at *Pokémon Go* (Niantic, 2016) gyms (spaces where players of the game congregate to battle each other) in hopes of "converting children and teens to HARDCORE NEO-NAZISM!" Although it is unclear whether this posting was a sincere call to action or a troll, Anglin did provide a PDF of the proposed flier and a map to various gym sites around the country to his readers, suggesting that even if this particular mission is just a joke, there are neo-Nazis who are thinking on some level about the logistics of using virtual worlds and multiplayer games to recruit young children (King & Cohen, 2016).

7 In fact, Mike Godwin himself recently showed his disdain for the Nazi-card-card when he Tweeted about the Unite the Right rally in Charlottesville and declared, "By all means, compare these shitheads to Nazis. Again and again. I'm with you" (Mandelbaum, 2017).

8 This is one of the main reasons that the alt-right and white supremacist groups were so incensed about *Wolfenstein 2: The New Colossus* (MachineGames, 2017). The *Wolfenstein* franchise has had Nazi enemies since its inception, but in this iteration, the Nazis are not just mindless automatons for

the player to mow down nor are they decontextualized from their genocidal politics. Instead, they are directly connected to both the Holocaust and to the resurgence of white supremacy in modern American politics. According to Grubb (2017), the game, which takes place in an alternate reality in which the Axis powers won WWII,

> paints a picture of a white America that abandoned its people, its principles, and its religions. That same America simultaneously embraced the Nazi's promise to secure the future of the white race. Some people are more enthusiastic about the new government than others, but everyone is – at the very least – standing with the Nazis. Throughout the game, you'll stumble across letters, notes, and conversations of "free" American people continuing to lead relatively normal lives. In one town, a pair of high-school-age boys talk about taking their dates to a wholesome, government-sanctioned film before casually mentioning the German lessons they have planned for the weekend. In that same town, a mother watches a parade and proudly boasts in her American accent about her son joining the Nazi military. Even the KKK give up their pseudo-libertarian ideology and Protestant Christianity in favor of Nazi socialism and German Catholicism. Machine Games is making the argument that white Americans are willing to give up their beliefs and accept Nazi rule because they don't value those things nearly as much as they cherish their position in a white-supremacist society – whether that was before or after the Nazis arrived.

9 Ironically, Trump then turned around and blamed video games for school shootings himself in the aftermath of the Parkland massacre (Tait, 2018).

References

Alexander, J. (2018). Top *CS:GO* commentator suspended by Twitch after using racist term. *Polygon*. Retrieved from https://www.polygon.com/2018/3/31/17184530/sadokist-counter-strike-twitch-suspension

Axford, W. (2017). *Wolfenstein* video game's slogan "Make America Nazi-free again" angers the alt-right. *The Houston Chronicle*. Retrieved from https://www.chron.com/news/nation-world/nation/article/Wolfenstein-alt-right-Nazi-video-game-America-12270440.php#photo-14328479

Beck, E. M., & Tolnay, S. E. (1995). Violence toward African Americans in the era of the white lynch mob. In D. Hawkins (Ed.), *Ethnicity, race and crime: Perspectives across time and place* (pp. 121–144). Albany: State University of New York Press.

Benson, J. (2015). The rise and fall of video gaming's most vocal enemy. *Kotaku UK*. Retrieved from http://www.kotaku.co.uk/2015/09/15/the-rise-and-fall-of-video-gamings-most-vocal-enemy

Campbell, A. (2018). Steam, your kids' favorite video game app, has a big Nazi problem. *The Huffington Post*. Retrieved from https://www.huffingtonpost.com/entry/steam-video-games-nazis_us_5aa006cae4b0e9381c146438

Capcom. (1988). *Bionic Commando* [NES video game]. Osaka: Capcom.

Colwill, T. (2017). Valve is not your friend, and Steam is not healthy for gaming. *Polygon*. Retrieved from https://www.polygon.com/2017/5/16/15622366/valve-gabe-newell-sales-origin-destructive

Condis, M. (2018). *Gaming masculinity: Trolls, fake geeks, and the gendered battle for online culture*. Iowa City: University of Iowa Press.

Cross, K. (2016). Press F to revolt: On the gamification of online activism. In Y. Kafai, G. Richard, & B. Tynes (Eds.), *Diversifying Barbie and Mortal Kombat: Intersectional perspectives and inclusive designs in games* (pp. 23–34). Pittsburgh, PA: ETC Press.

Deo. (2017). How white nationalism courts Internet nerd culture. *Medium*. Retrieved from https://medium.com/@DeoTasDevil/how-white-nationalism-courts-internet-nerd-culture-b4ebad07863d

Dewey, C. (2014). The only guide to Gamergate you will ever need to read. *The Intersect. The Washington Post*. Retrieved from https://www.washingtonpost.com/news/the-intersect/wp/2014/10/14/the-only-guide-to-gamergate-you-will-ever-need-to-read/?noredirect=on&utm_term=.53b2ab0d6458

Digital Illusions CE. (2002). *Battlefield 1942*. Redwood City, CA: Electronic Arts.

Dillon, B. (2018). White supremacists release video game where players shoot characters in Pulse-like gay club. *Gen*. Retrieved from https://gcn.ie/video-game-players-shoot-pulse-gay-club/

DreamWorks Interactive. (1999). *Medal of Honor*. [PlayStation video game]. Redwood City, CA: Electronic Arts.

Duffy, M. E. (2003). Web of hate: A fantasy theme analysis of the rhetorical vision of hate groups online. *Journal of Communication Inquiry*, 27(3), 291–312.

EJ. (2018). Who gets to be on the steam store? *Steam Community*. Retrieved from https://steamcommunity.com/games/593110/announcements/detail/1666776116200553082

Epic Games. (2018). *Fortnite* [PC video game]. Cary, NC: Epic Games.

Feinberg, A. (2017). This is the Daily Stormer's playbook. *The Huffington Post*. Retrieved from https://www.huffingtonpost.com/entry/daily-stormer-nazi-style-guide_us_5a2ece19e4b0ce3b344492f2

Futrelle, D. (2015). Weev: Gamergate is "the biggest siren bringing people into the folds of white nationalism." *We Hunted the Mammoth*. Retrieved from http://www.wehuntedthemammoth.com/2015/08/24/weev-gamergate-is-the-biggest-siren-bringing-people-into-the-folds-of-white-nationalism/

Gallagher, D. (2018). Dallas Fuel releases Félix Lengyel after second suspension over racist commentary. *Dallas Observer*. Retrieved from http://www.dallasobserver.com/arts/dallas-fuels-felix-lengyel-is-no-longer-on-the-team-after-posting-racially-insensitive-meme-10466185

Gamergate and the end of culture. (2014). *Radix Journal*. Retrieved from https://www.radixjournal.com/2014/09/2014-9-25-gamergate-and-the-end-of-culture/

Gamson, W. A. (1995). Constructing social protest. In H. Johnston & B. Klandermans (Eds.), *Social movements and culture* (pp. 85–106). Minneapolis: University of Minnesota Press.

Gao, M. (2018). A Nazi by any other name: Linguistics and white supremacy. *The Harvard Political Review*. Retrieved from http://harvardpolitics.com/culture/white-supremacy/

Godwin, M. (1994). Meme, counter-meme. *Wired*. Retrieved from https://www.wired.com/1994/10/godwin-if-2/

Grayson, N. (2018). Valve is quietly deleting hate groups, but it isn't solving Steam's big problem. *Steamed. Kotaku*. Retrieved from https://steamed.kotaku.com/valve-is-quietly-deleting-hate-groups-but-it-isnt-solv-1823849767

GreekRebel. (2014). Re: SPLC Jews add GamerGate to their "hatewatch." *Post 5*. Retrieved from https://www.stormfront.org/forum/t1071968/
Grubb, J. (2017). *Wolfenstein II: The New Colossus* review: Complicity in Nazi America. *Venture Beat*. Retrieved from https://venturebeat.com/2017/10/26/wolfenstein-ii-review-dear-white-people/
Hansen, S. (2017). *Overwatch* pro ends career with stream of racial slurs. *Destructoid*. Retrieved from https://www.destructoid.com/overwatch-pro-ends-career-with-stream-of-racial-slurs-432857.phtml
Hsu, T. (2018). When *Mortal Kombat* came under Congressional scrutiny. *The New York Times*. Retrieved from https://www.nytimes.com/2018/03/08/business/video-games-violence.html
id Software. (1992). *Wolfenstein 3D* [PC video game]. Garland, TX: Apogee Software.
id Software. (1993). *Doom* [PC video game]. Shreveport, LA: id Software.
id Software. (2016). *Doom* [PC video game]. Rockville, MA: Bethesda.
Infinity Ward. (2003). *Call of Duty*. [PC video game]. Santa Monica, CA: Activision.
Kalata, K. (2017). *Bionic Commando* (NES). *Hardcore Gaming 101*. Retrieved from http://www.hardcoregaming101.net/bionic-commando-nes/
Keipi, T., Näsi, M., Oksanen, A., & Räsänen, P. (2017). *Online hate and harmful content: Cross national perspectives*. London: Routledge.
Khosravi, R. (2017). Neo-Nazi gamer are modding their favorite titles to make them explicitly racist. *Mic*. Retrieved from https://mic.com/articles/173392/neo-nazi-gamers-are-modding-their-favorite-titles-to-make-them-explicitly-racist#.KPZEFnVjg
Kimmel, M. (2009). *Guyland: The perilous world where boys become men*. New York, NY: Harper Perennial.
King, J., & Cohen, A. (2016). Alt-right recruiting kids with "Pokémon Go Nazi challenge." *Vocative*. Retrieved from http://www.vocativ.com/357002/alt-right-pokemon-go-nazi-challenge/index.html
Lien, T. (2013). No girls allowed. *Polygon*. Retrieved from https://www.polygon.com/features/2013/12/2/5143856/no-girls-allowed
Love, N. S. (2017). Back to the future: Trendy fascism, the Trump effect, and the alt-right. *New Political Science, 39*(2), 263–268. doi:10.1080/07393148.2017.1301321
MachineGames. (2017). *Wolfenstein 2: The NewColossus* [PC video game]. Rockville, MD: Bethesda Softworks.
Maiberg, E. (2017). Steam is full of hate groups. *Motherboard*. Retrieved from https://motherboard.vice.com/en_us/article/d3dzvw/steam-is-full-nazi-racist-groups
Mandlebaum, R. F. (2017). Godwin of Godwin's Law: 'By all means, compare these shitheads to the Nazis'. *Gizmodo*. Retrieved from https://gizmodo.com/godwin-of-godwins-law-by-all-means-compare-these-shi-1797807646
McKeand, K. (2018). Videogames' portrayal of the Holocaust does a disservice to both players and victims. *PC Games N*. Retrieved from https://www.pcgamesn.com/jewish-opinions-on-nazis-in-videogames
Midway Games. (1992). *Mortal Kombat* [Arcade video game]. Chicago, IL: Midway Games.
Mojang. (2011). *Minecraft* [PC video game]. Redmond, WA: Microsoft Studios.

Mulkerin, T. (2017). PewDiePie's "apology" for Nazi jokes shows that he still doesn't get it. *Mic.* Retrieved from https://mic.com/articles/168883/pew-die-pie-s-apology-for-nazi-jokes-shows-that-he-still-doesn-t-get-it#.UuoyAps3H

Niantic. (2016). *Pokémon Go* [mobile phone game]. San Francisco, CA: Niantic.

Perlman, M. (2017). The key difference between "nationalists" and "supremacists." *Columbia Journalism Review.* Retrieved from https://www.cjr.org/language_corner/nationalist-supremacist.php

Perry, B. (2001). *In the name of hate: Understanding hate crime.* New York, NY: Routledge.

Peterson, A. (2015). Hillary Clinton's history with video games and the rise of political geek cred. *The Washington Post.* Retrieved from https://www.washingtonpost.com/news/the-switch/wp/2015/04/21/hillary-clintons-history-with-video-games-and-the-rise-of-political-geek-cred/?noredirect=on&utm_term=.f5f201df6e14

Picciolini, C. (2018). I am Christian Picciolini, a former white supremacist leader turned peace advocate, hate breaker, and author. Is America succumbing to hate again? Here, unfiltered, to answer your questions. AMA! *Reddit.* Retrieved from https://www.reddit.com/r/IAmA/comments/8umemf/i_am_christian_picciolini_a_former_white/

Reuben, N. (2017). I'm Glad Wolfenstein 2 Didn't Let Me Fight Hitler. *New Normative.* Retrieved from http://newnormative.com/2017/12/06/im-glad-wolfenstein-2-didnt-let-fight-hitler/

Riche, D. (2017). Toward a theory and pedagogy of rhetorical vulnerability. *Literacy in Composition Studies, 5*(2), 84–102. Retrieved from http://licsjournal.org/OJS/index.php/LiCS/article/view/171

Salter, M. (2017). From geek masculinity to Gamergate: The technological rationality of online abuse. *Crime, Media, Culture: An International Journal.* doi:10.1177/1741659017690893

Sarkar, S. (2017). JonTron being cut from Yooka-Laylee after spouting racist views. *Polygon.* Retrieved from https://www.polygon.com/2017/3/23/15039978/yooka-laylee-jontron-removed-playtonic

Sherr, I., & J. Carson. (2017). GamerGate to Trump: How video game culture blew everything up. *CNET.* Retrieved from https://www.cnet.com/news/gamergate-donald-trump-american-nazis-how-video-game-culture-blew-everything-up/

Sparrow, J. (2017). Milo Yiannopoulos's draft and the role of editors in dealing with the far right. *The Guardian.* Retrieved from https://www.theguardian.com/commentisfree/2017/dec/29/milo-yiannopouloss-draft-and-the-role-of-editors-in-dealing-with-the-far-right

Tait, A. (2018). Has Trump really alienated gamers? And will this affect him in 2020? *The New Statesman.* Retrieved from https://www.newstatesman.com/culture/2018/03/has-trump-really-alienated-gamers-and-will-affect-him-2020

Tamburro, P. (2018). Fortnite pro Ninja uses n-word on Twitch stream. *Game Revolution.* Retrieved from http://www.gamerevolution.com/news/378867-fortnite-pro-ninja-uses-n-word-twitch-stream

Ugilt, R. (2012). The Nazi-card-card. *International Journal of Zizek Studies, 6*(3), 1–16.

Valve Corporation. (2000). *Counter-Strike* [PC video game]. Bellevue, WA: Valve Corporation.

van Veen, T. C. (2015). Cognitive dissonance: A scholarly roundtable on GamerGate – Part II. *First Person Scholar.* Retrieved from http://www.firstpersonscholar.com/safeguarding-research-part-2/

WakeUpWhiteMan. (2014). SPLC Jews add GamerGate to their "hatewatch." *Post 1.* Retrieved from https://www.stormfront.org/forum/t1071968/

Weigel, D. (2005). Hands off Hitler! *Reason.* Retrieved from http://reason.com/archives/2005/07/14/hands-off-hitler

10 Theorycraft and Online Harassment
Mobilizing Status Quo Warriors

Alisha Karabinus

Boundaries, circles, thresholds, and doorways—these terms, connoting hard edges and divisions between game worlds and the so-called "physical" world, have long marked the ways scholars delineate between what is a game space and what isn't. As long as scholars have been studying play spaces, they have been studying this separation. Much of this research has focused on what players bring *into* game worlds: the embodied experiences they bring into Huizinga's (1955) clearly delineated play space, popularized as the "magic circle," or what Castronova (2005) framed as synthetic worlds. In this chapter, I argue that the current cultural moment requires a new focus: that the skills and lessons dedicated players have learned inside game spaces, and what they take with them when they cross back over from the threshold of the magic circle into the physical world, informs behavior in broader digital spaces.

This chapter traces a connection between digital activism and skills forged in ludic spaces, and positions the training offered by movements such as GamerGate as theorycraft and powergaming techniques adapted for other mediums, as techniques that can be spread beyond gaming. Powergaming refers to a focus on maximizing useful abilities in a game at the expense of other elements (Malone, 2009), while theorycraft, as Paul (2012) defines it, is the strategy of using deep, even mathematical analysis to optimize play for the biggest, most efficient results, but this approach can and has been adapted to other systems in order to manipulate them. Paul (2012), building from Consalvo's (2009) work, points to the paratexts resulting from such deep analysis as ways to reshape experiences to produce a desired result (p. 131), much like the work we see put into analysis of how to use social media campaigns to share information, dominate discussions, and infiltrate targeted spaces. Trice and Potts (2018) describe GamerGate members' strategies for targeting groups and individuals, and unpack ways attacks were planned and developed, but where did these necessary skills and techniques originate? This chapter draws a connection between analytical gameplay strategies—information flowing back out of the magic circle of virtual worlds as skills that gamers learn and later adapt to outside worlds—and the planning and carrying out of organized campaigns of dark activism.

Into the Magic Circle and Out Again

In the 2003 book *Rules of Play*, Salen and Zimmerman bring the physical boundaries of Huizinga's (1955) magic circle into sharp focus for digital games, and while they examine games and play as existing within a frame, it is their contention that this frame may not have solid boundaries for play like it does for (physical) games like tennis or baseball, for instance, games often played in clearly designated spaces. Castronova (2005) and Taylor (2006), writing in the context of massively multiplayer online role-playing games (MMORPGs) a few years later, saw that idea of the circle as increasingly more porous. In *Synthetic Worlds*, Castronova (2005) speaks of the boundaries of the magic circle as a membrane containing its own world with its own rules. "The membrane can be considered a shield of sorts, protecting the fantasy world from the outside world," writes Castronova, but he emphasizes that it's that fantasy world that needs to be separate, as it constitutes a space in which everyone adopts a new set of rules. But as he adds:

> In the case of synthetic worlds, however, this membrane is actually quite porous...people are crossing it all the time in both directions, carrying their behavioral assumptions and attitudes with them. As a result, the valuation of things in cyberspace becomes enmeshed in the valuation of things outside cyberspace.
> (Castronova, 2005, pp. 147–148)

Castronova (2005) opens the walls of the magic circle, talking of flow into and out of game spaces, only to retreat immediately back into it; when he speaks of these synthetic worlds, his expanded views of machine-based and human-based systems of power and politics, such as the rules of the game itself (the code) and then human-based systems (such as clan/guild rules), are focused internally. Castronova's (2005) permeable membrane consists of conversations that happen between players inside and outside of specific game spaces, that may incorporate game elements or not, but still encircle that game world without stretching out further into digital communities. Friendships, then, overlap these synthetic worlds and others; we retain our personal considerations as we move in and out of the membranous boundary.

Similarly, Taylor (2006) explores more of the human elements within the systems, and addresses some bleed over into social aspects of players' lives, but each examination is still limited to a particular game and its community. Taylor (2006) is still within the magic circle when discussing MMORPGs such as *Everquest* and *World of Warcraft*, and exploring each as its own sphere that extends beyond the game itself and into attached communities and fandoms. Taylor (2006) focuses on what entities bring into the spaces, but does not delve much into what goes with them when they leave again:

> And is there any danger in too much "real world" seeping in?... there is no firm line between these multiple worlds we move through. Keeping the real world out is not the battle to be won or lost. That is, I think, held on the terrain of equity, justice, fairness, and innovation.
>
> (p. 154)

Like Castronova (2005), however, Taylor (2006) is responding to a different cultural moment in games than the moment challenged by dark activism; in the mid-2000s, these scholars faced instead a need to determine the human and personal within the seemingly rigid system of rules that defined virtual worlds. More than a decade later, our focus has changed of necessity, as scholars work to determine the far-reaching impacts of social media interaction on political systems and personal lives, and how cultural factors—like gaming—may factor into those frames.

Taylor's (2006) work is useful for reminding readers that there are humans attached to characters, humans with messy lives and embodied experiences, but her focus is not on what happens when ideas and affect move outward from the game space. What is learned in game worlds that leaves those spaces, and what impacts might those lessons have? If game worlds have their own specific rules and procedures, then players who learn to operate in those spaces are taking something with them when they leave. After all, scholars working with educational games have written much about transferable skills from games (Chen, Siau, & Nah, 2010; Hobbs, Brown, & Gordon, 2006; Mozelius et al., 2015), so backflow from the magic circle from training and tactics practiced by "serious" gamers should follow a similar pattern, though it is never simplistic. As framed by Cross (2016),

> [a]t the heart of many recent cultural debates about gaming is whether or not (and, if so, how much) video games influence the views and behavior of individual players. While a consensus has emerged in academia that argues against simplistic causal notions of video games producing killers or other violent offenders, the more subtle and sophisticated forms of influence that prevail in all media (e.g., Collins, 1990; Moyer-Guse & Nabi, 2010) also obtain here.
>
> (p. 23)

Cross refers to the actions of GamerGate and adjacent groups as a form of "gamified activism," and Condis (2018) comes to a similar conclusion; Salter (2017) frames online harassment brigades as arising from "a dialectic relationship between reactionary formations of masculine identities and computing technology." In this chapter, a combination of these factors and others is presented as a complex explanation for the impetus behind and strategies employed by GamerGate that have spread to other groups. In short, this behavior predates the bounds of GamerGate, so it is no great surprise "gamified activism" spread beyond that ongoing effort as well. What is in question then is the source of those behaviors. The symptoms are visible in online interactions. The cause and inspiration are less clear.

Ludic Identities

> ...this group of cultural critics, the sort of people who've been marching through our universities, gender studies or cultural studies majors, set their sights on – well, they chose the wrong crowd. They chose the games. And gamers... they like to win.
> —(Christina Hoff Sommers, *Conversations with Bill Kristol*, 2015)

What is learned within and taken from the magic circle may also be a question of identity and connection. Perhaps scholars like Castronova (2005) and Taylor (2006) focused on social aspects of human players playing in order to present game spaces as viable locales for human connection, not just systems of rules that happened to engage players. Identity figures heavily into these discussions, and with so-called "hardcore" gamers, that very label—"gamer"—is at the heart of perceptions of the self. Particular emphasis has been placed by mainstream writers, scholars of digital culture, and games scholars alike, on toxic, mostly male-dominated communities of gamers, but since the rise of the GamerGate movement in August 2014 (Todd, 2015), GamerGate has become the overarching villain of all Internet dramas, synonymous with most online harassment linked to so-called "nerd culture." However, much of the coverage around GamerGate since its beginnings has overshadowed the movement's fractured roots; even as forces such as 4chan/8chan, reddit communities, and other online groups are acknowledged as impacting contentious digital spaces, harassing behaviors in game-adjacent spaces are often now simply labeled GamerGate action, and certainly the label serves as a convenient catchall title for something that had been previously difficult to name: widespread, loosely organized groups of restless Internet denizens with overlapping interests and the shield of anonymity.

But just talking about GamerGate without examining those roots, and the various tactics commonly employed across disparate factions, forces us into the trap of GamerGate itself: without true organization or leadership, there was no way to define an official "movement," but a movement existed regardless. Or, as Mortensen (2016) frames this amorphous identity:

> The swarm nature of GG, with anonymous participants and active denial using the "no true Scotsman" fallacy made it hard to prove that GG was behind doxing... and when a person had something unpleasant happen to him or her after he or she had spoken out against GG, GG would claim no responsibility. No true gamergater would harass, threaten, hack, or dox other people, and if it happened, either in the name of GG or not, it was supposedly the work of somebody unaffiliated with the movement.
>
> (p. 8)

Separation of "true" members of the movement from so-called "third party trolls" (or assumed unrelated bad actors using the hashtag for cover) points to a particular (and self-aware) identity shared by members. Independent researcher Christina Hoff Sommers, styled "based mom" for her support of GamerGate (Poland, 2016, p. 150), referred to a particular gamer identity common among GamerGate members in her 2015 interview with Bill Kristol: gamers are "opinionated and passionate about this hobby. And they have a reason to be passionate because they've always been disapproved of...." But the shifting nature of that passion, which allowed GamerGate to duck the blame for its worst elements, as Mortensen (2016) noted, also derailed the message with the outside world.

In *The Toxic Meritocracy of Video Games*, Paul (2018) outlines the difficulty of pinning down just what GamerGate's ostensible goal might be (Ethics in journalism? Hurt feelings? A series of meta arguments?) and finally quotes the anonymous essayist "Film Crit Hulk": "there is no world view. There is only the attack and the response" (p. 82). But attack and response are enough to get *a* message out into the world, and repetition keeps it in the spotlight. In order to maintain its position, members of GamerGate did not have to develop singular positions, or delve into inconvenient aspects of narrative: they only had to make noise. Falcão and Ribeiro (2013) indicate gamers in virtual worlds and online games are trained to seek concrete, achievable goals, a facet of play that becomes part of identity (p. 139), which may help explain the focus on forwarding these singular positions. Much of the operations' documents on creating social media trends via "thunderclaps," or coordinated posting campaigns, involve very strict instructions about *how* to post, with only loose guidelines on content. Trice and Potts (2018) describe this gaming of social media systems as "a perpetual state of invention" meant to disrupt and bend platforms, particularly Twitter, to their own aims (p. 2). Trice and Potts (2018) identified specific activities performed by members of GamerGate meant to maximize both the narrative of the movement itself and its reach: first, some tweets provided instructions for other members to participate, while a second group of tweets offered criticism of some "enemy" group, like feminists or games journalists, and a third group promoted artifacts, screenshots, evidence, or "morale boosts" (p. 6). None of these were meant for sustained argumentation, only volume.

In the early weeks of GamerGate, the "gamers are dead" articles published in late August–early September 2014 by Alexander, Johnston, Plunkett, and Wilson, and others engaged the notion of a prevailing "gamer" identity, declaring that the power and reach of the games industry meant that games no longer belonged solely to the stereotypical "gamer" for whom video games were more a lifestyle than a hobby; "gamers" didn't need to be at the forefront of gaming, because just about everyone is a gamer. Macris (2014), writing for *The Escapist*, disagreed, responding with a definition of "gamer" that might have been more palatable to members within the movement:

> Nowadays more people than ever play games, and that's a wonderful thing! But let us not be fooled: **Not everyone who plays games is a gamer**. A gamer is a **game enthusiast**, a person whose primary hobby or avocation is the enjoyment of games. The "enjoyment of games" is a deeper pursuit than merely playing them. It encompasses dedication towards their mastery; understanding of their history; commentary on the design; insight as to their relationships into the web of source material from which they are derived.
>
> (emphasis in the original)

Accepting this definition, then, gamers may be considered not only consumers seeking to be defined by consumption, but also dedicated hobbyists interested in learning more about and mastering games. With the "gamers are dead" media blitz, and mainstream responses to GamerGate, gamer-participants were able to cast themselves as underdogs fighting a never-ending series of battles, a mentality that continues on the subreddit KotakuInAction, where mentions of GamerGate as villains, harassers, or digital activists are continually catalogued and critiqued.

The GamerGate Question

But any exploration of a distributed, amorphous movement like GamerGate begs the question of its origins, and it is too simple to point to Eron Gjoni's 9,000-word condemnation of his ex-girlfriend, game developer Zoë Quinn, and the firestorm of rumors that grew into the cries of troubling ethics in game journalism (Todd, 2015). Gjoni's website *The Zoe Post* was a spark, but the fire had been burned before. A month before

Gjoni's website went live, Dr. Samantha Allen and Maddy Myers, after protesting gaming website Giant Bomb's hiring of two white male writers (the latest additions to a staff dominated by white male writers) (A. G. Wilson, 2014), were targeted for harassment on social media, harassment so brutal and extreme for Allen in particular—she was repeatedly misgendered, personally insulted, and told she should kill herself—that she announced she would no longer write about games. Months before that, Zoë Quinn had been in the spotlight again, after reporting harassment and threats, including threats sent to her physical address (Kotzer, 2014); before that, Anita Sarkeesian was targeted for Kickstarting her *Tropes vs. Women* video series (Kotzer, 2014). A long timeline of events in gaming precedes the beginning of GamerGate itself, many of which are impossible to disengage from gaming culture itself (Karabinus, 2015; Paul, 2018).

GamerGate self-styles as a leaderless "consumer revolt." While official definitions don't really exist—GamerGate's "official" documentation is spread across various social media hubs, and is largely concerned with timelines, examples, and links used as evidence—certain language repeats in a number of GamerGate hubs, like this oft-repeated description from GamerGate groups and documents:

> GamerGate is a consumer revolt against unethical practices in video game journalism and entertainment media, including (but not limited to) corruption and conflicts of interest, collusion, and the censorship of ideas and discussion. It is comprised of video game enthusiasts all over the world working together to eliminate ethical misconduct by industry professionals and promote fair and balanced video games media.
>
> As a group, GamerGate is leaderless and unstructured so all efforts and projects are collaborative endeavors agreed upon and fulfilled by the group's majority.[1]
>
> (GamerGate Wiki, 2018)

Trice (2015) has indicated that due to GamerGate's spread across numerous social media hubs—countless forums as well as reddit, 4chan and then 8chan, Twitter, YouTube, GitHub and then GitGud, among others—network analysis of GamerGate is largely impossible. Perhaps ultimately network analysis of such a movement is unsatisfying not because it proves difficult, maybe impossible, but instead because a network analysis in this case is only concerned with the *what* of GamerGate and the *how*—and the affective, larger question may still be *why*. Why did information spread as it did in the early days, and why do certain stories continue to gain traction and inspire action now while others do not? Why are certain so-called truths accepted without deeper analysis by a community that claims to privilege fact and objectivity over all else?

Paul's (2018) framing of the movement as a reflection of the (seemingly[2]) meritocratic system within games offers one explanation. Gamers have been taught—by sheer virtue of playing many games that reinforce this idea—that herculean effort pays off eventually. As an example, in a forum discussion on *Halo 5* (2015), "Droog Janus" posted asking for advice to improve in competitive play and identified the steps he was taking to improve, which involved watching tutorials, changing control schemes, and working to improve Internet connectivity. Respondents indicated that he was "on the right path. You probably just need to execute your plan for a few thousand games. Then you'll be good, or at least decent." This kind of advice—grinding for the hundreds of hours necessary to play "a few thousand games"—was not even questioned within the discussion, though it might only result in being a "decent" player.

These ludic lessons are part and parcel of the mastery gamers seek, per Macris's (2014) definition. Grinding, or the repetitive effort necessary to gain levels, skills, and loot, is continually reflected in GamerGate documentation for organized operations, such as e-mail campaigns, but this approach isn't unique to GamerGate operations; a handbook for posts on white supremacist hub *The Daily Stormer* (Feinberg, 2017) is equally specific and focused on small actions and choices in the quest for a greater eventual prize. The document, like any style guide, includes recommendations for phrasing and structure, but also recommends certain insults and epithets over others as more effective, and includes guidelines on how to comment on existing stories in the correct way to avoid removal from platforms such as Facebook. While these efforts to toe the line within systems and scrape by without penalty can look like general strategies, there are underlying links to ludic moves that connections between GamerGate (and its precursors) and alt-right groups bring into sharp relief.

Now You're Tweeting with Power: Enter the Theorycrafters

To return to the definition of the gamer as someone who is focused on learning, thinking, and doing more with games, in order to understand the foundational methods driving GamerGate and adjacent online groups, and how these movements spread, we must look at the ways gamers attempt to master their hobbies. Mastery means maximizing potential, both for player and system, and if "gamers," as defined earlier, are focused on mastery, how they do it becomes an essential part of that identity. Strategy guides, walkthroughs, and other such resources have long been tools for players looking to maximize their experiences (or just to find a way out of a tricky puzzle), but for the most serious gamers, theorycrafting—a deeply analytical approach to maximizing play efficacy—is the next level of dedication. Paul's (2012) examination of theorycraft in MMORPGs defines the practice as a way to change how game is played: "These theorycraftesque approaches work from outside the game to change how it is played, potentially in ways that were not anticipated by developers, radically expanding the influential forces relevant to games" (pp. 380–386).

Like the *Daily Stormer* style guide and instructions (Feinberg, 2017), GamerGate's documentation for using Twitter and participating in official operations demonstrate a deep analysis of how social media systems operate—how that game is played. Participants are handed playbooks defining how to create accounts, how to boost content, how to engage, how to argue, and which accounts and hashtags to target. 4chan's /pol/, the Politically Incorrect board, presents similar guides for gaining footholds in the social media marketplace of ideas, with different degrees of organization and stringency. Some are less formal, like this anonymous post from August 2017 suggesting strategies for "turning the Left antisemite"[3]:

> Recently I've seen quite a lot of hate from the left for Jewish republicans like Milo, Shapiro, Kushner and in the most recent Stephen Miller press conference where he went agaisnt the CNN "journalist" quoting the statue of liberty poem I've seen multiple lefties on youtube and twitter calling him Nazi and racist. So here is the Idea, we LARP as liberals and spread thinly veiled redpills[4] against these conservative Jews and Israel to the progressive community and see them turning against the Jews.
>
> (Turning the Left anti-Semite, 2017)

In contrast, the widely documented[5] Operation Lollipop seemed to have more specific instructions, tasking participants with creating fake social media accounts to push fractures within online feminist discourse. Participants created accounts with fake names and stock photos and inserted themselves into conversations in efforts to push extremist viewpoints through a long and slow campaign (Heppner, 2014). The instructions for doing so are not unlike the kinds of questions RPG players ponder when creating character backgrounds for story-driven tabletop role-playing games (RPGs). Also included are instructions for creating realistic Twitter handles and other accounts to increase presence, to look more realistic, as shown in Figure 10.1.

The questions for participants in Figure 10.1 are very like tips for creating strong character backstories in the tabletop RPG *Dungeons & Dragons* (Brierly, 2017; Ostrander, 2016): not only in both cases are these personas referred to *as* characters, but participants are also asked to think deeply about motivation, personality, and consistency, and even to consider things that may not come up at all, but still inform the creation of a person. Participants in these 4chan operations are also seen at

Design your character. Really get in touch with your feminine side and think about what kind of character you'd be good at impersonating, then answer the following questions:

What's her name?

Is your character female or transgendered?

What race is she?

Is she a Radical Feminist or an Intersectional Feminist (Read the Wiki pages on both of these).

What is her age?

What are her politics?

What are her hobbies?

What are her disabilities (disabilities are celebrated within the PoO community so don't be timid about inventing one)?

Set up Twitter account. Subtlety is key when creating a twitter account. Remember, we're trying to blend in. Follow these steps:

Create a new email account (http://www.hushmail.com is recommended).

Create a tumblr (http://www.tumblr.com) account (if you don't already have one) using your new email address.

Search tumblr with #Me and save a profile picture suitable to your character.

Sign up for a twitter (http://www.twitter.com) account using your character's name and your new email account.

You must also choose a twitter handle, which other users will use to contact you. It starts with an "@". Be creative, but be subtle. For example, if your character's name is Mikki Kelly, you could create a handle like "@MikkiRadFem" or "@KellyKickBoxer".

Figure 10.1 Operational instructions for creating fake online feminist accounts. Screencapture by A. Karabinus, 2019.

times as LARPing (participating in live action role-play, as seen earlier in the anonymous post about anti-Semitism), further strengthening that link between learned ludic behaviors and online interaction.

But the links extend far beyond creation and into operation and strategy, representing deep analysis into the inner workings of social media platforms. The turn-and-burn strategy of creating Twitter accounts for various GamerGate factions, for instance, works to circumvent Twitter's system that allows for muting, blocking, and other forms of ecology control, in order to maximize audience reach; individual accounts don't matter if all it takes to make a new one is a new e-mail address, a new avatar photo, and the same old strategy for pushing content toward trending status. Organized legions of dedicated users pushing the same goal toward the same end mean only the group matters, not the individual account (Trice, 2015). Since part of the strategy involves favoriting/retweeting anything on the hashtag, regardless of content, this, too, fits with Trice and Potts's (2018) analysis of how Twitter was leveraged to push the GamerGate narrative. GamerGate documentation, as captured in Figure 10.2 by Quinn (2014), demonstrates strategies for pushing GamerGate discussions and interests into greater visibility through constant retweeting/favoriting of content, creating ever-expanding circles of users who follow one another, and leveraging other hashtags as well to spread content further. At the time Quinn (2014) captured this image, the hashtags in question were related to PAX, the Penny Arcade Expo, a gaming convention. Trice (2015) has explored this onboarding documentation extensively, both in how these documents train new users and in how members of the movement have been able to exploit Twitter and leverage the system for their own gains (Trice & Potts, 2018).

Taylor's (2006) examination of powergaming might apply here as well:

> Straight, clear-cut cheating is not something I found to be a defining feature in the power gamers' style of play. Instead, it is just that somehow power gamers, while sharing the same world as their fellow players, seem to be at times too focused, too intent, too goal-oriented. To outsiders it can look as if they are not playing for "fun" at all.
>
> (p. 71)

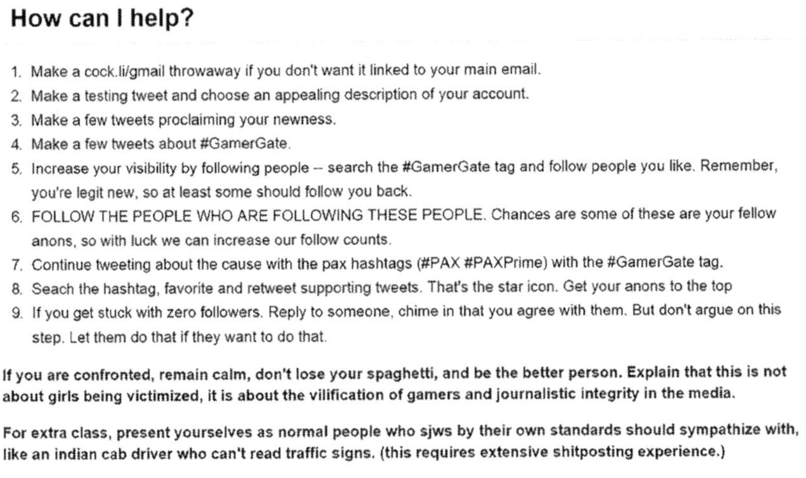

How can I help?

1. Make a cock.li/gmail throwaway if you don't want it linked to your main email.
2. Make a testing tweet and choose an appealing description of your account.
3. Make a few tweets proclaiming your newness.
4. Make a few tweets about #GamerGate.
5. Increase your visibility by following people -- search the #GamerGate tag and follow people you like. Remember, you're legit new, so at least some should follow you back.
6. FOLLOW THE PEOPLE WHO ARE FOLLOWING THESE PEOPLE. Chances are some of these are your fellow anons, so with luck we can increase our follow counts.
7. Continue tweeting about the cause with the pax hashtags (#PAX #PAXPrime) with the #GamerGate tag.
8. Seach the hashtag, favorite and retweet supporting tweets. That's the star icon. Get your anons to the top
9. If you get stuck with zero followers. Reply to someone, chime in that you agree with them. But don't argue on this step. Let them do that if they want to do that.

If you are confronted, remain calm, don't lose your spaghetti, and be the better person. Explain that this is not about girls being victimized, it is about the vilification of gamers and journalistic integrity in the media.

For extra class, present yourselves as normal people who sjws by their own standards should sympathize with, like an indian cab driver who can't read traffic signs. (this requires extensive shitposting experience.)

Figure 10.2 GamerGate instructions. Screencapture by Z. Quinn, 2014.

Some members of this wider ecology, working within GamerGate or without, see this sort of social media engagement as "fun," or at least chaos-inducing; like many aspects of chan culture, actions are undertaken simply to foment chaos—"for the lulz" (laughs). But gaming social media systems in this way "for the lulz" isn't just about creating chaos or humor: it is another form of mastery and control.

This ludic language is frequently utilized in digital communities that are a part of the wider GamerGate ecology. In organizing Twitter operations, instructions on 8chan's /gamergatehq/ read:

> As of now we have not yet used a tried-and-true tactic for twitter hashtags. A tactic we use in massively multiplayer online games every day. Every large scale attack in an MMO is planned and coordinated. We wouldn't go into an EVE online battle without a battleplan and without informing all captains when it takes place. For clan based attacks in browser games like TribalWars we set alarm clocks to 2am so we can surprise our opponents in their sleep.
>
> (GamerGate Leader, 2015).

GamerGate members weren't just trying to find the best way to spread their message; they were powerusers, pushing Twitter harder and in a more focused way than typical users. Further instructions suggested that members should track which posts and infographics received the most engagement, and reuse those items over and over in scheduled tweets. Not only does this strategy align with Trice and Potts's (2018) analysis of the perpetual invention of GamerGate members—a continued effort to sustain noise—it also bears a striking resemblance to Paul's (2012) discussion of training dummies in *World of Warcraft*. When theorycrafting became popular, Blizzard added training dummies within the virtual world that gave players targets they could attack over and over simply to test abilities and powers while measuring stats (Paul, 2012, p. 133), all in the pursuit of larger goals.

Sentiment and reach analysis of GamerGate tweets revealed that Twitter users active on the GamerGate hashtag were more involved on the platform than the average user—more followers, more interactions (Chatzakou et al., 2017). And they were more negative, less joyful, more apt to use words associated with hate. Perhaps surprisingly, that same team determined that GamerGate members' training and care in approaching Twitter resulted in participants being banned less often on Twitter than other users; operational documents allowed members to toe the line of what was acceptable on social media. Network and sentiment analysis both demonstrate GamerGate members' mastery of Twitter as a platform for spreading a very particular message—for gaming the system, as it were.

Theorycrafting a Virtualized Reality

When Cross (2016) calls GamerGate actions "gamified activism," she posits that this angle turns members' online actions into a game, a ludic scenario in which the day-to-day work of tweeting and e-mailing is grinding to level up. But perhaps most importantly, the "enemies" of GamerGate function in this virtualized reality as nonplayer characters (NPCs) in a game; they are obstacles, not people.

Furthermore, team operations help each member of GamerGate avoid feeling too responsible for any ill effects from the movement's actions. Poland (2016), in her book *Haters*, links the proclivity for and acceptance of the spread of negative messages to Kabay's (1998) work on deindividuation. Deindividuated users do not have to feel personally responsible for their actions, as responsibility is transferred to the group. GamerGate (as a whole) may be responsible, but users aren't. We see evidence of that groupthink in the official GamerGate description mentioned earlier: "As a group, GamerGate is leaderless and unstructured so all efforts and projects are collaborative endeavors agreed upon and fulfilled by the group's majority" (GamerGate Wiki, 2018).

But GamerGate, in particular, is more complex than just group identity; while Poland's (2016) assertions are certainly traceable in GamerGate actions (the planning of operations, the repetition of leaderless movements, and the willingness to accept and reject similar things as a group), there are other angles here too on this idea of deindividuation. Anything considered unsavory is often chalked up by members as the work of third-party trolls—Mortensen's (2016) "no true gamergater"— or one group will assign blame to another group. When former Nintendo employee Alison Rapp came under fire (Blackmon & Karabinus, 2016), users on KotakuInAction blamed doxxing, or the dissemination of personal information, on 8chan users while also agreeing to share information in private messages since it couldn't be posted on the subreddit, a move that allowed them to disassociate from the wrongdoing. They were only passing previously established facts, not performing the doxxing themselves. Similarly, while all the documentation on KotakuInAction insists that GamerGate does not harass, comments on Mortensen's (2016) article resulted in users posting her picture and calling for anyone who lived near her university to drop in to correct her work. The definition of harassment, then, may be seen as flexible.

Poland (2016) further draws on Kabay (1998) to write about the repetitive experiences of gaming or planning harassment operations, and the way participants lose themselves in the actions, creating increased tendencies for aggression and willingness to dehumanize targets. Popular GamerGate foci like Zoë Quinn and Brianna Wu have become "literally who" on KotakuInAction (a phrase used in lieu of their names) (GamerGate Wiki, 2018), despite their relative fame in those communities, an action that strips the human identities from these women. This dehumanization is a tool for separation that allows the "work" to continue without consideration for people who might be on the receiving end of GamerGate actions.

At the same time that GamerGate constructs its enemies as NPCs (nonplayer characters in games, or characters who exist only as part of the system and are not controlled by other, human, players) and its battles are stylized as raids, the fight is also very real. Raids are large-scale epic battles in which the player-heroes struggle and strategize together to take down big enemies, just as those who operate together in "thunderclaps" struggle toward the same large-scale goal. Members of GamerGate lashed out in response to "gamers are dead" articles, referring to their persecution and victimization at the hands of interloping games journalists who had forgotten what gaming was really all about: the consumers. Not only did this separation feed into the "Us versus Them" battle mentality, but it demonstrated how keenly felt anti-gamer slights were to members of GamerGate, even as members in IRC chats were doxxing anyone with any ties to Zoë Quinn (Johnston, 2014b).

On the other hand, GamerGate social media actions were written off as "just words." Not only did this allow members to duck any accusations they were harassers, it returned the combat to a state of unreality:

> Harassing behaviour, such as hundreds of Twitter users piling into the mentions of a prominent target like Brianna Wu to hurl abuse at her, were seen by GamerGaters as "disagreement" rather than harassment. The fact that the Tweets were "just words" was repeatedly emphasised, as was the idea that GamerGate's opponents had no right to "not be offended." In one instance, extreme transphobic abuse (a user calling transgender opponents of GamerGate "trannies" that no one should "give a fuck about" who were "retarded... autistic fucks") was excused by another GamerGater as "distasteful comedy" that should not be "policed," dismissing the harms of such statements as "hurt feelings."
>
> (Cross, 2016, p. 27).

This negotiation indicates that while GamerGate members didn't see the virtual world and actions there as "real," they simultaneously felt real injury when their own selves and identities were attacked. Hansen (2004), by way of Bay and Rickert (2008), sees these virtual/physical negotiations as reflecting "the demands of embodied perception," and gamers, in perceiving themselves as victim-heroes in the grand battle of ethics, have created a war they must fight and win (p. 213), though part of doing so is selectively determining what holds meaning, and what doesn't. The communities of GamerGate—the image boards, subreddits, hashtags, and documentation hubs—as a space for gathering demonstrate the tension of emergent virtual dwelling places in Bay and Rickert's (2008) work with Facebook. There is both a real and not-real feeling to this form of digital activism; participants are very serious about the tasks they are undertaking, while at the same time mitigating certain inconvenient impacts of those. This, too, might be considered part of theorycrafting: ignoring the inconvenient and charging ahead in the effort to win.

Win Conditions

Trice and Potts's (2018) discussion of perpetual rhetorical invention describes a strategy of success for GamerGate actors, but also, as they point out, diminished the potential for a tangible conclusion. In comparing GamerGate to "mission-based activism" like the Arab Spring, Black Lives Matter, and even the MAGA campaign, Trice and Potts (2018) point out that "[GamerGate's] ever-expanding list of targets and arguments" prevented the development of any resolution or potential outcome; the movement continued for the movement's sake. Without any clear, overarching "win condition," then, the focus lingered on individual moments and particular targets. Pushing a particular "operation" or "thunderclap" was its own win, much like an individual raid in an MMORPG.

In a gaming-focused issue of *Technical Communication Quarterly*, issue editors deWinter and Vie (2016) wrote:

> Games provide frameworks for interaction. They are rule systems that are teleological in nature. However, games themselves exist within complex cultural and economic structures, which require scholars to interrogate the actors and discourse that influence game creation, consumption, and deployment in game- and non-game-like arenas.
>
> (p. 151)

More and more, we're seeing tactics, skills, and motivations spread from game-arenas to the physical. While we cannot directly fix the platforms that have been impacted, we can point out misuse of these platforms, by outlining the strategies employed, as well as their sources and developments, as a practical application for rhetorical theory. Unpacking these actions and placing them within a broader context is necessary, too; to those not directly impacted, GamerGate can too easily be seen as an individual movement, a flash in the pan—nothing too serious. It is tempting, too, to write off GamerGate and other movements, even the sprawling, distributed network of the alt-right, as general use of social media that simply *happens* to have resulted in harassment. Harassment can be written off as an unfortunate by-product, as those in power (with the ability to change platforms) are too often insulated from the worst actions. The response then is so often, "well, sometimes threats happen; block the bad eggs and move on."

But the actions of GamerGate and similar movements are anything but standard use of social media; these are highly organized campaigns drawing on particular organizational tools and strategies to produce results—to "game" the system. By drawing connections between learned skills in the past, and interconnected cultural shifts, such as the rise of the alt-right, scholars can more easily point to potential solutions for platforms to undertake, and help dismantle efforts to write off such organized campaigns as standard behavior. We must rely on social media platforms to "make clear-headed choices about how conflation of platform purpose and user experience makes them vulnerable to abuse and potentially undermines their goals as both a media platform and an activist supraplatform" (Trice & Potts, 2018). As scholars, our duty is to shine a light on the darker uses of the platforms that connect us. With that, though, comes real danger; researchers working on uncovering tactics like these become targets themselves, if they weren't already, and concern over the potential risks involved in undertaking such research has given some scholars pause (Andrew, 2016; Chess & Shaw, 2016).

Our job, then, beyond simply bringing tactics to light and connecting the dots between the various platforms, actors, and sources of such social media campaigns, is to ensure as educators that information literacy pedagogy engages not just traditional media and new media artifacts but also social media. We must teach students and other users to recognize fake accounts and support and amplify those who are already doing such work. Countercampaigns dedicated to unmasking troll accounts (Poland, 2016) and organizations such as Zoë Quinn's Crash Override (Crash Override, n.d.), with its cybersecurity guides and documentation on online protection, are key tools in fighting an ongoing battle against online harassment and supporting and spreading the word about such efforts is a simple and effective stopgap solution. Working, too, to change the mindset that what happens in online spaces is not "real" is a necessary action for teacher-scholars to take. By exploring how ideas, skills, and strategies can move out of game worlds and into other spaces, we can work to restructure those spaces, creating change where platforms will not.

Notes

1 This particular definition was taken from the "official" GamerGate wiki but the language is repeated whole or in part on documents on the GamerGate Steam group, on the subreddit KotakuInAction, and other sites.
2 "Seemingly" here because, as Paul (2018) says himself, the skill-based structure of most games is only truly meritocratic to a certain point, and as it extends through game culture, a host of other factors begin to impact who gains skills and whose skills matter.
3 Retrieved from a 4chan archive: https://archive.4plebs.org/pol/thread/136118832/.
4 A meme with roots in the *Matrix* films, the "red pill" represents the so-called knowledge about the deeper, darker "truths" others happily ignore.

5 Operation Lollipop was famously exposed by Twitter user @sassycrass (Shafiqah Hudson) with the #YourSlipIsShowing campaign after the #EndFathersDay hashtag trended in mid-2014 (Poland, 2016).

References

Alexander, L. (2014, August 28). 'Gamers' don't have to be your audience. 'Gamers' are over. *Gamasutra*. Retrieved from gamasutra.com

Andrew, A. D. (2016, July 11). Even doing academic research on video games puts me at risk. *The Establishment*. Retrieved from https://medium.com/the-establishment/

Bay, J., & Rickert, T. (2008). New media and the fourfold. *JAC, 28*(1/2), 209–244.

Blackmon, S., & Karabinus, A. (2016, March 31). Another woman, another loss: Nintendo terminates Alison Rapp. *NYMG*. Retrieved from nymgamer.com

Brierly, T. (2017, January 23). More of Tom's GM tips: How to create an interesting character for Dungeons & Dragons. *Medium*. Retrieved from medium.com

Castronova, E. (2005). *Synthetic worlds: The business and culture of online games*. Chicago, IL: University of Chicago Press.

Chatzakou, D., Kourtellis, N., Blackburn, J., De Cristofaro, E., Stringhini, G., & Vakali, A. (2017, July). Hate is not binary: Studying abusive behavior of #gamergate on twitter. In *Proceedings of the 28th ACM Conference on Hypertext and Social Media* (pp. 65–74). New York, NY: ACM.

Chen, X., Siau, K., & Nah, F. F. H. (2010). 3-d virtual world education: An empirical comparison with face-to-face classroom. In *Proceedings of the 31st International Conference on Information Systems* (p. 260). St. Louis, MO: ICIS.

Chess, S., & Shaw, A. (2016). We are all fishes now: DiGRA, feminism, and GamerGate. *Transactions of the Digital Games Research Association, 2*(2), 21–30.

Collins, P. H. (1990). *Black feminist thought: Knowledge, consciousness, and the politics of empowerment*. New York, NY: Routledge.

Condis, M. (2018). *Gaming masculinity*. Iowa City: University of Iowa Press.

Consalvo, M. (2009). *Cheating: Gaining advantage in videogames*. Cambridge, MA: MIT Press.

Conversations with Bill Kristol: Christina Hoff Sommers. (2015, June 28). Transcript. Retrieved from conversationswithbillkristol.org

Crash Override. (n.d.). Retrieved from crashoverridenetwork.com

Cross, K. (2016). Press F to revolt. In Kafai, Y. B., Richard, G. T., & Tynes, B. M. (Eds.), *Diversifying Barbie and Mortal Kombat: Intersectional perspectives and inclusive designs in gaming* (pp. 23–34). Pittsburgh, PA: ETC Press.

deWinter, J., & Vie, S. (2016). Games in technical communication. *Technical Communication Quarterly, 25*(3), 151–154.

"Droog Janus." (2015, December 23). Help a casual player 'git gud.' *Halo Waypoint*. Retrieved from www.halowaypoint.com

Falcão, T., & Ribeiro, J. C. (2013). The whereabouts of play, or how the magic circle helps create social identities in virtual worlds. In Crawford, G.,

Gosling, V. K., & Light, B. (Eds.), *Online gaming in context* (pp. 145–155). New York, NY: Routledge.

Feinberg, A. (2017, December 13). This is the Daily Stormer's playbook. *The Huffington Post*. Retrieved from www.huffingtonpost.com

GamerGate Leader. (2015, April 5). OP Earthquake. /gamergatehq/. Retrieved from 8ch.net

GamerGate Wiki. (2018). GamerGate Wiki. Retrieved from ggwiki.deepfreeze.it

Hansen, M. B. N. (2004). *New philosophy for new media*. Cambridge, CA: MIT Press.

Heppner, D. (2014, February 21). Black propaganda in feminism part II. *Return of Kings*. Retrieved from www.returnofkings.com

Hobbs, M., Brown, E., & Gordon, M. (2006). Using a virtual world for transferable skills in gaming education. *Innovation in Teaching and Learning in Information and Computer Sciences, 5*(3), 1–13.

Huizinga, J. (1955). *Homo ludens: A study of the play-element in culture*. Boston, MA: The Beacon Press.

Johnston, C. (2014a, August 29). The death of the "gamers" and the women who "killed" them. *Ars Technica*. Retreived from arstechnica.com

Johnston, C. (2014b, September 9). Chat logs show how 4chan users created #GamerGate controversy. *ArsTechnica*. Retrieved from arstechnica.com

Kabay, M. E. (1998, March). Anonymity and pseudonymity in cyberspace: Deindividuation, incivility and lawlessness versus freedom and privacy. *Annual Conference of the European Institute for Computer Anti-Virus Research (EICAR)*, Munich, Germany.

Karabinus, A. (2015, November 13). Our long dark history: A timeline of sexism in gaming. *NYMG*. Retrieved from www.nymgamer.com

Kotzer, Z. (2014, January 24). The sexist BS women who make video games have to deal with. *Vice*. Retrieved from vice.com

Macris, A. (2014, September 8). Publisher's note: The state of gaming. *The Escapist*. Retrieved from www.escapistmagazine.com

Malone, K. L. (2009). Dragon kill points: The economics of power gamers. *Games and Culture, 4*(3), 296–316.

Mortensen, T. E. (2016). Anger, fear, and games: The long event of #GamerGate. *Games and Culture*. doi:10.1177/1555412016640408

Mozelius, P., Wiklund, M., Westin, T., & Norberg, L. (2015, June). Transfer of knowledge and skills from computer gaming to non-digital real world contexts. In *International Conference on e-Learning* (p. 235). Reading, UK: Academic Conferences International Limited.

Moyer-Guse, E., & Nabi, R. (2010). Explaining the effects of narrative in an entertainment television program: Overcoming resistance to persuasion. *Human Communication Research, 36*, 26–52.

Ostrander, K. (2016, September 16). 5 steps to writing a killer RPG character backstory. *Geek & Sundry*. Retrieved from geekandsudry.com

Paul, C. A. (2012). *Wordplay*. New York, NY: Routledge.

Paul, C. A. (2018). *The toxic meritocracy of video games: Why gaming culture is the worst*. Minneapolis: University of Minnesota Press.

Poland, B. (2016). *Haters: Harassment, abuse, and violence online*. Lincoln, NE: Potomac Books.

Plunkett, L. (2014, August 28). We might be witnessing the 'death of an identity.' *Kotaku*. Retrieved from kotaku.com

Quinn, Z. (2014, December 5). Gamergate is about ethics in games journalism—But not in the way you think. *The Daily Dot*. Retrieved from www.dailydot.com

Salen, K., & Zimmerman, E. (2003). *Rules of play: Game design fundamentals*. Cambridge, MA: MIT Press.

Salter, M. (2017). From geek masculinity to Gamergate: The technological rationality of online abuse. *Crime, Media, Culture, 14*(2), 247–264.

Taylor, T. L. (2006). *Play between worlds*. Cambridge, CA: MIT Press. Retrieved from http://www.ebrary.com

Todd, C. (2015). Commentary: GamerGate and resistance to the diversification of gaming culture. *Women's Studies Journal, 29*(1), 64.

Trice, M. (2015, July). Putting GamerGate in context: How group documentation informs social media activity. In *Proceedings of the 33rd Annual International Conference on the Design of Communication* (p. 37). New York, NY: ACM.

Trice, M., & Potts, L. (2018). Building dark patterns into platforms: How GamerGate perturbed Twitter's user experience. *Present Tense: A Journal of Rhetoric in Society, 6*(3). https://www.presenttensejournal.org/volume-6/building-dark-patterns-into-platforms-how-gamergate-perturbed-twitters-user-experience/

Turning the Left anti-Semite. (2017, August 4). Retrieved from archive4plebs.org

Wilson, A. G. (2014, July 4). Bombs, silence, building a better culture. *Silverstring Media*. Retrieved from silverstringmedia.com

Wilson, D. (2014, August 28). A guide to ending "gamers." *Gamasutra*. Retrieved from gamasutra.com

11 Volatile Visibility
How Online Harassment Makes Women Disappear

Bridget Gelms

For the majority of my online life, I've fluctuated between being visible and invisible, as I find myself making decisions about how much or how little I want to be "seen" online. For example, in the days leading up to an important 2016 U.S. House of Representatives vote regarding health care, I used my public Twitter account to circulate my representatives' contact information via relevant hashtags, hoping to be seen. In 2010, I decided to decrease my visibility by deleting my Facebook account after several unsettling experiences on the platform, one of which involved someone taking a picture of me from my profile and using it, without my permission, in a meme. Yet, decisions about our visibility online often occur outside of our own agency. For instance, my Facebook visibility lives on, in one form or another, through my inevitable shadow profile.[1] On Twitter, my visibility can decrease through the engagement-driven algorithm, keeping me hidden from my followers' feeds until my tweets are deemed popular enough, and it can increase through being added to user-generated lists, circulating me among certain circles without my consent. On several occasions, usually after having discussed the gendered aspects of online harassment, I've been added to lists with violent names created by people with nefarious intentions—lists used as a mechanism to surveil or menace women online. This is just one of many examples of how, for women, being visible online can quickly and easily turn dangerous. This condition, what I call volatile visibility, or the correlation between being "seen" online and the amount of harassment experienced, is rapidly altering the shape, tenor, and populations of our digital environments right before our eyes.

In this chapter, I share the stories of two women, Kate and Ella—one who has been highly visible on social media by going viral and one who has rendered herself highly invisible as a preemptive measure to guard against harassment. Their stories, while all too common, aren't of the variety that commands mainstream attention as narratives of online harassment are typically filtered through the lens of celebrity (for example, Leslie Jones, Kelly Marie Tran, and Millie Bobby Brown, to name a few, who all left social media at one time or another in the wake of harassment). High-profile instances of celebrities being harassed online have done much to bring the issue to greater public consciousness, but what about the untold stories of the countless harassed women who aren't celebrities? What happens to the women who lack the support mechanisms of fame, money, or privilege to be able to leave social media behind in the face of relentless harassment? What potentially irrevocable effects is harassment having on our digital cultures, public discourses, and the women who experience it regularly? In what follows, I'll describe how online harassment significantly alters women's relationship to social media and technology, informing their attitudes about being "seen" online and causing them to retreat, even if temporarily, from public view. These new norms hold serious implications for how we think about digital ethics, circulation, and the future of our digital public spheres.

Defining Online Harassment

Rhetoric and composition has a rich history of taking up research questions that directly intersect with spaces, identities, and concerns of online harassment in a variety of ways. Notably, computers and writing scholars have long examined issues of design, politics, and cultures of the Internet and how they influence public writing and rhetoric online (Arola, 2010; Edwards & Gelms, 2018; Herbst, 2009; Reyman, 2013; Selfe & Selfe, 1994; Wysocki & Jasken, 2004). More pointedly toward online harassment, scholars have also explored how antagonism and exclusionary tactics online affect writing, rhetorical practice, and pedagogy (Blair, 1998; Bomberger, 2004; DeWitt, 1997; Gruwell, 2015; Laflen & Fiorenza, 2012; Lane, 2015; McKee, 2002). Such work has done much to uncover the rhetorical dimensions of the Internet, uniquely positioning us to connect these topics more directly to the current state of online harassment, as locations, targets, and definitions of online harassment evolve alongside the landscape of our digital publics.

Online harassment is commonly misconceived as affecting everyone evenly because of its widespread nature. Indeed, online harassment is pervasive and frequent—the Pew Research Center, for example, categorizes harassment as a "common part of online life" (Duggan, 2014)—yet, the varieties and degrees of harassment people experience change across social categories. For instance, online harassment disproportionately targets women (Barak, 2005; Cole, 2015; Jane, 2014b; Penny, 2013; Poland, 2015), as evidenced in a recent survey finding that the most common type of abusive tweets employs misogynistic language (Warzel, 2016). Furthermore, online harassment takes on additional dimensions for LGBTQIA+ women (Herring et al., 2002; Sparby, 2017; Warzel, 2016), women of color (Citron, 2014a; Gruwell, 2017; Mantilla, 2015), and women who engage in social justice and feminist discourses (Davies, 2015; Jane, 2014a). For these women, everyday participation and circulation on social media come at a cost.

Of course, men (particularly gay, bisexual, queer, and transgender men) experience online harassment too, even that which uses misogyny in its construction (Citron, 2014a), but the kinds of harassment men experience are vastly different from what women are subjected to (Chemaly, 2014). For instance, according to the Pew Research Center, young women are the most vulnerable population to "sexualized forms of abuse," as "21% of women ages 18–29 experience sexual harassment online" as compared to the 9% of men in the same age range (Duggan, 2017). Furthermore, while men are more likely to be called names, women are far more likely to be stalked or sexually harassed (Duggan, 2014). Women are also more likely to be victims of sustained, prolonged attacks by groups of people rather than singular incidents perpetrated by a lone harasser (Jane, 2014b; Mantilla, 2015) and are more likely to suffer more serious aftereffects of harassment than men (Duggan, 2017).

Given the intersectional nature of how harassment is leveraged and experienced, it can be a term that is difficult to define—there is not a one-size-fits-all model, and yet the phrase "online harassment" is commonly used to describe the miscellaneous vitriol present on most social platforms, muddying the ways in which many of these transgressions are distinctly violent, misogynistic, racist, homophobic, and transphobic. Citron (2014b) defines online harassment as "online expression [...] targeted at a particular person that causes the targeted individual substantial emotional distress and/or fear of bodily harm." Certainly, this framework helps us narrow our thinking about what constitutes online harassment, but it's imperative we examine how often emotional distress and fear stem from abuse that employs existing cultural attitudes about women that aim to shame, silence, and victimize them both online and offline. Perpetrators of *this* kind of online harassment engage in covert and overt sexism and misogyny, much of which has been institutionalized, for a political and ideological purpose—to police women and feminist ideologies out of public spaces and discourses. This kind of harassment carries long-term effects on individual victims as well as the social makeup of online spaces in that it dictates who is allowed to contribute to the conversations that happen online—it has a massive impact on who and what circulates on social media safely.

The prominence of gendered online harassment is facilitated by an underlying patriarchal ideology that women should not move about in public, let alone participate in public discourses, without being regulated in ways that privilege male bodies and patterns of discourse. As Citron (2014a) puts it so simply, "men are more often attacked for their ideas and actions," while women are attacked for their very being (pp. 14–15). The devaluation of women as an embedded part of our culture acts as a foundational precedent for sexist online harassment. Beard (2014) points out that history provides evidence of women being consistently shut out of public discourse, and women who have dared to speak in public forums "still have to pay a very high price for being heard," in the form of suffering sustained harassment (p. 12). Beard (2014) argues, "it doesn't much matter what line you take as a woman, if you venture into traditional male territory, the abuse comes anyway" (p. 13).

Yet, the public perception that online harassment does not necessarily occur on gendered lines persists. Experts in online harassment have worked hard to illuminate this fallacy by debunking narrow claims that men receive more abuse than women. Chemaly (2014), for example, argues, "For girls and women, harassment is not just about 'unpleasantries.' It's often about men asserting dominance, silencing, and frequently, scaring and punishing them." The very real likelihood of women experiencing or witnessing harassment while on social media influences how they interact and *exist* in online spaces. Megarry (2014) writes, "Equality online is dependent not only on the ability to occupy a space, but to be able to influence it and speak without fear of threat or harassment" (p. 46). Mainstream utopic visions of the Internet highlight its democratizing potential, but Megarry's assertion reminds us that we are far from women holding an equitable place online so long as volatile visibility remains such a large part of our digital realities.

Stories of Online Harassment and Volatile Visibility

Before I discuss two stories of online harassment, I want to issue a content warning that points to an ever-present methodological dilemma in researching and writing about online harassment and should be of interest to those pursuing work in the realm of digital ethics. As you continue reading, you will encounter narratives of rape threats, stalking, and other forms of abuse. There are many sticky ethical considerations regarding the use of traumatic language in our academic work and how we represent such experiences. I believe that when we censor the language of abuse or sanitize the experiences of the abused, we create a functional cloaking mechanism, keeping the realities of what women experience out of sight and, as the saying goes, out of mind. With that said, I'm sensitive to those who may suffer emotional distress while reading about the trauma of others, so please read with caution.

Takayoshi (1994) argues that there's a significant gap between theory and the "reality [women] live" (p. 25), meaning we haven't done enough to actually *talk to and with* women about their day-to-day realities of experiencing harassment. Therefore, I use interviews as a method of documenting their stories. The women I discuss in this chapter came to be interviewed by way of a survey I conducted as part of a larger project about online harassment. Survey respondents were asked if they would be interested in participating in an interview about their online harassment experiences, and the interviews were conducted either through e-mail or over the phone, depending on the participant's preference.

During these conversations, I was influenced by Selfe and Hawisher (2012), who note that conventionally structured interviews have significant limitations, especially when it comes to feminist research. They maintain that less structure allows for a more reciprocal conversation where participants help to shape the questions. This approach gives more agency to the participants in how they're represented through the research, a crucial aspect of my work given the personal and sensitive nature of online harassment. While I was guided by several main concerns and topics, I went into the interviews hoping to have a dialogic conversation, where the participant could help steer the interview. I wanted to foster a sense of collaboration, where participants became active shapers of the questions—where the conversations could unfold more organically and be tailored to individual experience, where I could simply *listen* to their stories and what they deemed to be relevant (Lather, 1988; Royster & Kirsch, 2012).

In their ethnography *Troubling the Angels: Women Living with HIV/ AIDS* (1997), Lather and Smithies describe a methodology of person-based research in which researchers should become comfortable with "both getting out of the way and getting in the way" (p. xiv). By this, they mean that while sometimes it's important for us to participate along with our participants, we have to recognize when it's time to get out of the way and simply listen to the stories being told. To that end, in writing about these conversations, I want these women to tell their own stories in their voices, and therefore, I try to centralize their own words as much as I can.

Kate's Story: Circulation as Volatile Visibility

Kate,[2] who has been on Twitter for over nine years, begins our interview saying, "I definitely don't experience [harassment] on a daily basis, but it's not so irregular to be harmless." She tells me, "the instances when I've experienced harassment have seemed to fall into a few pretty clear categories." Kate has seen a lot of targeted dogpiling—Internet slang for when droves of people engage in sustained denigration of a single user. Dogpiling drives harassment to her account in hordes. This kind of harassment, the kind that is highly concentrated, voluminous, and deployed over a short period of time, is one of the "clear categories" she speaks to throughout our interview.

Kate, a lawyer and a mom, tweets most often about politics, law, and feminism and has amassed a following with similar interests. Primarily, if she experiences abuse, it's when one of her tweets "gets legs," defined as when she's retweeted by a celebrity or quoted in a news article. These instances of wide circulation, Kate observes, almost always result in sexist online harassment. The first story she tells me about took place in April of 2016, shortly after an announcement that Harriet

Tubman would replace Andrew Jackson on the twenty-dollar bill. This announcement was met with backlash from some who felt that in order to be featured on American currency, Tubman should look happier. Kate responded to these critiques on Twitter, lampooning the notion that Harriet Tubman should be smiling. Her tweet went viral, and then the harassment began.

"I was getting replies to that for weeks," she tells me. The variety of responses she got ranged from general vitriol and antagonism to full on violent threats. She doesn't downplay the impact even the perceivably lesser offenses had on her. "I got quite a few replies from men [telling me] to stop whining and making a big deal about expecting women to smile," she says. "It definitely wasn't the most abusive I've seen, but the number of randoms replying was huge because of how many people saw it and from how defensive men get when we say not to tell us to smile." Even though she doesn't categorize these kinds of tweets high on the abusive scale, they still affected her largely because of the sheer number of them.

The Harriet Tubman tweet wasn't the only time Kate has experienced high volume harassment. Two other examples had to do with her commentary on rape charges and accusations brought against comedian Bill Cosby[3] and NFL player Ben Roethlisberger.[4] In both of these instances, she didn't have high visibility from her tweets going viral, but her visibility came in the form of her account being unlocked and therefore publicly searchable. Kate speculates that harassers found her because they were patrolling keyword searches of "Bill Cosby" and "Ben Roethlisberger," looking for people to target. She was told by harassers that "Bill wouldn't even want to rape me," and the harassment surrounding her comments on Roethlisberger was relentless, causing her to have to spend an inordinate amount of time blocking other users.

Twitter's blocking mechanism didn't always stop blocked users from attacking her, however. "One guy," she says, "manually retweeted me, even after I blocked him and deleted my tweets," meaning he typed out her handle and the words of her original tweet. This is in contrast to using the retweet button to recirculate an intact tweet from the originating account. His manual retweet functioned as a call for his followers to harass Kate since he was now unable to interact with her behind the block, and they did so in droves. They all "started tweeting at me, calling me gendered insults and weirdly mocking the fact that I was a lawyer and didn't understand 'innocent until proven guilty.' One guy told me to quit law and 'hit the pole.'" The *amount* of abusive comments is what rattled Kate the most in this case. "That was one of the few times I felt the need to lock my account for a while until the wave of replies was done," she says. And while she had experienced online harassment in the past, she explains, "it was the first time I had experienced *targeted* harassment from people, and it really overwhelmed me."

Kate has developed specific strategies for dealing with online harassment and the "negativity" that comes along with it. For instance, she's learned from experience to obscure her discussion in ways that make her less visible to harassers who are looking for targets. Now, "if I ever talk about Roethlisberger," she explains, "I say 'Ben R' or something along those lines." She also intentionally misspells words or phrases that are likely, in her experience, to inspire harassment, such as "GamerGate" or "Trump." Some of her other go-to responses are to utilize features of Twitter, like blocking and Twitter's "quality filter," a feature that was added in late 2016, and, according to Twitter, "can improve the quality of Tweets you see by using a variety of signals, such as account origin and behavior" ("New Ways to Control," 2016). Using it works as a gatekeeping mechanism by filtering out content that is likely to have been sent by bots or spam accounts. In theory, it helps limit the amount of harassment someone might see, but there are significant limitations. As Kate points out, there's no way to tell what it filters out or if it has filtered anything at all, and, therefore, Kate has "no idea how much that has impacted things." This along with harassers' circumvention of the blocking function demonstrates that women looking for platform features that directly address harassment are left with few viable options.

As Kate touched on throughout our interview, she has experienced a wide range of harassment styles, but it's the moments of visibility that produce the kinds that have stuck with her. Unfortunately, her experiences with harassment have resulted in her withdrawal, even if sometimes temporary, from public conversation, pointing to a key impact that online harassment has on public discourse: it limits *who* participates and *what* is discussed.

Ella's Story: Invisibility as Avoidance of Online Harassment

At the beginning of our interview, Ella explains that the only social media she's on is Twitter, which she has used since 2009 through a locked and anonymized account. Her avatar is not her picture, nor is it a picture of a human. Ella elaborates, "the parts that are viewable to the public are not gendered in anyway, and that's deliberate." Her choice to suppress her identity as a woman by using avatars that are nonhuman and genderless is partly about privacy but also "because I don't want to attract the sort of harassment I see happening when people are known to be gendered on Twitter as female." Ella tells me that she knows people, both offline and through Twitter, who "have had to either leave Twitter, take extended breaks from Twitter, or locked their account specifically because they've received harassment." Her choice to remain locked is informed in part both by witnessing harassment and by experiencing it first-hand, conditioning her to leave as few tracks online as possible.

Ella's job requires her to frequently appear in the media—on television, in magazines, in newspapers, and on the radio—and she's extremely cognizant about her public persona. Therefore, she's understandably careful about what she adds to the Internet as her "real" self. But her skills regarding extreme privacy were honed as a direct result of harassment experiences. The first she tells me about occurred while she was in college in the early 2000s and changed the way she thinks about privacy and the Internet. Unbeknownst to her, a long-term boyfriend "granted himself super-user access to my personal computer so that he could, without my knowledge or consent, log in remotely and basically see anything that I had on my computer." She learned he had done this years later after they broke up when he "pleaded with me to change my password because he couldn't stop himself from logging onto my computer." This moment, this experience of being stalked by digital means, was pivotal for Ella and her relationship to digital technologies. She solemnly tells me, "Every account I've ever opened up online, every new computer I purchase, I think about that experience." This happened over 15 years ago but has traumatized her well into adulthood.

At this point in our conversation, I'm thinking a lot about the nature of definitions. Ella's story about a long-term boyfriend installing backdoor surveillance mechanisms on her computer isn't necessarily the one that I would typically see in research about online harassment because so much of the conversation is dominated by experiences of strangers, often anonymous, lobbing insults and threats at women via social media or e-mail. In my view, Ella's story absolutely meets the criteria of sexist online harassment in that her perpetrator surveilled her whereabouts, physical and digital, without her consent and in doing so reified cultural patterns of men's subjugation of women. And yet Ella is hesitant to classify her experience as harassment.

She uses our interview to work through her thinking about this, rhetorically asking, "Stalking is harassment, right?" before moving on:

> If I were to tell the parallel story of like, this same individual also hung around outside the *one* exit to my dorm knowing I would have to leave my dorm and confront him. He planted himself there. That would be understood as a harassing thing to do. But if someone were to just ask me like you did at the beginning, "tell me about your experiences with harassment online," the thing that I think of are comments that people leave on posts or doxxing or stuff like that. I wouldn't have necessarily, on my own, thought of this example that has been actually really instrumental in pretty much all of my behavior around technology.

It's important to dwell on the point Ella implicitly makes here because it encapsulates why work on sexist online harassment is so necessary: she notes that the scope of conversations surrounding online harassment does not include her experience, and therefore, she hasn't thought of them necessarily as harassment. In other words, our cultural narratives about online harassment shape victims' perceptions about who it affects as well as its severity, validity, and extent. As Ella indicates, there seems to be a popular dichotomy made between offline and online harassing actions; Ella was comfortable categorizing her harasser waiting around at her dorm uninvited as stalking, and while she knew that his *digital* stalking was wrong, she wasn't quick to deem it in such severe terms, perhaps because she had never seen those kinds of acts described as online harassment.

As if this traumatizing experience Ella had with her college boyfriend isn't enough, she also shares with me the time, also in college, that another former boyfriend doxxed her. Setting the stage, she tells me that although she was in college "before social media was a big thing" (Facebook debuted in her junior year), the culture at her school was fairly digitally social. A lot of people shared what they were up to through blogging platforms like LiveJournal or Xanga much in the same way someone might do on Facebook or Twitter today. Her doxxer had his own personal blog "where he talked about his life and it was pretty popular and well-read among people on campus." One of the things his blog became known for was how he would write, as Ella describes it, "in plain view" but also "put personal stories in the comments, commented out in the actual coding of the website," hidden from the front view of the page. "People who read his website and were a little tech savvy could go read these things that wouldn't necessarily appear on the website but were embedded in the code."

Ella and this person broke up after only having casually dated for less than three months, and, upset by the breakup, he started spreading vicious and bizarre rumors about her "both in *plain view* and in code on the website." His harassment of her, then, was embedded in the actual structural fibers of his blog. Both of the experiences she described to me revealed to Ella the ways in which tech-savvy men can use technology and the Internet against women, causing her to retreat from digital publics and seek out ways to be less visible.

I ask Ella how online harassment, either experiencing or witnessing it, has impacted or changed how she uses social media. She says, online harassment "means I don't say very much on social media at all. And what I do say, I put behind a lock." She tells me about a personal rule she has developed: she only approves followers whom she has met in person, explaining, "I'm not just gonna follow a friend of a friend. I want to have my information on lockdown." Strictly following this rule, she says, mitigates the risk that her social network on Twitter expands such that suddenly she's sharing personal information with strangers. Establishing a certain amount of trust with someone before she approves them as a follower is, in a sense, an anti-harassment strategy. As discussed with Kate, many anti-harassment strategies that are readily available to women are deployed *after* harassment has already happened. Ella, conversely, takes *preemptive* measures. Yet, her strategies, conditionally, are predicated on removing herself from visibility to a broader network of people and discourses, and, in some ways, don't even succeed in shielding her from the harm of online harassment. "Even just having that strategy," she says, "means I am, every day, online operating from a place of fear."

Ella sees what friends or public figures who have experienced severe sexist, homophobic, or racist online harassment have gone through, and it scares her. She says,

> For me, the witnessing part or witnessing even women that I don't know personally but are Twitter famous, like Zoë Quinn[5] or various women who are nerds or in the science fiction community or in the tech community... seeing what happens to them, seeing them get harassed off of Twitter or off the internet or having to move, seeing these things... the emotional fallout from that is one of fear.

Much like Kate, Ella's awareness of sexist online harassment makes her fearful to participate or interact online. In Ella's case, a lot of this fear has been facilitated by simply seeing other women get harassed. Her own personal experiences with being stalked and doxxed in college, she says, instill fear and paranoia, causing her to be extremely cautious with her technology use. For her, these emotional resonances translate into "doing as little of public interacting on the Internet as possible." Remaining silent or hidden from public view is what keeps online harassment and all of the emotional fallout that comes with it at a necessary distance.

I also ask Ella if she has seen any harassment among the small group of people she *does* include in her network on Twitter, and while she doesn't immediately consider it harassment, she mentions that she sees a lot of subtweeting, a cultural practice on Twitter of tweeting *about* someone without tagging them or directly naming who is being talked about. Subtweeting is akin to gossiping but doing so knowing fully well that the person being gossiped about will hear it. Ella admits, for her, that subtweeting probably falls more in line with general antagonism than it does with harassment, but she wavers on this point. She works out her thinking by porting this example into an offline context: "Okay, somebody at work... if I were in a cube and my coworkers were in the cube next to me talking to a third person about me purposefully loud enough so that I could hear them saying nasty things, I would consider that harassment," she says. I ask, "But it's your instinct to *not* consider that harassment when it's in a digital space?" "Yeah," she replies. This moment in our interview was one of a few like it where Ella was quick to comparatively analyze offline analogs to some of the examples of online harassment we talked about. In these instances, comparing the two seemed to complicate or change her defining criteria for what constitutes online harassment.

She says she is hesitant to put her three personal experiences, the stalking, the doxxing, and the subtweeting, all in the "harassment basket," and I ask her why. She responds,

> It's clear to me that those are fucked up things that shouldn't happen. But they seem distinct fucked up things that shouldn't [be classified as] harassment necessarily. Not saying that they don't rise to the level of harassment, but maybe harassment isn't the right word to describe what they are. But I don't know what that word is.

Ella goes on to say that she has a tendency to compare her experiences with the experiences of others and that

> there's this internal monologue of, 'what happened to me was not comparable to what has happened to other people.' It would feel like I'm stealing something from those people who were wronged *more* than I was, to call what happened to me harassment.

I was surprised, frankly, to hear Ella say that her experiences with stalking and doxxing are not on par with others' experiences or are somehow less severe, and as we talked more, it became clear that Ella is sensitive to the problem of those who co-opt oppression for personal gain. "I don't want to cheapen the victimization of other folks by lumping my experiences in with theirs," she says. "And yet you feel like you don't have the language to describe your experience?" I ask, gesturing toward her comment that she doesn't know what the word is for her experiences. "Yeah," she replies.

Ella hypothesizes that her reservations about describing her experiences necessarily as harassment might be because of *where* these experiences took place (online) and how many times (a few). But as she talks through her feelings on this, she realizes that our propensity to take physical space more seriously than online space, in many facets, may be an influencer on her thinking. For example, she notes that street harassment is very recognizable to her, "and I have no problem calling that harassment." She says, "One dude catcalls me and I'm like, that guy just harassed me." For Ella, the ubiquity of street harassment or even workplace sexual harassment "feels distinct" from the examples of online harassment we discussed "because it's like a single action that happens but has had consequences for me ever after." She pauses before saying,

> As I'm thinking through that, I'm like, well [the digital stalking and doxxing are] also ubiquitous because I just got finished describing to

you that my entire behavior on the Internet has been conscientiously focused and changed because of those things in the same way that when I walk home from work, I have a particular route that is designed to avoid catcalling. Cognitively, there's something about the fact that it's an online space. And it feels, because it's relegated to online space and we privilege physical space over that, it feels like it's a different category. But honestly, as I'm talking through this I realize that it's not.

One of the ways in which women *can* actually control the amount of online harassment they experience is through silence and self-erasure, and as such, Ella has taken great measure to ensure that she remains as invisible as possible in avoidance of online harassment.

The Complex Legacies of Online Harassment

Observations made by Kate and Ella all point to several incredibly important takeaways that add to our understandings of online harassment, the first being online and offline harassments are deeply connected, but it's difficult to know where online starts and offline begins. Ella's examination of online harassment, for example, has always operated within a framework that positions offline spaces as holding more importance than online ones and excludes certain acts from the spectrum of what's popularly considered online harassment. But both Kate and Ella have suffered "offline" as much as online. Kate, for example, struggled with anxiety and insomnia following the harassment associated with her viral tweet. Ella, in addition to her constant worry about information security, laments the professional ramifications stemming from her lack of online presence. These are just scratching the surface of the ways in which concerns about online harassment seep into women's offline lives. Yet, we have to ask: considering how many facets of our daily lives are deeply entangled in the digital, are we ever truly "offline?" Popular discourses dichotomizing online from offline drive perceptions that, for example, offline forms of harassment are more serious and consequential than online ones, but we must be mindful that such perceptions influence how women contextualize and share experiences of online harassment.

Inaccurately describing online harassment or only documenting and sharing the stories of what's considered to be the "most severe" shapes cultural connotations of what "counts" as harassment. A creation of a hierarchy of harassment experiences, then, may lead to some women understanding their harassment experiences as trivial or not understanding them to be harassment at all, as evident in Ella's story. I sympathize with Ella's concerns about immediately labeling her experiences as harassment. I too find myself hedging away from language of online harassment when describing some of the things I've experienced myself. I sometimes wonder if ranking our harassment experiences, labeling one worse than another, does more harm than good. Certainly, there are levels of severity influenced by hierarchies of gender, race, and sexuality, but I'm concerned that popular narratives about online harassment cause those who experience it infrequently or in small doses to believe that their experience doesn't matter or isn't somehow representative of larger cultural issues.

Furthermore, we can learn from these women's stories that women don't have to have first-hand experience with harassment in order to feel its effects. Witnessing or knowing about online harassment can be traumatizing, fear-inducing, and silencing. Kate, for instance, specifically described the fear she experienced in the wake of GamerGate, having seen journalists, public intellectuals, and other everyday women doxxed and harassed to life-changing degrees. Ella too cited GamerGate target Zoë Quinn's experience as the one she watched with horror and still thinks about with regard to her use of social media and hesitations to participate. Online harassment alters women's behaviors in reactive ways, often erasing them from public view. For Kate and Ella, both witnessing and experiencing online harassment have profoundly changed the way they interact with technology and the Internet. Arguably, such experiences have made them more reflective users when it comes to issues of privacy and surveillance, but it has also shaped them in ways that hinder their circulation and participation in public discourse online.

These are enormously complicated problems, but it's evident that by talking to women about online harassment, about the volatility of being a visible woman online, we continue to learn more about the intricate nature of the issue and its effects. As researchers interested in digital ethics and rhetoric, we should continue to capture narratives of online harassment, especially those that may not look like the harassment experiences of public figures. But furthermore, we should seek out places in our communities, both online and offline, where we can make meaningful interventions in online harassment and the threats it poses to digital publics, discourses, and people. Online harassment, by design, creates overpowering boundaries for the identities, ideas, and behaviors that diverge from those that are readily enfranchised in our culture. Such boundaries work to remove women from digital environments and maintain the Internet as a place where women aren't welcome, and it's incumbent on us as scholars, teachers, and community-members to work toward more equitable, inclusive, and just digital futures.

Notes

1 A shadow profile refers to Facebook's practice of collecting data on potential users, or people who have never signed up for an account, and keeping data on former users like me.
2 The women I discuss are pseudonymed and were invited to make amendments or suggest changes to the write-up of their stories.

3 Cosby has been accused of sexual assault by over 60 women and stood trial in 2017, which ended in mistrial when the jury deadlocked. Prosecutors retried the case in 2018 and Cosby was found guilty of three counts of aggravated indecent assault.
4 Roethlisberger has been accused of sexual assault by two women, one of whom filed a civil suit that Roethlisberger settled out of court. The other woman did not press charges.
5 After conducting this interview, Quinn came out as nonbinary/agender on her blog, though later removed the post. In response to the removal, they write, "I just don't want to friggin talk about my gender shit or have it be A Big Thing. The thing I wrote said as much but really had the opposite effect, which honestly, I should've figured" (Quinn, 2018).

References

Arola, K. (2010). The design of Web 2.0: The rise of the template, the fall of design. *Computers and Composition, 27*(1), 4–14.

Barak, A. (2005). Sexual harassment on the internet. *Social Science Computer Review, 23*(1), 77–92.

Beard, M. (2014). The public voice of women. *London Review of Books, 36*(6), 11–16.

Blair, K. (1998). Literacy, dialogue, and difference in the 'electronic contact zone.' *Computers and Composition, 15*(3), 317–329.

Bomberger, A. M. (2004). Ranting about race: Crushed eggshells in computer-mediated communication. *Computers and Composition, 21*(2), 197–216.

Chemaly, S. (2014, September 9). There's no comparing male and female harassment online. *Time*. Retrieved from http://time.com/3305466/male-female-harassment-online/

Citron, D. (2014a). *Hate crimes in cyberspace*. Cambridge, MA: Harvard University Press.

Citron, D. (2014b, October 23). Defining online harassment. *Forbes*. Retrieved from https://www.forbes.com/sites/daniellecitron/2014/10/23/defining-online-harassment/#27e47bbd28de

Cole, K. (2015). "It's like she's eager to be verbally abused": Twitter, trolls, and (en)gendering disciplinary rhetoric. *Feminist Media Studies, 15*(2), 356–358.

Davies, M. (2015, September 25). Amelia Bonow explains how #ShoutYourAbortion 'just kicked the patriarchy in the dick.' *Jezebel*. Retrieved from https://jezebel.com/amelia-bonow-explains-how-shoutyourabortion-just-kicke-1732379155

DeWitt, S. L. (1997). Out there on the web: Pedagogy and identity in face of opposition. *Computers and Composition, 14*(2), 229–243.

Duggan, M. (2014). Online harassment. *Pew Research Center*. Retrieved from http://www.pewinternet.org/2014/10/22/online-harassment/

Duggan, M. (2017). Online harassment 2017. *Pew Research Center*. Retrieved from http://www.pewinternet.org/2017/07/11/online-harassment-2017/

Edwards, D., & Gelms, B. (2018). The rhetorics of platforms: Definitions, approaches, futures. *Present Tense: A Journal of Rhetoric in Society, 3*(6), Retrieved from http://www.presenttensejournal.org/editorial/vol-6-3-special-issue-on-the-rhetoric-of-platforms/

Gruwell, L. (2015). Wikipedia's politics of exclusion: Gender, epistemology, and feminist rhetorical (in)action. *Computers and Composition, 37*, 117–131.

Gruwell, L. (2017). Writing against harassment. Public writing pedagogy and online hate. *Composition Forum, 36*, n.p. Retrieved from http://compositionforum.com/issue/36/against-harassment.php

Herbst, C. (2009). Masters of the house: Literacy and the claiming of space on the internet. In K. Blair, R. Gajjala, & C. Tulley (Eds.), *Webbing cyberfeminist practice: Communities, pedagogies and social action* (pp. 135–152). New York, NY: Hampton Press.

Herring, S., Job-Sluder, K., Scheckler, R., & Barab, S. (2002). Searching for safety online: Managing 'trolling' in a feminist forum. *The Information Society, 18*(5), 371–384.

Jane, E. A. (2014a). 'Back to the kitchen, cunt': Speaking the unspeakable about online misogyny. *Journal of Media and Cultural Studies, 28*(4), 558–570.

Jane, E. A. (2014b). 'Your a ugly, whorish, Slut': Understanding e-bile. *Feminist Media Studies, 14*(4), 531–546.

Laflen, A., & Fiorenza, B. (2012). "Okay, my rant is over": The language of emotion in computer-mediated communication. *Computers and Composition, 29*(4), 296–308.

Lane, L. (2015). Feminist rhetoric in the digital sphere: Digital interventions & the subversion of gendered cultural scripts. *Ada: A Journal of Gender, New Media, and Technology, 8*, n.p. Retrieved from https://adanewmedia.org/2015/11/issue8-lane/

Lather, P. A. (1988). Feminist perspectives on empowering research methodologies. *Women's Studies International Forum, 11*, 569–81.

Lather, P. A., & Smithies, C. S. (1997). *Troubling the angels: Women living with HIV/AIDS*. Boulder, CO: Westview Press.

Mantilla, K. (2015). *Gendertrolling: How misogyny went viral*. Santa Barbara, CA: ACB-CLIO, LLC.

McKee, H. (2002). 'YOUR VIEWS SHOWED TRUE IGNORANCE!!!': (Mis)communication in an online interracial discussion forum. *Computers and Composition, 19*(4), 411–434.

Megarry, J. (2014). Online incivility or sexual harassment? Conceptualizing women's experiences in the digital age. *Women's Studies International Forum, 47*, 46–55.

"New Ways to Control Your Experience on Twitter." (2016, August 18). *Twitter*. Retrieved from https://blog.twitter.com/official/en_us/a/2016/new-ways-to-control-your-experience-on-twitter.html

Penny, L. (2013). *Cybersexism: Sex, gender and power on the internet*. New York, NY: Bloomsbury Publishing.

Poland, B. (2015). *Haters: Harassment, abuse, and violence online*. Lincoln. University of Nebraska Press.

Quinn, Z. (2018, October 17). Anonymous asked: You're not nonbinary/agender anymore? [Tumblr post]. Retrieved from https://thezoequinn.tumblr.com/post/166511931338/youre-not-nonbinaryagender-anymore

Reyman, J. (2013). User data on the social web: Authorship, agency, and appropriation. *College English, 75*(5), 513–533.

Royster, J. J., & Kirsch, G. E. (2012). *Feminist rhetorical practices: New horizons for rhetoric, composition, and literacy studies*. Carbondale: Southern Illinois University Press.

Selfe, C. L., & Hawisher, G. E. (2012). Exceeding the bounds of the interview: Feminism, mediation, narrative, and conversations about digital literacy.

In L. Nickoson & M. P. Sheridan (Eds.), *Writing studies research in practice: Methods and methodologies* (pp. 36–50). Carbondale, IL: Southern Illinois University Press.

Selfe, C. L., & Selfe, R. J. (1994). The politics of the interface: Power and its exercise in electronic contact zones. *College Composition and Communication, 45*(4), 480–504.

Sparby, E. M. (2017). Digital social media and aggression: Memetic rhetoric in 4chan's collective identity. *Computers and Composition, 45,* 85–97.

Takayoshi, P. (1994). Building new networks from the old: Women's experiences with electronic communications. *Computers and Composition, 11,* 21–35.

Warzel, C. (2016, September 22). 90% of the people who took BuzzFeed News' survey say Twitter didn't do anything when they reported abuse. *BuzzFeed News.* Retrieved from https://www.buzzfeed.com/charliewarzel/90-of-the-people-who-took-buzzfeed-news-survey-say-twitter-d?utm_term=.vjQDOpXQj#.lhjmQpoGe

Wysocki, A. F., & Jasken, J. I. (2004). What should be an unforgettable face... *Computers and Composition, 21*(1), 29–48.

Part IV
Circulation and Amplification of Digital Aggression

12 Confronting Digital Aggression with an Ethics of Circulation

Brandy Dieterle, Dustin Edwards, and Paul "Dan" Martin

Sharing writing is a ubiquitous feature of networked life. Generally, sharing invokes positive, if not saccharine, feelings (who, after all, would make an argument *against* sharing?). On social media platforms, the directive to share elicits seemingly progressive values of social participation and building toward a better, more connected, world. As John (2016) noted in *The Age of Sharing*, "sharing, we are told, is caring, and as such, has a warm glow around it" (p. 3). Despite its general warm glow, our contention in this chapter is that sharing is not always caring—indeed, sharing can cause harm to individuals, communities, and publics. While sharing or circulating texts does important world-building work, the (re)circulation of writing on social media has also been utilized for shaming, harassment, and bullying, forms of digital aggression that have only intensified in the last decade.

This chapter bridges scholarship in circulation studies and rhetorical ethics to address ethical relationality in social media circulation. To do so, we argue that the act of circulating preexisting writing *is* writing; it is a curatorial and rhetorical practice that invites participation, assumes an exigence and audience, prompts further circulation, and so on. Second, we position (re)circulating writing as a "habit of citizenship" (Wan, 2011), a world-building act that has implications for public discourse in an algorithmic age. Finally, we conceptualize an ethics of circulation, arguing that sharing preexisting writing—retweeting, forwarding, sharing, reblogging, and so on—assumes and constructs a rhetorical relationship with others and thereby deserves thoughtful contemplation about what such a relationship entails. Paying specific attention to acts of digital aggression (Sparby, 2017), we advocate for circulatory writing practices that promote inclusivity, social justice, and mindful contemplation in a current political climate where, in some cases, politicians and other influencers exemplify the exact opposite.

To more fully explain our argument, we briefly explain the ethical complexities of circulation in two particular cases. Our first case example examines the development and curation of a GIF of Donald Trump tackling a CNN logo (Trump, 2017) and what Trump's tweeting of the GIF means as a form of online harassment and digital aggression.

This GIF originated on a subreddit known for sharing misogynistic, sexist, racist, ableist, and other problematic content, which Trump then recirculated on Twitter to make a claim about CNN being "fake news." The location where the GIF originated is problematic, as is the content of the GIF itself as it promotes violence and aggression toward the news media specifically. With our framework, we also consider the ramifications of (re)circulating such content, either in support of or in critique of the message, because by sharing content, the user provides further exposure across more networks and, essentially, amplifies the message. Our second case example follows the reverberations of the online harassment Leslie Jones received after the release of the *Ghostbusters* movie trailer on YouTube. After briefly detailing how such aggression emerged on Twitter and other platforms, we note how individuals and communities mobilized to confront the racism and misogyny attached to the harassment and violence Jones experienced. Drawing attention to circulatory practices such as those used in coordination with hashtags (e.g. #StandWithLeslie and #BlackMenSupportLeslie), we use our second case example to highlight how circulatory practices can amplify support and solidarity for those facing gendered and racialized violence. We do not presume to arrive at any definitive or easy answers related to the dynamics of circulation. Rather, through our framework and these two cases, we have formulated a set of guiding principles and questions for navigating ethical sharing that we hope initiates further research and discussion on what is and is not ethical behavior for spreading content and being part of a network.

Circulation, Writing, and Ethics

Indicating speed, flow, and movement, "circulation" refers to processes of cultural, rhetorical, and affective transmission and transformation. Circulation, what Gries (2018) identified as an emerging threshold concept for rhetoric and composition/writing studies, has also emerged as a key concept for digital rhetorics. Though circulation is nowhere near a new concept (Rickert, 2018), circulation has paved the way for a new wave of scholarship at the intersections of rhetorical theory, practice, and method (Brooke, 2009; Eyman, 2015; Gries, 2015, 2018; Porter, 2009; Ridolfo & DeVoss, 2009, among others). We want to acknowledge the wealth of work that has emerged in circulation studies, but we also want to pay attention to the *unfinished* work of conceptualizing ethical frameworks that can come to grips with a concept marked by speed, change, and dynamism.

For example, we are wary about how virality has come to mark "rhetorical success." Widespread circulation, while important for digital economies of writing, should not be the benchmark for "good" or "successful" rhetorical practice (Bradshaw, 2018; Brooke, 2015). This concern is made palpable in examples of viral compositions that spread for racist, sexist, homophobic, classist, or otherwise problematic reasons. As we highlight in this chapter, the spread of insensitive, injurious, or violent content can be damaging for particular individuals or communities.

There's a more mundane dimension to our argument, too. In an age of retweets, shares, and reblogs, it's often easy and expedient to recirculate already flowing content without fully interrogating its origins or anticipating what its further spread may accomplish. Once someone decides to share content, the person sharing becomes, in a sense, a coauthor of that content. Authorship in digital writing environments takes many nonconventional forms and is embedded in the value and currency of increased share counts, comments, and likes (Beer, 2016). The expansion of intertextual entrances for liking, remixing, and sharing online harassment increases the kairotic opportunities for trolls to generate and spread hate. In addition, sharing, liking, and commenting on content obfuscate the responsibilities for authorship a circulator assumes when engaging with harassment and expanding its reach (Prentice, 2015). In the sections that follow, we work through the framing assumptions embedded in our ethics of circulation framework.

(Re)circulating Is Writing

Sharing writing today is rather easy. Those with access to networked technologies can boost already existing writing with the click of a button. Not a particularly laborious act, continuing the circulation of writing, it would seem, carries little intellectual energy and, as such, may not seem like a worthy topic of concern for writing and rhetoric researchers. Thus, it may be easy to write off sharing already existing writing as something other than writing. There are lots of stand-in conceptualizations for such work (many of which we've already used in this chapter: sharing, circulating, delivering, and redistributing). Why, then, would we want to call such activities "writing acts?" What would be the purpose or use value of *that*?

For us, situating circulation practices as writing practices, as a kind of authorship, ascribes a certain amount of accountability and consequentiality to circulating content. As mentioned, and not unlike other kinds of writing practices, choosing—or not choosing—to boost writing teems with material and rhetorical consequentialities. Furthermore, beyond individual choice in any simple sense, the ways in which networks and platforms order and arrange our circulations likewise entail ethical decision-making. In both cases, situating acts of (re)circulation as a kind of writing practice demonstrates the need for ongoing research and pedagogical reflection on matters that may otherwise be written off as too mundane or inconsequential. In other words, such an orientation suggests that *recirculating writing matters*—that it's a topic and practice that should enter our critical discussions in scholarship and pedagogy.

And yet, such a notion—(re)circulating writing (a text) *is* writing (an activity)—cannot be understood as a new claim. We take our cue from a number of rhetoric and writing scholars who have expanded what constitutes the work we do—or might do—in our scholarship and classrooms. To give more coherence to our claim, we especially draw on Kennedy's (2016) work with textual curation and Dush's (2015) work with writing content. Kennedy (2016) defined textual curation as an arrangement-driven "compositional craft" (p. 177). Drawing on expansive definitions of writing and discussion of curation from varied disciplines, Kennedy positioned textual curation as a category of writing that disrupts traditional understandings of authorship, agency, and writing labor. Not a singular author composing alone, textual curation designates a kind of distributed writing practice that undergirds all digital writing platforms. Warner (2017) described curation as "grabb[ing] existing utterances and populat[ing] them," thus making the text half ours and half someone else's (p. 139). In Kennedy's terms, textual curation involves packaging, filtering, tagging, recomposing, and—we would add—recirculating texts across writing ecologies. Textual curation, Kennedy argued, *is* writing, though it may sound unfamiliar to traditional understandings of writing.

Similar to Kennedy, Dush (2015) noted changing dynamics of writing on digital platforms. "Good writing practice," Dush argued, "involve[s] both crafting well-written posts and optimizing these posts as transportable, findable content" (p. 173). Dush positioned writing *as* content to point out a few key characteristics of writing today: writing is often *conditional* (made malleable and remixable), *computable* (given numerical representation in the form of digital data), *networked* (connected to wider discursive and infrastructural systems that allow for easy distribution and circulation), and *commodified* (made into monetizable assets). In current contexts, Dush argued, the work of writing not only involves inventing new kinds of content but also managing flows of content. To combine Kennedy (2016) and Dush (2015), writing entails thinking through the "rhetorical velocity" (Ridolfo & DeVoss, 2009) of texts already in motion. In other words, circulatory practices—considering not only one's own writing but also already circulating writing within given ecologies—are central to the activity of writing.

Throughout this chapter, we use the term circulatory writing practices to signal a range of interventional procedures that writers use to work with—or against—flows of content. Discussed both in academic scholarship and in Internet vernacular, circulatory writing practices include activities such as sharing, signal boosting, amplifying, redistributing, and forwarding, among others. We recognize we risk broadening our understanding of writing too much when we include such practices under the definitional sign of "writing." Nevertheless, we open the door of definition to suggest that we will be in a better position to see circulation through an ethical lens and as arising from practices that have consequences for civic participation in a digital age, a line of questioning we take up next.

Circulation Practices Are Habits of Citizenship

Prior to the proliferation of networked technologies, much counter/public sphere theory noted the transformational capacities of the ongoing and reflexive circulation of texts, ideas, and bodies. In many landmark works (Fraser, 1990; Habermas, 1989; Warner, 2005), scholars noted that circulation works to bring about change and build lifeworlds. In digital contexts, similar arguments have been made about the importance of circulation for public participation, citizenship, and activism (Hawk, 2012; Jenkins, Green, & Ford, 2013; Penney & Dadas, 2014; Sheridan, Ridolfo, & Michel, 2012; Simmons, 2018). Indeed, without the circulatory architectures of networked platforms, it would be difficult to imagine many tactics of digital counter/public work. Take, for example, practices such as digital activism, hashtag activism, and networked protest—all of these practices require pathways of circulation, where multimodal assemblages of text and affect accumulate throughout time and space (Edwards & Lang, 2018). From print to digital economies, circulation has always been inextricably linked to civic and counter/public work.

Yet, because such work takes place on platforms owned by private companies, digital circulation is subject to algorithmic gatekeeping (Tufekci, 2015). Gatekeeping control over circulation is not a new problem per se, but one marked by acceleration and opaque platform politics (Edwards, 2018). Moreover, circulating digital content is more than sharing visible writing with an immediate audience; it also shares streams of data with a range of corporate, third-party, and government entities (Beck, 2017; Reyman, 2013), leaving data trails that intimately map the kinds of content you are likely to share. In other words, when we recirculate writing, we also recirculate data, and the circulation of that data can have profound consequences for how we understand, encounter, and interact with others in networked publics (Beer, 2016).

For example, software engineers at Twitter explained that a user's timeline is determined based on a number of factors. They noted:

> In order to predict whether a particular tweet would be engaging to you, our models consider characteristics (or features) of:
>
> - The tweet itself: its recency, presence of media cards (image or video), total interactions (e.g., number of Retweets or likes)
> - The tweet's author: your past interactions with this author, the strength of your connection to them, the origin of your relationship
> - You: tweets you found engaging in the past, how often and how heavily you use Twitter. (Koumchatzky & Andryeyev, 2017)

In other words, Twitter's algorithmic timeline is determined, in part, by what kinds of content the user has (re)circulated in the past. Though digital circulation is choreographed by way of many economic, cultural, and computational factors, users' own circulation practices can fold back on the kinds of circulations they may encounter in the future. Put otherwise, (re)circulating digital writing—regardless of intent—has meaningful consequences for the production of publics.

Given the relationship between circulation and public work, then, we position circulation practices through Wan's (2011) understanding of "habits of citizenship." Though not without critique, citizenship is a category that often describes the kinds of attributes needed for participating in public life. As Wan (2011) argued, citizenship has long been a cornerstone of rhetoric, writing, and literacy education. Rather than pinpointing a prescriptive list of attributes of citizenship, Wan (2011) suggested that citizenship "is located in more everyday activities that may be mediated through habits and practices like the literate skills learned in classrooms and beyond" (p. 45). Such habits, which Wan grounds in political theorist Danielle Allen's (2004) work, are the "deep rules" that determine appropriate behaviors and practices among citizens. As we explore next, digital writers need to cultivate habits that are responsive to the conditions of algorithmic circulation outlined earlier. In other words, considering the role of circulation is one habit among many that affects how citizens encounter and engage the world.

Toward an Ethics of (Re)circulation

Given the two stances we articulated earlier (re/circulating writing *is* writing and circulatory writing practices constitute habits of citizenship), we proceed here by sketching what we call the ethics of (re)circulation and describe how circulation is always caught up in a process of relating to networked others. To further support what we've discussed in the previous sections, we draw on Porter's (1998) rhetorical ethics, Brown's (2015) networked ethics, and politics of affect to demonstrate the tenets of our ethical framework.

To begin, we reiterate that practices of circulation—as writing activities—are never neutral or inconsequential. According to Porter (1998), "all acts of writing are also ethical actions... in that they always inevitably assume a 'should' for some 'we'" (p. xiv). If, as we have argued, acts of (re)circulation constitute a kind of writing, it follows that circulating writing assumes a relationship with others. This is not to say, however, that such a relationship is determined once and for all. Porter's (1998) rhetorical ethics contends that ethical actions are kairotic; they are contingent, situational, and circumstantial. Negotiating ethical decisions, asking what is right and what should be, is always entangled in rhetorical practice. We would likewise suggest that managing flows of circulation involves making ethical decisions.

Of course, the writing environments Porter described in 1998 are quite different from what we encounter today. As such, building from Porter, though diverging from him by grounding his discussion in Derrida's notion of hospitality, Brown (2015) argued that we would also do well to account for how writing spaces themselves configure ethical relations. As Brown explained, "Any attempt to account for ethical action in networked life must account not only for individual choice but also for the digital environments that determine how those choices take shape." For Brown, and as we explained in the previous section, network infrastructures come to bear on ethical relations: they shape how we relate to and encounter one another. Brown figured his discussion of ethics in terms of "ethical programs," which he explained has a dual meaning, evoking "both the computational procedures of software (a computer program) and the procedures we develop in order to deal with ethical predicaments (a program of action)." Furthermore, "an ethical program, computational or otherwise, is a set of steps taken to address an ethical predicament." Like Porter's (1998) discussion of rhetorical ethics, ethical programs, when considered from the perspective of the human rhetor, are not easily arrived at—they demand a kind of puzzling through, a questioning that won't arrive at absolute answers.

To this end, recirculating writing doesn't necessarily imply that one ideologically supports the message. Rather, as we explore in the cases later, the writer may be further circulating the message for purposes of exposure, protest, or critique—so that others can interrogate the message in question. Though recirculating aggressive content often works to amplify sentiments of warning and/or critique, part of the ethical challenge here is the need to consider the affective and citational politics of (re)circulating writing. When highly circulatory content moves in networked spheres, it brings with it a surge of affective intensities. For example, Edwards and Lang (2018) described the circulation of affect in their study of #YesAllWomen, noting that affect—not emotion per se, but a kind of atmosphere that emerges in particular ecologies (Edbauer, 2005)—piles up and accumulates to have certain kinds of rhetorical effects. In other words, recirculating harassment for the purpose of offering critique may have difficulty breaking through the affective swell of the already flowing content.

In short, there are no clear-cut answers, as we need to explore ethics of circulation on a case-by-case basis. Developing an ethical stance toward circulation will always be somewhat of a moving target due to the changing dynamics of networked environments. Still, digital writers would benefit from understanding that mundane actions of (re)circulating content are not without consequence. As scholars and teachers of digital rhetoric, we would do well to include into our habits of citizenship fuller understandings of how circulation creates public lifeworlds that are central to civic action.

Ethics of Recirculation in Action

The remainder of this chapter considers the ethical implications of circulating writing in two particular cases of online aggression and harassment. We chose the following cases because they best demonstrate the rhetorical complexity of circulation and how circulation is a form of writing and authorship. The first case considers a tweet from Donald Trump that prominently featured a GIF of him tackling the CNN logo, which he deemed to be "fake news" (Trump, 2017). By applying a rhetorical and ethical frame of circulation and curation to this tweet and the origins of the GIF, we are able to examine how sharing harassing content increases the impact of that harassment and thus entails a set of fraught ethical relationships. The second case examines the harassment Leslie Jones garnered after the release of the *Ghostbusters* movie trailer on YouTube. We examine how supporters of Jones countered the online aggression she received using ethical circulation approaches to spread positive messages and support for Jones. While the first case largely focuses on the rhetorical–ethical work accomplished by the recirculation of a single text and its modification, the second case explores how people can use similar circulation techniques to offset online harassment.

Case 1: Donald Trump, Fake News, and Aggression

On July 2, 2017, U.S. President Donald Trump tweeted a GIF of him tackling the CNN logo shortly after he made claims they were "fake news" (Trump, 2017). The accompanying caption read, "#FraudNewsCNN #FNN." The GIF depicted a clip from a 2007 recording of Wrestlemania that featured Trump tackling another person, but the GIF had been modified by a redditor depicting the "person" being tackled as the CNN logo. The post originally appeared on the subreddit "r/The_Donald," a space that often circulates racist, misogynistic, ableist, and other problematic content. The user who modified the GIF ("HanAssholeSolo"), who had a history of circulating aggressive content, has since deleted the original post alongside other content and issued an apology. At the time this was taking place, Trump had ramped up his attacks on the news media, expressing his view that news stories were biased and attempting to silence what was really taking place. Often, his comments on "fake news" targeted news media outlets that included unfavorable coverage. The White House claimed that the GIF was not taken from reddit, although they didn't identify where it came from, and at the time of writing this (almost one year later), the tweet had approximately 136,000 comments, 346,000 shares, and 570,000 likes on Twitter, making it his most retweeted tweet of 2017 (Kelsey, 2017).

Of course, we can discuss the potential harm Trump caused in recirculating the curated content. We can deduce that Trump wants to frame himself as machismo, as exerting strength and unafraid confidence, even if the imagery of the GIF emerges from a scripted television show. In the process of recirculating the GIF, Trump sets up a series of relationships—between himself and the reddit poster; between himself and the press; between himself and his supporters; and between himself and those who oppose him. Considering the rhetorical value of this GIF prior to its recirculation, the spread of the GIF by @realDonaldTrump gave this object even more power and velocity. In essence, in establishing a relationship between himself and someone who expressed extremist views, Trump promoted a violent and aggressive rhetorical position that rippled out toward others who may encounter the GIF through its recirculation.

In addition to the ethics of Trump sharing the GIF, we are more interested in the everyday acts of recirculating Trump's use of the GIF. When the GIF began to circulate on Twitter and other social networks, we recall a range of people in our own networks recirculating the tweet for a number of reasons. Some retweeted the message in support of the president, while others amplified the message to oppose it. For those in opposition to the GIF, we suspect people began to recirculate the tweet to make sense of and question what had actually happened. As CNN responded, "It is a sad day when the President of the United States encourages violence against reporters" (Stelter, 2017). Recirculations were, as we see it, attempts to bring such a statement to the fore.

Though we acknowledge the many reasons someone might recirculate content, in retrospect, we wonder what those kinds of recirculations accomplish. As mentioned earlier, the affective atmosphere generated from widespread circulation should not be discounted. How might contributing to the velocity of text already in motion contribute to an atmosphere that was manufactured from the start? According to the report "Media Manipulation and Disinformation Online," Marwick and Lewis (2017) described "strategic amplification" as a tactic used to control media messages where content is purposefully "amplified beyond its original scope" (p. 39). Looking particularly at the role of traditional news media (but we'd include everyday citizens, too), Marwick and Lewis (2017) noted:

> For manipulators, it doesn't matter if the media is reporting on a story in order to debunk or dismiss it; the important thing is getting it covered in the first place. The amount of media coverage devoted to specific issues influences the presumed importance of these issues to the public. This phenomenon, called agenda setting, means that the media is remarkably influential in determining what people think about.
> (p. 39)

We might think of such agenda setting through strategic amplification as constructing an affective atmosphere that limits the kinds of responses that are likely to emerge. Of course, we don't want to suggest that opposition is unimportant or not worthwhile; rather, we question the efficacy of participating in a pre-framed affective atmosphere where oppositional voices can easily be drowned out.

Relatedly, in an age where data circulations and "metric power" (Beer, 2016) determine the contours of networked encounters, there is a need to consider the deeper logics of recirculating content. The continued recirculation of this GIF increases its value as it spreads and expands across networks, and in this way the object develops its own power and authority as a result. Brown (2015) argued for paying attention to how digital environments program ethical relations. In this case, if we consider how reddit and other social networks promote sharing, sometimes sharing content isn't necessarily intended to advocate for the content. Instead, it may be something that the person sharing found to be funny, amusing, touching, critique-worthy, thought-provoking, and any number of other reasons. Furthermore, when we consider the design of these digital environments, they are constructed to make the recirculation of such content easy. One click and a text is shared to a whole other network of connections. One screenshot and an uploaded image moves texts across platforms. However, regardless of intention, the ethical implications of these acts of writing are that the people who shared this GIF are advocating suspicion of and aggression toward news agencies and journalists by presenting an anti-news agenda.

Case 2: Ghostbusters, Leslie Jones, and Counter-Circulations of Anti-racism

The second case we detail here focuses on how circulatory writing practices can work to counter online harassment and aggression. In other words, where we largely focused on the damaging effects of circulating content in the first case, we focus attention here on the more positive effects of amplifying content in efforts to redress and reroute already existing streams of harassment and aggression. We examine the reverberations of a well-known case of targeted harassment in recent years: the coordinated effort to harass actress and comedian Leslie Jones following the debut of the women-led *Ghostbusters* reboot. The hate and violence Jones faced cannot be detached from her positionality as a Black woman on the Internet, as the barrage of vitriol Jones faced was—and continues to be—sexist and racist in nature. Because we want to outline how circulatory practices are tethered to issues of social justice, we look at the ways in which coalition-building and anti-racist praxis circulated in response to the harassment Jones faced.

The harassment of Jones began in the comments section of a YouTube movie trailer for *Ghostbusters* before quickly hardening into a sustained form of brigading. As of March 2018, over 44 million people have viewed the movie trailer, and over 275,000 people have made comments on the trailer. Thousands of users wrote racist and misogynistic comments about Jones and the other women in the film and then circulated the trailer, along with the comments and memes, within their social media networks. According to *The Guardian*, the *Ghostbusters* movie trailer is the tenth most disliked video on YouTube (Shoard, 2016). This public dislike of the film set in motion an additional barrage of online harassment, starting with Milo Yiannopoulos, who wrote a sexist and racist review of *Ghostbusters* for *Breitbart* that over-energized white supremacist groups and further accelerated the spreading and intensity of hate for and violence against Jones and the other women in the film. The harassment drastically escalated when it connected to trending algorithms on platforms like Twitter, YouTube, and Facebook. Harassers implemented hashtags like #freemilo to directly coordinate the circulation of hate-filled tweets, and they made fake Twitter accounts for Jones, assuming her identity and tweeting out falsehoods. Jones left Twitter for a short period of time to escape the hatred. After months of harassment, Jones's website was hacked and nude photographs of her were posted in a case of what many have called revenge porn (Sanghani, 2016).

In relation to such harassment and violence, we find that the argument from our first case stands—that is, recirculating harassment regardless of one's position, intentions, or ideology can participate in the further amplification of said harassment, violence, and/or aggression. So instead of focusing on the initial circulatory practices that framed the coordinated effort to harass Jones, we examine how networks of support emerged to amplify anti-racist and intersectional sentiments. In response to Jones's visible harassment, several individuals and groups organized efforts to challenge and redirect the circulatory practices that brought the initial swell of harassment against Jones to a roar. Instead, many people engaged in circulatory practices that advocated for solidarity and support of Jones in particular, while also calling attention to the experiences of being harassed as a Black woman in general.

For example, in reference to the revenge porn posted to Jones's website, pop star Katy Perry (2016) tweeted, "Do not give your eyeballs to this racist, hate-filled, misogynoir crime. I #StandWithLeslie." Invoking misogynoir here, Perry is calling attention to Black feminist Moya Bailey's term for describing the anti-Black racist misogyny Black women experience in daily life (Bailey & Trudy, 2018). Such a response—and the decision to create a new hashtag—works not only to draw attention away from the strategic amplification of harassment but also to redirect circulation flows into a discussion about the unique violences women of color experience. Similarly, the tag #BlackMenSupportLeslie emerged to vocalize the cybercrime inflicted upon Jones, while also affirming the experiences of other Black women. For example, the tag was often recirculated with variations of Malcolm X's famous quote, "the most disrespected person in America is the Black woman." As activist April Reign (2016) wrote on Twitter, "#BlackMenSupportLeslie. It is really important that y'all stand up for us, too." Here, we can see the double work of the hashtag at play—not only does it confront the harassment of Jones without keying into already toxic circulation flows (e.g. recirculating racist content), but it also broadens the discussion to include the lived experiences of other multi-marginalized people. Taken together, these examples demonstrate how mindful circulation techniques can combat online aggression with great effect. Sharing positive messages that function to dismantle online harassment is an example of ethical circulation acting rhetorically to disrupt the social norms that shelter and perpetuate that online harassment.

From a platform policy and computational angle, other hashtags such as #BanNero (@Nero was Yiannopoulos's Twitter handle) were also circulated to draw attention to Twitter's consistent failure as a platform to address and punish this type of aggressive behavior. In addition to Jones publicly commenting about Twitter's lack of response, other high-profile supporters directed efforts to banning some of the most vocal promoters of harassment on the platform. For example, the director of *Ghostbusters*, Paul Feig, publicly denounced the harassment of Jones and became the central catalyst for setting the hashtag activism for Jones into motion. Feig facilitated the circulation of these hashtags into the news feeds of prominent public figures and well-known celebrities so they could help spread support for Jones through their networks. Increasing the exposure of the message within larger social networks widened the support for Jones and brought more awareness to these forms of online injustices and to the frequency at which they occur. In the end, Yiannopoulos's account was removed from Twitter, though it should be mentioned that it took significant and coordinated effort for the removal to happen.

Such coordinated pushback on online aggressors functions much like an "ethical program" (Brown, 2015). Brown maintained that ethical programs are the approaches and steps individuals take to solve ethical issues, concerns, and problems. The retaliation to the harassment that Jones received, with the use of multiple hashtags and the controlled spreading within particular networks that allowed for the most rhetorical traction, operates as an ethical program that resulted in a permanent Twitter ban for Yiannopoulos, and, according to *Think Progress*, the New York Department of Homeland Security investigated the harassment of Jones in 2016. An ethical program for circulation can result in social justice. Put otherwise, circulating support for Jones as a means to confront digital aggression is the type of "habits of citizenship" (Wan, 2011) for circulation and world-building we advocate for in this chapter. The ethics of circulation we propose support these forms of sharing because they promote the inclusivity, social justice, and mindful contemplation needed to navigate dense and complex social and political cultures.

Conclusion

In the past decade, the circulatory nature of the web has led to more participatory writing environments. Yet, from these case examples, we can see that the ease of circulation within and across networks can propagate harm, harassment, and violence. In our experiences, many digital writers do not consider sharing instances of online harassment as a kind of writing practice, nor do they consider the ways in which circulation participates in the formation of digital aggression. These cases suggest that we all have a responsibility to consider who is in our networks, how our networks function, and how the movement of content into our networks can bolster the circulation of online harassment. Given the complexities of the aforementioned cases, we end this chapter by briefly considering how researchers, teachers, and writers may better understand the ethical implications of recirculation. Below, we provide some guiding questions to consider when contemplating an ethics of circulation on digital platforms. We envision these questions as a place to formalize discussions about what constitutes ethical circulation writing practices and to move these conversations forward for greater consideration.

What are the ideological and political assumptions attached to the circulation of the content? Are there traces of cyberbullying, harassment, or aggression? Circulating content puts your name—and digital identity (Beck, 2015)—behind those messages and in front of more and more people. Regardless of intent, circulation draws an association between yourself and the original message espoused as you enter and engage in conversations surrounding the content. Such an association could have larger implications than considered at the time of circulation.

Is the content circulated with a sense of care, empathy, and compassion? If there is something that needs to be shared to make a statement, such as wanting to speak out against cyberbullying or harassment, consider the potential harm caused by recirculating the content. For example, during a talk about this topic and research at a national conference, an author of this chapter chose not to share the GIF referenced in the first case example. She described it and discussed her concerns with it, but she specifically avoided sharing the GIF in an effort to weaken its circulation.

How might the content be reshaped as it circulates in and beyond your own network? Attempt to understand whom you are connected to and how those connections could potentially engage or enhance online harassment. Consider how far your network reaches and the ways in which writing gets reshaped as it moves through and beyond your network. Think about how some of your connections may be connected to other, more dangerous, networks that you may be unaware of and cannot see.

What role do platform policies, architectures, and data practices play in amplifying and/or diminishing aggressive content? Because platforms use distinctive computational procedures, it's important to consider how circulation flows are ordered and filtered differently across social media. Furthermore, because individual platforms employ distinctive community guidelines and algorithmic procedures to manage reports of harassment and aggression, further research on platform policies and procedures, as well as careful and kairotic contemplation of the affordances and constraints of individual platform architectures, can be helpful starting points for considering the role platforms play in boosting and/or suppressing harmful content.

How can scholars, teachers, and writers rethink logics of speed and slow down the circulation process to strive for circulatory practices that are meaningful for the long-term vitality of communities? Bradshaw (2018) has emphasized the need for researchers and citizens to consider how the speed of circulation can facilitate and/or impede the goals of particular communities. In an all-things-viral era, it's important to consider how community goals can be achieved through deliberate acts of "slow circulation."

How do you account for anonymous communication and make sure to provide accurate representation of yourself without placing yourself in danger? Brock and Shepherd (2016) contended that we need to avoid using social media that supports anonymous interaction, and that this avoidance is a form of ethical social media use and resistance. The anonymity and ease at which we can spread content around the Internet aid new forms of online harassment that are restructuring how we interact with each other in digital spaces, and how the circulation of new media and digital writing shapes our identity.

Ultimately, we advocate approaching circulation with attention toward inclusivity and social justice. Ethical sharing takes into account how spreading content creates a powerful force that can both hurt people *and* amplify socially just causes. The dialogue that arises from recirculating hateful, aggressive, or problematic content brings needed awareness and conversation, but here we argue that digital writers and digital scholars should approach engaging in that dialogue in thoughtful and critical ways. We've focused here on redressing online harassment by cultivating habits of citizenship—in our scholarship, classrooms, and public work—that recognize the ethics and responsibility embedded in everyday acts of sharing writing. Making a world worth living in is a shared project. When habits are cultivated to sustain more ethical circulation practices, we might find ourselves in a better position to realize that shared goal.

References

Allen, D. (2004). *Talking to strangers: Anxieties of citizenship since Brown v. Board of Education*. Chicago, IL: University of Chicago Press.

Bailey, M., & Trudy. (2018). On misogynoir: Citation, erasure, and plagiarism. *Feminist Media Studies, 18*(4), 762–768.

Beck, E. N. (2015). The invisible digital identity: Assemblages in digital networks. *Computers and Composition, 35*, 125–140.

Beck, E. N. (2017). Sustaining critical literacies in the digital information age: The rhetoric of sharing, prosumerism, and digital algorithmic surveillance. In D. Walls & S. Vie (Eds.), *Social writing/social media: Publics, presentations, and pedagogies* (pp. 37–52). Boulder: University Press of Colorado.

Beer, D. (2016). *Metric power.* London: Palgrave Macmillan.

Bradshaw, J. L. (2018). Slow circulation: The ethics of speed and rhetorical persistence. *Rhetoric Society Quarterly, 48*(5), 479–498.

Brock, K., & Shepherd, D. (2016). Understanding how algorithms work persuasively through procedural enthymeme. *Computers and Composition, 42*, 17–27.

Brooke, C. G. (2009). *Lingua fracta: Toward a rhetoric of new media.* New York, NY: Hampton.

Brooke, C. G. (2015). Cognition in the wild(fire): Peak virality and digital rhetorics. *YouTube.* Retrieved from https://www.youtube.com/watch?v=0hWh6mU24i0

Brown, J. J. (2015). *Ethical programs: Hospitality and the rhetorics of software.* Ann Arbor: University of Michigan Press.

Dush, L. (2015). When writing becomes content. *College Composition and Communication, 67*(2), 173–196.

Edbauer, J. (2005). Unframing models of public distribution: From rhetorical situation to rhetorical ecologies. *Rhetoric Society Quarterly, 35*(4), 5–24.

Edwards, D. W. (2018). Circulation gatekeepers: Unbundling the platform politics of YouTube's Content ID. *Computers and Composition, 47*, 61–74.

Edwards, D. W., & Lang, H. (2018). Entanglements that matter: A new materialist trace of #YesAllWomen. In L. Gries & C. G. Brooke (Eds.), *Circulation, writing, and rhetoric* (pp. 118–134). Logan: Utah State University Press.

Eyman, D. (2015). *Digital rhetoric: Theory, method, practice.* Ann Arbor: University of Michigan Press.

Fraser, N. (1990). Rethinking the public sphere: A contribution to the critique of actually existing democracy. *Social Text, 25/26*, 56–80.

Gries, L. E. (2015). *Still life with rhetoric: A new materialist approach for visual rhetorics.* Logan: Utah State University Press.

Gries, L. E. (2018). Introduction: Circulation as an emergent threshold concept. In L. Gries & C. G. Brooke (Eds.), *Circulation, writing, and rhetoric* (pp. 3–24). Logan: Utah State University Press.

Habermas, J. (1989). *The structural transformation of the public sphere.* Cambridge, MA: MIT Press.

Hawk, B. (2012). Curating ecologies, circulating musics: From the public sphere to sphere publics. In S. Dobrin (Ed.), *Ecology, writing theory, and new media: Writing ecology* (pp. 160–179). New York, NY: Routledge.

Jenkins, H., Ford, S., & Greene, J. (2013). *Spreadable media.* New York, NY: New York University Press.

John, N. (2016). *The age of sharing.* New York, NY: Polity.

Kelsey, A. (2017, December 29). President Trump's most popular tweets of 2017. *ABC News.* Retrieved from https://abcnews.go.com/Politics/president-trumps-popular-tweets-2017/story?id=52032464

Kennedy, K. (2016). Textual curation. *Computers and Composition, 40*, 175–189.

Koumchatzky, N., & Andryeyev, A. (2017). Using deep learning at scale in Twitter's timelines. *Twitter*. [blog]. Retrieved from https://blog.twitter.com/engineering/en_us/topics/insights/2017/using-deep-learning-at-scale-in-twitters-timelines.html

Marwick, A., & Lewis, R. (2017). *Media manipulation and disinformation online*. New York, NY: Data & Society Research Institute. Retrieved from https://datasociety.net/output/media-manipulation-and-disinfo-online/

Penney, J., & Dadas, C. (2014). (Re)Tweeting in the service of protest: Digital composition and circulation in the occupy wall street movement. *New Media & Society, 16*(1), 74–90.

Perry, K. (2016, August 24). Do not give your eyeballs to the racist, hate-filled, misogynoir crime [Tweet]. Retrieved from https://twitter.com/katyperry/status/768540189043986432?lang=en.

Porter, J. E. (1998). *Rhetorical ethics and internetworked writing*. Greenwich, CT: Albex.

Porter, J. E. (2009). Recovering delivery for digital rhetoric. *Computers and Composition, 25*(4), 207–224.

Prentice, M. (2015). Managing intertextuality: Display and discipline across documents at a Korean firm. *Signs and Society, 3*(S1), S70–S94.

Reign, April. [ReignOfApril]. (2016, August 25). It is really important that y'all visibly stand up for us, too [Tweet]. Retrieved from https://twitter.com/ReignOfApril/status/768867273197035520

Reyman, J. (2013). User data on the social web: Authorship, agency, and appropriation. *College English, 75*(5), 513–533.

Rickert, T. (2018). Circulation-signification-ontology. In L. Gries & C. G. Brooke (Eds.), *Circulation, writing, and rhetoric* (pp. 308–314). Logan: Utah State University Press.

Ridolfo, J., & DeVoss, D. N. (2009). Composing for recomposition: Rhetorical velocity and delivery. *Kairos: A Journal of Rhetoric, Technology, and Pedagogy, 13*(2). Retrieved from http://kairos.technorhetoric.net/13.2/topoi/ridolfo devoss/intro.html

Sanghani, R. (2016). We need to call Leslie Jones's nude hack what it is: A hate crime. *The Telegraph*. Retrieved from https://www.telegraph.co.uk/women/life/we-need-to-call-leslie-joness-nude-hack-what-it-is-a-hate-crime/

Sheridan, D. M., Ridolfo, J., & Michel, A. (2012). *The available means of persuasion: Mapping a theory and pedagogy of multimodal public rhetoric*. West Lafayette, IN: Parlor Press.

Shoard, C. (2016, May 2). Ghostbusters trailer is most disliked in YouTube history. *The Guardian*. Retrieved from https://www.theguardian.com/film/2016/may/02/ghostbusters-trailer-most-disliked-in-youtube-history

Simmons, M. (2018). Engaging circulation in urban renewal. In L. Gries & C. G. Brooke (Eds.), *Circulation, writing, and rhetoric* (pp. 43–60). Logan: Utah State University Press.

Sparby, E. M. (2017). Digital social media and aggression: Memetic rhetoric in 4chan's collective identity. *Computers and Composition, 45*, 85–97.

Stelter, B. [brianstelter]. (2017, July 2). CNN statement responding to the president [Tweet]. Retrieved from https://twitter.com/brianstelter/status/881521068078505985

Trump, D. J. [realDonaldTrump]. (2017, July 2). #FraudNewsCNN #FNN [Tweet]. Retrieved from https://twitter.com/realDonaldTrump/status/881503147168071680

Tufekci, Z. (2015). Algorithmic harms beyond Facebook and Google: Emergent challenges of computational agency. *Journal on Telecommunications and High Technology Law, 13*, 203–218.

Wan, A. (2011). In the name of citizenship: The writing classroom and the promise of citizenship. *College English, 74*(1), 28–49.

Warner, J. (2017). *Adolescents' new literacies with and through mobile phones.* New York, NY: Peter Lang Publishing.

Warner, M. (2005). *Publics and counterpublics.* New York, NY: Zone Books.

13 The Banality of Digital Aggression
Algorithmic Data Surveillance in Medical Wearables

Krista Kennedy and Noah Wilson

Krista

When the alarm goes off each morning, the first thing I do is pull my hearing aid out of its case and put it in my ear. After that, my day as a deaf professor is much like any other professor's day. I watch streaming videos to catch up on the news and get ready to head to campus. I spend my day teaching classrooms full of students, chairing or participating in meetings, mentoring and being mentored. On some days, my colleagues and I examine graduate students in defenses. On some other days, I present my own work and negotiate question and answer sessions. I close my office door for some scheduled writing time and listen to music while I write. As often as not, on the commute home I stop off at the grocery store, the dry cleaners, or the public library to transact small bits of business. All in all, there's nothing to see here.

But someone, *something*, is recording every modulation, every step. The Starkey Halo smart hearing aid that I wear is a significant improvement over the other hearing aids I've worn for the past 40 years. My hearing aids are by necessity always newish ones, somewhere between one and the max life of around four years old, a mandatory purchase that costs approximately $2,500 in order to have the level of power required for me to do my job. Throughout the day, I work very closely with it to do my listening.[1] Multiple algorithms automatically adjust sound. Directional mics switch intelligently to draw in sound, which is then analyzed by two intersecting algorithms that classify input every six milliseconds and adapt to diminish noise between syllables every 20 milliseconds. I tinker with the volume and settings via the TruLink app on my iPhone, which is itself an integral part of the system. Geo-tagged "sound memories" rely on the phone's telemetry to trigger calibrated settings when it senses that I've entered the tagged space. If the iPhone senses that I'm moving at more than five miles per hour, the system assumes that I am in a car and begins to automatically detect and filter out car noise. Each movement, each bit of tinkering with the volume, each millisecond of adjustment is algorithmically recorded, tracked, analyzed, and repurposed.

The data (I do not call it *my* data because I neither own it nor have access to it) is used by my audiologist in consultation with me to more precisely calibrate the aid's settings for my hearing range. This process has significantly improved the ways I'm able to use my aid. However, it is also anonymized as big data by the manufacturer for research and development purposes, stored for an indefinite amount of time at an undisclosed data storage facility, and most likely resold to other vendors in both identifiable and de-identified forms. My geographic movement data is likely tracked by Apple via their contracted satellite and Apple Maps for Apple's own research and development purposes. Their Region Monitoring API provides location monitoring data on individual iPhones to the TruLink app in order to trigger setting toggles when a geotagged location is entered. All of the data is variously transmitted through satellites, cell phone towers, wireless transmission, and direct uploads or downloads.

At the point of sale, I was informed of the ways that my audiologist and I would benefit from having personalized data to work with. I neither consented nor withheld consent, as my consent was not required. Data use was presented as simply a fact, and one that I largely appreciated based on the direct benefits for me. No educational literature was offered regarding the algorithms or their data collection protocols, which may be considered trade secrets. The Health Insurance Portability and Accountability Act (HIPAA) (United States Department of Health & Human Services, 2013), which requires clear disclosures of information handling practices and consent, isn't much help in this instance since hearing aids are rarely covered under insurance and consequently, hearing aid data collection may not be regulated under this act.[2] Despite that, I have worn this aid for around 15 hours each day for the past four years, knowingly generating data at every waking moment. It remains an essential component of my everyday private and professional lives.

Noah

If I can find the time, a normal day for me as a graduate student begins with a run. Back in the days when I trained for long-distance races, I opted to wear my heart rate monitor. It was the cheapest monitor I could buy as an undergraduate student in 2009, with no GPS tracking or run logging. More recently, I was able to afford a single-purpose, transparent piece of technology that simply read my heart rate and generated a visual representation of it. I only used the device for running and it only told me what I wanted to know. Since I don't require a medical wearable for anything other than fitness tracking, I only wore it when I decided that this data would be beneficial to me. That data was neither saved nor transmitted nor repurposed nor sold.

These days, I don't competitively run anymore, since the continued wear and tear on my joints is not worth my impending, hereditary arthritic future. When I do run in the mornings, I don't bring any digital technologies along. I opt to not carry my phone, I don't listen to music, and I don't track my time or distance. I step away from my desk and screens, and I just run.

One of us decides daily how much data they will generate and how much they will let their body be tracked. The other of us simply generates data, which is simply tracked. Only one of us consents or resists because only one of us can opt out of wearing the device in question without significant repercussions in their life. Many late-deafened folk do opt out of wearing hearing aids, of course, but with that decision comes an increased risk of social isolation and dementia, among other health risks (Lin et al., 2011). In this sense, wearing such a vital device is similar to wearing a pacemaker, insulin pump, or other crucial wearable that supports the daily functions, movements, and activities of life. Wearers simply don't have an easy option to not wear the device and thus not generate data, and the implications of that data collection bring complex benefits and drawbacks.

This relentless data harvesting constitutes an increasingly pervasive form of digital aggression. In this chapter, we focus on essential medical wearables as a venue for digital aggression in the form of algorithmic data surveillance. Our case study investigates the ways that bodily and informational surveillance function as aggression for wearers[3] of smart hearing aids, a reality which exemplifies the pervasive surveillance issues posed by many medical wearables. Specifically, we examine issues related to opacity and expediency, both of which are central elements of banal aggression in algorithmic data surveillance. The implications reach beyond our study to wearers who opt in to wearing health trackers such as Fitbits, Apple Watches, and the like, as well as to the ways that all users' data is harvested in contemporary digital environments. As Gouge and Jones have argued, these devices and the bodies that wear them create new rhetorical ecologies and therefore new rhetorical effects and consequences (2016). This emerging rhetorical landscape should shape the ways that instructors approach teaching cutting-edge digital rhetorics in the contemporary writing classroom, since both we and our students are constantly faced with the political realities of data harvesting.

Our central case study focuses on the Starkey Halo smart hearing aid, first introduced in 2014. As one of the best-selling smart hearing aids currently on the market, the Halo presents a significant site for studying algorithmic data surveillance as a core design feature of critical medical wearables. Part of its significance lies in its unremarkableness: the device and its data infrastructure are hardly unusual. Like most medical wearables, this device aggressively surveils wearers and transmits data—all under an intentional opacity meant to protect corporate intellectual property interests. All of the data collection described is conducted in compliance with U.S. law, which heavily regulates the safety of medical devices but often not the collection or transmission of data. No laws are overtly broken, and the transaction is entirely business as usual.

A pervasive technocapitalist ethic of expediency and the intentional opacity and dehumanization it engenders are central to our concerns in this chapter, given the ways that it shapes the design and deployment of these wearables. What Banner (2017) has called "communicative biocapitalism" relies on dehumanization by design in order to more effectively capitalize on disabled bodies and the data that they produce. In this context, she writes, "the patient's voice… serves as free labor for private corporations, with few protections given to the individual's voice, and with no choice about its entry into privatized medical research" (p. 2). This operationalization requires "historical neglect of structural inequalities and the economic logics scaffolding medicine itself" (p. 2). Maintaining intentional opacity surrounding the design of data-harvesting algorithms and the extent to which data is harvested and deployed further removes the possibility of any real consent on the part of the patient, reducing them to a data derivative (Amoore, 2011) rather than a human living a full life and making informed decisions about that life.

***

Digital aggression is human. Digital aggression is loud, even on the screen, when everything becomes ALL CAPS. Digital aggression is virulent disagreement, trolling, flaming, stalking, and revenge porn. Digital aggression is hacking, doxxing, and tracking. Digital aggression is hateful. Digital aggression is active, present, on your screen, in your inbox, in your texts, in your social media, and in your face. Digital aggression is always symbolic communication, always grounded in language and images.

Except when it's *none* of those things. As others in this collection suggest, aggression also happens under the surface in the code that lies beneath all of our interfaces. It is systemic in every sense of the word, built into the design and coding of platforms, systems, and algorithms (Brown, 2015; Noble, 2018). These design choices are in fact political, reflective of the driving ethos of late capitalism and a culture that has come to accept surveillance as a matter of course in social media, shopping, CCTV, smart home devices such as Alexa, and even the toasters that sit on our counters (Gunkel, 2017). Biometric data gathered from Fitbits powers multiple big data uses as insurance companies offer bonuses to wearers who share their data while fitness tracking data can also reveal the location of military bases (Hern, 2018). Pharmaceutical companies vie for access to patient health records in order to assess the efficacy of their products (Hirschler, 2018).

What makes surveillance dangerous is that its aggression is normalized through the opacity and complexity of its practices. We do not question the tremendous amount of data collected on a daily basis because the full range of uses for that data are so opaque to us. Unseen surveillance approaches us on all fronts, whether government, corporate, or private. It scrapes, collects, and makes decisions on our behalf without our knowledge—and we individuals sometimes rightfully want to reap the benefits of this automated surveillance. As surveillance studies scholar Gary Marx points out, the realities of surveillance are nuanced (1998, 2015). While most often associated with governmental overreach, surveillance is also conducted by private institutions and corporations. Aggressive surveillance and coercive policies are intensively problematic and present a host of ethical issues. And yet, the potential for abuse is often entangled with significant benefits for individuals.

In the case of medical wearables, the promise of individualized data, vital adjustments made in real time, and careful management of disability disclosure offer compelling benefits that drive wearer acceptance of surveillance. Even casual wearers of products such as Fitbits and the Braggi DashPro, a smart, in-ear fitness monitor, value personalized data collection to the extent that they are willing to accept external tracking by the manufacturer as well as, in some cases, their insurance company and employer. Wearers of medical devices also benefit from big data-driven R&D that draws on aggregated use data to revise factory settings and interfaces. Consequently, we proceed with the baseline assumption that surveillance is not inherently bad and may even be beneficial in some contexts. This suggests the importance of intentionality in the design and deployment of surveillance systems: what systems are surveilling *and* for whose benefit and to what ends.

Data Surveillance in Medical Wearables

Venues for aggression are limited only by human reach, stretching past screens into our daily lives—and into our bodies. Today's wearable medical devices move code onto, into, and through the human body, integrating algorithms in the daily activities of our flesh (Gouge & Jones, 2016; Pedersen, 2013). These technologies are increasingly Internet-tethered, mobile-enabled, and reliant on both algorithms and artificial intelligence, themselves owned by parties both known and unknown to us. Devices such as pacemakers, bedside monitors, and insulin pumps no longer rely only on periodic calibration in order to function. Instead, multiple algorithms constantly monitor the device's immediate surroundings (whether it be a body or a room), comparing tracked data to existing user-based settings and adjusting the device's performance based on sensed data. They also gather data on wearer behavior, tracking aspects such as blood sugar and alcohol levels, heart rate and blood pressure, and even wearer location and rate of speed. AI utilities make simple decisions based on wearer behavior, including recalibrating devices without human intervention.[4] In the process, devices maintain near-continuous tethering with institutional servers, transmitting a stream of personalized data back to health care providers—and, importantly, to corporations who gather this data for research and development purposes as well as reselling it to multiple buyers.

The tremendous amount of data generated by medical wearables is an increasingly valuable commodity that, while tied to the wearer whose daily actions produce it, is practically never owned by that wearer. As Reyman (2013) has argued concerning user data on the social web, understanding the implications of user data ownership is an important area of inquiry for the field of writing studies because it offers new insights into rhetorical agency and the commodification of individual performances. The same is true for medical wearables, particularly as they track the wearer's agile, intensive collaborations with algorithms that often reveal creative responses to managing communicative environments. In either context, data is understood as a by-product rather than a creation of the user or wearer (Reyman, 2013, p. 516). Given the naturalization of corporate ownership of user data in almost any technological context, most owners of smart technologies likely have little expectation of owning their data.

Wearers may, however, have a reasonable expectation of knowing what data is in fact being collected and the implications of that collection.[5] As a result of working closely with their physician to manage their health, wearers frequently understand and value the benefits that result from their own physician having access to personalized data collected by their devices (PwC Health Research Institute, 2014). However, while wearers may have some general indication that organizations are collecting data through these devices, they may very well not be aware of the full range or extent of data being collected or how that data is being used (Lupton & Michael, 2017).

Wearers of the Halo may feel that this ambiguity is worth the trade-off for personalized data that facilitates iterative calibration of aid functions for their individual hearing ranges. They may also opt into this surveillance-heavy system because it enhances their perceptions of rhetorical agency in disability disclosure, a particular concern for the late-deafened older wearers who constitute the primary market (Kennedy, 2017), and that in itself may make trading one's data seem worthwhile. It is also the case that the disabled, whether they explicitly identify as disabled or not, have long been accustomed to surveillance of their bodies and actions by the state (Schweik, 2009), educational institutions (Harmon, 2013; Stuckey, 2014), workplace norms (Erevelles, 2001), and private individuals (Cox, 2013).

For the d/Deaf, successfully negotiating (and often subverting) pervasive surveillance is frequently connected to the basic need to earn a livelihood: public perceptions of d/Deaf people as less intelligent, less capable, or simply difficult to accommodate contribute to a 50% average unemployment rate for this group. Safety in a culture that fosters ableist aggression is another central impetus. Sometimes, this stems from the quotidian need to avoid micro- and macro-aggressions in social situations. At other times in history, the inability to appear to be "normal" has imposed far more dire consequences, as when the Nazi T-4 program targeted disabled individuals for forced sterilization, medical experimentation, and involuntary euthanasia (Brueggemann, 2009). Given the crucial need for safety, whether daily or epochal, it is no surprise that wearers will surrender an extensive amount of privacy.

Provided that wearers are likely both accustomed to and aware of various sorts of surveillance and may well feel that the functionality the device offers is a useful trade-off, can the algorithmic data surveillance imposed by these devices be considered to be aggression? It can and it should, due to a pervasive technocapitalist ethic of expediency (Katz, 1992) that drives the purposeful opacity imposed by corporations in the service of protecting their intellectual property and the dehumanization of data used for research and development purposes. The result is an inherently banal performance of aggression in the service of technological capitalism, one that ignores the humanity of the wearer in service of automated data harvesting that is understood to be simply the way business is done. As in Arendt's (1964) germinal arguments concerning the banality of evil, this aggression is an unthinking deployment of an existing social order and agenda.

The Halo's algorithms are part of this relentless push for algorithmic collection and analysis of biometric and soundscape data. As Katz (1992) argues in his foundational article, technological capitalism's ethic of expediency is simultaneously a means to both practical and ethical ends (p. 257). As with any instance of private surveillance of a consumer base, Starkey's data collection is driven by its ideology, ever bent on efficiently generating wealth through the exchange of goods and information. To be clear, while Katz's case study focused on technical documents of the Third Reich, we do not imply that the intentions of modern health surveillance systems necessarily have such innately nefarious goals. Rather, we argue that an ethic of expediency drives the decision to dehumanize the central R&D data set in order to create a disembodied representation of the "consumer," one that commoditizes the human wearer.[6]

This ethic also forestalls the possibility of dialectical exchange (Katz, 1993) and, indeed, even disclosure of the full scope of the algorithms at work or the scope of data collection implications. Since the Halo's algorithms deeply shape the wearer's life in both short-term and long-term ways, as Kennedy (2017) has argued elsewhere, this ethical stance enacts not just aggression but violence against its wearers, a violence that "harbors within itself an additional element of arbitrariness" when it imposes results that are beyond human actors' control (Arendt, 1972, p. 106).

This is a violence that is enacted because it can be one done in the service of what is understood to be quotidian research and profit. Katz

(1992) locates this perceived objectivity of technology as a central aspect of expediency:

> Science and technology embody the ethos of objective detachment and truth, of power and capability, and thus the logical and ethical necessity for their own existence and use. ... Technological expediency actually subsumes political expediency and becomes an end in itself.
> (pp. 264–265)

The widespread perception of algorithmic data collection as an objective, scientific means of data collection and analysis is currently indeed an end to itself within contemporary technological capitalism, one that has subsumed the rights of individual citizens to understand and access the informational goods that they themselves produce. The algorithm's technological ethos of "rationality, efficiency, speed, productivity, power" (Katz, 1992, p. 266) instead assumes precedence, privileging the production of profit over the rights of dis/abled bodies.

This prioritization is true across the landscape of medical wearables, but it has more direct impact on disabled bodies who wear these technologies for essential bodily maintenance or disability negotiation rather than as an opt-in technology for fitness tracking. Tucker (2017) describes this targeted aggression as "technocapitalist disability rhetoric" that "attributes agency to technology and tech companies and simultaneously revokes it from disabled people." While she does not frame her discussion within the notion of expediency, it often intersects with this concept as she examines a rhetoric that views disabled bodies as "a test site for profitable innovation."[7] Disabled people are more likely to be the targets of such aggression than the able-bodied, whether in the advertisements she examines or in the devices that they rely on.

Despite manufacturers' framing of themselves as supporters of the disabled and disability rights, the rhetoric of their advertising and promotional materials remains exploitative and focuses on the wonders of technology-as-accessibility rather than disabled bodies as the central narrative, she writes, arguing that "such rhetoric reframes a human rights issue—disability rights—as merely a technical problem to be solved through product development" (Tucker, 2017, n.p.). Disabled people, then, are market solutions rather than humans who collaborate closely with smart technologies in order to negotiate daily life. Similarly, from the perspective of an organization collecting data, wearers *are* data under current algorithmic data collection policies. Expediency drives design, deployment and collection—and also disclosure and consent.

Opacity and Dehumanization

We turn our attention now to two of the most central aspects of banal aggression: opacity, which prevents the wearer from making informed decisions, and dehumanization through an ethic of expediency surrounding data collection, repurposing, and sale. In doing so, we attend to what Marx (1998) has termed "the data collection context" with an eye toward building contextual understandings of surveillance ethics. Published well before the emergence of smart medical wearables, Marx's concerns remain startlingly applicable to today's algorithmic surveillance technologies. In proposing concrete ways that data collection regulations should expand to account for electronic surveillance, he poses a series of questions that address the contexts of data collection. Elements of these address awareness, consent, the opportunity for human review, the right of the surveilled to inspect and challenge the data, and the necessity of adequate data stewardship and protection (Marx, 1998, p. 174). The surveilled individual, he argues, should have among other basic rights the right to awareness that their data is being collected, the opportunity for meaningful consent, the opportunity to access the data and challenge inaccuracies or misuses, and the assurance that their data is used exclusively for agreed-upon purposes and adequately protected from cybersecurity threats. Anything less constitutes a violation of trust and ethics—in other words, aggression. In the 20 years since the publication of Marx's essay, none of these guidelines have found their way into U.S. law. Despite extensive deliberation by the Federal Trade Commission,[8] there is still no U.S. provision that requires manufacturers or providers of medical wearables to even inform wearers that data is being collected for use by multiple entities for multiple purposes (Tschider, forthcoming).

The politics at work here are evident in the design of the aid's algorithmic aspects. Technological design necessarily enacts forms of power and authority (Winner, 1980). Algorithms are no different from hardware in the inherent politics of their design and deployment (Brown, 2015; Vee, 2017). The lines of code that comprise algorithms are hardly neutral; rather, they are "motivated by quite specific epistemic standards that can radically delimit what counts as valid or meaningful" (Ingraham, 2014, p. 64). Noble (2018) further argues that algorithmic design is "predicated on specific values from specific kinds of people—namely, the most powerful institutions in society and those who control them" (p. 29). These institutions necessarily enact social visions, and consequently the algorithms they develop are inevitably modeled on outcomes typically serving commercial interests and agendas (Beer, 2018). The Halo's multiple algorithms enact a complex political stance, one that does in fact provide valuable individualized data that enhances daily negotiations of disability. The benefits come with attendant downsides, given that this system operates entirely within the framework of technological capitalism that relies on an ethic of expediency both as a design philosophy and as a tautological argument for aggressive opacity and dehumanization of data.

Opacity

This aggression begins with opacity at the point of sale, when wearers are not offered sufficiently granular information about what algorithms are deployed in their wearable and its ancillary devices, what data they will produce, and how that data will be collected, transferred, stored, and used. With device manufacturers benefitting from the long-term protection of trade secrets rather than the shorter-term protections of patents or copyrights, the incentive to profit through corporate policies of nondisclosure outweighs the incentive to educate patients.[9] The unavailability of such shorter-term protections for algorithms has driven manufacturers to protect their own self-interests through algorithmic opacity.

Often, the procedures and processes through which algorithms operate are obscured from users even as those algorithms are active participants in shaping users' pathways, access to knowledge, and daily engagement with the world around them (Ingraham, 2014). In the case of the Halo, this information does not appear in promotional materials, point-of-sale materials, professional materials for audiologists, or any patent filing for the device. Under the law, patents provide an important notice function by offering limited monopoly to an invention while simultaneously disclosing invention functionality to the public. Although several Starkey patents have been issued, none of those we identified explicitly reference algorithmic usage or cross-platform functionality, mobile device app data transmissions, or integration into a common device data set.

This intentional opacity is therefore a crucial element of multiple aspects of a wearable; limited education is the consequence of these nondisclosure policies. As a Halo wearer, Krista was verbally informed that her audiologist would download data for calibration purposes and that Starkey would repurpose that data in a big data pool for research and development purposes. This data is uploaded from the audiologist's office and also downloaded directly by Starkey any time the aid is sent to them for repair. No consent form was offered, nor was any opportunity for access to or review of the information and attendant data handling and use practices. There is no avenue for challenging the data and no information is available about its transmission or storage.

As a result, any potential for real dialogue between manufacturer and wearer about data collection and use are effectively forestalled unless the wearer calls the central service number or pursues legal avenues. Even when the possibility of asking questions exists, due to the aforementioned issues only limited information may be shared, if at all. Instead, the technology's capabilities function as a tautological argument for pervasive deployment. This technological ideology functions culturally as a form of phronesis, producing the accepted practical wisdom that more data is always better and that algorithmic collection data is ultimately both necessary and beneficial. In his follow-up article on praxis and expediency, Katz (1993) argues that

> the dialectic of technological ideology is aware only of its own values. Only technical criteria (or legal force) teleologically embody and lead to the 'ethically correct' rational (i.e. technological) end. The audience is to be persuaded based on technological values only....
>
> (p. 56)

Once the ideology of technological capitalism supersedes the needs of citizens, he contends, the need for deliberative rhetoric is obliterated. If there is no need for dialogue between manufacturer and wearer because the technology is presumed to be beneficial based on its own values, then the wearer's education or consent becomes unnecessary. Instead, "technological politics set the agenda for the debate through its initiatives and power, which is rooted in the ideology of expediency based on a rationality deeply embedded in Western culture" (Katz, 1993, p. 58). The wearer is reduced to a subject whose function is to wear the device, benefit as much as they can, and most importantly, to generate data at every possible moment.

Dehumanization

Consequently, although the wearers' data is certainly present in research and development processes, the wearers themselves are never present as complete human beings. Instead, what is present is the wearer's shadow form: their data. Human complexity is not efficient within the scope of technological capitalism. What is collected is not so much the subject in their totality but rather what is observable, discernible, and trackable. This dehumanized data is pooled, analyzed according to big data methodologies to map broad use patterns, and then relied on as the basis of design updates. The likely intention is to drive an efficient development and deployment process. However, this process enacts a long-standing form of ableist violence which operates within historical medical models of disability that view disability as a problem to be fixed or cured by experts who work upon disabled bodies rather than in collaboration with them. The lack of direct communication or consultation that occurs when data is understood to stand in for humans (particularly when no avenue of direct dialogue has been established) reveals a lack of commitment to disability rights or, indeed, to the disabled themselves. The phrase "nothing about us without us" has become a defining principle of the Disability Rights Movement, demanding that disabled representatives be included in real conversations and negotiations about their care. "At the heart of the Disability Rights Movement (DRM) as indicated even by the resonant phrase 'nothing about us without us' are issues of representation... How is disability being represented? Who is doing the representing?

And for what purpose?" ask disability scholars Brueggemann et al. (2012, p. 65). To that we would add, *what* is doing the representing?

The algorithms and the data are doing the representing, of course. The resulting dehumanization of data has been a central concern for surveillance studies scholars. While we recognize data as a vital element of research, it should hardly be considered the only reliable or most valuable element. Surveillance systems are created for the explicit purpose of categorizing people and actions, demarcating certain portions of the population along arbitrary standards, argues Lyon (2003): "It classifies and categorizes relentlessly, on the basis of various—clear or occluded—criteria" (p. 8). Furthermore, data generated, analyzed, and processed by one surveillance system might be used in another's processes as companies transfer data among internal teams or sell it to other corporations without any legal need to notify the wearers who produced the data.

Another cause for concern is that algorithmically generated data does not necessarily remain an unaltered end product but is often reprocessed. The data generated by one algorithm may be used in calculations by another algorithm, with the resulting output becoming an exponentially further removed and abstracted representation of the original person's data. Amoore (2011) refers to this exponential abstraction as a "data derivative," which "comes into being from an amalgam of disaggregated data—reaggregated via mobile algorithm-based association rules.... The relation between the elements is itself changed" (p. 28). This data derivative is less a direct representation of its subject as it is a calculated potential of various actions. These actions might include a novice hearing aid wearer's propensity to turn the volume up or down inappropriately, or extensive fiddling with the TruLink interface in restaurant environments that feature babble and clatter in the background.

This is only a part of the surveillance story; algorithms continue to process our data, combine it with other decontextualized data, and then recalculate and recontextualize what this data *means*, forecasting anticipated behaviors of the user/wearer. At this stage, aggression lies in the process of categorizing or inscribing the wearer when multiple data sets are analyzed side by side. Those calculations, those de-contextualized abstractions of a person, are used to make decisions about the lives and capabilities of the original, data-generating bodies. Algorithmic data collection goes further than observing and collecting data; it also categorizes people and establishes relations between them that did not exist before. Algorithmic surveillance systems create a disembodied, dehumanized commodity for sale to both capitalist and governmental institutions.

Among the implications is the potential for class-based aggression. In the case of the Halo, as the resulting data is disassociated from the humans who produced it, material aspects of their humanity are also dissociated from the data pool that is used to make decisions about their hearing and experience of future wearers who may access this expensive technology at a later date when it will likely be lower in price. The Halo's current data pool necessarily relies on a largely well-off demographic who can afford hearing aids that currently retail for $2,000–$3,000 apiece or $4,000–$6,000 for a set, plus the cost of an iPhone, which currently hovers between $1,000 and $1,350. The collective data that Starkey relies on consequently reflects the needs of a heavily white and/or affluent audience, a significant number of whom are retired. This data advances a very different development trajectory than the one that would benefit blue-collar wearers who regularly encounter the noise-intensive environments of construction sites, factory floors, or food service environments—in other words, the very wearers who will likely encounter this technology years from now as the price drops.

Conclusion

The implications of algorithmic data collection that we have explored are the new norm for medical wearables, whether integrated with bodies to track biometric fitness data or to ensure that a heart continues beating. The reach of pervasive surveillance will continue to extend through these technologies as each generation becomes more enhanced. For example, hearing aids that collect biometric data through their proximity to the thin skin and heavy blood flow of the ears were introduced as this collection went to press. Very shortly, it may no longer be possible for a hearing aid wearer to continue to opt out of biometric data tracking. It will simply become compulsory by virtue of its inclusion in a vital medical wearable.

These present and near-future developments require close investigation by scholars of rhetoric and writing studies. The banal aspects of these algorithms and the ways that they quietly write and rewrite identities, prescribe activities and movements, and facilitate or prohibit communication demand our attention and inquiry. The encompassing ideology of technological capitalism demands accounting for as we further investigate material rhetorics and their designs. Algorithms' impacts on intimate human/machine interaction and collaboration have profound implications for our conceptualizations of rhetorical agency. As we increasingly live among and within algorithms throughout the moments of our lives, we have an obligation to understand the ways that they are shaping us even as we shape them.

Developing and facilitating this understanding means that contemporary digital writing and rhetoric pedagogies are a vital arena for developing literacies for navigating increasingly complex information networks. Most fundamentally, it requires us to foster literacies that facilitate core understandings of the ubiquity of algorithms and the ways that these algorithms increasingly write our lives, our data, and our world, as we have seen in the fallout of the 2016 U.S. presidential election. In doing so, we must consider the ways that we write with and alongside algorithms, responding to Yancey's (2018) call to develop "on the ground practices" that reflect the demands of emerging multimodalities. Likewise,

Hart-Davidson (2018) maps the facets of automation that writing teachers and students must address now rather than in a future world. How, he asks, should humans consider writing in a world of cyborg writing? How do we talk about writing—and about doing research? What should writing machines do and how should they do it? As Laquintano and Vee (2017) write in their important piece "How Automated Writing Systems Affect the Circulation of Information Online," another essential element of algorithmic literacies is a basic understanding of the ways that algorithms create and circulate news, shaping national and international discussions in ways that have devastating consequences for responsible discourse. To these essential areas, we add another: developing core understandings of our existence as subjects within a data economy. As we have suggested in this chapter, this applies to all bodies in the classroom, as each in the course of their digital and physical travels creates the individual data that make up the big data that the world is concerned with and increasingly constructed by. To develop algorithmic literacy means understanding the ubiquitous nature of algorithmic data surveillance, the data's rhetorical construction of individuals, and the ethical implications for the human beings whose performances have been harvested. Taken together with those areas suggested by our colleagues in the field, these potential components of algorithmic literacies represent a tall pedagogical order—but one that is squarely in line with our field's core tenets of source evaluation, argument contextualization, informed tool use, and rhetorical ethics.

Notes

1 For extensive discussion of human/machine collaboration with smart hearing aids, see Kennedy (2017).
2 The Health Insurance Portability and Accountability Act was originally created to address insurance-related issues related to job lock, or the inability to transfer insurance in the event of job transfer. Although HIPAA does not specifically limit HIPAA applicability to insurable activities, the conditions under which Protected Health Information would be transmitted by a Covered Entity typically involve insurable activities. See United States Department of Health & Human Services (2013): "These transactions include claims, benefit eligibility inquiries, referral authorization requests, or other transactions for which HHS has established standards under the HIPAA Transactions Rule." It is important to note that most consumer-type transactions that involve hearing aid sales may not establish Covered Entity status, as typically retailers will not be considered health care providers (one of three covered entity statuses) unless PHI is transmitted in connection with such activities described earlier.
3 Following Potts (2013), our use of the term "wearer" in place of "user" is intended to emphasize the intensive human/machine collaboration between wearers and their devices.
4 For discussion of the rhetorical agency of algorithms in interaction with humans, see among others Gillespie (2014), Gunkel (2012), Kennedy (2009, 2016, 2018), Miller (2007), Propen (2012), and Reyman (2013, 2018).
5 This is increasingly true in EU contexts; this expectation led to the General Data Protection Regulation policies that went into effect in May 2018.

The GDPR requires companies to comprehensively and specifically disclose the extent of data collection and offer consumers a meaningful way to consent or to opt out. At this writing, U.S. regulations offer no such broad protection.

6 This ethic is hardly limited to Starkey or even to other manufacturers of medical wearables; as Katz (1992) notes, "the ethical problem is even deeper and more widespread than the ethos of a single bureaucracy" (p. 258). While this purely capitalist representation is efficient in an economic sense, displacing the human in this user/device "wearer" hybrid has implications that reach further than any utility granted to the device.

7 For more on the disabled body as a site of capitalist oppression, see Abberly (1987), Banner (2017), Erevelles (2001), and Galer (2012).

8 Relevant meeting records and white papers can be found at ftc.gov; examples include Negash and Meso (2017) and "Comments on the Future of Privacy Forum Re: The Internet of Things, Project No. P135405."

9 This opacity is comprehensive; Starkey did not respond to our requests for interviews.

References

Abberly, P. (1987). The concept of oppression and the development of a social theory of disability. *Disability, Handicap & Society, 2*(1), 5–19.

Amoore, L. (2011). Data derivatives: On the emergence of a security risk calculus for our times. *Theory, Culture & Society, 28*(6), 24–43.

Arendt, H. (1964). *Eichmann in Jerusalem: A report on the banality of evil.* New York, NY: Penguin Books.

Arendt, H. (1972). On violence. In *Crises of the republic* (pp. 105–198). San Diego, CA: Harcourt Brace & Co.

Banner, O. (2017). *Communicative biocapitalism: The voice of the patient in digital health and the health humanities.* Ann Arbor: University of Michigan Press.

Beer, D. (2018). Envisioning the power of data analytics. *Information, Communication & Society, 21*(3), 465–479.

Brown, Jr., J. (2015). *Ethical programs: Hospitality and the ethics of software.* Ann Arbor: University of Michigan Press.

Brueggemann, B. J. (2009). *Deaf subjects: Between identities and places.* New York, NY: New York University Press.

Brueggemann, B. J., Brewer, E., Hetrick, N., & Yergeau, M. (2012). Current issues, controversies, and solutions. In B. J. Brueggemann & G. L. Albrecht (Eds.), *SAGE reference series on disability: Arts and humanities* (pp. 63–99). Thousand Oaks, CA: SAGE.

Comments on the Future of Privacy Forum re: Internet of things, project no. P135405. (2014). Retrieved from https://www.ftc.gov/sites/default/files/documents/public_comments /2014/01/00013-88250.pdf

Cox, P. (2013). Passing as sane, or how to get people to sit next to you on the bus. In J. A. Brune & D. J. Wilson (Eds.), *Disability and passing: Blurring the lines of identity* (pp. 99–110). Philadelphia, PA: Temple University Press.

Erevelles, N. (2001). In search of the disabled subject. In J. C. Wilson & C. Lewiecki-Wilson (Eds.), *Embodied rhetorics: Disability in language and culture* (pp. 92–114). Champaign: Southern Illinois University Press.

Galer, D. (2012). Disabled capitalists: Exploring the intersections of disability and identity formation in the world of work. *Disability Studies Quarterly, 32*(3), Retrieved from http://dsq-sds.org/article/view/3277/3122

Gillespie, T. (2014). The relevance of algorithms. In T. Gillespie, P. J. Boczkwoski, & K. Foot (Eds.), *Media technologies: Essays on communication, materiality, and society* (pp. 167–194). Cambridge, MA: MIT Press.

Gouge, C., & Jones, J. (2016). Wearables, wearing, and the rhetorics that attend to them. *Rhetoric Society Quarterly, 46*(3), 199–206.

Gunkel, D. (2012). *The machine question.* Cambridge, MA: MIT Press.

Gunkel, D. (2017). The Internet of things: When your toaster and self-driving car start talking about you behind your back. *Emerging Media Ecologies, 16*(2–3), 251–254.

Harmon, K. C. (2013). Growing up to become hearing: Dreams of passing in oral deaf education. In J. A. Brune & D. J. Wilson (Eds.), *Disability and passing: Blurring the lines of identity* (pp. 167–198). Philadelphia, PA: Temple University Press.

Hart-Davidson, B. (2018). Writing with robots and other curiosities of the machine age. In J. Alexander & J. Rhodes (Eds.), *The Routledge handbook of digital writing and rhetoric* (pp. 248–255). New York, NY: Routledge.

Hern, A. (2018, January 28). Fitness tracking app Strava gives away location of secret US army bases. *The Guardian.* Retrieved from https://www.theguardian.com/world/2018/jan/28/ fitness-tracking-app-gives-away-location-of-secret-us-army-bases

Hirschler, B. (2018, March 1). Big pharma, big data: Why drug makers want your health records. *CNBC.* Retrieved from https://www.cnbc.com/2018/03/01/reuters-america-analysis-big-pharma- big-data-why-drugmakers-want-your-health-records.html

Ingraham, C. (2014). Toward an algorithmic rhetoric. In G. Verhulsdonck & M. Limbu (Eds.), *Digital rhetoric and global literacies: Communication modes and digital practices in the networked world* (pp. 62–79). Hershey, PA: IGI Global.

Katz, S. (1992). The ethic of expediency: Classical rhetoric, technology, and the Holocaust. *College English, 54*(3), 255–275.

Katz, S. (1993). Aristotle's Rhetoric, Hitler's Program, and the ideological problem of praxis, power, and professional discourse. *Journal of Business and Technical Communication, 7*(1), 37–62.

Kennedy, K. (2017). Designing for human-machine collaboration: Smart hearing aids as wearable technologies. *Communication Design Quarterly, 5*(4) 40–51.

Kennedy, K. (2009). Textual machinery: Authorial agency and bot-written texts in Wikipedia. In M. Smith & B. Warnick (Eds.), *The responsibilities of rhetoric* (pp. 303–309). Long Island, NY: Waveland Press.

Kennedy, K. (2016). *Textual curation: Authorship, agency, and technology in Wikipedia and Chambers's Cyclopaedia.* Columbia: University of South Carolina Press.

Laquintano, T., & Vee, A. (2017). How automated writing systems affect the circulation of political information online. *Literacy in Composition Studies, 5*(2), 43–62. Retrieved from http://www.licsjournal.org/OJS/index.php/LiCS/article/view/169/219

Lin, F. R., Metter, E. J., O'Brien, R. J., Resnick, S. M., Zonderman, A. B., & Ferrucci, L. (2011). Hearing loss and incident dementia. *Archives of neurology, 83*(2), 214–220.

Lupton, D., & Michael, M. (2017). 'Depends on who's got the data': Public understandings of personal digital dataveillance. *Surveillance & Society, 15*(2), 254–268.

Lyon, D. (2003). *Surveillance as social sorting: Privacy, risk, and digital discrimination*. London and New York, NY: Routledge.

Marx, G. T. (1998). Ethics for the new surveillance. *The Information Society*, 14, 171–185.

Marx, G. T. (2015). Surveillance studies. *International Encyclopedia of the Social & Behavioral Sciences*, 23, 733–741.

Miller, C. R. (2007). What can automation tell us about agency? *Rhetoric Society Quarterly*, 37(2), 137–57.

Negash, S., & Meso, P. (2017). Privacy concerns in the age of smart devices. *Federal Trade Commission*. Retrieved from https://www.ftc.gov/system/files/documents/ public_comments/2017/11/00028-141795.pdf

Noble, S. U. (2018). *Algorithms of oppression: How search engines reinforce racism*. New York, NY: NYU Press.

Pedersen, I. (2013). *Ready to wear: A rhetoric of wearable computers and reality-shifting media*. Anderson, SC: Parlor Press.

Potts, L. (2013). *Social media in disaster response: How experience architects can build for participation*. New York, NY: Routledge.

Propen, A. (2012). *Locating visual-material rhetorics: The map, the mill, and the GPS*. West Lafayette, IN: Parlor Press.

PwC Health Research Institute. (2014). Health wearables: Early days. *PwC*. Retrieved from https://www.pwc.com/us/en/health-industries/top-health-industry-issues/assets/pwc-hri-wearable-devices.pdf

Reyman, J. (2013). User data on the social web: Authorship, agency, and appropriation. *College English*, 75(5), 513–533.

Reyman, J. (2018). The rhetorical agency of algorithms. In A. Hess & A. Davisson (Eds.), *Theorizing digital rhetoric* (pp. 112–125). New York, NY: Routledge.

Schweik, S. M. (2009). *The ugly laws: Disability in public*. New York: New York University Press.

Stuckey, Z. (2014). *A rhetoric of remnants: Idiots, half-wits, and other state-sponsored inventions*. New York, NY: SUNY Press.

Tschider, C. (forthcoming). The consent myth: Improving choice for patients of the future. *Washington Law Review*.

Tucker, B. (2017). Technocapitalist disability rhetoric: When technology is confused with social justice. *Enculturation: A Journal of Rhetoric, Writing, and Culture*. Retrieved from http://enculturation.net/technocapitalist-disability-rhetoric

United States Department of Health and Human Services. (2013). Summary of the HIPAA privacy rule. *HHS.gov Health Information Privacy*. Retrieved from https://www.hhs.gov/hipaa/for-professionals/privacy/laws-regulations/index.html

Vee, A. (2017). *Coding literacy: How computer programming is changing writing*. Cambridge, MA: The MIT Press.

Winner, L. (1980). Do artifacts have politics? *Daedalus*, 109(1), 121–136.

Yancey, K. B. (2018). "With fresh eyes": Notes toward the impact of new technologies on composing. In J. Alexander & J. Rhodes (Eds.), *The Routledge handbook of digital writing and rhetoric* (pp. 61–72). New York, NY: Routledge.

14 Fostering *Phronesis* in Digital Rhetorics
Developing a Rhetorical and Ethical Approach to Online Engagements

Katherine DeLuca

Introduction: What We Do Online Matters

It did not take long in the history of the Internet or social media for patterns of rhetorical behaviors and communicative practices to emerge. From the development of ways of speaking (from 1337speak to LOLcats to the linguistic conventions of ironic and surreal memes) to ways of rhetorically engaging, there have been clear trends. And they haven't always been good.

One needn't look far for examples of the ways that people use their writing and communications in digital venues to hurt others. From harassment (see, for instance, Poland, 2016; Sparby, 2017a, b) to threats of violence (which, regrettably, often correspond with acts of violence online and offline), the rhetorical and ethical impacts of online communications—both online and offline—are readily apparent.

From U.S. President Donald Trump's tweets to followers' cruel comments on celebrity social media accounts, from students sharing faux pas in interactions with professors (see, for instance, one student's account of turning in a paper directed toward "Professor Whats His Nuts" (2018)) to amateur sleuths using social media to solve crimes (which I will discuss later in this chapter), the rhetorical velocity (Ridolfo & DeVoss, 2009; Sheridan, Ridolfo, & Michel, 2012) and virality of imprudent online compositions and communications demonstrate both the swiftness and the spread of such texts as well as the appeal of such modes of rhetorical engagement.

In this chapter, I build upon the ideas of scholars who have examined the circulation of digital texts (Bradshaw, 2018; Edwards, 2018; Gries, 2013; Ridolfo & DeVoss, 2009; Sheridan, Ridolfo, & Michel, 2012) as I consider what instructors of digital rhetorics and writing, and related fields, might do to intervene in these commonplace rhetorical behaviors and communicative practices. I propose a pedagogical approach that balances impulses toward hasty, rash communications, and compositions with prudent judgment and practical wisdom, and I advocate for the integration of pedagogy that aids students in developing *phronesis* in digital rhetorics and writing classrooms.

I begin this chapter by discussing *phronesis*, or prudent judgment and/or practical wisdom (Aristotle, 2002), and its relationship to *mêtis*, or cunning intelligence, another form of rhetorical and ethical judgment and intellect which many scholars (Dolmage, 2009; Edwards, 2018; Hawhee, 2004; Yergeau, 2017) have positioned as a key rhetorical strategy. But where *mêtis* may guide digital citizens' desire to be cunning, wily, and the first to leave a comment on a thread (Powers, 2017), I suggest that we can teach students to foster *phronesis*, developing active habits and engagements (Sachs, 2002) that encourage prudent judgment and practical wisdom in digital contexts. I situate this active engagement of *phronesis* as a way to balance impulses toward sometimes imprudent rhetorics.

In developing this theoretical positioning, I briefly turn to two illustrations from reddit, sometimes called the front page of the Internet and positioned as a "source for what's new and popular on the web" (Potts & Harrison, 2013) for its tendency to highlight and house much of the web's viral content. Although I use rhetorical events from reddit to demonstrate modes of engagement in online spaces, I see them as examples of which many may be found across digital and online spaces. Thus, following this discussion of *phronesis* and *mêtis* through these examples, I offer pedagogical suggestions for fostering *phronesis* and encouraging students to attend to the rhetorical and the ethical simultaneously as they engage in digital spaces. I link these theoretical concepts to praxis targeted toward the development of thoughtful, engaged citizens—here, digital citizens—in the tradition of the classical rhetorical education.

Instructors of rhetoric and writing studies are well situated to encourage students to engage with the rhetorical and ethical implications of their online compositions and communications. Accordingly, I suggest that we can teach students to understand their responsibilities as digital citizens by helping them to foster a rhetorical–ethical perspective in our classrooms, helping them to understand that what they do online matters and to consider the potential impacts their rhetorical compositions and communications may have on others.

Phronesis and *Mêtis*: Moving toward Balance in Online Engagements

Building upon the concepts of rhetorical velocity (see Ridolfo & DeVoss, 2009; Sheridan, Ridolfo, & Michel, 2012) and futurity (Gries, 2015), I emphasize a specific dimension for considerations of future impacts and potentials of any given composition: the ethical. If *mêtis* can be linked to virality and to an ethic of fast circulation (Bradshaw, 2018), I connect *phronesis* with a different approach—aligned with Bradshaw's (2018) ethic of slow circulation and rhetorical persistence. *Phronesis*, I argue, is something we can teach. By encouraging students to engage the rhetorical *and* the ethical simultaneously, instructors can aid students in the development of a rhetorical–ethical perspective that puts *phronesis* first and encourages digital citizens to consider and weigh the potential impacts of their texts. I see this rhetorical–ethical perspective as making use of *phronesis* as not only a consideration of circulation, and thus rhetorical velocity (Ridolfo & DeVoss, 2009; Ridolfo, Sheridan, & Michel, 2012) and futurity (Gries, 2015), but also as an ethical issue with real, often embodied, effects on others.

Although, as Ridolfo and DeVoss (2009) make clear, one cannot know for certain the future of a circulated text, considering that the potential ethical impact of a text can enable digital citizens to more fully understand the rhetorical import and significance of their online and offline communications and engagements. Instructors of rhetoric and writing studies can encourage students to engage with the lives, communications, and compositions they create and influence across spaces from a rhetorical–ethical perspective that is simultaneously rhetorically prudent and forward looking while also being situationally responsive.

To situate this rhetorical–ethical perspective as an active engagement and orientation by individuals toward others and the world around them, I compare two ways of knowing and rhetorically responding: *mêtis*, or cunning intelligence (see Dolmage, 2009; Edwards, 2018; Hawhee, 2004; Knudsen, 2005; Yergeau, 2017), and *phronesis*, or practical wisdom and prudent judgment derived from social practice and experience (see Aristotle, 2002; Knudsen, 2005; Moss, 2011; Sachs, 2002). I begin with *mêtis* as a way of exploring and characterizing how I see many digital citizens engage rhetorically in online spaces before turning to *phronesis* as an alternative mode of active engagement and ethical habit to foster through education.

As I discuss both of these rhetorical concepts, I illustrate them in action by turning to two examples from reddit. Although both events may seem long past now, as they come from 2012 and 2013, especially when considering the pace at which viral events and memes move in online spaces, both demonstrate characteristics of rhetorical interactions and behaviors that endure. Furthermore, as Potts and Harrison (2013) argue, spaces like reddit are "cultures, rhetorically constructed by their communities." In this culture, certain conventions of rhetorical engagement are valued, including using *mêtis* to promote virality in content created and circulated on the site and beyond. In the examples used later, I highlight how *mêtis* and *phronesis* could, and sometimes do, operate in digital spaces, to lay the basis for the rhetorical–ethical perspective that I recommend instructors incorporate into their digital rhetorics and writing pedagogy.

Defining Mêtis—*Embodied, Cunning Intelligence*

According to Dolmage (2009), *mêtis* has "always been associated with trickery—those with mêtis can see the world slightly differently" (p. 9). As Hawhee (2004) defines this embodied intelligence, *mêtis* is the ability "to cunningly and effectively maneuver a cutting instrument, a ship, a chariot, a body, on the spot, in the heat of the moment"; it is a way of navigating the world that relies on mind and body using knowledge responsively (p. 47). Edwards (2018) explains, "*mêtis* represents a flexible, kairotic, and cunning mode of intelligence" (p. 72).

Knudsen (2005) explains that *mêtis* is "ethically ambiguous," and "depending on the context, the wiles of *mêtis* may be interpreted as cheating, lies and manipulation, and/or they can be admired as taking advantages of a minimum of means to reverse a seemingly inevitable outcome" (p. 61). Although *mêtis* is sometimes characterized as wily, its ethical ambiguity potentially aids its adaptivity and responsiveness in any given situation. As Dolmage writes, "*mêtis* is timely, flexible, and practical," and not unlike rhetoric as Aristotle defines it *mêtis* locates the best means for responding to a situation as it arises.

Mêtis, as Dolmage (2009) and Yergeau (2017) highlight, is also deeply embodied. *Mêtis* connects intelligence to the physical, embodied realities of our experience. And this embodiment is particularly significant when considering the ethical dimensions of digital citizens' rhetorical responsiveness—though technologies mediate the rhetorical exchange, the responses originate from embodied individuals and are received by embodied individuals. This embodiment is also key to understanding the appeal of *mêtis*—the satisfaction of feeling cunning and wily, of the joy applying this rhetorical strategy at just the right moment and in just the right way. It can feel good to go viral or to be first, and that embodied relationship to rhetorical engagements can impel rhetors to push forward, further, and faster.

Thus, I see *mêtis* as a central rhetorical strategy and way of knowing in the pursuit of what Powers (2017) terms firstness—a "metaculture that plays a role in making culture circulation faster" (p. 165). Firstness, which encompasses both being first in an online discussion and a notion of superlativity, according to Powers (2017), and *mêtis* contribute to the rhetorical velocity of a text and help construct, as Bradshaw (2018) terms it, "viral circulation," an ethic of communication grounded in speed and reach, which he defines in juxtaposition to an ethic of slow circulation. *Mêtis* impels rhetors in Bradshaw's (2018) and Powers's (2017) respective rhetorical models. But, as Bradshaw (2018) argues, "viral circulation" does not account for or fit every rhetorical context and moment of circulation. Additionally, I argue, it sometimes is misapplied to rhetorical events when another intellectual and rhetorical approach may be more prudent.

When Mêtis *Falls Short: The Boston Marathon Bombing and reddit*

Mêtis has many potential benefits for the rhetor who uses it. It can enable quick, effective, and kairotic responses to rhetorical events and situations, but the impact of those rhetorics may not always yield the intended or a positive result. I turn here to an illustration of what I see as unchecked *mêtis*—wiliness and cunning that do not consider the implications of its rhetoric: the Boston Marathon bombing and the subsequent false accusations of responsibility made against an innocent college student, Sunil Tripathi, on r/findbostonbombers. I situate this example as *mêtis* because, in many ways, the rhetorical engagements demonstrated here are sophisticated and persuasive, if imprudent.

As Potts and Harrison (2013) explain, reddit "describes itself as 'a pretty open platform and free speech place,'" made up of participants, or redditors, who contribute to various communities, or subreddits, across the site. Furthermore, as Potts and Harrison (2013) argue, the rhetorical events and circulations of communications on reddit following the marathon bombing were not characteristic of the site and its community members; rather, they write:

> Overall, the efforts and attitudes in FindBostonBombers are not indicative of reddit as a whole, as evidenced by the behavior after these events. On reddit, there was a sense of regret and anger over what occurred in FindBostonBombers. The rhetorical structures of the culture of reddit, with its need for evidence, hierarchy information flows, and link structure, is not a good fit for the kind of activity that went on in FindBostonBombers. It will be interesting to observe how their interface might change further to support these cultural beliefs about these kinds of activities, namely manhunts, in the future.

Although perhaps uncharacteristic of the space and community, and some years past now, as an illustrative example, this event shows how *mêtis* can guide rhetors toward their goals, especially when that goal may be characterized by firstness and a desire for viral circulation (Powers, 2017 and Bradshaw, 2018, respectively), but may fall short of considering the ethical implications and impact of their circulated texts and communications.

In April 2013, two explosions occurred near the finish line of the Boston Marathon route. More than 5,000 runners were yet to cross the finish line ("2013 Boston Marathon," 2018). The explosions injured an estimated 264 people, and killed three individuals, including an eight-year-old boy from Dorchester, MA ("Boston Marathon Bombings," 2018). As with so many events in our contemporary digital culture, media coverage of the event was immediate and pervasive—extending from established forms of media distribution, including print and television media, to newer and more immediate channels of information sharing, like social media sites.

On reddit, however, users did not limit their discussions to grieving and remembrance; they also began calling for justice, and redditors began investigative efforts to locate the person or persons responsible. As redditors' pursuit of their culprit began, the textual compositions—from tweets, to photo analyses, and in-depth discussion threads—gained traction, creating seemingly unforeseen rhetorical and ethical effects. In short, this communicative event illustrates some digital citizens' failure to consider the circulation and rhetoricity of their compositions and communications, and moreover, demonstrates a failure to reflect upon the potential ethical implications of their communications.

Redditors took to specialized threads and subreddits to share information and develop theories on the identity of the Boston bombers. Seemingly guided by *mêtis*, and the desire to be both cunning and kairotic (Edwards, 2018) and first (Powers, 2017), redditors pooled their resources and insights to identify leads in the case. One such subreddit was "/r/findbostonbombers," which has since been made private (and thus the threads of the subreddit itself inaccessible to uninvited redditors). See Figure 14.1 for a screencapture of the /findbostonbombers/ front page. As Potts and Harrison (2013) explain, redditors on this subreddit "were focused on tracking down the suspected terrorists. Before the subreddit was shut down by reddit's leadership team, the participants in this subreddit had wrongfully named several innocent people as terrorists." It is this thread of the event—the misidentification of innocent people—that I want to focus on here, as it most clearly displays the potential ethical impacts upon others. Perhaps beyond what the redditors responsible for those false accusations may have predicted, the naming of one suspect, Sunil Tripathi, had far-reaching effects.

Sunil Tripathi, known to his family as "Sunny," was an undergraduate student at Brown University. Tripathi went missing on March 16, 2013, after "having suspended his studies due to bouts of depression" ("Sunil Tripathi," 2018). Following his disappearance, the Tripathi family worked with the F.B.I., university officials, and others in an effort to find Sunil.

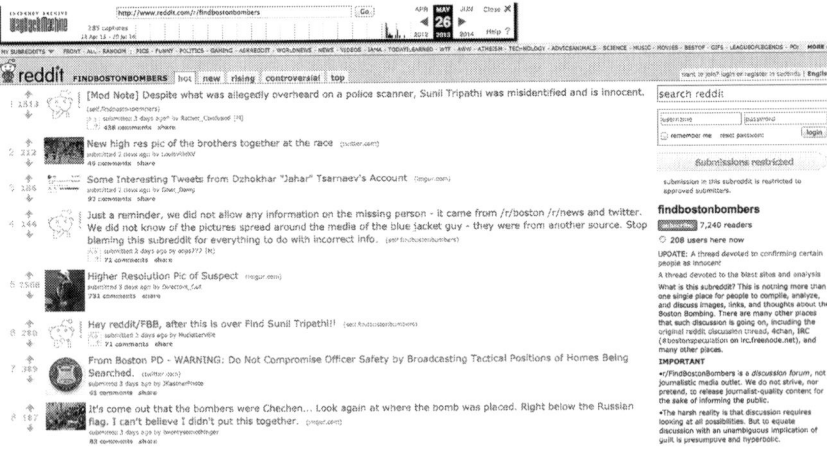

Figure 14.1 Front page of the subreddit r/findbostonbombers/, by Internet Archive Wayback Machine, 2013. Screencapture by K. DeLuca, 2014.

The family also set up a Facebook page dedicated to finding Sunil, which was entitled "Help us Find Sunil Tripathi" and "included video messages from family and friends and recent images of Sunil" (Kang, 2013). The page was set up "with the hope that if Sunil searched for himself [online], he would find loving messages from his family and friends" (Kang, 2013).

When the F.B.I. released photos of the bombers to the media three days after the bombing, a woman named Kami Mattioli tweeted that Suspect 2 resembled Sunil Tripathi, whom she had attended high school with but had not seen for three years (Kundani, 2013). Following Mattioli's tweet, a redditor "pizzatime," "(who saw Mattioli's tweet but who never knew Tripathi) confirmed that Tripathi looked exactly like Suspect 2, [and] a subreddit devoted to the bombing confirmed it was Tripathi" (Kundani, 2013). Users on the subreddit "posted side-by-side pictures comparing Sunil's facial features with the face that would later be identified as Dzhokhar Tsarnaev. The pictures were accompanied by speculation about Sunil's disappearance and the F.B.I.'s involvement in his search" (Kang, 2013). Taken together, members of the subreddit viewed these texts as credible evidence, using it as a cause to pursue Tripathi, via his family, as a suspect.

Though initially just one tweet, the effects of one woman's accusations were far-reaching, traveling from one online space to be reiterated in multiple others, like reddit where the discussion seemed to galvanize others, to be taken up by media outlets whose reach extended both online and offline, and finally to affect the private lives of a suffering family in very public ways. Despite assurances from law enforcement that Sunil Tripathi was not a suspect, his family received threatening and abusive messages online and offline. As discussion of Sunil as a suspect circulated, the "volume of threatening Facebook messages" on the page that the family created to help find their son grew, and the family "now worried that [Sunil] would see what was being written about him and take drastic measures to harm himself" and took down the page at around 11:00 p.m. (Kang, 2013). Sadly, the Tripathi family's efforts to stem the flow of abuse and rumors directed toward their son and brother did not stop speculation about Sunil's assumed guilt, and it did little to prevent the family from receiving extensive harassment.

The Tripathis "received hundreds of threatening and anti-Islamic messages," and a friend "called a homeless shelter in Philadelphia to see if Sunil had been there and was told that the shelter did not aid terrorists" (Kang, 2013). Sunil's mother summarized the traumatic experience succinctly:

> All the sentiment and help we had received to help find Sunil switched over and said he was a terrorist. And you know the irony is… Sunil was so gentle, and he was a victim of all that damn scandal, and he was a victim of his depression. It was just so ugly.
>
> (2013)

Already enduring the trauma of having their son go missing, the family was forced to reckon with the anger and harassment of strangers pursuing so-called justice.

As the redditors were "playing detective" (Potts & Harrison, 2013), they relied on wiliness and cunning alone, pursuing the high of firstness (Powers, 2017) as they tried to outwit the Boston Bomber. In spite of the investigative efforts of members of this subreddit, the second suspect of the bombings was identified as Dzhokhar Tsarnaev, who was apprehended in Watertown three days after the bombings amid a massive manhunt by police. And in spite of their desire and efforts to achieve justice, these redditors contributed to the suffering of a worried and grieving family, further traumatizing them as they already feared the worst. On April 23, 2013, five days after the redditors named him as a suspect, Sunil Tripathi's body was recovered from the Providence River.

Although this rhetorical event is just one example of unchecked *mêtis*, I think it is an important one, as it demonstrates not only the visceral, embodied connection between our digital rhetorics and *mêtis* but also the potential wiliness of rhetorical velocity and futurity. As Ridolfo and DeVoss (2009) and Gries (2015) argue, we cannot know how our rhetorical creations will be taken up in the future, and part of what I suggest we can teach students is a stronger consideration of how things might be taken up and how that may impact others. When *mêtis* impels us toward rhetorical action, we can help students develop active rhetorical and ethical habits (Sachs, 2002) that encourage prudence and are mindful of rhetorical velocity *and* ethical impact.

Defining Phronesis—Prudent Judgment and Practical Wisdom

Had the digital citizens on r/findbostonbombers engaged this rhetorical event with *phronesis*, their responses may still have been quick and cunning, but they might have been balanced by prudence and a greater consideration of the potential effects that their words and discussions might have had on others. Of course, their personal ethics may have dictated that they respond to this rhetorical event in exactly the manner that they did, but I advocate for creating the space and possibility for other responses by providing digital citizens the rhetorical education and lessons that might help guide them through such contexts.

I view *phronesis* as an alternative model for rhetorical engagement in digital spaces that considers both rhetorical and ethical impacts. In the *Nichomachean Ethics* (2002), Aristotle defines *phronesis* as being "concerned with human things and things about which is it possible to deliberate" and as being "not only about what is universal... [but also as about] the particulars as well, since it has to do with action, and action is concerned with particulars" (1141b, p. 109). *Phronesis*, like *métis*, is oriented toward action (Knudsen, 2005)—toward making choices about how best to respond to situations and events effectively and ethically.

In his reading and translation of the *Nichomachean Ethics*, Sachs (2002) argues that *phronesis* is an "active condition by which someone discerns the right means to the right end in particular circumstances" (p. 209). *Phronesis*, thus, is a form of virtue and intellect (Moss, 2011), and it is a way of understanding and acting in the world. Furthermore, like *métis*, it is rhetorical, guiding our responses to others and their communications, in the best, most kairotic way in a given situation. Sachs (2002) situates virtue, like *phronesis*, as *hexis*, "an active having-and-holding that depends on the effort of concentrating or paying attention" (p. xii). Although frequently viewed as habit (*ethos*), Sachs argues that virtue is better understood as *hexis*, as it emphasizes the active engagement of the individual in the development and maintenance of their virtue. This active ethical engagement can build toward *ethos*—moving toward the development of an ethical habit or character while acknowledging the active practices that enable that development. This active engagement characterizes not only the responsiveness of *phronesis* but also its rhetoricity.

Moss (2011) also argues that *phronesis* is practicable, a form of intellect that can be further fostered and developed through habituation: "*phronesis* is a virtue of practical intellect rather than theoretical, and its closest analogue is therefore not wisdom…but craft" (p. 257). Like *métis*, *phronesis* is concerned with action and movement toward rhetorically effective responsiveness, and like *métis*, *phronesis* is a form of intellect, a way of knowing and understanding the world that shapes individuals' responses to it. And while *métis* is ethically ambiguous (Knudsen, 2005), *phronesis* is concerned with making decisions aimed at the good, fostered through virtue and character and habit (*ethos*) (Moss, 2011, p. 206).

Phronesis, thus, can be understood as an active mode of engaging with the world, and as an active means for understanding, measuring, and responding to any given rhetorical event. Thus, a rhetorical–ethical perspective that puts *phronesis* first becomes a means for actively, responsively engaging in communicative events that simultaneously encourages prudence and forward-thinking, considering the potential ethical impacts of any given rhetorical engagement. Furthermore, it becomes a mode of engagement that we can aid students in developing through practice and education.

Phronesis can provide a holistic approach for making sense of particular rhetorical situations and applying knowledge to mutable contexts to respond rhetorically and ethically. Through education and practice, these ways of knowing and responding to the world can shape digital citizens' rhetorical and ethical perspectives over time. I turn again to an example, also from reddit, that elucidates how *phronesis* can intervene in such moments and can reshape and reframe digital interactions.

240 *Katherine DeLuca*

Phronesis *as Intervention: Responding to Haters Online*

In September 2012, a reddit user with the username "european_douchebag" posted a photo to the subreddit "r/funny." Taken in line at Ohio State University's Thompson Library café, without the subject's knowledge, the image featured a young Sikh woman looking at her phone. The young woman was dressed like many other students her age, wearing a t-shirt, yoga pants, and flip-flops, with a backpack hanging from one shoulder. She also wore a dastar, or turban, as representative of her faith. But what seemed to prompt the reddit user to post the photo to this subreddit with the caption "I'm not sure what to conclude from this" was the subject's facial hair (european_douchebag 2012).

Perhaps viewing the woman's appearance as a curiosity in a culture that rather strongly encourages women to rid themselves of so-called "excess" body hair by any means necessary, european_douchebag was apparently motivated enough by her appearance to take her photo and post it to a subreddit entitled "funny"—signaling that this image was worthy of mocking and laughter. As one journalist put it:

> The mind of european_douchebag was SO INCREDIBLY BLOWN by the fact that women have hair on their bodies—and, yes, faces—and that some women are bold, self-assured, and pious enough not to cave to western beauty standards (and gender expectations), there was nothing for him to do but post her photo online and wait for the abuse to flood in.
>
> (West, 2012)

Some individuals immediately responded to european_douchebag's post by criticizing him for posting an image without securing permissions from the subject, and others suggested that being amused by a woman with a beard was juvenile. For instance, one respondent wrote,

> What you should conclude from this is that it's not ok to take photos of strangers and post them on the internet without permission. … I'm objecting to op [original poster] taking a picture without this woman's knowledge or permission.
>
> (Taylorsiem, 2012)

Other users' comments indicated that they too found the image humorous, expressing mock confusion over the subject's gender identity (see Figure 14.2).

Although european_douchebag's thread received some responses, the post itself did not garner much attention overall from reddit's front page or other media outlets until, as West (2012) wrote, "…something totally lovely and unexpected happened. The woman in the photo responded."

Fostering Phronesis *in Digital Rhetorics* 241

> [-] **Taylorselm** 265 points 1 year ago*
> What you should conclude from this is that it's not ok to take photos of strangers and post them on the internet without permission.
> edit: so that my position is clear. I'm objecting to op taking a picture without this woman's knowledge or permission and then posting it without her knowledge or permission. This is really easy to fix. Getting her permission is not hard to do, op just had to ask, they were obviously standing pretty close by. And if op asked and she said no then op is a dick, and we should all strive not to be dicks.
> permalink
>
> > [-] **Clown_Vomit** -1 points 1 year ago
> > Well now that you've chided him, he probably wont do it again. So thanks for that.
> > permalink parent
> >
> > > [-] **Taylorselm** 23 points 1 year ago
> > > Sometimes otherwise good people do inappropriate things simply because they haven't thought about them. I didn't insult the op, I just reminded them that some people might not like having their picture posted online when the end result will be the picture being mocked. So yes, hopefully now that I've chided them, they won't do it again.
> > > I will admit when I posted that I did not notice the username european_douchebag.
> > > permalink parent

Figure 14.2 Comments about image posted to reddit by european_douchebag. Screencapture by K. DeLuca, 2014.

The subject of the photo, who revealed herself to be a university student named Balpreet Kaur, posted to the reddit thread to begin a dialogue about her appearance and choices regarding her body hair. In her message, Kaur uses *phronesis*, practical wisdom, and prudent judgment to formulate her response. In making a response directly to the post, Kaur is able to change and challenge the existing rhetorics and reconceptualize the ethics at play.

Kaur wrote the following message and posted it to the thread:

> Hey, guys. This is Balpreet Kaur, the girl from the picture. I actually didn't know about this until one of my friends told on facebook. If the OP wanted a picture, they could have just asked and I could have smiled :) However, I'm not embarrased or even humiliated by the attention [negative and positve] that this picture is getting because, it's who I am. Yes, I'm a baptized Sikh woman with facial hair. Yes, I realize that my gender is often confused and I look different than most women. However, baptized Sikhs believe in the sacredness of this body—it is a gift that has been given to us by the Divine Being [which is genderless, actually] and, must keep it intact as a submission to the divine will.... By transcending societal views of beauty, I believe that I can focus more on my actions. My attitude and thoughts and actions have more value in them than my body because I recognize that this body is just going to become ash in the end, so why fuss about it?... However, my impact and legacy will remain: and, by not focusing on the physical beauty, I have time to cultivate those inner virtues and hopefully, focus my life on creating change and progress for this world in any way I can.... I appreciate all of the comments here, both positive and less positive because I've gotten a better understanding of myself and others from this.
>
> (Kaur, 2012, brackets Kaur's)

Kaur's prudent, measured response drew quite a bit of attention—from outpourings of support from other reddit users to news stories on sites from around the world (for instance, a story posted on French news site 20minutes.fr, A.L., 2012). Kaur's post helped to transform the tone and the conversations that emerged from this reddit thread. Conversations moved from questioning Kaur's gender expression to genuine inquiries about different cultural and religious practices and even discussions about gender roles and cultural issues more broadly. Apart from generating productive discussion about issues relevant to the thread that pushed it beyond a space to mock another individual, Kaur's response also inspired something nearly unheard of on the Internet: a sincere apology from the original poster.

After Kaur posted her message, european_douchebag went back to the thread and offered an apology. european_douchebag wrote that he recognized that the post he made was not funny, and instead, he wrote, "put simply it was stupid. Making fun of people is funny to some but incredibly degrading to the people you're making fun of. It was an incredibly rude, judgmental, and ignorant thing to post" (european_douchebag as quoted in West, 2012). Kaur's post inspired him to "read more about the Sikh faith," and he gestured particularly to a point Kaur had made in her post writing: "it makes a whole lot of sense to work on having a legacy and not worrying about what you look like. I made that post for stupid internet points and I was ignorant" (european_douchebag as quoted in West, 2012). He further stated that he had reached out to Balpreet via e-mail and had even made plans to meet up with her the next time he was on Ohio State University's campus.

Reading Kaur's response as making use of *phronesis*—of prudent judgment and practical wisdom actively engaged by choosing the most virtuous and appropriate response to the situation—creates an opportunity for seeing how a rhetorical-ethical perspective and approach to digital rhetorics could intervene to create change in rhetorical exchanges and communications. Where european_douchebag was guided by *mêtis* and firstness, Kaur relied upon *phronesis* to reframe the rhetorics of the thread. Kaur's response created change, challenging misconceptions and prejudices and pushing the original poster to reconsider not only his views on broader issues but also potentially the ethical impacts of his digital rhetorics on real people.

As digital citizens, including students, rhetorically engage across spaces—from spaces like reddit to other forms of social media—developing an ability to navigate through and across these spaces in a rhetorical *and* ethical way seems paramount. Thus, in the remainder of this chapter, I advocate for teaching digital citizens how to move through these spaces from a rhetorical-ethical perspective grounded in *phronesis* that considers not only the speed and reach (Bradshaw, 2018) of their compositions and communications but also the impact of those rhetorics on others.

Equipping Digital Citizens with Rhetorical and Ethical Perspectives

Teaching students about a rhetorical–ethical perspective that values the prudent, reflective judgment of *phronesis* can enable students to imagine and think beyond their current kairotic moment. Students can be encouraged to consider the ethical possibilities for their communications and compositions and to make choices that value others and their lived experiences. In short, students need to be equipped with knowledge and practice for engaging rhetorically with others across spaces—both in their roles as students and as digital citizens.

Encouraging students to actively consider the ethical and rhetorical impacts of their communications can help them to become responsible and responsive digital citizens. Instructors of rhetoric and writing can encourage their students to attend to texts from a rhetorical–ethical perspective by asking them to think actively and carefully about not only when and how a text might be recomposed and redistributed (Gries, 2015; Ridolfo & DeVoss, 2009; Sheridan, Ridolfo, & Michel, 2012) but also what effects that recomposition and redistribution might have on real people. To aid students in their development of *phronesis* as *hexis*, I offer a few pedagogical suggestions, building first from the examples presented in this chapter before turning to my own classroom practice, to demonstrate how this theoretical concept might be merged with praxis.

Using Examples as Ethical Case Studies

Reddit's etiquette page—aptly named "reddiquette"—is described as "an informal expression of the values of many redditors" ("Reddiquette," 2018). Notably, the reddiquette page is not a terms of service agreement; rather, it offers suggestions. The etiquette guide begins with a simple, but important, mandate: "Remember the Human" ("Reddiquette," 2018). The authors of the guide suggest to readers:

> when you communicate online, all you see is a computer screen. When talking to someone you might want to ask yourself 'Would I say it to the person's face?' or 'Would I get jumped if I said this to a buddy?'
>
> ("Reddiquette," 2018)

In short, redditors are asked to be *good* digital citizens, to engage ethically with other individuals and to remember the human element of online discussions—indeed, to remember the embodied aspects of seemingly disembodied interactions.

In light of this exhortation to remember the human, I see the illustrative examples discussed earlier as potentially useful case studies for students to engage as they consider what it means to be a good digital citizen. These examples demonstrate two forms of rhetorical engagement in digital spaces—one demonstrating an ethical and rhetorical response based only in *mêtis* and the other highlighting the role *phronesis* might play in rhetorical negotiations. Together, they can provide students insights into alternative pathways for engaging and communication with others in digital spaces that moves beyond cultures of firstness (Powers, 2017) and viral circulation (Bradshaw, 2018).

The examples presented in this chapter could function as case studies for engagement in the classroom. To practice *phronesis* and develop their rhetorical–ethical approach to communications and situations, students might be asked to consider how they would respond to such situations, imagining themselves as inhabiting the rhetorical perspective of these redditors. Undergirding both of these examples or issues concerning embodied rhetorics and ethics—issues of race, gender, culture, and religion—all of which can be discussed and considered, focusing on how *mêtis* may impel us to initially respond to such issues before considering how *phronesis* might reframe our reactions and rhetorics. Building upon this exploration, as students examine the potential rhetorical and ethical impacts of a given composition or situation, they might also trace out the lines of circulation and the publics that may potentially be impacted by such an event, highlighting the real people, ethical concerns, and rhetorical dimensions at stake.

Practicing Phronesis *Together in the Rhetoric and Writing Classroom*

Understanding *phronesis* as *hexis* (Sachs, 2002) and this rhetorical–ethical approach as a means for actively engaging in both rhetoric and virtuous practices can enable instructors to bring these theoretical concepts together with classroom praxis. The classroom can become a space for actively practicing *phronesis*, helping students to develop strategies and habits for employing *phronesis* in their everyday rhetorical engagements.

Phronesis can function as a heuristic for invention. As Yergeau (2017) argues, "invention is always located, but it is not fixed or fixable: it is an ecology in movement" through which rhetors "might come to know" (p. 181). Aligning with Yergeau's definition of invention, I situate the rhetorical–ethical perspective I advocate for here as an active heuristic and approach for both creating and responding to rhetorics. Emphasizing *phronesis* as a way of knowing as they encounter and compose rhetorics and publics, students can productively locate (and relocate and revise and reconsider) sites of invention that actively engage prudent judgment while remaining situationally responsive. Students can practice, through invention via these ways of knowing, developing their rhetorical and ethical responsiveness, both immediate and forward-looking.

In my own classroom, I have used *phronesis* as a heuristic for invention by challenging students to incorporate and engage with the ethical dimensions of their compositions throughout the composing process. In undergraduate multimodal writing courses, for instance, this has taken the form of actively engaging students in discussions of ethics and the capturing of others' voice or image with recording devices—including how and when they record others and what permissions they seek. Together, we discuss the experience of having our image or voice captured without consent—not unlike Balpreet Kaur's experience described earlier—and the impact it has on us. From there, we make connections between the kairotic moment and impulse to capture someone else's image or voice without permission, and discuss how we can make more prudent choices by seeking permission from subjects. Bringing this consideration into our discussions from the beginning of their composing process aids students in inventing prudent and practical approaches to their composing that considers the ethical and embodied impacts of their texts.

In graduate courses in professional writing and communication on social media and writing for the web, we collaboratively foster this rhetorical–ethical perspective and *phronesis* by continually confronting and engaging the ethical dimension of the work of social media professionals. In assignments—from reading works on digital ethics and algorithms (Noble, 2018; Reyman, 2017) to developing a social media style guide and composing a social media campaign—students are asked to consider the potential ethical implications of their social media communications and compositions for others, be it clients, consumers, or any person who might engage with their compositions. Accordingly, ethical considerations play a role as they imagine what inventing such documents—both as students and as professionals—from a rhetorical–ethical perspective would entail. Especially as students preparing to enter workforces where the ever-changing and fluid nature of technologies and rhetorics may make best practices a moving target, developing students' rhetorical–ethical perspectives through practice, moving toward habit, seems especially valuable.

Through this active engagement and practice, students may develop the rhetorical–ethical perspectives that enable them to actively engage the rhetorical events that they encounter. Understanding and employing *phronesis* as an active mode of engagement that builds toward habit and character (*ethos*) can aid students in seeing the stakes of their everyday rhetorics—whether participating in subreddits or writing e-mails to their congresspeople. Fostering a rhetorical–ethical perspective centered on *phronesis* can encourage students to think about others' experiences and perspectives, enacting a first step toward asking questions about the ethical implications of their ideas, position, arguments, and ultimately, their compositions.

References

2013 Boston Marathon. (2018, June 26). *Wikipedia*. Retrieved from Wikipedia. org: https://en.wikipedia.org/wiki/2013_Boston_Marathon

A.L. (2012). Une 'femme à barbe' moquée répond sur Reddit. Retrieved November 1, 2018 From 20minutes.fr: https://www.20minutes.fr/web/1011113-20120926-femme-barbe-moquee-repond-reddit

Aristotle. (2002). *Nichomachean ethics*. (J. Sachs, Trans.), Newburyport, MA: Focus Publishing.

Boston Marathon Bombings. (2018, June 26). *Wikipedia*. Retrieved from Wikipedia.org: https://en.wikipedia.org/wiki/Boston_Marathon_bombing

Bradshaw, J. L. (2018). Slow circulation: The ethics of speed and rhetorical persistence. *Rhetoric Society Quarterly, 48*, 1–20.

Dolmage, J. (2009). Metis, *mêtis*, mestiza, and Medusa: Rhetorical bodies across rhetorical traditions. *Rhetoric Review, 28*, 1–28.

Edwards, D. (2018). Circulation gatekeepers: Unbundling the platform politics of YouTube's content ID. *Computers and Composition, 47*, 61–74.

european_douchebag. (2012). I'm not sure what to conclude from this. *Reddit*. Retrieved from https://www.reddit.com/r/funny/comments/109cnf/im_not_sure_what_to_conclude_from_this/?sort=new#c6bmnym

Gries, L. E. (2013). Iconographic tracking: A digital research method for visual rhetoric and circulation studies. *Computers and Composition, 30*(4), 332–348.

Gries, L. E. (2015). *Still life with rhetoric: A new materialist approach for visual rhetorics*. Boulder: University of Colorado Press.

Hawhee, D. (2004). *Bodily arts: Rhetoric and athletics in ancient Greece*. Austin: University of Texas Press.

Kang, J. C. (2013). Should reddit be blamed for the spreading of a smear? *The New York Times Magazine*. Retrieved from https://www.nytimes.com/2013/07/28/magazine/should-reddit-be-blamed-for-the-spreading-of-a-smear.html

Kaur, B. (2012). Re: I don't know what to make of this. *Reddit*. Retrieved from https://www.reddit.com/r/funny/comments/109cnf/im_not_sure_what_to_conclude_from_this/?sort=new#c6bmnym

Knudsen, F. (2005). *Seamanship and anthropoship: Reflecting on practice*. Arbejdsmedicinsk Afdeling: Sydvestjysk Sygehus.

Kundani, L. (2013). When the tail wags the dog: Dangers of crowdsourcing justice. *New American Media*. Retrieved from http://newamericamedia.org/2013/07/when-the-tail-wags-the-dog-dangers-of-crowdsourcing-justice.php

Moss, J. (2011). "Virtue makes the goal right": Virture and phronesis in Aristotle's ethics. *Phronesis, 56*, 204–261.

Noble, S. U. (2018). *Algorithms of oppression: How search engines reinforce racism*. New York, NY: NYU Press.

Poland, B. (2016). *Haters: Harassment, abuse, and violence online*. Lincoln, NE: Potomac Books.

Potts, L., & Harrison, A. (2013). Interfaces as rhetorical constructions: Reddit and 4chan during the Boston Marathon bombings. Retrieved from: http://williamwolff.org/wp-content/uploads/2013/09/PottsHarrison_reddit4chan.pdf

Powers, D. (2017). First! Cultural circulation in the age of recursivity. *New Media & Society, 19*, 165–180.

Professor Whats His Nuts. (2018). *KnowYourMeme*. Retrieved from https://knowyourmeme.com/memes/events/professor-whats-his-nuts

Reddiquette. (2018). *Reddit*. Retrieved from Reddit.com: https://www.reddit.com/wiki/reddiquette

Reyman, J. (2017). The rhetorical agency of algorithms. In A. Hess & A. Davisson (Eds.), *Theorizing digital rhetoric* (pp. 112–125). New York, NY: Routledge.

Ridolfo, J., & DeVoss, D. N. (2009). Composing for recomposition: rhetorical velocity and delivery. *Kairos, 13*, Retrieved from http://kairos.technorhetoric.net/13.2/topoi/ridolfo_devoss/intro.html

Sachs, J. (2002). Introduction. *Nichomachean ethics*. (J. Sachs, Trans.), Newburyport, MA: Focus Publishing.

Sheridan, D. M., Ridolfo, J., & Michel, A. J. (2012). *The available means of persuasion: Mapping a theory and pedagogy of multimodal public rhetoric*. Anderson, SC: Parlor Press.

Sparby, E. M. (2017a). Digital social media and aggression: Memetic rhetoric in 4chan's collective identity. *Computers and Composition, 45*, 85–97.

Sparby, E. M. (2017b). *Memes, 4chan and haters, oh my! Rhetoric, identity, and online aggression*. (Doctoral dissertation). Available from ProQuest Dissertations and Theses database. (UMI No. 10282254).

Sunil Tripathi. (2018). *Wikipedia*. Retrieved from https://en.wikipedia.org/wiki/Sunil_Tripathi

Taylorsiem. (2012). Re: I don't know what to make of this. *Reddit*. Retrieved from https://www.reddit.com/r/funny/comments/109cnf/im_not_sure_what_to_conclude_from_this/?sort=new#c6bmnym

West, L. (2012). Reddit users attempt to shame Sikh woman, get righteously schooled. *Jezebel*. Retrieved from https://jezebel.com/5946643/reddit-users-attempt-to-shame-sikh-woman-get-righteously-schooled

Yergeau, M. (2017). *Authoring autism: On rhetoric and neurological queerness*. Durham, NC: Duke University Press.

Index

Note: *italic* page numbers refer to figures and page numbers followed by "n" denote endnotes.

abuse *see* aggression
academic freedom: *1940 Statement on Principles of Academic Freedom and Tenure* 134; *Keyishian v. Board of Regents* 134
Adams, Paul 111
aggression: and anti-Semitism 133, 134, 137; effects of 6, 11, 36, 92, 118, 143, 151, 172, 180, 181, 191, 203, 206, 216, 233, 236–8, 243; and LGBTQ+ xix, xx; and politics 10, 44, 104, 116, 123, 128, 143, 150, 155n8, 161, 180, 183, 201–3, 222, 224; prevalence of 54, 70, 151; and race 10, 51, 88, 98, 143, 153n2, 155n8, 191, 244; responses to 1, 7, 8, 17, 24, 48n2, 58, 62, 64, 108, 124–6, 132, 136, 137, 165, 184, 185, 205, 219, 234, 238–40; and women 1, 6, 9, 10, 17, 18, 36, 48n3, 51–4, 56, 70, 73, 74, 87, 88, 90–2, 94–6, 98, 99, 105, 108, 114, 116, 173, 179–92, 206, 207, 240, 241
algorithmic data collection 221, 224–6
algorithmic data surveillance 216, 220, 225; in medical wearables 218–21
algorithms 222; automated systems and 4; data-harvesting 217; engagement-driven 179; for gendered harassment on-line 17
Almjeld, J. 92
alt-right groups 10, 11, 27, 28, 104, 106, 143, 151, 154n8
Amoore, L. 223

anonymity 20, 22, 24, 28, 37, 38, 40, 42, 51, 110, 163, 210
"antibody rhetoric" 118, 119
Arendt, H. 220
Aristotle 126, 127, 238
Arola, K. L. 75, 76
ARPANET 35
Association of Internet Researchers 2
audience 1, 34, 76, 80, 96, 98, 100, 124–38, 197, 201
Auernheimer, Andrew "Weev" 147
automation *see* algorithms

Baldwin, Adam 41
Banner, O. 217
Barthes, R. 130, 131
Bay, J. 173, 174
Beard, M. 96, 181, 182
Beck, E. 3
Beyer, J. 104, 111, 119
Bitzer, L. 125–7
Blair, K. 92
Blakely, K. 92
bluepill 113, 115, 120n7
Blumler, J. G. 34
Boase, J. 132
Bond, Sarah E. 96
Boston Marathon bombing 234–8, 236; Tripathi, Sunil 235–8
boyd, d. 132, 133
Boyle, C. 71, 79, 80
Bradshaw, J. L. 210, 234
Brand, Stewart 39
Brock, K. 208
Brown, J. J., Jr. 2, 3, 9, 11, 12, 19, 71, 76, 77, 202, 203, 206
Brueggemann, B. J. 225

Index

bullying 75, 197
Bumble 70, 73, 74
Bush, V. 35, 37
BuzzFeed 28

Campbell, E. 111, 114
Carnegie, T. M. 71
Castronova, E. 160–3
Ceraso, S. 71
Cernovich, Mike 41
de Certeau, M. 99
*chan: 4chan 20, 21, 40, 43, 51, 104–8, 110–12, 114–17, 119, 166, 168; 8chan 107, 163, 166, 171, 172; Holla Forums 107, 109; /pol/ 27, 104, 107, 109, 112, 113, 115, 116, 168
Charlottesville, Virginia *see* Unite the Right rally
Chemaly, S. 182
The Chronicle of Higher Education 124, 136
Ciccariello-Maher, George 123–4, 128, 130–2, 138
circulation practices 198–9; ethical complexities of 197; habits of citizenship 201–2; practices of 202; relationship between public work and 202; writing 200 (+ sharing)
Citron, D. 181
Citron, Jason 28, 29; *see also* Discord
civility 4–7, 70, 106, 114
Clinnin, K. 4
code of ethics 35–7; American Institute of Electrical Engineers 35; National Society of Professional Engineers 35
Coleman, G. 104, 107, 112, 119
Coleman, S. 34
Condis, M. 10, 11, 163
Consalvo, M. 160
community: communities of harm 9, 33, 35; virtual communities 38, 39
content creators 8, 52, 58, 67
content moderation *see* moderation
Costanza-Chock, S. 29
Crash Override 175
Cross, K. 145, 162, 163, 172
Cushman, E. 89

The Daily Stormer 146, 150, 154n6, 167, 168
data collection and tracking: fitness trackers 215, 217, 221, 226; medical wearables (*see* disability, medical wearables); *see also* surveillance
death threats 6, 126
dehumanization 173, 221–2, 224–6
DeVoss, D. N. 233, 238
digital activism 160, 174, 201
digital citizens: habits of citizenship 201–3, 208, 210; netizenship 34, 36
disability: d/Deaf 219–20; Disability Rights Movement 224; Health Insurance Portability and Accountability Act (HIPAA) 215, 227n2; medical wearables 11, 214–28; Starkey Halo smart hearing aid 11, 214, 216
Discord 18, 19, 23–30
Dogpiling 33, 48n2, 183
Dolmage, J. 234
Doom 147, 151
"don't feed the trolls", inadequate response 5, 6, 51
doxxing 33, 48n1, 172, 187–9
Duffy, J. 75
Duggan, M. 93
Duncan, P. 118
Dush, L. 200

"e-bile" 21
Eble, M. F. 35, 37
Edwards, D. W. 203, 234
ethics of care 73
embodied knowledge 80, 108
ethic of expediency 36, 217, 220, 222
ethical programs 2, 203, 208
ethic of responsibility 1–12
enthymeme 125–9, 131
ethos 239, 245; of digital spaces 38; enthymemes 127; onsite 108; of service to humanity 36; WELL 39

Facebook: Cambridge Analytica 1; LeftBook 9, 33, 34, 36, 43–8; moderation on (*see* moderation); shaming groups 33, 34, 36, 43–7; and visibility 179
fake news 198, 204
Falcão, T. 164
Feinberg, A. 146, 167, 168
Fibreculture 104, 116, 117
Flusser, V. 129, 130, 132–3
free speech: and academic freedom (*see* academic freedom); First Amendment xix, xx, 18

Gage, J. 127
Galloway, A. 69
GamerGate: Anita Sarkeesian 166; on reddit 33, 34, 39, 41–3, 48, 163, 166; on Twitter 10, 41, *41*, 43, 164, 166, 168–71, 173, 185; *The Zoe Post* 165–6; Zoe Quinn 40, 165, 166, 172, 173, 175, 188, 191
gamers: axioms of online culture 143–4; definition of 165; hardcore 163; in online games 164; recruitment of 151; rhetoric used by 150; in virtual worlds 164
gaming communities 1, 27
Gamson, W. A. 146
gatekeeping 1, 105, 185; academic 111, 118; algorithmic 201; control over circulation 19
Gelms, B. 10, 11, 92–3
Ghostbusters 206–8
Gillespie, T. 6, 8, 51
Godwin, Mike 147, 154n7; Godwin's Law of Nazi Analogies 148
Google 5, 47, 80, 91
Gouge, C. 216
Gries, L. E. 198, 238
Gurak, L. 3

Haas, A. M. 35, 37
harassment, definitions of 180–2; *see also* aggression
Harrington, D. 3
Harrison, A. 233, 235, 236
Hart-Davidson, B. 227
hate speech *see* aggression
Hatreon 18–19
Hauser, G. 137
Hawhee, D. 233–4
Hawisher, G. E. 183
Heineman, D. S. 4
Herring, S. C. 17, 18, 28, 51
Heyer, Heather *see* Unite the Right rally
Hodson, J. 96
Holt, N. 112
Huizinga, J. 160, 161

Imzy 19, 21, 73
Inside Higher Ed 96, 124
Instagram 69
interface design: and aggression 9, 20, 29, 69, 70–2, 74–6, 78, 80, 81; design justice 9, 12, 28–30;

ethical interface production 69–82; hateware 9, 17–30
Internet Relay Chat (IRC) 17, 51
Isocrates xvi

Jane, E. A. 21, 90, 92, 111
Jenkins, H. 34
Jeong, S. 5
John, N. 197
Johnson-Eilola, J. 3
Jones, J. 216
Jones, Leslie 10–11, 198, 206–8

Kabay, M. E. 172
Kalven Committee 134
Katz, S. B. 36, 220–1, 224, 228n6
Kaur, Balpreet 241–2, 245
Keipi, T. 144
Kennedy, K. 11, 200, 214–15, 220
Kessler, Jason 29
Kirsch, G. E. 89
Kirstein, P. N. 136
Knudsen, F. 234
Knuttila, L. 107
KotakuInAction (KiA) 33, 34, 37, 40–3, *42*, 48, 172; GamerGate (*see* GamerGate)

Lai, C.-H. 132
Lang, H. 203
LaPoe, V. 114
Laquintano, T. 227
Lather, P. A. 183
law: Communications Decency Act of 1996 22; *Fields v. Twitter* 23; First Amendment (*see* free speech); *Keyishian v. Board of Regents* (*see* academic freedom); law enforcement 18, 19, 29, 237; Ninth Circuit Court of Appeals 23; and responsibility 18, 19, 22, 23, 28, 29, 136, 148, 183, 184, 216, 222, 223, 237; Section 230 18, 22, 23, 25, 30
Leiter, B. 136
Levy, S. 38
Lewis, R. 205
ludic identity 163–5, 167, 171, 172
Lyon, D. 225

McComas, Dan 19, 73
McKee, H. A. 90, 93
McMillan Cottom, Tressie 96
Macris, A. 165, 167
Maiberg, E. 152

Manivannan, V. 10, 11
Manthey, K. 4
Mantilla, K. 108
Marwick, A. 132, 133, 205
Marx, G. T. 218, 222
Massanari, A. L. 20, 94
medical wearables *see* disability
Meggary, J. 182
"memetic rhetoric" 20
mētis 116, 232–9, 242, 244
Milner, R. M. 4, 5, 30, 51
moderation: content moderators 7, 25; platform providers 23; policies 152; rules-based 9, 33, 34, 44; tools 52, 54–8, 57, 66
morality 105, 106
Mortal Kombat 151
Mortensen, T. E. 164, 172
Moses, G. 106
Moss, J. 239
Murthy, D. 132

Naaman, M. 132
Nasi, M. 157
Nazi: Nazi-card 148, 154n7; neo-Nazis 27, 144–8, 150–3, 153n2, 154n6; recruitment 144–7, 153; representations of in video games 143–7, 149–51, 154n8
netizenship 34, 36
The New York Times 27, 55, 136
Noble, S. U. 91, 222

Oksanen, A. 157
Olson, C. 114
Ong, W. 126
Ott, B. 108
Overstreet, M. 105, 118
Overwatch 24

Paul, C. A. 160, 164, 167, 171, 175n2
pedagogy 69–82, 175, 180, 199, 231, 233
peer review: @RealPeerReview 97, 97, 98; Reviewer #2 105, 106, 108–15, 117–19
Perry, D. 136
PewDiePie 143
Pew Research Center 1, 180, 181
Phillips, W. 4, 104, 112, 119
phronesis 232–3; defined as 238–9; as intervention 240–2; prudent judgment and practical wisdom 238–9; in rhetoric and writing classroom, digital citizens practicing 244–5
Poland, B. 4, 6, 51, 52, 172
Porter, J. E. 1, 90, 93, 202, 203
Poster, C. 126
Potts, L. 9, 11, 75, 160, 164, 170, 171, 174, 227n3, 233, 235, 236
Powell, K. M. 89
Powers, D. 234
privacy 1, 3, 4, 28, 87, 98, 100, 100n2, 185, 186, 191, 220; *see also* data collection and tracking; surveillance
PUBG 54

Quinn, Zoe *see* GamerGate

Radix 146
Ramus, P. 126
rape threats 182
Rasanan, Peter 126
Raymond, J. C. 127
Reddit: GamerGate (*see* GamerGate); r/findbostonbombers (*see* Boston Marathon bombing); r/funny (*see* Balpreet Kaur); r/kotakuinaction (*see* KotakuInAction (KiA)); r/The_Donald 204
redpill 111, 113–15, 118, 120n2, 168
research: autoethnography 106, 110–12, 114–17; feminist methodologies 10, 87–100; feminist scholars 92, 96, 111; hazards of 91; interviewing 75, 94, 95; safety of researchers 98; tactical resistance 10, 12, 88, 98–100
responsibility: and accountability 1, 2, 4, 7, 35–7, 41, 42, 48, 96, 108, 199; outsourcing of 17–30
Reyman, J. 219, 227n4
Rheingold, H. 33, 38, 39, 47
rhetorical ethics 3, 202, 203; rhetorical–ethical perspective 232, 233, 239, 242–5
rhetorical situation 10, 125, 126, 133, 134, 137, 138, 239
rhetorical velocity 200, 231–4, 238
rhetorical vulnerability 143, 151
Ribeiro, J. C. 164
Riche, D. 143, 151
Rickert, T. 173, 174

Ridolfo, J. 233, 238
Roberts, S. 6
role playing games: MMORPGs 161, 162, 168; *World of Warcraft* 162, 171
Royster, J. J. 89

Sachs, J. 239
Salaita, Steven 133–6, 138
Salvo, M. J. 75
Salen, K. 161
Salter, M. 152, 163
Sarkeesian, Anita *see* GamerGate
Section 230 *see* law, Section 230
Selfe, C. L. 3, 69, 183
Selfe, R. J. 3, 69
sexually explicit aggression 56, 58–60
shaming 1, 33, 34, 36, 43–7, 197
sharing 11, 24, 27, 54, 69, 132, 170, 187, 190, 197–201, 204–6, 208–10, 231, 235; *see also* circulation
Shepherd, D. 210
Smithies, C. S. 183
social justice 11, 34, 37, 43, 48, 87, 88, 144, 180, 197, 206, 208, 210; feminism 40, 74, 88, 116, 145, 183
Sommers, Christina Hoff 164
Sparby, E. M. 20
Spencer, Richard 146
stalking 1, 6, 91, 182, 187, 189
Stallman, Richard 38
Steam 24, 152, 153, 175n1
surveillance 4, 11, 98, 186, 191, 214–28; *see also* data collection and tracking
SWATting 18

Takayoshi, P. 89, 182
Tannen, D. 106, 118
Tarsa, B. 19
Tarsa, R. 76, 77
Taylor, T. L. 161–3, 170
technical image 127–33, 137, 138
Tinder 74
Trice, M. 9, 11, 160, 164, 166, 170, 171, 174
Tripathi, Sunil *see* Boston Marathon bombing
trolling: academic trolls 10, 105–19; counter-trolling 10, 117; gendertrolling 108, 114; *see also* don't feed the trolls

Trump, Donald 11, 123, 143, 155n9, 197, 198, 204–6, 231
Tucker, B. 221
Tufekci, Z. 34
Twitch 52, 143; Amazon subsidiary 53; community moderation 63–6; factors moderating harassment 52; gendered harassment 56; harassment of women on 51, 56; language of 55; limitations 55; moderation practices 58–63; moderation tools 56–8, 57; recorded livestreams 55; streamer selection 54–5; written policies 53–4
Twitch streamers 52, 53
Twitter: academic speech on 128, 133; academic trolls *see* trolling; circulation on 198, 201, 202, 204, 205, 207, 208; and interface design 78; Leslie Jones 179, 198, 204, 206; @RealPeerReview *see* peer review; and visibility 179, 183–5, 187, 188

Ugilt, R. 148
Unite the Right rally 27, 29, 154n2, 154n7; Heyer, Heather 19, 27, 29
Universal Declaration of Human Rights xvii
user testing, as ethical activity 79–80

value systems 7
Vee, A. 227
Vie, S. 174
Vera-Gray, F. 93, 96, 111, 114
video games: GamerGate *see* GamerGate; gamers *see* gamers; magic circle 160–3; theorycraft 10, 160–76; Twitch *see* Twitch
video games, as alt-right recruitment tool 10, 11, 27, 28, 54, 94, 104, 106, 143–7, 149–51, 154n6, 154n8, 167, 174, 175
virtue ethics 70, 72–3, 75, 77, 81–2
visibility 1, 10, 104, 170, 179–92
Vitanza, V. 118, 119

Walker, J. 127, 128
Wall, S. 112
Wan, A. 202
Warner, J. 200
Warnick, B. 4

WELL (Whole Earth 'Lectronic Link) 33, 36, 39, 40, 42, 48n3
West, L. 240
white genocide 123, 125, 128–30
white nationalist 143, 148, 150, 151, 153n2
white privilege 70, 127
white supremacist 11, 27, 29, 123, 128, 143–55, 167, 207; KKK 154n2, 155n8
Wikimedia Foundation Research Committee (RCom) 94–5
Wikipedia 34; ethos and *netizenship* 36; gender gap 94; homophobic practices in communities 91; person-based study of women writers 94
deWinter, J. 174

Wired 38
Wolfe Herd, Whitney 70, 73–5; *see also* Bumble
Wu, Brianna 172

Yancey, K. B. 226
Yergeau, M. 234, 244
Yiannopoulos, Milo 143
YouTube 40, 41; gaming celebrities 143; *Ghostbusters* movie trailer on 206–8; harassment on 92; homophobic practices in communities 91
Young, Cathy 41

Zimmerman, E. 161
Zittrain, J. 34, 36